PENGUIN BOOKS
THE ULTIMATE OPERA QUIZ BOOK

KENN HARRIS was born in New York City, where he heard his first opera at the age of eight. He considers himself fortunate that his formative years coincided with the age of spectacular singing that followed the Second World War. A graduate of the University of Rochester, Kenn feels, however, that his favorite and best teachers were the phenomenal artists who reigned at the Metropolitan Opera and on the Broadway stage. Kenn spent night after night hearing Tebaldi, Corelli, Price, and the other unrivaled singers of that time, honing his powers of observation and criticism.

He returned to New York after completing his education and worked in a variety of jobs in the publishing and music industries. In 1978, he made his debut as host and critic-in-residence on the cable television program *What's On*, remaining with that program for twelve years; he also hosted *Gotham Odyssey*. In 1990, he was rewarded with *The Kenn Harris Show* on Channel J. Kenn's other books include *Opera Recordings: A Critical Guide*, a biography of Renata Tebaldi, and the first edition of *The Ultimate Opera Quiz Book*. He has written theatre and opera criticism for many periodicals. Since 1977 Kenn has been in charge of opera sales for New York's most prestigious music store, J & R Music World. He currently lives on Manhattan's Upper West Side, with his two musical cats, Anzoleta and Momolo.

KENN HARRIS

THE *Ultimate* OPERA QUIZ BOOK

The Passionate Operagoer's Companion

REVISED AND EXPANDED

PENGUIN BOOKS

PENGUIN BOOKS
Published by the Penguin Group
Penguin Books USA Inc., 375 Hudson Street,
New York, New York 10014, U.S.A.
Penguin Books Ltd, 27 Wrights Lane, London W8 5TZ, England
Penguin Books Australia Ltd, Ringwood, Victoria, Australia
Penguin Books Canada Ltd, 10 Alcorn Avenue,
Toronto, Ontario, Canada M4V 3B2
Penguin Books (N.Z.) Ltd, 182–190 Wairau Road,
Auckland 10, New Zealand

Penguin Books Ltd, Registered Offices:
Harmondsworth, Middlesex, England

First published in Penguin Books 1982
This revised and expanded edition published in Penguin Books 1997

1 3 5 7 9 10 8 6 4 2

Photograph credits
Author's collection: no. 1; Stephen Leopold: 2, 42; Winnie Klotz/Metropolitan
Opera: 3, 4, 5, 6, 7, 12, 13, 14, 15, 24, 25, 26, 28, 38; John Anderson: 8, 9, 10,
11, 40; Robert E. Weiss: 16, 17, 18, 19, 20, 21, 22, 23, 29, 30, 31, 32, 33,
34, 35, 36, 37, 39; Robert Pilnick: 27; Lucine Amara: 41;
C. Robert Wessler: 43; Lois Kirschenbaum: 44.

LIBRARY OF CONGRESS CATALOGING IN PUBLICATION DATA
Harris, Kenn, 1947–
The ultimate opera quiz book: the passionate operagoer's
companion/Kenn Harris.—Rev. ed.
p. cm.
ISBN 0 14 02.5390 4
1. Opera—Miscellanea. I. Title.
ML1700.H36 1997
782.1—dc21 96-39323

Printed in the United States of America
Set in Adobe Garamond · Designed by Francesca Belanger

I happily dedicate this book to my mother, Marion Harris,
an incandescent combination of Mrs. Miniver, Molly Goldberg,
and Madame Rose—the ultimate "page" mother.
To paraphrase Tennessee Williams:
Skina-marinka dinka du, Big Mama.
I love you.

Preface

❦

It was, as Annina in *La Traviata* might have put it, *una giòia improvvisa* when it was suggested to me that I revise and expand my *Ultimate Opera Quiz Book*. The creation of the first edition of this book brought me great pleasure, and the realization that there *were* people who had enjoyed the book filled me with satisfaction. This book has not been devised to "humble" the reader or to flail him or her with information that they do not possess. On the contrary, playing along with these quizzes and whimsical guessing games should reveal to the reader how much he or she already knows about the world of opera, and its denizens. If, on the journey, one picks up a few facts, *tanto meglio*, as Adriana Lecouvreur used to say!

In preparing the new edition of this book, I began by rereading and re-evaluating all the questions found in the 1982 edition, retaining the material that still seemed relevant, updating answers where necessary, and "retiring" those items that no longer seemed to fit properly. After all, certain careers that had flourished in the 1980's had withered in recent years. Some artists' achievements require re-evaluation, and, sadly, the passage of more than a decade meant that a number of people had died and verb tenses needed to be changed. Then too, some artists who were children when the first edition was published have recently won acclaim and deserve to be mentioned.

The Ultimate Opera Quiz Book has been expanded in two ways. First, new questions have been added to most of the original quizzes. Secondly, fifty new quizzes ranging from the factual— "Early Verdi" or "Cecilia Bartoli"—to the more fanciful—"Four Gals Named Leonora" and "Don't Sing with Your Mouth Full." I hope that readers find these new quizzes *down* to my usual standard!

Most of the answers required by these questions are factual. After all, there is no getting around the fact that Hagenbach is killed by an avalanche in the fourth act of Catalani's *La Wally*, is there? However, certain questions are subject to different interpretations, while others might be resolved by different examples than I've used—If I offer twenty cases of operatic adulteresses, I know people will find at least that many other examples of that phenomenon, as well. If you come up with an answer that differs from mine, feel free to "write it in", as long as you can defend it. Heaven forbid that I be as rigid as Princess Turandot concerning the answers to my enigmas!

One innovation that readers familiar with the previous edition of *The Ultimate Opera Quiz Book* will note is that, in the present book, each question is rated from one to four on an ascending scale. This indicates the relative challenge that each question represents. Readers who consider themselves operatic novices will be pleased with themselves when they answer several "4"s correctly in one sitting. More jaded operaphiles might blush if they stumble over a "1."

Don't despair—unless you are betting on answers! Everything herein is primarily intended to celebrate opera and to encourage interest in *la lirica*.

A problem inherent in writing about opera is that no printed words can adequately describe the beauty and wonder of the human voice singing the incredible melodies of Bellini and Verdi, Mozart and Wagner. I am totally in awe of all people involved in creating and singing opera! Even when I am being satirical or exercising my right to debunk a few artists who have become legends in their own minds, I hope that my love of opera is never obscured by a cynical or skeptical remark.

As an avid collector of recordings and videos, I took special pleasure in creating the sections that deal with those media. Opera videos were quite scarce in 1982, but now, one can find multiple versions of many works, and wonderful recitals by the greatest singers of the past fifty years. It is remarkable that any book about opera can compete with the "real thing."

I hope you enjoy the anecdotes. Many of them have been passed down from standee to standee for decades. Others concern more recent events. A number of these stories actually unfolded in my presence!

So, Opera Quizzées, welcome to the feast! I hope you find everything to your liking. A word of advice. If you're stumped in identifying a particularly nutty operatic plot, just guess that it's Ponchielli's *La Gioconda*—you're probably right!

KENN HARRIS
Laguna Beach, California 1996

Acknowledgments

❧

I'll begin by saying that I have more friends than I could possibly deserve, and I would like to offer each *amico mille grazie.*

Let me begin by thanking my creative and indomitable literary agent, Sam Fleischman, and his superb associate, Maddie Perrone, for their faith in me and for everything they have done to make this new edition of *The Ultimate Opera Quiz Book* a reality.

I am eternally grateful to my visionary editor, David Stanford and to his resourceful associates Kris Puopolo and Paul Morris at Penguin U.S.A. for their skillful shaping of this book, allowing its best qualities to emerge, while at the same time offering tactful yet constructive criticism and saving me from my lowest impulses where (alleged) humor was concerned. These folks believed in this book's potential from the start, so much so that my reply, when told of Penguin's abiding interest—"That's very nice but I can't talk now because I have a fever of 104 and am on my way to the hospital"—where I was swallowed up for days in medical red tape—did not kill their enthusiasm!

I am proud to mention the heroic efforts in my behalf by Charles D. Lieber, who represented me on the first edition of this book, as well as the excellent handling of the original material by the editor of the 1982 edition, Martha Kinney.

Many artists whom I loved on the operatic stage encouraged me in my work on this book, and also contributed—or confirmed—anecdotes that appear here. These wonderful people include, in no particular order, Lucine Amara, Maria Spacagna, Giuseppe di Stefano, Elisabeth Soederstroem, Samuel Ramey, Mirella Freni, Jerome Hines, Robert Merrill, José Carreras, Carlo Bergonzi, Franco Corelli, Harolyn Blackwell, Katia Ricciarelli, Régine Crespin, Teresa Stratas, Jarmila Novotna, Giulietta Simionato,

Leontyne Price, Birgit Nilsson, Ljuba Welitsch, and Miss Renata Tebaldi.

I will not forget the courtesy of New York City's First Opera Fan, the Hon. Mayor Rudy Giuliani, who allowed me to live a few moments of uniquely Gothamesque operatic history. Special thanks also to the Mayor's Director of Communication, Cristyne Lategano.

I take this opportunity to thank Joe and Rachelle Friedman of J and R Music World and my many friends there for their invaluable aid and encouragement: Sue Vovsi, Doug Diaz, Mary Jane Glaser, Margaret Lynch, Bill Kennedy, Ray Knight, Sea Jan Shu, Clint Witsil, Rupert Hewitt, Matt Ziruk, Roger Davis, Ken Spence, et al.

Much of this book was written at my favorite place in the whole world (except for Milan), the Laguna Beach Riviera. The unforgettable seascapes and comfortable outdoor furniture of that delightful Orange County hostelry allowed me to write under circumstances worthy of a *divo*. Grazie tanto to Bruce Willats and his marvelous staff for allowing me to work so happily, and for fending off questions from other guests about "that nut who does nothing but scribble all day underneath the palm trees!"

When I began work on this book, I was owned by two fabulous cats. One, a large, fluffy "marshmallow with legs" known as Shtuppë, died in May of 1995. Ever since, whenever a portion of the MS fell inexplicably fell from my desk to the floor, I knew Shtuppë was, somehow, with me. The other cat, my sleek, glamorous Fedora, is so jealous of my work that she destroyed two word processors, but at 15, she's still here and I don't dare leave my work unattended!

I offer special thanks to Mrs. Doris Urman for keeping my fighting spirit at full boil! Extra special thanks to my cardiologist, Dr. Howard Kloth, for keeping me alive thus far.

Three dear and wonderful friends of mine did not live to see this book in its final form. I cherish the memory of Bobbi Tillander, a terrific mentor and unforgettable character, Joe Bartomioli, a loving and gentle friend for more than a quarter century, and Shaya Schultz, who taught me the basics of the record industry, kept me supplied with Diet Coke and shared many laughs with me.

How can I properly thank Harvey Silbert and Louis Putallaz for putting up with my mood swings and anxiety attacks during the writing of this book? All the dinners I kvetched through, and the plays, movies, and operas I muttered through! That's not mere loyalty, that's heroism! Many others cheered me up and calmed me down. My love to Gillian Hyde, Rhoda Feuer, Linda Sinkus, the Stevens clan of Minneapolis, Dan Plotkin, Marshall Boyler, Cherry Munson, Tom Jacobson, David Runzo, Todd Lichtenstein, Richard Sherr, Barry Bruckner, Mimi Bowling, Carl and Joan Saslow, Roy Herschaft, Tom Savage, Richard Harcourt, Bob Weiss, Rodenick Jordan, Carrie Tenoglia, and a special "thank you" to Bob Wessler, who so generously provided me with a typewriter at exactly the right moment!

My family, particularly Fay, Bonnie, Gwen, Mort, Joan, and Harriet was as supportive of me as anyone could possibly be. Anyone else I haven't listed, you know who you are!

Kenn Harris

Contents

II. *Opera Stars and Supernovas* 51

III. *Unforgettable Characters* 126

IV. *And Then What Happens? Opera Plots and Plotting* 164

V. *A Potpourri* 183

THE ANSWERS

THE Quizzes AND Anecdotes

❀ ❀ ❀

I

The Operas
and Their Composers

1. AMERICAN OPERA

1. Although born in Italy, this composer has spent most of his adult life in America. Among his many credits is the first opera to have been commissioned for television. Name the composer and the opera. (3)

2. First performed in 1958, this opera was composed with Maria Callas in mind for the title role. Callas rejected the score. Who created the title role in this opera? (4)

3. Beverly Sills had one of her first successes in an opera based on an incident in American history. Name the opera and its composer. (3)

4. At the time of his murder, Marc Blitzstein was at work on an opera dealing with a controversial American court case. What was the case? (4)

5. Jack Beeson's most popular opera is based on the life of a notorious New Englander. Can you identify the opera? (To the disappointment of many in the audience, the score does *not* include the well-known folk song about its title character.) (2)

6. One of Arthur Miller's best-known plays was adapted into a splendid opera some years ago, with its political message left intact. Name Miller's play and the composer of the opera it inspired. (3)

7. Although first produced on Broadway and later made into a Hollywood film, this wonderful work has slowly begun to

make its way into the repertories of opera houses in America and around the world. Who were the composer, librettist, and its three original stars? Which important American singer received her first "break" in a 1953 revival of this work? (2)

8. Can you remember the title of Howard Hanson's opera, which was performed at the Metropolitan Opera during the 1930s? (4)

9. The great American soprano Helen Traubel, peerless in Wagner and a radio favorite when clowning with Jimmy Durante, made her Metropolitan Opera debut in a now-forgotten American opera. What was it? (4)

10. A famous American playwright's Broadway success was used as the basis for this American opera that transplanted a Greek legend to American shores. Name the dramatist, play, opera, composer, and the New York–born soprano who starred in its world premiere at the Met. (3)

11. The late Marie Powers had a great personal success as the tormented title character of this opera. The work premiered on Broadway and was later seen on television and around the world. Identify the work and its prolific composer. (2)

12. As far as we can ascertain, there is only one opera that has a crucial scene set in a New York subway station. Can you name it? In case you were wondering, "Take the A Train" is not heard in this score! (4)

13. Gertrude Stein wrote the whimsical libretto for an opera dealing with a famous fighter for women's rights. Name the opera, the composer, and the protagonist. (3)

14. This opera transplanted a biblical episode to the New World. Identify the opera, its composer, the biblical story in question, and tell where the opera was set. Where and when was the work premiered? Who starred in the first New York performance? (3)

15. Can you name two operas based upon works by Charles Dickens that premiered in the United States and were composed by U.S. citizens? (4)

16. Do you know which of Philip Glass's operas is about Christopher Columbus's travels to the New World? It had its first

performance in October 1992. Do you know at which American opera house? (3)

17. We bet you can't come up with the name of Aaron Copland's one opera! (3)

18. A well-remembered American play had its central character created on Broadway by Tallulah Bankhead. The film version boasted Bette Davis in that role. Name the operatic version of the play, the composer, and the woman who created the pivotal character. In what way is soprano Brenda Lewis important in the history of this work? (4)

19. Lawrence Tibbett sang two indigenous American roles during his years of Met stardom. What were they? (4)

20. Who wrote the libretto for John Corigliano's opera *The Ghosts of Versailles*, which had its world premiere at the Metropolitan Opera in 1991? (3)

21. Which Mozart comedy is related to *The Ghosts of Versailles*? (2)

22. Two veteran North American divas delivered much admired performances in the first production of *Ghosts*. Who are they? (2)

23. Name Lee Hoiby's opera based on a Tennessee Williams play. Geraldine Page created the leading character in the play. Who sang the role at the opera's premiere, given in 1971 at the New York City Opera? (4)

24. Angela Lansbury created the leading female role in a hybrid work by Stephen Sondheim that was first produced on Broadway, but has turned up in the repertories of many American opera companies. Singer/director Rosalind Elias was the first artist to perform the role at the New York City Opera. Name the work, and the role that Lansbury and Elias sang. (1)

Answers on page 261.

2. ENGLISH OPERA

1. Name the first English opera composer and three of his operas. (2)

2. Did you know that one of Benjamin Britten's operas is based on a novel written by an American? Identify the opera and the novelist. (3)

3. Another of Britten's operas is based upon the exploits of an American folk hero. Who was he? (3)

4. Dame Joan Sutherland, in her early days at the Royal Opera, Covent Garden, sang in a contemporary opera composed by Sir Michael Tippett. To which masterpiece are we referring? (4)

5. During the 1970s the work of a contemporary British woman composer was in vogue. Can you name her and two of her operas? (4)

6. What has become of the former Sadler's Wells Opera Company? (2)

7. American-born impresario Matthew Epstein headed an important British lyric theater for several successful years in the 1990s, overseeing its transformation from a regional to an internationally renowned company. What is the name of the company? (3)

8. What is the name of the singer most often associated with the operas of Benjamin Britten? (2)

9. In Britten's opera *Peter Grimes*, how did Grimes's first apprentice die? (2)

10. Who created the title role at the world premiere of Britten's *Billy Budd*? (4)

11. With what company does the Royal Opera share Covent Garden? (1)

12. For which British company did director Jonathan Miller create his controversial production of *Rigoletto*, set not in Mantua but in Manhattan's Little Italy, updating Verdi's opera to the 1950s? (3)

13. Who was the German-born composer who lived in London for many years, composing operas to both English and Italian texts? (2)

14. Who composed the opera commissioned for the coronation of Queen Elizabeth II? Name the opera and identify, if you please, its subject. (2)

15. When Maria Callas canceled a series of performances of *Tosca* at Covent Garden in 1965, she was replaced by a young soprano from a former territory of Great Britain. Who was she? (4)

16. The late British soprano Amy Shuard was acclaimed throughout Europe for a Puccini role. Which one? (3)
17. Three of the following artists are Dame Commanders of the British Empire. Reveal to us which one is still a "commoner."
    1. Kiri Te Kanawa
    2. Margaret Price
    3. Gwyneth Jones
    4. Clara Butt (2)
18. What is the name of the mute character so crucial to the plot of Britten's *Death in Venice*? (3)
19. In what theater does the English National Opera perform in London? (2)
20. Two Italian composers settled in London at the turn of the twentieth century, giving music lessons and writing songs. One of them composed several operas, including a work that was once quite popular. Name both composers, and provide, if you can, the titles of several of the operatic composer's works for the lyric stage. (3)
21. What British-born tenor was well known in the 1970s for singing and recording Wagnerian roles in English? (3)
22. Can you name (and spell that name!) the young Welsh baritone who created a sensation in the early 1990s singing Mozart, Strauss, and Wagner operas in Europe and the United States? (2)
23. Name four operatic roles composed by Benjamin Britten for Sir Peter Pears. (3)
24. Which British opera festival is celebrated for its superlative Mozart and its fancy dress rules? (1)
25. Please identify the composers of the following English operas:
    a. *Fennimore and Gerda* (4)
    b. *Riders to the Sea* (3)
    c. *Troilus and Cressida* (2)
    d. *The Little Sweep* (2) (3)
26. What is Frederick Delius's best-known opera? (4)

Answers on page 263.

3. FRENCH OPERA

1. Name two operas by Ambroise Thomas. (3)
2. List three operas composed by Verdi for the Paris Opéra. (3)
3. Who wrote the libretto for *Carmen*? On whose novel is it based? (2)
4. Do you know at what Paris opera house Verdi and Donizetti experienced early successes? (3)
5. Name four operas (not necessarily by French composers) dealing with the French Revolution. (2)
6. Please identify the soprano who created the role of Mélisande in Debussy's *Pelléas et Mélisande*. (3)
7. Identify the following characters from French operas. Name the opera and composer, and briefly describe the character.

    a. Zuniga (2)
    b. Spalanzani (2)
    c. Philine (4)
    d. Sièbel (3)
    e. Blanche de la Force (3)
    f. Charlotte (2)
    g. De Brétigny (3)
    h. Schlémil (3)
    i. Mercédès (2)
    j. Rachel (3)
    k. Leïla (3)
    l. Cassandre (3)
    m. Athanaël (4)
    n. Abimelech (3)
    o. Nicklausse (3)

8. Anyone can name one opera by Gustave Charpentier, but can you name two? (4)
9. Which French composer authored an opera dealing with Britain's King Henry VIII? (3)
10. Poulenc's *Dialogues des Carmélites* ranks among the outstanding operas by French composers of this century. At which opera house did the world premiere take place? (3)
11. Who was the American soprano for whom Jules Massenet composed *Esclarmonde*? (4)
12. Name two French cities where opera festivals are held each summer. (2)
13. What was the title of the opera left unfinished by Debussy at his death? (3)

14. Which three Offenbach operettas were recorded by the un-forgettable French soprano Régine Crespin? (2)
15. Which of the following is *not* a French opera: *Le Roi d'Ys; Robert le Diable; Le Coq d'Or; Le Roi de Lahore*? (2)
16. Who among the following is *not* a French operatic conductor: Pierre Boulez, Jean Morel, Wilfred Pelletier, Georges Prêtre? (3)
17. What is the current name of the Parisian theater formerly known as the Opéra-Comique? (2)
18. List Hoffmann's four great loves in Offenbach's *Les Contes d'Hoffmann*. (2)
19. From which operas do the following arias come? Give the title, the composer's name, and the character who sings each.
    a. "Pourquoi me réveiller, ô souffle du printemps?" (2)
    b. "Les oiseaux dans la charmille." (1)
    c. "Vois ma misère, hélas! Vois ma détresse." (3)
    d. "Je dis, que rien ne m'épouvante." (1)
    e. "Connais-tu le pays où fleurit l'oranger?" (2)
    f. "Ah! je ris de me voir si belle en ce miroir!" (2)
    g. "Avant de quitter ces lieux." (2)
    h. "Pleurez mes yeux!" (4)
    i. "Ô souverain, ô juge, ô père." (4)
    j. "Enfin, je suis ici." (4)
    k. "Il m'en souvient." (4)
    l. "Sois immobile." (2)
    m. "Ah! fuyez, douce image." (1)
    n. "Ah, quel dîner je viens de faire." (2)
    o. "Où va la jeune Hindoue?" (3)
20. Who is the composer of *Les Martyrs*? What is the title of the better-known, Italian version of this opera? (3)
21. What is the name of the new home of the Paris Opéra? What has become of the former home of that company, one of the great treasures of the City of Light? (2)
22. Who is the American maestro appointed director of the Paris Opéra in 1995? (2)
23. A duet for two female voices from a half-forgotten French opera found great popularity in the United States ever since

an airline commercial featured it as its theme song. Name the duet, the opera, the composer, and the characters who sing it. (3)

24. In addition to the Paris Opéra and the Paris Opéra-Comíque (Salle Favart), there is now a third major opera company in Paris, which takes its name from the venerable theater in which it performs. Can you name the company and the theater? (3)

25. Do you remember the name of the soprano who, in the 1950s and 1960s, was closely associated with the operas of Poulenc? (3)

Answers on page **265**.

4. GERMAN OPERA

These questions concern operas not *composed by Wagner or Richard Strauss.*

1. Name two operas by Albert Lortzing. (3)
2. Who composed *Die Lustigen Weiber von Windsor*? (2)
3. Who is the composer of *Margarete*? (3)
4. Where and when was *Fidelio* first performed? (3)
5. When this beloved artist took one of her children to a performance of *Hänsel und Gretel* in which she sang the role of the witch, the child caused pandemonium. Seeing his mother being thrown into the oven, he began to scream, "They're killing my mama!" Who was this artist? Where did this take place? (3)
6. Who wrote the play on which Alban Berg based the opera *Wozzeck*? (4)
7. Who are the trio who torment Wozzeck throughout Berg's opera? (3)
8. Name Friedrich von Flotow's most enduring work. (2)
9. What are the names of the tenor and soprano lovers in *Der Freischütz*? (3)

10. "Ozean! Du Ungerheuer" comes from what opera? Who is the composer? (3)

11. Who completed the orchestration of act three of Berg's *Lulu*, left unfinished at the composer's death? (4)

12. What held up the completion of *Lulu* for more than forty years? (3)

13. Where and when did the premiere of the completed *Lulu* take place? Name the conductor and the soprano who performed the title role. (3)

14. When Hans Werner Henze's opera *The Young Lord* was first produced by the New York City Opera, what famous operatic personality played an important, if mute, role? (4)

15. The Bavarian State Opera produced, in 1978, a new opera based on a Shakespearean tragedy that Verdi had once attempted but failed to make work as a music drama. Name the opera, its composer, and the artist who sang the title role. (4)

16. Name the three major opera companies found in Berlin. (2)

17. Which of Richard Wagner's children composed several operas? Name two of the operas. (4)

18. Can you identify the composers of the following German operas?

    1. *Der Evangelimann* (4)
    2. *Euryanthe* (2)
    3. *Dantons Tod* (3)
    4. *Violanta* (3)
    5. *Jonny Spielt Auf* (3)

Answers on page **268**.

5. ITALIAN OPERA

1. Name the two operas by Gioacchino Rossini that feature a leading tenor named Lindoro. (2)

2. What is the title of the opera that Gaetano Donizetti left unfinished at the time of his death? (3)

3. Johann Simon Mayr was the principal teacher of which famous Italian composer? (3)

4. Who was Amilcare Ponchielli's most successful student of composition? (3)

5. What was the occupation of Giuseppe Verdi's father? (2)

6. Alfredo Catalani composed two operas highly regarded by Arturo Toscanini, who named one of his children after the title character of one. What are the two operas? (3)

7. Saverio Mercadante's mid-nineteenth-century opera *Il Giuramento* is based on the same source as a much more famous Italian opera composed a few years later. Name the source, its author, the better-known opera, and its composer. Don't worry about summarizing the plot. It can't be done! (3)

8. Which Italian opera is sometimes referred to as "the Italian *Tristan*"? (3)

9. A Jesuit priest composed an opera for a beautiful and famous soprano, who spent part of her childhood in New York. Name the composer, the opera, and the lady for whom it was composed. (2)

10. For each aria title listed below, name the opera it is from, as well as the composer, and the character who sings it.
    a. "Dai campi, dai prati" (3)
    b. "Quando le sere al placido" (1)
    c. "Son pochi fiori" (3)
    d. "Voce di donna o d'angelo" (2)
    e. "Il cavallo scalpita" (2)
    f. "Quanto è bella, quanto è cara" (2)
    g. "Ah! non credea mirarti" (3)
    h. "Nemico della patria" (2)
    i. "A lui che adoro" (4)
    j. "Paolo, datemi pace" (4)

11. Why did the Austrian censors (servants of the government that occupied Northern Italy in pre-Risorgimento days) object to the libretto for Verdi's *Un Ballo in Maschera*? (3)

12. The following are titles of choruses from Italian operas. For each, give the title and composer of the work from which the chorus is taken.
    a. "O Pastorelle, addio!" (3)
    b. "Trema, Banco!" (2)
    c. "Regina Coeli" (2)

      d. "Guerra, guerra!" (3)

      e. "Va pensiero, sull'ali dorate" (1)

13. Name the famous composers of these relatively obscure Italian operas.

    a. *Emilia di Liverpool* (3)

    b. *La Cena delle Beffe* (4)

    c. *Alzira* (3)

    d. *Gemma di Vergy* (3)

    e. *Chatterton* (4)

    f. *Giulietta e Romeo* (4)

    g. *Adelson e Salvini* (3)

    h. *I Promessi Sposi* (4)

    i. *Nerone* (name two) (2)

    j. *La Finta Giardiniera* (3)

    k. *Edgar* (3)

    l. *Tancredi* (3)

    m. *Il Mondo della Luna* (4)

    n. *Le Maschere* (3)

    o. *Amelia al Ballo* (3)

    p. *Un Giorno di Regno* (2)

    q. *Orlando Furioso* (4)

14. Giuseppe Verdi started and abandoned several times a work based on what celebrated tragedy? (2)

15. What Italian opera house still displays a ceiling plaque dedicated to "Il Duce, Benito Mussolini"? (4)

16. What is the name of the honor awarded distinguished singers by the city of Busseto each year? (4)

17. Which one of the following Italian operas did *not* have its world premiere at La Scala, Milan?

    a. *Madama Butterfly*

    b. *Otello* (Verdi)

    c. *Nabucco*

    d. *Aida*

    e. *I Lombardi* (2)

18. What is the famous Roman venue for lavishly staged outdoor opera performances each summer? (1)

19. Which Italian opera house boasts a superb museum of operatic and theatrical memorabilia? (1)

20. Who was the head of La Scala throughout the years that Maria Callas sang there? (3)

21. Name the Italian cities in which the following opera houses are situated.

    a. La Fenice (1)

    b. Teatro San Carlo (3)

    c. Teatro Massimo (2)

22. For which Italian opera house does conductor Riccardo Muti serve as musical director (as of 1996)? (2)

23. Which Italian music publishing house championed the careers of such composers as Bellini, Donizetti, Verdi, and Puccini? (2)

24. At what Italian opera house did Maria Callas and Giuseppe di Stefano codirect an opera in 1971? What was the opera? (4)

25. What Italian city boasts a notoriously demanding opera-going public? (2)

Answers on page 269.

6. RUSSIAN OPERA

1. Who was the librettist for Modest Mussorgsky's *Boris Godunov*? (3)

2. Name two Russian composers who tampered with the orchestration of *Boris Godunov* after Mussorgsky's death. Which of the three versions of *Boris* is most often performed today? (3)

3. What are the sources of Pyotr Ilich Tchaikovsky's *Pique Dame* and *Eugene Onegin*? (2)

4. Music from Alexander Borodin's *Prince Igor* was adapted for a Broadway musical. One piece, with a new, "American" lyric, has become a popular standard.
   a. Name the Broadway show in question. (2)
   b. Identify the section of the opera from which most of the music was adapted. (3)
   c. Who did the adaptation? (4)
   d. Name the song that became a popular hit. (1)
   e. Who sang that song on Broadway in the musical's original production, and who sang the hit recording? (3)

5. In *Eugene Onegin*, there is an aria known as the Letter Scene. Who writes the letter, to whom is this missive addressed, what are the letter's contents, and what ultimately happens between the sender and the recipient? (3)

6. Under what circumstances did the U.S. premiere of Serge Prokofiev's *War and Peace* take place? (4)

7. With what work did the Bolshoi Opera open its first engagement in the United States in 1975? Who sang the title role? Can you name the tenor and mezzo-soprano headliners of that performance? At what American theater did all this occur? (3)

8. Who was the first Bolshoi soprano to sing at the Metropolitan Opera? Which roles has she sung there, and in what languages? (3)

9. After the first production of *Boris Godunov*, Mussorgsky was urged to make a certain addition to his opera that would make the work more enjoyable to the audience. The composer took the advice. What did he do? (4)

10. Prokofiev created an opera based on Tolstoy's *War and Peace*. He also created an opera based on a novel by Feodor Dostoevsky. Which one? (4)

11. Which of the following works is *not* a Russian opera: *The Czar's Bride*, *The Czarevitch*, or *A Life for the Czar*? Name the composer of the "impostor," as well as the composers of the two truly Russian works. (3)

12. In Tchaikovsky's *Pique Dame*, who is Hermann's rival for the hand of Lisa? (3)

13. Can you identify the following Russian operatic luminaries?
    a. Dmitri Hvorostovsky (2)
    b. Irina Archipova (2)
    c. Tamara Milashkina (4)
    d. Feodor Chaliapin (1)
    e. Maria Guleghina (3)

14. Who are the composers of the following operas?
    a. *The Maid of Orleans* (2)
    b. *Khovanschina* (2)
    c. *Ruslan and Ludmila* (3)
    d. *Aleko* (4)
    e. *Sadko* (3)

15. After the demise of the Soviet Union, one of Russia's most distinguished opera companies, the Kirov, changed its name back to its original, pre-revolutionary appellation. The city in

which this great company is situated did something similar. What are the Soviet and pre-Soviet names of both the company and the city in question? (2)

Answers on page 271.

7. *AIDA*

1. What is the name of the god worshiped by the Egyptians in *Aida*? (3)
2. How does Amneris trick Aida into revealing her true feelings about Radames? (2)
3. Who created the role of Aida, and in what other way was this artist important to Verdi? (3)
4. What change did Verdi make in the score of *Aida* after the first performance in Egypt and before the Italian premiere at La Scala? (4)
5. Describe the two endings Verdi composed for Radames' aria "Celeste Aida." (3)
6. In a well-known Italian film of *Aida*, a popular screen beauty was cast in the title role, and the singing was dubbed by an equally beloved artist. Who is seen and who is heard in this 1953 film? (3)
7. Aida, with her father offstage eavesdropping, tricks Radames into revealing the route the Egyptian soldiers are planning to take. What route is that? (2)

The great conductor Sir Thomas Beecham was presiding over a performance of *Aida* beset by many stylistic problems, not the least of which was a camel that relieved itself on the stage during the Triumphal Scene. As Sir Thomas watched the camel, he was heard to mutter to himself, "Terribly vulgar, but, Lord, what a critic!"

8. *Aida* was the only opera conducted by Arturo Toscanini to be telecast, albeit in concert form, in the United States. A recording of this performance has been available since 1957. A video edition was issued in 1990, although it was withdrawn in 1994. Name the recording company that issued these historic documents. Who are the artists who perform Aida, Amneris, Radames, Amonasro, and the Priestess? (3)

9. A performance of *Aida* in Mexico City became one of the most remarkable evenings in Maria Callas's career. What was the reason for all the excitement? (4)

10. Who wrote the libretto for *Aida*? (2)

11. Name the outstanding Mississippi-born soprano who was acclaimed in Moscow for singing the title role of *Aida* with a visiting troupe from La Scala, before she sang the role at the Met. (1)

12. What misdeed does Radames accuse Amneris of committing in their confrontation in the fourth act of *Aida*? (2)

Answers on page 274.

8. *CARMEN*

1. In Act I, Micaela brings Don José three gifts from his mother. What are they? (2)

2. What is the fight about between Carmen and her coworker in the cigarette factory? (2)

3. What is the coworker's name? (3)

4. Which of Bizet's operas was composed first, *Carmen* or *Les Pêcheurs de Perles*? (2)

5. What objections were voiced by the management of the Paris Opéra-Comique to Carmen's onstage activities? (3)

6. Which of Carmen's two smuggler friends is the chief of the outlaws, El Remendado or El Dancairo? (3)

7. Who composed the music to the recitatives in the revised, "operatic" version of *Carmen*? (3)

8. When the bullfighter Escamillo duels with José, he spares the

corporal's life, giving a specific reason for doing so. What is his reason, and how does José repay him? (4)

9. Unfavorable reviews of the first production of *Carmen* accused its composer of being in the thrall of what other well-known nineteenth-century opera composer? (2)

10. Who was the famous American Carmen who graduated to that role after many performances of the role of Micaela? (3)

11. Who directed the landmark 1952 production of *Carmen* at the Metropolitan Opera that starred Risë Stevens and Richard Tucker? (4)

12. Victoria de los Angeles sang the title role in *Carmen* onstage only twice, both times in the United States. With which two companies? (4)

13. Which one of the following baritones did *not* make a complete recording of the role of Escamillo?
   - a. Tom Krause
   - b. Leonard Warren
   - c. Robert Merrill
   - d. Robert Massard
   - e. José van Dam (3)

14. In Act III, why does Micaela seek José in the smugglers' mountain hideaway? (2)

15. In what ways did Geraldine Farrar's film performance of *Carmen* differ from her acclaimed performance in the opera house? (4)

Answers on page 275.

9. *CAVALLERIA RUSTICANA*

1. Why has Santuzza been excommunicated? (2)
2. Who was the first Santuzza? (4)
3. What is the name of Turiddu's married girl friend? (1)
4. When Alfio refuses the glass of wine that Turiddu offers him, what reason does he give for not taking the drink? (2)
5. During his "Addio" aria, Turiddu asks his mother, Mamma Lucia, to do three things for him. What are they? (3)

6. What curse does Santuzza hurl at Turiddu at the climax of their quarrel? In what way might it be said to have been fulfilled? (2)

7. Name the soprano from Zagreb who was for more than twenty-five years the most acclaimed Santuzza in America? (2)

8. Mezzos Rosalind Elias and Carol Smith recorded the role of Lola in *Cavalleria Rusticana*. Can you recall the tenor who sang Turiddu opposite each lady? (4)

9. Who wrote the novella on which Mascagni's opera is based? (3)

10. Leonard Bernstein made one of his rare appearances at the Metropolitan Opera in 1970, conducting what was then a new production of *Cavalleria*. Who sang Santuzza and Turiddu? (There is a recording of this performance.) (4)

Answers on page 276.

10. *LES CONTES D'HOFFMANN*

1. On whose work is the libretto of this opera based? (1)

2. Name the opera's librettists. (3)

3. At which opera house was *Les Contes d'Hoffmann* premiered? (2)

4. What are the names of the evil men who pursue Hoffmann throughout the opera? (3)

5. Which characters sing the following arias or musical numbers in *Les Contes d'Hoffmann*?
    a. "Scintille, diamant" (3)
    b. "J'ai des yeux" (4)
    c. "Belle nuit, ô nuit d'amour" (1)
    d. "Il était une fois à la cour d'Eisenach" (2)
    e. "Elle a fui . . ." (3)

6. What has Giulietta taken from Schlémil? (3)

7. What two things does Hoffmann take from Schlémil? (3)

8. What does Giulietta take from Hoffmann? (2)

9. Lucine Amara, Victoria de los Angeles, and Jarmila Novotna were all famous exponents of what role in *Les Contes d'Hoffmann*? (2)

10. In Act I of *Hoffmann*, what is the name of Olympia's "father"? (2)

11. In the version of *Les Contes d'Hoffmann* recorded by Joan Sutherland for Decca/London, what variation of the plot is there in the "Giulietta Act"? (4)

12. A contemporary musicologist has pieced together a version of this opera that supposedly reflects Offenbach's true intentions concerning the score at the time of his death, before the opera was completed. Who is he? (3)

13. An entirely American-born and -trained cast, led by a French conductor, triumphed in the Metropolitan Opera's 1955 production of *Les Contes d'Hoffmann* (available on CD). Can you name the artists who sang Hoffmann, the Four Villains, Olympia, Giulietta, and Antonia? Who was the conductor? (4)

14. How many times has Plácido Domingo recorded *Les Contes d'Hoffmann*? Who are his leading ladies? (3)

15. Which of the following tenors is *not* a famous exponent of the role of Hoffmann?
    a. Jon Vickers
    b. Nicolai Gedda
    c. Neil Shicoff
    d. Alfredo Kraus (1)
    Answers on page 277.

11. *DON GIOVANNI*

1. What is the opera's subtitle? (4)
2. Who wrote the libretto? (2)
3. Why is Leporello standing on guard duty at the beginning of Act I? (1)
4. To which character does Leporello sing the Catalog Aria? (1)
5. Please name the characters in *Don Giovanni* who sing the following pieces:
    a. "Vedrai, carino" (3)
    b. "Dalla sua pace" (2)
    c. "Or sai chi l'onore" (2)

    d. "Là ci darem la mano" (1)

    e. "Ho capito, signor sì" (2)

6. Name the once-popular dance that is heard toward the end of the first act. (1)

7. Who are the three maskers who "crash" Don Giovanni's party? (2)

8. Who among the following singers has *not* been a famous Don Giovanni during the past fifty years?

    a. Jerome Hines

    b. Nicolai Ghiaurov

    c. Thomas Hampson

    d. Hermann Prey

    e. George London (3)

9. Although Leontyne Price was a noted Donna Anna, she is featured in a recording of *Don Giovanni* singing another role. What was it? Bonus: Who sings Donna Anna on that recording? (3)

10. Describe the final act of defiance that seals Don Giovanni's doom. (1)

11. Name the role in *Don Giovanni* that Zinka Milanov, Ljuba Welitsch, and Eleanor Steber all sang. (2)

12. Which two arias from *Don Giovanni* were recorded by Maria Callas, who never performed the opera on stage? (3)

Answers on page ***278***.

12. *L'ELISIR D'AMORE*

1. What is the theme of the book Adina reads to the assembled villagers in the opening scene? (2)

2. What is the name of the aria that Nemorino sings in the first scene? (2)

3. To what mythological character does Sergeant Belcore compare himself upon his entrance in Act I? (3)

4. Name the tenor with whom the role of Nemorino is indelibly associated, even though there are few still living who actually heard him in the part. (1)

5. How much does Dr. Dulcamara propose to charge the crowd for his cure-all medicine? (4)

6. Why is Nemorino at first unconcerned when Adina announces plans to marry Belcore? What happens to frighten Nemorino? (3)

7. What is the name of the song that Dr. Dulcamara invites Adina to sing with him at her wedding celebration? (3)

8. Which of the following tenors did *not* record a complete version of *L'Elisir d'Amore*?
   a. Jussi Bjoerling
   b. Nicolai Gedda
   c. Luigi Alva
   d. Giuseppe di Stefano (3)

9. What is the real reason that the village girls start to pay attention to Nemorino? To what does Nemorino attribute his new-found success with the ladies? (2)

10. What character sings "Una furtiva lagrima"? (1)

11. Name the aria that immediately follows "Una furtiva lagrima." Who sings it? (3)

12. Dame Joan Sutherland, Mirella Freni, and Rosanna Carteri have each recorded the role of Adina. Who sings Nemorino opposite each soprano? (3)

13. Which of the following basses never sang Dr. Dulcamara?
   a. Salvatore Baccaloni
   b. Renato Capecchi
   c. Paolo Montarsolo
   d. Ezio Pinza (2)

   Answers on page 279.

13. *FAUST*

1. Which aria from *Faust* was composed to an English text for the opera's first London production? What is the aria's first couplet in English? Who sings it? (4)

2. When Méphistophélès first appears to Faust, he asks him what

he wants from the Devil. Faust immediately lists three items. What are they? (2)

3. Which characters in *Faust* sing the following musical numbers?
   a. "Le veau d'or" (1)
   b. "Il était un roi de Thulé" (2)
   c. "Salut! demeure chaste et pure" (2)
   d. "Gloire immortelle de nos anciens aïeux!" (3)
   e. "Il ne reviendrà plus" (3)

4. Who were the two brothers who often sang the roles of Faust and Méphistophélès together in the nineteenth century? (4)

5. Can you identify the opera house that presented *Faust* so frequently that some wags referred to it as the "Faustspielhaus"? (3)

6. Who designed and staged the famous Metropolitan Opera production of *Faust* that moved the time of the action forward from the Middle Ages to the time of the opera's composition, in the 1850s? (4)

7. What is the name of Marguérite's foolish neighbor, whom Méphistophélès pretends to woo in order to give Faust and Marguérite some time together? (2)

8. Name the soprano, tenor, and bass who recorded *Faust* together twice in a period of five years. What is the principal difference between the recordings? (3)

9. There is a legend that the ballet music for Gounod's *Faust* was actually the work of another composer, one even better known than Gounod. Can you guess his identity? (4)

10. Enrico Caruso recorded sizable excerpts from *Faust* with a famous soprano and bass. Who were they? (4)

11. The title role in *Faust* was the last role to be performed at the Metropolitan by one of the following great tenors. Who?
    a. Giuseppe di Stefano
    b. Jan Peerce
    c. Jussi Bjoerling
    d. Ferruccio Tagliavini (3)

12. Can you name at least five basses who were famous for singing both Gounod's Méphistophélès and Boito's Mefistofele? (2)

13. What characters in *Faust* sing the opera's final trio? (1)

14. Can you name four sopranos who were well known for both Gounod's Marguérite and Boito's Margherita? (3)

15. There is a scene in *Faust* that is very often cut from performances and recordings. Name the characters who appear in it. What happens? (4)

16. Who staged the New York City Opera's *Faust*, performed at Lincoln Center in the 1960s and 1970s? What alteration in the opera's plot was made in this version? (4)

17. Which of the following sopranos was *not* a famous Marguérite?
   a. Dorothy Kirsten
   b. Beverly Sills
   c. Eleanor Steber
   d. Patrice Munsel
   e. Pilar Lorengar (3)

18. With what kind of anachronistic dance does the Kermesse Scene of *Faust* conclude? (3)

Answers on page 280.

14. *MADAMA BUTTERFLY*

1. Puccini based his opera *Madama Butterfly* upon a play by David Belasco. Belasco, in turn, based his drama upon a short story by a then-noted American author. Who wrote that original story? (4)

2. Early in *Madama Butterfly*'s first act, Pinkerton describes the lease on the house he has rented. What were the lease's two clauses, and what relationship does one of them have to the marriage contract between Butterfly and Pinkerton? (3)

3. When Butterfly shows Pinkerton a few of her possessions, he shows displeasure at one of them, which Butterfly promptly discards. What arouses Pinkerton's disapproval? (2)

4. At *Madama Butterfly*'s world premiere at La Scala, one of the many things that the hostile audience carped at was a seemingly inadvertent quotation from another Puccini opera. What tune was quoted (give the opera, too, of course) and where does the intrusion occur? (2)

5. One of the most famous recordings of *Madama Butterfly* was made in Rome shortly before the outbreak of World War II. This recording is still available. Who sing the roles of Butterfly and Pinkerton on this album? (2)

6. When does Pinkerton promise that he will return to Butterfly? What happens when Butterfly asks Consul Sharpless about this? (2)

7. Where in Japan does *Madama Butterfly* take place? (1)

8. After *Madama Butterfly's* disastrous first performance, Puccini withdrew the opera from La Scala and made a series of revisions before he would allow the opera to be produced again, several months later in Brescia. Four of these changes are important enough to be noted here. Describe them. (4)

9. Name the four sopranos who have each recorded the title role of *Madama Butterfly* twice. Name the tenors on each of the eight recordings. (3)

10. What is the name of the wealthy suitor to whom the marriage broker Goro introduces Butterfly while she is still waiting for Pinkerton to return to Japan? (1)

11. Who was the first tenor to sing Pinkerton at the Metropolitan Opera? (2)

12. In Act II, the heroine orders the American consul to leave her home at once, although she immediately reconsiders. What has Sharpless done to incur Butterfly's wrath? (2)

13. Who is the first soprano to record an absolutely complete *Madama Butterfly*, a set in which all existing versions of the opera are included? (4)

14. Maria Callas sang the title role of *Madama Butterfly* in only one American city. Name it. Who sang Pinkerton on that occasion? What newsworthy event occurred backstage after the first performance? (3)

15. Tenor Richard Tucker sang the role of Pinkerton on two recordings of *Madama Butterfly*. For which labels did Tucker record the opera? Name Tucker's two leading ladies. (3)

*Answers on page **281**.*

15. VERDI'S *OTELLO*

1. What publisher worked very hard to persuade Verdi to compose *Otello*? (3)
2. What special stipulation did Verdi insist upon in his contract to have *Otello* produced for the first time? (4)
3. Name the other famous Italian composer who created a successful opera based on Shakespeare's *Othello*. (2)
4. Which entire act of Shakespeare's tragedy was omitted from Verdi's opera? (2)
5. Identify the characters who sing the following phrases:
   a. "Già della notte densa estingui ogni clamor . . ." (2)
   b. "Era la notte, Cassio dormia . . ." (2)
   c. "Ed io t'amavo per le tue sventure, e tu m'amavi per la mia pietà . . ." (3)
   d. "Era più calmo?" (2)

One of the most catastrophic yet hilarious gaffes I have ever seen in an opera house occurred during a performance of *Die Walküre*. The first act was spectacularly cast—Birgit Nilsson was Sieglinde and Jon Vickers sang Siegmund. The performance grew from strength to strength musically, and then came that powerful moment when Siegmund pulls his father's sword from the tree into which it had been thrust by Wotan. Vickers pulled, Nilsson gasped in awe—and the sword fell apart into little pieces across the floor of the stage! How the two singers managed to finish the act without dissolving into hysterics, I'll never know. (Vickers, of course, has been known to erupt into fury on lesser provocation.) Undaunted, Siegmund led his sister off to conceive Siegfried, and it can only be hoped that the Wälsungs' night of love went off more smoothly than their escape from Hunding.

6. Lauritz Melchior sang only one act of *Otello* at the Metropolitan Opera, during a gala concert. Which act did Melchior sing? (4)

7. Can you name the artist who was not only a superb Otello but, later in his career, was a formidable Iago as well? (4)

8. Mario del Monaco broadcast *Otello* three times from the Metropolitan Opera. Leonard Warren was the Iago in each performance. Who were the two sopranos who sang Desdemona in these broadcasts? (You can find transcriptions of these performances on CDs.) (3)

9. What action of Otello's horrifies the Venetian ambassadors during the opera's third act? (1)

10. What, to Otello, is conclusive "proof" that Desdemona has been unfaithful to him? (1)

11. Name the Russian baritone who has had successes as Iago in key world opera houses in the 1990s. (2)

12. Baritone Ettore Bastianini was dismissed from a recording of *Otello* when the conductor found him ill prepared. Who replaced Bastianini? Who was the dissatisfied maestro? (3)

13. Who was the outstanding Otello in America during the 1930s and 1940s? (2)

14. What was the extent of Maria Callas's professional involvement with Verdi's *Otello*? (2)

15. Who starred in Herbert von Karajan's film version of *Otello*? What parts of Verdi's score did Karajan abridge? (3)

16. When James McCracken returned to the Metropolitan Opera in 1963 to sing the title role in *Otello*, he was heard in his second role in that opera at the Met. What role had McCracken sung at the Met previously?

17. What was the only scene from *Otello* that Caruso and Bjoerling, decades apart, recorded? Name the artists who collaborated with them. (2)

18. Mirella Freni sang only two excerpts from *Otello* at the Met, each on a special occasion. Name each event, and identify the scenes that Freni sang. Who were her colleagues? (3)

19. Which of the following sopranos did *not* sing Desdemona?

        a. Maria Spacagna
        b. Beverly Sills
        c. Zinka Milanov
        d. Shirley Verrett (3)

20. What character in *Otello* leads the work's "brindisi"? (1)

Answers on page 283.

16. *PAGLIACCI*

1. In the original score of *Pagliacci*, which character is given the opera's final line? (3)
2. What *is* that final line? (1)
3. On what source did Ruggiero Leoncavallo base *Pagliacci*? (4)
4. What is the name of Nedda's lover? (1)
5. What advice does Tonio give Canio after the latter's unsuccessful pursuit of Nedda's lover? (2)
6. Who is the only major tenor in recent years who has made a practice of singing Turiddu in *Cavalleria Rusticana* and Canio in *Pagliacci* on the same evening? (2)
7. Who sang Canio and Tonio in a San Francisco Opera performance in 1962, when Marilyn Horne sang Nedda? (4)
8. Which of the following sopranos, all of whom have recorded the role of Nedda, never actually sang the role on stage?
        a. Maria Callas
        b. Lucine Amara
        c. Gabriella Tucci
        d. Teresa Stratas (3)
9. What are the first two words of the opera's "Prologo"? (2)

Answers on page 284.

17. *DER RING DES NIBELUNGEN*

1. In *Das Rheingold*, in order to steal the gold from the Rhinemaidens, what does Alberich have to do? (2)
2. What are gods Wotan and Fricka worried about when we first meet them in scene 2 of *Das Rheingold*? (3)

3. What is Freia's special contribution to the gods' lifestyle? (2)
4. How does Alberich make himself invisible? (2)
5. What is the name of the gods' new home? (1)
6. Kirsten Flagstad, arguably the greatest Brünnhilde of all time, appears on the first complete studio recording of the *Ring* (led by Solti on Decca/London) singing what role? (3)
7. Who helps Wotan outwit Alberich? (2) How is this done? (3)
8. What mode of transportation does Fricka employ in Valhalla? (3)
9. How does Siegmund react when Brünnhilde tells him about the fate that awaits him? (2)
10. How does Wotan initially plan to punish Brünnhilde for having defied him by trying to aid Siegmund in his battle with Sieglinde's husband? What mercy does she ultimately receive from him? (3)
11. In Act III of *Die Walküre*, what does Brünnhilde tell Sieglinde, and what does the Valkyrie give to the Valsung? (3)
12. Why is *Siegfried* often refered to as the "scherzo" of the *Ring*? (3)
13. What happens to Siegfried after he tastes the blood of the dragon that he has slain? (3)
14. Why does Siegfried kill Mime? (3)
15. How does Siegfried learn of Brünnhilde's existence? (2)
16. Who is the Wanderer? (1)
17. Early in Act III of *Siegfried*, the Wanderer encounters earth goddess Erda, who makes her first appearance on stage since *Das Rheingold*. What, however, has happened between these characters since then? (3)
18. In the first scene of the prologue to *Götterdämmerung*, what are the three Norns doing? When this activity is interrupted, what is foreshadowed? (2)
19. Name the musical interlude played between the second scene of *Götterdämmerung's* prologue and scene 1 of Act I. (2)
20. Why does Waltraute visit Brünnhilde? (2)
21. In what order were the libretti for the *Ring* operas written? (4)
22. Who wrote the libretti for the *Ring*? (1)

23. What reason does Hagen give for killing Siegfried? (2)
24. What is the name of Brünnhilde's horse? (2)
25. Name five orchestral highlights of the *Ring*. (1)
26. Who wrote the English translation of the *Ring* used by the English National Opera and the Seattle Opera, and heard in the ENO's recording of the *Ring*? (4)
27. In *Die Walküre*, why does Fricka insist that Wotan protect Hunding in his fight with Siegmund? (1)
28. What is Wotan's relationship to Siegmund? (2)
29. What is Brünnhilde's relationship to Siegmund? (2)
30. Therefore, what is Brünnhilde's relationship to Siegfried? (1)
31. What are Brunnhilde's first words upon waking up at Siegfried's kiss? (3)
32. What does Siegfried say upon seeing the sleeping Brünnhilde for the first time? (3)
33. Which *Ring* opera requires the services of a chorus? What is the scene in which the chorus performs? (2)
34. Who devised the so-called neo-Bayreuth style of staging the *Ring* (and other Wagnerian works) that, after World War II, helped remove the Nazi stigma from these operas? (3)
35. Name five famous Brünnhildes who also were celebrated for singing Sieglinde. (4)
36. Who was the principal American Brünnhilde during World War II, when Flagstad was trapped in her native Norway? (3)
37. Who conducted the notorious 1975 Bayreuth *Ring* cycle, which incited much booing from the audience? (This unorthodox *Ring* was set in an industrialized, seemingly nineteenth-century Europe.) (3)
38. Where did Herbert von Karajan first stage his own controversial *Ring* production? What opera house subsequently produced a *Ring* based on Karajan's interpretation? (3)
39. In the 1970s, a British soprano known for singing Brünnhilde in English as well as German had the unenviable task of replacing Birgit Nilsson in *Götterdämmerung* when Nilsson injured herself in a backstage accident at the Metropolitan. Can you identify her? (3)
40. At what opera house was there a performance that had Nilsson

as Brünnhilde and Montserrat Caballé as Sieglinde? Who sang Siegmund? (4)

41. Maria Callas sang the *Walküre* Brünnhilde in Italy, in Italian. Can you tell us the name of the theater where this performance took place, and who was the conductor? (4)

42. Arturo Toscanini recorded vocal excerpts from *Die Walküre* and *Götterdämmerung* for RCA during the 1940s. What scenes were recorded, and who were the soprano and tenor? (4)

43. The role of Wotan was shared by what two artists on the von Karajan recording of the *Ring*? (2)

44. Who are the two Brünnhildes on the von Karajan recording of the *Ring*? (3)

45. A soprano who is world-famous in an entirely different repertoire than Wagner performed a tiny part on the Solti recording of the *Ring*. Name the lady and the role she sang. (2)

46. In the years between the *Ring* performances of Helen Traubel and Birgit Nilsson, who was the principal Brünnhilde at the Metropolitan Opera? (4)

47. Please name the American soprano who achieved great success as Brünnhilde at the Bayreuth Festival in the 1950s. (3)

48. What curse does Alberich place on the ring, and why does he do so in the first place? (2)

49. Who conducted the first post–World War II *Ring* cycle at La Scala? Who was the Brünnhilde? (Note, this cycle has been available for many years as a recording.) (3)

*Answers on page **285**.*

18. *RIGOLETTO*

1. Why does Count Monterone set a "father's curse" upon Rigoletto? (1)

2. Which Mantuan courtier is Rigoletto's next-door neighbor? Why is this important to the plot? (2)

3. What is Sparafucile's price list for murders and assassinations? (3)

4. Which aria in *Rigoletto* is preceded by the words *"Ciel, dammi corragio"*? (3)

5. Why were the Venetian censors so confounded by *Rigoletto*? (3)

6. What was the title character's name in Verdi's original version of the opera? (4)

7. To which of the Duke's courtiers does Rigoletto plead in vain for mercy in the opera's second act? (2)

8. What event interrupts Gilda and Rigoletto in their duet of reconciliation in the second act? How does that interruption affect Rigoletto? (2)

9. How many times is "La donna è mobile" sung in Act III? (3)

10. How does Verdi make use of the chorus in the final act of *Rigoletto*? (3)

11. Can you identify the author of the libretto for *Rigoletto*? (3)

12. Which character in *Rigoletto* sings a cabaletta in the second act? What is the name of the piece (which is often cut from performances and recordings, probably because it concludes with a ringing high D-flat)? (3)

13. A live recording of a World War II–era performance of *Rigoletto* starring Leonard Warren, Jussi Bjoerling, and Bidù Sayão is still available on compact disc. From what opera house was it taken? (3)

14. Can you identify the British stage director responsible for a production of *Rigoletto* set in New York's Little Italy in the 1950s? In this version, the Duke is a gangster who sings "La donna è mobile" after slipping a dime into a jukebox in Sparafucile's seedy bar. Which opera company commissioned the production? (4)

15. Which of the following sopranos did *not* record the role of Gilda?

        a. Hilde Gueden
        b. Erna Berger
        c. Gianna D'Angelo
        d. Mattiwilda Dobbs (4)

16. What article of clothing does Gilda lose as the courtiers are abducting her from her home? (3)

17. When Joan Sutherland sang Gilda at the Metropolitan in 1972, what change in the staging was made necessary because of the soprano's generous proportions? (3)

*Answers on page **289**.*

19. *DER ROSENKAVALIER*

1. What are the nicknames that the Marschallin and Octavian have for one another? (2)
2. What is Baron Ochs's full name? (3)
3. Who is Leopold? (3)
4. Octavian feels quite dispirited when the suddenly melancholy Marschallin dismisses him. What does his lover offer to allow him to do as a way of cheering him up? (3)
5. Why does the Marschallin summon little Mohammed at the end of the first act? (2)
6. Describe Ochs's reaction when he discovers Sophie and Octavian in each other's arms in Act II. (3)
7. In Act II what choice concerning her future does Faninal give his daughter Sophie? (2)
8. In the well-known film made at the Salzburg Festival, who are the artists who portray the Marschallin, Octavian, Sophie, and Ochs? Who conducts? (3)
9. In the famous 1930 abridged recording of *Der Rosenkavalier* (currently available as an EMI CD) who are the artists in the same roles listed in Question 8? Who conducts? (4)
10. Why is Annina furious with Ochs as Act II draws to a close? (2)
11. In Act III, the Marschallin gives advice first to Ochs and then to Sophie. What does she say to each? (4)
12. Why does Mohammed come back onstage at the very end of the opera? (1)
13. Name the German-born soprano who was closely identified with the role of the Marschallin in the United States in the 1930s and 1940s. (3)
14. Can you name the father and son who, over the years, have each conducted recorded performances of *Der Rosenkavalier*? (3)

15. What role does Ljuba Welitsch sing on Herbert von Karajan's first recording of *Der Rosenkavalier*? (4)

Answers on page 291.

20. *TOSCA*

1. Name the playwright who wrote *La Tosca* and the actress who made the play a success. (3)
2. Puccini, with the help of publisher Giulio Ricordi, convinced what composer to relinquish the rights to the play on which the opera is based? What reason did they give to lure the gullible chap away from *La Tosca*? (3)
3. Who, without being aware of it, is the model for Mario Cavaradossi's painting in the Church of Sant' Andrea delle Valle? In what other ways is this person important to *Tosca*'s plot? (3)
4. From where does the prisoner Angelotti escape? (1)
5. Why does Tosca return to the Church of Sant' Andrea delle Valle after her first meeting with Mario Cavaradossi? (2)
6. Which aria in *Tosca* did Puccini come to dislike, and why? (3)
7. When Scarpia prepares a safe-conduct for Tosca, what route does she ask him to follow? (3)
8. How did the tradition of singing the aria "Vissi d'arte" from a prone position on the floor originate? (3)
9. Why was the world-premiere performance of *Tosca* interrupted moments after the opera began? (4)
10. Who composed the music for the cantata that Tosca is heard singing offstage during the second act? (4)
11. Two videotapes of Renata Tebaldi singing the title role of *Tosca* have been published. From what cities do they come, and who sing the roles of Mario and Scarpia in each? (4)
12. What complete act of *Tosca* starring Maria Callas has survived on videotape and laser disc? In fact, two separate performances of this act are available. Where and when was each performed, and who were Callas's colleagues in the roles of Mario and Scarpia in each performance? (3)

Russian diva Galina Vishnevskaya had a scary experience singing *Tosca* in Vienna. Having stabbed Scarpia, the soprano searched the dead man's desk, looking for the safe-conduct that would allow her and Mario to leave Rome. Vishnevskaya inadvertently brushed her head against a candle and her wig caught fire. Fortunately, her Scarpia was lying "dead" with his eyes open and saw his colleague was in danger of performing a non-Wagnerian immolation scene. He leapt up, ran to the still-oblivious soprano and began whacking the flames in her hair with his bare hands. Vishnevskaya screamed, unsure whether her colleague had gone mad or was indulging in a bizarre new piece of stage business. Only after the act ended did Vishnevskaya realize that her resurrected Scarpia had saved her life.

🌿 🌿 🌿

13. Who sang the soprano, baritone, and tenor leads in the production of *Tosca* that was telecast "live" all across the world, from the actual Roman locations for Puccini's opera? Who conducted? Who directed the production? What company issued audio and video recordings of the event? (3)
14. Who was the famous Italian soprano who once sang *Tosca* in English in San Francisco? (A recording of the first act of this performance has survived.) (4)

Answers on page 292.

21. *TRISTAN UND ISOLDE*

1. Some of the music associated with Tristan and Isolde's love appears elsewhere in Wagner. Where? (3)
2. Why is Isolde so furious with Tristan at the beginning of the opera? (2)
3. Where did *Tristan und Isolde* have its world premiere? (4)

4. How does Brangäne, Isolde's handmaiden, deceive her mistress? (1)
5. What is the name of the soliloquy sung by Isolde in the opera's first act? (2)
6. Why is Isolde heartbroken when King Marke comes to claim her as his bride? (2)
7. What is Melot's contribution to the plot? (2)
8. Which of the following sopranos is *not* an acclaimed Isolde?
   a. Leonie Rysanek
   b. Frida Leider
   c. Helen Traubel
   d. Astrid Varnay (3)
9. When Birgit Nilsson made her Metropolitan debut as Isolde, who sang the role of Tristan? (4)
10. Identify the recording of *Tristan* in which the services of three women were used, even though the opera has roles for only two female singers. Who were the singers, and how were they employed? (4)
11. What character in *Tristan und Isolde* sings the Liebestod? (1)
12. What character keeps a vigil during the lovers' tryst but isn't able to warn them in time that King Marke has returned? (2)
13. Who conducts the recording of the second-act love duet from *Tristan* with Kirsten Flagstad and Lauritz Melchior recorded in the United States shortly before World War II began? (4)
14. Birgit Nilsson recorded *Tristan und Isolde* twice commercially. Who sings Brangäne on each? (3)
15. Who dies first, Tristan or Isolde? (2)

*Answers on page **294**.*

22. *LA TRAVIATA*

1. Where and when did *La Traviata* have its world premiere? (3)
2. The opera's first performance was not a success. What were the two main reasons that *Traviata* failed to please its audience? (3)
3. Who is Violetta's protector at the beginning of the opera? (1)

4. Name the six "solo" guests at Violetta's party. (1)
5. What character sings "De' miei bollenti spiriti"? (2)
6. Why is Alfredo's father so insistent that Violetta break off her liaison with Alfredo? (1)
7. How does the elder Germont know that Alfredo is heading for Flora's party? (2)
8. What are Papa Germont's words after he witnesses Alfredo insulting Violetta, and why might they seem hypocritical? (3)
9. Who sang the principal roles in the famous 1955 *La Traviata* at La Scala, immortalized on a broadcast tape now published by EMI? Who was the conductor? Who was the designer and stage director? (3)
10. Toscanini led a famous broadcast of *La Traviata* long available as a commercial recording on the RCA label. Who were the artists singing Violetta, Alfredo and Germont? (3)
11. Violetta's poignant outburst "Ah!, Gran Dio, morir sì giovane" comes after what sign that she is dying? (2)
12. What are Violetta's final, inappropriately ecstatic words? (1)
13. Baritone Robert Merrill recorded the role of Germont three times. For what record companies did Merrill sing this role? Who sings Violetta and Alfredo on each recording? (2)
14. Which of the following tenors was *not* famous for the role of Alfredo in *La Traviata*?
    a. Nicolai Gedda
    b. Jan Peerce
    c. Franco Corelli
    d. Giuseppe Campora
    e. Alfredo Kraus (3)
    Answers on page **295**.

23. I'VE HEARD THAT BEFORE

Operatic composers occasionally pay other composers the compliment of quoting someone else's aria in their own scores. Below are listed a number of operas (including some of today's "pop operas") in which such occasions occur. Give the name of the opera quoted, its composer, and the reason that the quotation is made.

1. *Don Giovanni* (2)
2. *Il Tabarro* (3)
3. *Les Contes d'Hoffmann* (2)
4. *Die Meistersinger von Nürnberg* (2)
5. *Madama Butterfly* (2)
6. *The Phantom of the Opera* (3)
7. *Cats* (3)
8. *Les Misérables* (4)

Answers on page **297**.

24. WAGNER I

1. What was Wagner's first opera? (3)
2. Name Wagner's first wife. (3)
3. Who was the influential music critic whom Wagner hated and used as the basis for a nasty character in one of his operas? Name the character and the opera. (3)
4. The original version of *Tannhäuser* is known by the city in which it was first produced. The revised version of that opera, first staged elsewhere, is also known by the city of its "birth." Name both cities, and describe the principal difference between the two versions. (2)
5. Name the monarch who, for many years, was Wagner's principal patron. (3)
6. Name Wagner's second wife. Who was her father? (1)
7. What was Mathilde Wesendonck's relationship to Richard Wagner? (3)
8. Which of Wagner's works is foreshadowed in themes found in the Wesendonck Lieder? (2)
9. A brilliant and celebrated Briton adored Wagner's music and wrote a famous book on the subject. Can you name the author and his book? (2)
10. Which of Wagner's operas involve relationships between fathers and sons? (2)
11. In what circumstance did Wagner hit upon the idea of composing *Der Fliegende Holländer*? (3)
12. The Viennese soprano Leonie Rysanek is especially admired for her Wagnerian roles. What are they? (3)

13. A young composer, who eventually achieved fame with a very popular opera of his own, once served as an assistant at Bayreuth during the preparation for the world premiere of *Parsifal*. In fact, this chap synthesized a few bars to be added to an orchestral interlude to facilitate a scene change. Identify the composer and his most famous opera. (4)

14. For what occasion was the *Siegfried Idyll* composed? (3)

15. In which of Wagner's operas do the following characters appear? Briefly discuss each one in terms of his or her importance to the operas in question.
    a. Melot (3)
    b. Henry the Fowler (3)
    c. Wolfram (2)
    d. Erik (4)
    e. Fafner (2)
    f. Mary (4)
    g. Pogner (3)
    h. Waltraute (1)
    i. Woglinde (2)
    j. Brangäne (4)

16. Which Wagnerian characters sing the following well-known lines?
    a. "Amfortas, die Wunde!" (1)
    b. "In fernem Land" (2)
    c. "Du bist der Lenz" (2)
    d. "Die Frist ist um" (3)
    e. "Mild und Leise" (1)
    f. "Weia! Waga!" (2)
    g. "Dich, teure Halle" (3)
    h. "O sink hernieder" (4)
    i. "Gerechter Gott, so ist's entschieden schon" (4)
    j. "So ist es denn aus mit den ewigen Göttern" (4)

17. Klingsor, the villain in *Parsifal*, had once been a Knight of the Grail. Why is this knight different from all other knights? (3)

18. In *Parsifal*, why has Kundry been condemned to her miserable existence? (3)

19. What was Wagner's final opera? (1)

20. Where and when did Wagner die? (3)

21. Name two sopranos who, within six years of one another, made extraordinarily successful Metropolitan Opera debuts singing Sieglinde in *Die Walküre* during Saturday matinee broadcast performances. (3)

22. Birgit Nilsson occasionally sang two roles in the same performance of this Wagnerian opera. Which one? (3)
23. Which of Wagner's operas was not, according to the composer's wishes, supposed to be performed anywhere outside Bayreuth? (1)
24. What two birds serve as boat drivers for Lohengrin? (1)
25. How do the following characters die in Wagner's operas?
    a. Senta (2)
    b. Telramund (4)
    c. Hunding (3)
    d. Mime (2)
    e. Fasolt (3)

*Answers on page **298**.*

25. WAGNER II

1. Name the onetime operetta singer who, under the tutelage of Herbert von Karajan, became a noted exponent of Lohengrin, Rienzi, and Walther. (3)
2. Who was the first American artist to sing at the Bayreuth Wagner festival? (4)
3. What was Cesare Siepi's one Wagnerian role? (4)
4. What is the name of Tristan's loyal servant? (1)
5. When the wounded Tristan was being cared for by Isolde (in Ireland, months before the action of the opera begins), what alias does he use? (2)
6. Which of the following characters does *not* appear in a Wagnerian opera: Herzelaide, Ortrud, Brangäne, or Magdalene? (2)
7. Which of the following artists has never sung a Wagnerian role in the opera house: Renata Tebaldi, Leontyne Price, or Mario del Monaco? (2)
8. Name the celebrated comedienne who for years convulsed audiences with her satirical lectures on Wagner's music? (1)
9. One of the greatest of Wagnerian conductors was Italian. He stormed away from the Bayreuth Festival to protest the Nazi regime in Germany. Who was he? (2)

10. In which of Wagner's stage works is a musical theme from *Tristan* quoted? Describe the dramatic situation. (3)
11. Name all of the Mastersingers. (4)
12. Which of Wagner's operas is devoid of all supernatural elements? (2)
13. Who was the British conductor who led the English-language performances and recordings of the *Ring* given at the English National Opera in the 1970s? (3)
14. What Wagnerian role did Nellie Melba foolishly insist upon singing, nearly wrecking her voice in the process? (3)
15. Who was the "Schwarze Venus" of Bayreuth? (3)
16. Who sang the role of Brünnhilde in the controversial Bayreuth Festival *Ring* cycle in 1976, in which the action was moved forward to the nineteenth century? (3)
17. "Dolce, calma, sorridente" is the Italian translation of the opening words of which famous Wagnerian scene? (4)
18. Why are the works of Richard Wagner never performed in Israel? (1)

Answers on page 302.

26. MOZART

1. What is the title of Mozart's first opera, and how old was he when he wrote it? (2)
2. What is the familial relationship between Fiordiligi and Dorabella in *Così Fan Tutte*? (1)
3. Listed below are several arias, duets, and ensembles from Mozart operas. For each, identify the opera it is from, and the character or characters who sing it.
    a. "Dalla sua pace" (2)
    b. "Ein Mädchen oder Weibchen" (1)
    c. "Vedrò mentr'io sospiro" (3)
    d. "Un'aura amorosa" (3)
    e. "Pace, pace, mio dolce tesoro!" (2)
    f. "Bei Männern, welche Liebe fühlen" (3)

4. In which of Mozart's operas do the characters listed below appear?
   a. Sesto (4)   d. Masetto (2)
   b. Elettra (4)   e. Astrafiammante (4)
   c. Don Curzio (3)   f. Guglielmo (3)

5. For which single Mozart role was soprano Zinka Milanov celebrated? (3)

6. Which two of Mozart's greatest operas had their world premieres in Prague? (1)

7. Which of Mozart's operas is a thorough debunking of the world of opera? (2)

8. Two of the most famous arias in *Don Giovanni* were inserted after that work's first performance. Name them. (2)

9. Which of the following operatic conductors was *not* renowned for his Mozart performances: Bruno Walter, Fritz Busch, Clemens Krauss, or Josef Krips? (3)

10. Richard Strauss was a great admirer of Mozart. Two of Strauss's operas are acknowledged homages to Mozart works. Name these two operas and the Mozart operas that, in a sense, inspired them. (3)

11. At the end of *Don Giovanni*, the six surviving characters announce their plans for the future. For each of these people—Donna Anna, Don Ottavio, Donna Elvira, Zerlina, Masetto, and Leporello—describe their projected activities. (3)

12. In *Die Zauberflöte*, what is Monostatos's reward for telling Sarastro of Pamina's attempt to escape? (1)

13. Which Mozartean character is a "valentine" to the composer's wife? (2)

14. Which of the following celebrated basses was *not* a great exponent of *Le Nozze di Figaro* and *Don Giovanni*: Feodor Chaliapin, Cesare Siepi, Ezio Pinza, or George London? (3)

15. Identify the Mozart aria occasionally sung in concert by Maria Callas. (Callas was rarely associated with Mozart's music.) (3)

16. Who directed the 1979 film of *Don Giovanni*? Who conducted the performance? Who sang the roles of Don Giovanni, Donna Anna, Donna Elvira, and Zerlina? (3)

17. Actor Alfred Lunt staged a Metropolitan Opera production of

one of Mozart's most brilliant operas that established that work as a repertory opera in the United States. Name the opera. Who sang the tenor lead in that production's first performance? (4)

18. When Ingmar Bergman filmed *Die Zauberflöte* in 1974, he made a major change in one aspect of the opera's plot. What was this alteration? (3)

19. Name two European music festivals traditionally associated with Mozart operas. (2)

20. What is the name of the love song that Cherubino has written in honor of the Countess Almaviva in *Le Nozze di Figaro*? (1)

21. At the ripe old age of fourteen, Mozart was commissioned by an Italian theater to compose an *opera seria*. Name the work that resulted. (4)

22. Name the three libretti written for Mozart by Lorenzo da Ponte. (2)

23. Freemasonry is the ever-present theme of which opera by Mozart? (1)

24. Dame Janet Baker won plaudits for her work in a rather infrequently performed Mozart opera on a classical subject. What is the opera? (3)

25. Marc Chagall created the decor for a landmark production of a Mozart opera in a major opera house. Name the opera and the theater. (2)

26. A young stage director who became active in the 1980s has created several bizarre productions of Mozart operas. In one production, the opera's aristocratic, seventeenth-century characters were transplanted to a ghetto in New York City. A Mozart comedy was reset in a diner owned by the opera's principal servant. Name the director, and identify the Mozart operas he mangled. (3)

27. Who is the American baritone whose Don Giovanni has been hailed by many reviewers as the finest since Cesare Siepi's? (1)

28. In the years following World War II, a red-haired soprano from Eastern Europe was renowned as Donna Anna in *Don Giovanni*. What was her name? (3)

29. Sopranos Elisabeth Schwarzkopf, Gundula Janowitz, and Lu-

cia Popp are all heard in one recording of a Mozart opera.
Identify the opera, the label that recorded it, and the role each
diva sings in it. (2)

30. George Bernard Shaw makes many references to *Don Giovanni*
in one of his plays. Name the play and the portion of its third
act that combines Shaw's genius with Mozart's. (2)

Answers on page 303.

27. PUCCINI RARITIES

1. Where and when was Giacomo Puccini born? (2)
2. Who is the tenor who sings the title role in the RCA recording
   of the second act of Puccini's second, seldom-heard opera,
   Edgar? (4)
3. Who sang the title role at the world premiere of *Turandot*? (3)
4. Name the country town where Puccini had his beloved hunting lodge. (3)
5. What was the title and who were the playwright and star of
   the hit American show that Puccini saw in London and that
   inspired him to compose *Madama Butterfly*? (2)
6. From which composer did Puccini steal the idea for his opera
   La Bohème? (2)
7. Name the four Puccini operas that had their world premieres
   at the Metropolitan Opera. (2)
8. Puccini once auditioned a young singer and said to him,
   "Who sent you to me? . . . God?" Whom was he addressing? (1)
9. Who were the first artists to sing the roles of Minnie, Johnson,
   and Rance in Puccini's *La Fanciulla del West*? Who conducted
   the premiere? (3)
10. Who were the librettists for Puccini's "big three"—*La
    Bohème, Tosca,* and *Madama Butterfly*? (2)
11. A famous recording was made of a performance that celebrated
    the fiftieth anniversary of the world premiere of *La Bohème*.

Where was this performance given? Who were the conductor and the principal artists? (3)

12. A famous playwright turned down Puccini's request for the operatic rights to one of the author's most successful plays. Who was the recalcitrant dramatist? What reason did he give for his refusal, and what was the eventual fate of the play in question? (4)

13. Where and when did Renata Tebaldi sing her only staged performances of Minnie in *La Fanciulla del West*? Who was her leading tenor? (4)

14. Which of Puccini's works was influenced by the poet Dante Alighieri, and in what ways? (3)

15. In which Puccini opera does the leading baritone get to punch the leading tenor? (2)

Answers on page 305.

Enrico Caruso and Geraldine Farrar, the first Metropolitan Pinkerton and Cio-Cio-San, were set to record the love duet from Puccini's *Madama Butterfly* one fine day at the RCA studios in Camden, New Jersey. The diva was first to arrive at the studio and discovered, when the tenor checked in a few moments late, that Caruso had had a drink or two en route from Manhattan. The normally fastidious Caruso even had a slight trace of liquor on his breath. Miss Farrar decided to immortalize the incident. When the recording session was underway, Farrar's Butterfly replied to Caruso's Pinkerton, when the latter sang "Ti serro palpitante. Sei mia." ("I hold you trembling, be mine!") by singing "He had a highball!" (instead of "Yes, for life!"). The two phrases have the same number of syllables. Caruso giggled, rendering his next line unintelligible. The recording survives on CD.

28. EARLY VERDI

1. Italian audiences found this leading character funny because he was not only a minister cuckolded by his wife, but he forgave her, too. (2)
2. This opera, climaxed by a magnificent trio, begins in Milan and ends a continent away. (3)
3. In this opera, the soprano, tenor, and baritone conspire to kill the basso, who is a historical character. (2)
4. About as early a Verdi opera as one can find, it is said to exist in an even earlier, lost, version, entitled *Rocester.* (2)
5. In his letters, Verdi refers to this opera as "really ugly." (4)
6. In this revised but still unsuccessful version of an early Verdian bomb, the title character is no longer a minister but a knight. He is still saddled, however, with a wayward wife. (3)
7. This not too merry, but not too unpleasant comic opera was composed shortly after the deaths of Verdi's first wife and their two children. It is practically never performed. (3)
8. This opera contains an immortal chorus sung in unison, and a "killer" aria for the soprano. Name each. (2)
9. One of Verdi's "patriotic" operas, this rarely performed work requires its hero to make a spectacular leap off a balcony. (3)
10. A father and son are the protagonists of this opera, which involves torture, dungeons, marital frustration, and has no comic relief. (3)
11. The bass aria "Infelice!" and the baritone aria "Oh, de' verd' anni miei" are just two of the highlights of this work. (2)
12. In this opera, Medora and the slave, Gulnara, are rivals for the love of Corrado. (4)

Answers on page 307.

29. VERDI I

1. Where was Verdi born? (1)
2. What was the name of Verdi's influential patron and father-in-law? (2)

3. What did the slogan "Viva Verdi" actually mean? (2)
4. Which of Verdi's twenty-six operas were composed to French texts? (2)
5. Name the opera Verdi composed for soprano Jenny Lind. (3)
6. What was the name of Verdi's country estate? (1)
7. Verdi revised *Simon Boccanegra* in 1881. Who worked on the reworked libretto, and what was the principal addition to the opera? (2)
8. To whom did Verdi dedicate his *Requiem*? (1)
9. Who was the librettist for *Rigoletto*? (1)
10. Name three nonoperatic songs by Verdi. (4)
11. Who was the second cellist at the world premiere of *Otello*? (3)
12. What Verdi chorus became a patriotic anthem for the newly unified Italy? (1)
13. In which of Verdi's operas did the woman who was to become the composer's second wife create the leading soprano role? What was her name? (2)
14. Identify the artist who created the title role in *Falstaff*. (3)
15. Which Verdi work was made into a propaganda film by the Allies in World War II? (3)
16. Why did Verdi decide not to compose an opera based on Sardou's play, *La Tosca*? (4)
17. Where did Verdi die? (3)
18. What was the charitable organization created by Verdi? (1)
19. Can you name an opera referred to in various letters of Verdi's whose existence has never been substantiated? Name this hypothetical opera, and the opera that it probably became. (4)
20. Which of the following German sopranos listed here was a noted Aida?

      a. Elisabeth Grümmer
      b. Elisabeth Schwarzkopf
      c. Elisabeth Rethberg
      d. Anneliese Rothenberger (3)

Answers on page 307.

Fans of the illustrious Mary Garden loved to tell this story. It seems that Miss Garden, during her brief but adventurous tenure as "Directa" of the Chicago Opera back in the 1920s, found herself at a dinner party where a certain elderly financier spent the entire evening ogling the diva, who was wearing a stunning and nearly backless gown. Finally, the tempestuous soprano demanded to know what the dinner guest was staring at.

"Miss Garden," stammered the D.O.M., "I can't begin to guess what it is that is holding up your dress."

"Two things," snapped La Garden: "Your age and my discretion!"

30. VERDI II

1. In which operas do the following female characters appear: Giselda, Federica, Fenena, and Odabella? (3)
2. The aria "La mia letizia infondere" is from which of the following Verdi operas: *Alzira, Un Giorno di Regno, I Lombardi alla Prima Crociata*, or *Simon Boccanegra*? Who sings it, and for what kind of voice is it written? (3)
3. Ernani, in Verdi's fifth opera, is offered a choice of two means of killing himself. What are they, and which does the poor tenor choose? (2)
4. Who is the author of the libretto for *Nabucco*? (3)
5. In Verdi's *Macbeth*, the aria for Lady M., heard early in the second act of the revised version of the opera, is completely different from that composed for the original 1847 production. Name the aria heard in the second version, and also the one it replaced. (4)
6. What Verdi opera is based on a poetic drama by Lord Byron? (3)
7. In what country does Verdi's *Un Giorno di Regno* take place? (4)

8. Verdi attempted to compose an opera based on Shakespeare's *King Lear* but never completed it. Although Verdi destroyed most of the music, one aria was later used in another famous work. Name the aria, the opera, and the character who sings it. Who was the character in *Lear* for whom it was intended? (4)

9. Verdi borrowed the musical theme from one of his early songs and gave it to the heroine of one of his most popular operas. Name the song, the opera in which it appears, the aria, and the character who sings it. (4)

10. Verdi often portrayed tender relations between fathers and daughters in his operas. Perhaps he was drawn to such themes because he lost his own two children when they were still very young. Here is a list of daughters in operas by Verdi. For each, provide the name of her father and the title of the opera in which they appear.

    a. Amelia Grimaldi (3)
    b. Abigaille (2)
    c. Nannetta (2)
    d. Gilda (1)
    e. Leonora di Vargas (2)

11. Although there are many drinking songs in Verdi's operas, only one major Verdian character is shown to be drunk. Name the character, the opera, and the significance of the character's inebriation. (3)

12. Which of the following plays is *not* the source of a Verdi opera: *Die Räuber, Henry V, La Fuerza de Sino,* or *Henry IV, Part I*? (2)

13. Anna Moffo and Teresa Stratas starred in theatrical film versions of what beloved Verdi opera? (2)

14. Which characters in operas by Verdi die and return as ghosts? (3)

15. Soprano Mirella Freni has sung, at different times in her career, a mother and daughter in a Verdi opera. What is the title of the opera, and which roles did Freni sing? (3)

16. Which of the following Verdian baritone roles is *not* a villain?

    a. Count di Luna
    b. Don Carlo di Vargas
    c. Paolo Albiani

      d. Rodrigo, Marchese di Posa

      e. The Thane of Cawdor (2)

17. What was the first Verdi opera to be performed at the new Metropolitan Opera House at Lincoln Center, in 1966? Who were the soprano, tenor, and baritone stars? (3)

18. Maria Callas recorded a duet from this Verdi opera in the 1960s but it wasn't published until more than a decade after her death. Name the duet, the opera from which it comes, the recording company involved, and the tenor who partnered Callas in the selection. (3)

19. Who is the only saint to figure in a Verdi opera? Name the opera. How does the ending of the opera differ from the generally accepted account of this person's demise? (3)

20. Which Verdi opera is known in German as *Die Macht des Schicksals*? (3)

Answers on page 309.

II

Opera Stars and Supernovas

31. BARITONES

Try to identify the baritones from the clues given below.

1. Celebrated for his Verdi, this artist died on the stage of the Metropolitan Opera on March 4, 1960. (3)
2. Skipping out on his Metropolitan contract to make a film called *Aaron Slick from Punkin Crick* almost cost this artist his career with that opera company. (3)
3. Renowned as a frightening Baron Scarpia, this singer, who died in 1984, was also a noted stage director, painter, and teacher. (2)
4. This heroic baritone continued to sing although suffering from cancer of the vocal cords; he died at a young age. (3)
5. He created the roles of Iago, Falstaff, and Tonio. (2)
6. Although alcoholism shortened his career, this baritone enjoyed great popularity at the Met, on radio, and through his recordings. (2)
7. This American baritone was brave enough to talk back to the gallery patrons at the opera in Parma and was punched in the jaw by the stage manager of that opera house. (3)
8. This Teutonic baritone excelled in the operas of Strauss, Mozart, and Wagner and once was married to a famous artist with whom he frequently appeared in performance. (3)
9. This baritone, admired in many contemporary operas, excelled in music by Mozart and once costarred in a Broadway musical with Phil Silvers and Nancy Walker. (4)
10. He sang at the Metropolitan for thirty-three consecutive seasons, setting a record for longevity in that theater by a leading

artist. He was best known for some exotic villains. Jerome Hines broke this gentleman's longevity record in 1983. (4)

11. Although he is a star all over the world, this baritone has sung exactly one performance at the Metropolitan Opera, replacing Leonard Warren after that artist's sudden death. (3)

12. A farm boy from Illinois, this gentleman has been the handsome villains in Verdi operas from Hamburg to San Francisco, and all points in between. (1)

13. This baritone had a distinguished career throughout the United States and Latin America, and costarred with Maria Callas in many of her early triumphs. Most Americans know him as the star of a Frank Loesser musical. (3).

14. This baritone, as famous for singing Neapolitan songs as for Italian operas, costarred with Anna Moffo in a film version of a Verdi opera. Name baritone and opera. (3)

15. A versatile Welshman, this artist was knighted by Queen Elizabeth in appreciation of his outstanding career performing the music of Mozart, Strauss, and Britten. (3)

16. One of the first American singers to make a career in postwar Europe, he was noted for his versatility and acting prowess. Ill health forced him to end his career prematurely. (3)

17. He was the first African-American male to sing at the Metropolitan Opera. His son is a famous jazz artist. (4)

18. A redoubtable Viennese baritone, this artist aged gracefully from leading man to character singer. He was well known for his work in operetta and briefly headed the Vienna State Opera. (3)

19. This Cairo-born artist began his long career as a baritone, but in recent years he has displayed comic gifts as a basso buffo. (3)

20. In his five-decade-long career, this singer has recorded each of Schubert's songs written for male voice and has sung operas by Gluck, Berg, Busoni, and virtually everybody else. (1)

21. Once married to a celebrated Octavian, this veteran baritone is a Rossini specialist and a pillar of the Glyndebourne Festival. (3)

22. One of the few French artists to enjoy an international career,

this baritone has gone from villains to character roles, always impressing as an actor and linguist. (3)

23. A product of the New York City Opera, this baritone sings everything from *Il Barbiere di Siviglia* to *Billy Budd* in opera houses throughout the world. (3)

24. Beloved as a character singer for forty years, this baritone was married to a great soprano noted for her Verdi. (4)

25. A stage actor and director of great skill and charm, he called himself a baritone and sang the villain in a popular operetta broadcast from the Met four times. (3)

26. This American baritone is as at home singing operas by Mozart and Rossini as he is in the songs of Mahler and Stephen Foster. (1)

27. He created the role of Porgy at the Metropolitan Opera premiere of *Porgy and Bess.* (3)

28. Although born and trained in Siberia, this young baritone has shown a natural gift for the music of Verdi. Not surprisingly, he often performs and records songs by Russian composers. (2)

29. This baritone alumnus of the Kirov Opera sang the role of Stankar in the first Metropolitan Opera performance of Verdi's *Stiffelio* and has recorded the baritone leads in *Luisa Miller* and *Trovatore*, among other Verdi works. (3)

30. This baritone once sang "Home on the Range" as an impromptu encore after a performance at the Chicago Opera. (4)

Answers on page 311.

32. BASSES

1. This bass was prevented from making his Metropolitan Opera debut because of questions about his political affiliation in his native land. (3)

2. This bass sang such roles as Mefistofele and Giulio Cesare at the New York City Opera but never sang at the Metropolitan. (2)

3. This basso buffo was a favorite of Arturo Toscanini and once

Many performers have nightmares in which they find themselves standing naked on stage. Imagine how basso Samuel
Ramey must have felt when the director of a production of
Don Giovanni at the New York City Opera informed him
that he would be called upon to sing the Champagne Aria
without benefit of costume. After all, the director reasoned,
Don Giovanni was dressing for a party, so why wouldn't he
relax in the nude for a few moments before putting on dou-
blet and hose. Ramey is known for his cheerfulness and read-
iness to be a part of an ensemble, and thus, not surprisingly,
he agreed. At rehearsals, Ramey played the scene in his
shorts, apparently wanting to reduce his modesty little by
little.

The story, however, ends a bit anticlimactically, for,
shortly before the dress rehearsal, the director reconsidered
and decreed that Ramey could play the scene stripped only
to the waist, with a pair of tights covering his lower half.
We'll never know whether Ramey was relieved, or a little bit
disappointed!

performed the Disney hit "Bibbity Bobbity Boo" on American
radio. (3)
4. This bass sang Hagen on the Solti *Ring*. (2)
5. This attractive basso had the honor of being introduced on
   radio by none other than Tallulah Bankhead, before performing "September Song." (3)
6. This rotund basso, a fixture at the Met for nearly twenty
   years in the sixties and seventies, claimed to speak almost
   no English, although his wife was born and reared in New
   York. (4)
7. This bass, known for both his Mozart and his Mussorgsky, is
   married to soprano Lucia Evangelista. (3)

8. This basso regularly accuses his wife of adultery—they often appear together in *Don Carlo*. Name the lady, as well. (2)

9. This gentleman sang Ramfis on the Caniglia/Gigli EMI recording of *Aida*, and was chosen by Toscanini to appear in the concert that celebrated the opening of the rebuilt La Scala, after the Second World War. (4)

10. This bass made his Metropolitan Opera debut in a small role when he was twenty-one years old. Three years later he sang a lead at the Met's inaugural performance at its new home in Lincoln Center. (3)

11. No, this Golden Age artist was *not* named for a parrot! (4)

12. A student of Rosa Ponselle, this bass sings as much Wagner as he sings Verdi. Another opera in his repertoire is by Britten. (2)

13. His primitive, frightening interpretation of Boris Godunov helped establish Mussorgsky's opera in America and Western Europe. (1)

14. This wonderful basso-buffo was noted for his Leporello and Dr. Dulcamara. His last performance took place at the Met, in *Don Pasquale*, in the company of Beverly Sills and Alfredo Kraus in 1978. (3)

15. This bass, whose name suggested his multicultural roots, often sang opposite both Maria Callas and Renata Tebaldi. (3)

16. This talented American sang at La Scala before he reached the Metropolitan Opera but remained at the Met for more than two decades. He dubbed the singing voice of Rossano Brazzi in the film *South Pacific*. (2)

17. This versatile German sings such diverse roles as Osmin, Hunding, and Ochs with distinction. (4)

18. A noted Boris, this imposing Finn was adept in such a comic role as Kecal in *The Bartered Bride*, too. (2)

19. First choice in the 1990s for Hagen, this bass has been televised in such operas as *Der Ring* and *Der Fliegende Holländer*. (1)

20. This handsome Italian has starred in a film of *Don Giovanni* and has sung and recorded the title role of *Boris Godunov* in Russian. (2)

21. This artist once mistook a weather-related newspaper headline for an enthusiastic greeting upon his return to London after World War II. (3)

22. This bass bowed at the Met shortly after the Second World War, then sat out the entire Bing era (1950–72), later accepting James Levine's invitation to resume his career there in 1976. The basso sang character roles for more than the next decade. (3)

23. This barrel-chested gent was a familiar figure in operas in America and Europe in the 1950s and 1960s, often singing operas by Verdi. His brother was a noted composer. (3)

24. A member of the "home team" at the Rome Opera, this bass sang many important roles on recordings, including Alvise Badoero in the recording of *La Gioconda* that starred Milanov, Di Stefano, and Warren. (4)

25. This American artist was famed for his outstanding diction in English, and his interest in contemporary opera. He took part in the Metropolitan's last English-language broadcast performance of *Così Fan Tutte*. (4)

26. This singer actor is my personal choice for the designation "the artist who most deserved to sing at the Met (and other major opera houses) but didn't." He often sang scenes from *Boris Godunov* in concerts and recitals. (3)

Answers on page 312.

33. MEZZOS

Try to identify these mezzos from the clues given below.

1. The most famous Carmen of her time, this mezzo once made a movie with Bing Crosby. (1)

2. This beautiful lady invaded the United States with the Bolshoi and conquered audiences as Marina in *Boris Godunov*. She has made many recordings and scored triumphs at La Scala, the Vienna State Opera, the San Francisco Opera, and the Met. (3)

3. Although she started her career singing small roles at La Scala, this artist eventually set the world standard for such roles as Azucena, Amneris, Adalgisa, and Santuzza. (2)

4. She was the first American Carmen. (4)

5. This large lady from Germany helped the American war effort in World War I, although two of her sons fought in the Kaiser's army. (3)

6. Samuel Barber's aunt, she sang Dalila and Suzuki in the company of Enrico Caruso. (3)

7. This mezzo is married to a leading bass at La Scala and is beloved for her searing performances as Amneris and Azucena. She broadcast *La Gioconda* from the Met with Renata Tebaldi and Carlo Bergonzi. (3)

8. Making her Metropolitan debut as a "boy" in *Die Zauberflöte*, this artist has charmed audiences in the ensuing years as Cherubino, Mélisande, Octavian, and Hänsel. (1)

9. This mezzo, who eschewed high fashion onstage and off, was one of the very finest singers of this century. Her performances opposite Maria Callas in *Norma* and *La Vestale* were greatly admired. (3)

10. Before becoming a soprano, this mezzo stunned her audience by singing both Cassandra and Dido in the long-overdue Met premiere of Berlioz's *Les Troyens*. (2)

11. Once a soprano, this New York–born artist lowered her vocal range and became a famous Dame Quickly and Carmen. (2)

12. The artist in Question 10 replaced this singer at the last moment in the role of Dido in the first Met *Les Troyens*. A beloved German mezzo who retired in 1993, she soon recovered from the illness that had sidelined her. (1)

13. A famous Bolshoi Carmen, this lady sang that role in Russian opposite Mario del Monaco, who, on a visit to Moscow, performed that night in a mixture of French and Italian, in a performance preserved on videotape. (3)

14. A favorite of Toscanini, this exciting mezzo's voice failed her quite early, ending a brilliantly promising career. (4)

15. This American mezzo, active in the 1930s, '40s, and '50s,

recorded excerpts of *Carmen* with Ramón Vinay, and retired to Florence. (4)

16. This mezzo was a namesake of the soprano heroine of a verismo opera, which she occasionally sang herself. (2)

17. Having made her Metropolitan Opera debut in 1954, this mezzo remains active there to this day. She sang two world-premiere performances at the Met, both Hänsel and the Witch in *Hänsel und Gretel*, and is a much sought after stage director. (2)

18. An unforgettable Cherubino and Rosina, this mezzo also recorded arias by Handel and was enchanting in the zarzuela repertory. (2)

19. Although she sang such soprano roles as Nedda and Musetta, this mezzo was at her best singing the *bel canto* operas of Rossini, Bellini, and Handel. (1)

Answers on page 313.

34. SOPRANOS

Try to identify these sopranos from the clues given below.

1. Forty years old when she achieved stardom, this lady provided a glorious voice that could accomplish miracles with the music of Wagner, Gluck, or Beethoven. She also sang the first performance of Strauss's "Four Last Songs." (1)

2. She was the first Metropolitan Cio-Cio-San, coached in the role by the markedly unenthusiastic Puccini. (3)

3. Her operatic debut was televised throughout the United States and, within a few years' time, her Verdi interpretations were acclaimed throughout the world. (2)

4. Whether singing Mozart, Verdi, or Samuel Barber, this lady, who frequently appeared on TV's *The Voice of Firestone* concerts, impressed with her beautiful tone and handsome stage presence. She learned the score of a brand-new opera within a few weeks, and after its world premiere the critics believed that the role had been composed for her alone. (3)

5. She recorded *Carmen*, an interpretation that is considered a classic, twenty years *before* she sang that role on the stage. (1)
6. This famous Marschallin had a celebrated career as a recitalist, then retired to California, where she taught for the last two decades of her life. Several of her former pupils (Grace Bumbry, Régine Crespin, and Frederica von Stade) are themselves famous singers. (2)
7. Toscanini told her that she had the voice of an angel, and throughout her career, her fans swore that she had a similarly angelic personality. (2)
8. One of the most thrilling Verdi sopranos of all time, this temperamental but endearing artist was a notable Gioconda, Santuzza, and Norma. Many of her best roles were recorded in the company of such artists as Leonard Warren, Jussi Bjoerling, and Fedora Barbieri. (2)
9. This pretty lady is noted for her Violetta, Butterfly, and Lucia, but she has also starred in a horror movie, a Hollywood extravaganza, and had her own television show in Italy. (2)
10. This woman made her debut at the Royal Opera in a tiny role, then sang dramatic soprano parts for several seasons until one night when, apparently cast "against type," she stunned the world with her abilities as a coloratura soprano at the premiere of a new production of a *bel canto* favorite. (1)
11. This exciting artist started her career as a mezzo-soprano, then let her voice fly upward until her repertoire included Lady Macbeth, Norma, and Tosca. In 1994 she played Nettie in a Lincoln Center revival of *Carousel*. (1)
12. A beautiful woman with a heavenly voice, this artist had a great career in Europe and America despite her alleged former association with Nazi politics. (2)
13. The first American to sing at Bayreuth, she was known as the "Yankee Diva." (4)
14. She sang more than 700 performances at the Metropolitan Opera in a career that spanned five decades. She is known for her ability to step into a role at a moment's notice. Among her best roles are Aida, both Verdi Leonoras, Nedda, and Micaela. (2)

15. The modern world's greatest Wagnerian soprano, this artist elected to give up her American career rather than accept defeat in a tax case. Once the matter was settled, she returned to the United States triumphantly. (1)

16. She made her New York debut (at Carnegie Hall) as a last-minute replacement for Marilyn Horne. Within a year she was a star at the Metropolitan Opera, and everywhere else. When she actually appeared she was often glorious, but her reputation as a "canceler" was all too well deserved. (1)

17. For more than four decades, this Viennese artist sang Verdi and Puccini roles as brilliantly as she performed the heroines of Strauss and Wagner. (2)

18. Caruso insisted that this woman sing with him at the Met. Her voice has been called one of the greatest in history, but her chronic stage fright led to an early retirement. Although synonymous with Verdi, this lady was a fabled Norma and a controversial Carmen. (1)

19. A plane crash cut short the life of this beautiful American

A Spanish soprano celebrated for her glorious *pianissimi* found herself singing her first *Aida* in a major opera house with an understudy replacing Plácido Domingo as Radames. This gentleman was singing the role for the first time in his career. The lady acquitted herself nobly, and the understudy, who usually sang the messenger, performed well, too. However, as the end of the Tomb Scene drew near, the diva decided to take no chances. In an aside clearly audible in the house (and preserved on numerous in-house tapes), she stopped singing for a moment and directed the tenor, *"Canta piano"* (Sing softly). The poor tenor obeyed his Aida, but many in the house were laughing too loudly to hear the high note!

soprano who combined Hollywood stardom with a career as an operatic prima donna. (3)

20. Her every move seemed to guarantee her headlines, yet the constant publicity, much of which was unjustly negative, could not obscure the fact that she was one of the most brilliant operatic artists of all time. (1)

21. Brooklyn-born, she achieved fame singing queens from Egypt, Scotland, and England, and spent a decade running a major opera company. (1)

22. This petite soprano boasted a voice that could soar an octave *above* high C. (3)

23. This diminutive diva stirred controversy wherever she went. Her roles ranged from Lauretta and Amina to Norma and Lady Macbeth. More than four decades after her debut, this artist added the Marschallin to her repertoire. (2)

24. In her day a fine coloratura, she is perhaps best remembered because a chicken recipe takes its name from her. (3)

25. Although she never sang with a major opera company, this charming lady's humorous treatments of Wagner, Verdi, and "The Art of the Lied" endeared her to music lovers around the world. (1)

26. An unparalleled singing actress, she was the only artist who escaped unscathed when the Metropolitan Opera made a poorly received visit to Paris, in 1965. (3)

27. A child actress on Broadway, this lady sang a small but well-noticed part in the original production of *West Side Story* years before her Metropolitan Opera debut as Rosina in *Il Barbiere di Siviglia*. (3)

28. This American soprano made her Metropolitan debut as Leonora in *Il Trovatore* in 1990. Rumored to be extremely temperamental, she has nonetheless become quite prominent in the Mozart and Verdi repertoire. (2)

29. This Wagnerian stalwart narrowly escaped injury when she was struck on the head by a falling prop at the same moment a trap door was mistakenly opened during a performance of *Götterdämmerung* at the Metropolitan.

30. This soprano's career lasted fourteen years, taking place si-

multaneously with those of Tebaldi and Callas. She made few recordings but has countless fanatical admirers around the world, thanks to the many "live" tapes that circulate. (3)

31. This soprano sang the title role in the first complete compact-disc recording of Mascagni's *Lodoletta*. (3)

32. This Turkish-born soprano often "stood by" for Callas in Italy, but she later achieved fame in a number of Callas's roles and other *bel canto* rarities. (3)

33. This vivacious New Yorker created the role of Kitty Scattergood in the American premiere of Menotti's *The Last Savage* at the Metropolitan Opera. (3)

34. This blond charmer sang such diverse roles as Rosalinde in *Die Fledermaus*, Fiora in *L'Amore dei Tre Re*, and the title role in *Tosca*. As a band singer, she worked with Frank Sinatra. (3)

35. Long a stalwart at the New York City Opera, this singer had an exceedingly varied repertoire that included *The Crucible*, *Manon*, and *La Traviata*. (3)

36. This lady's first husband was a conductor. Her current husband is an opera singer. In 1993 she added the title role in Giordano's *Fedora* to her long list of heroines. She has sung many times with a tenor who hails from her native town of Modena, Italy. (1)

37. Although she rarely sang outside her native Italy, record collectors around the world prize her lovely recording of *La Traviata*, which she made in the company of Cesare Valletti, Leonard Warren, and Pierre Monteux. (4)

38. This soprano, married to Canadian conductor Wilfred Pelletier, sang the title role in the historic broadcast/recording of *Fidelio*, led by Toscanini. (3)

39. This soprano sang under the baton of Tullio Serafin in several complete recordings made in Rome in the 1930s and '40s, including *Tosca*, *Aida*, *Andrea Chénier*, and *Un Ballo in Maschera*. (3)

40. This soprano, who retired from singing in 1973, made headlines in 1994 when she loudly booed a new production of *Madama Butterfly* at the Met, because she objected to the staging. (3)

Theatergoers laughed when Lily Tomlin, playing an engagement at a Broadway theater, listed Zinka Milanov as her
understudy in the playbill. Someone reported this to Madame Milanov, who immediately slapped a multimillion-dol-
lar libel suit on Ms. Tomlin, claiming great anguish and
damage to her image (note that this was twelve years after
Milanov's retirement from singing), since the diva never
served as anyone's understudy. The suit was settled out of
court. Fortunately for playwright and opera-buff Terrence
McNally, Madame Milanov never saw his play *The Ritz*.
This farce, set in a gay bathhouse, ends with the show's
villain being thrown into a baggy green dress and named
winner of the "Zinka Milanov Look-alike Contest." One
imagines the diva sniffing, "Ve are NOT amused!"

❧ ❧ ❧

41. This Roman soprano appeared at the Metropolitan in a wide
    range of leading roles between 1961 and 1972. She was an
    especially poignant Violetta and a memorable Aida. (3)
42. Originally a junior high school guidance counselor, this
    woman became one of the world's foremost Aidas in the 1960s
    and '70s. (2)
43. Once a dramatic soprano in Europe and America, this lady
    now is the director of Dischi Melodram, the Milan-based pro-
    ducer of "live" recordings of operas. (4)
44. In Paris, she created the role of Mme. Lidoine, in *Dialogues
    des Carmélites*. In America, years later, she electrified audiences
    singing the role of Mme. de Croissy, the Old Prioress, in the
    same opera. (2)
45. This Canadian artist was the "house soprano" at Covent Gar-
    den in the 1960s and '70s. (4)
46. This Scottish beauty created the role of Mélisande in Debus-
    sy's opera. A star wherever she sang, she never was a member

of the Metropolitan Opera Company, singing instead for Oscar Hammerstein's rival organization. (2)

47. This lady is the only soprano in the history of Verdi's *Nabucco* who has sung the cruelly taxing role of Abagaille for more than twenty years, without doing her voice irreparable harm. (2)

48. This soprano sang the title role in Strauss's *Arabella* in English in America, and in German in Europe. Before singing that role, she sang the role of the heroine's sister, Zdenka, at the Salzburg Festival, under Karl Böhm's direction. (3)

49. This soprano from the Iberian peninsula was a beloved figure at the Metropolitan Opera in the first half of this century. She made several recordings with John McCormack. A famous Violetta, she had a successful run in the American opera *Peter Ibbetson*, opposite Lawrence Tibbett. (4)

50. She is the only woman to sing music by Arnold Schoenberg at the Metropolitan. Her other roles there have included Cassandra, Dido, and Kundry. (2)

Answers on page 313.

35. TENORS

Try to identify these tenors from the clues given below.

1. Italian journalists nicknamed this feisty divo "Golden Calves" because his handsome appearance thrilled people nearly as much as his charismatic singing. (3)

2. Not content with being a leading singer in theaters around the world, this tenor also conducts in opera houses around the world and has also served as head of two important opera companies in the United States. (1)

3. This tenor began his career as a baritone, achieved his greatest successes as Tristan and Otello, and ended his career singing basso buffo roles. (3)

4. This artist once took part in a bizarrely comic fund-raising act for the Met, in which he was photographed doing an Apache dance with a celebrated prima donna with whom he had

rarely, if ever, shared the stage. Name the tenor and his dancing partner. (4)

5. These two tenors, brothers-in-law, were stars for decades and would not speak to each other. (3)

6. At the age of eighty, this famous artist sang a small role in an opera in which he had often sung the tenor lead. (4)

7. Equally at home in operetta and grand opera, he fled the Nazis and died prematurely in England. (2)

8. Although he only sang one fully staged opera performance in his entire life, this tenor was chosen to portray Enrico Caruso in a famous movie. (1)

9. After singing a particularly thrilling high C, he stopped the performance to announce that the note had been dedicated to a newspaper critic who, a few days earlier, had written that the tenor could no longer hit high C. (3)

10. After missing his entrance in *Lohengrin*, this tenor made the oft-repeated request to a chorister: "What time does the next swan leave?" (3)

11. Many boy sopranos turn out to be basses, but this boy (who once turned down the opportunity to hear Caruso in order to go to a silent film instead) was often hailed in later life as Caruso's "successor." (3)

12. Although he sang in many operas, this tenor made many fans through his appearances in Broadway musicals, including *Candide* and *Man of La Mancha*. (3)

13. Although he was five feet eight inches tall, much shorter than the two ladies with whom he costarred most frequently, this brilliant tenor was considered one of opera's most potent sex symbols during the peak of his career. (2)

14. Although he is as Italian as the tower at Pisa, this tenor received his first major engagements in Australia and England. (1)

15. This gentleman recorded one of his best roles in an opera that has the rare distinction of being conducted by its composer in this recording. Name the tenor, the opera, the role he sang, and the work's composer. (3)

16. This Polish-born tenor made life miserable for Grace Moore (and was repaid in kind) whenever the two sang together. (2)

17. During a performance of *Tristan und Isolde*, this glorious but temperamental tenor once got up from the dying hero's bed to demand that noisy members of the audience "stop their damned coughing." (3)

18. His recorded roles range from Sandor Barinkay to Grigori, and also included Almaviva, Don Jose, and Werther. A master singer of songs from around the world, this now semiretired tenor still occasionally appears on the operatic stage. (3)

19. He rarely sang in staged operas, but his way with songs made him one of the most popular concert stars of his age, as his recordings still testify. (2)

20. In between engagements at the world's leading opera houses, this outstanding tenor (whose admittedly bland stage presence led one exasperated critic to compare him to a trained seal) runs an inn in Verdi's hometown. (3)

21. Although he excels as Faust, Hoffmann, and Werther, this aristocrat is not French at all and, in fact, made his operatic debut in Cairo. (3)

22. Beginning his career in such tiny roles as Parpignol and Roderigo, this hefty gentleman eventually earned a place for himself in many opera houses in such roles as Samson, Otello, Canio, and Tannhäuser. (3)

23. This tenor made some of his first recordings while interned in a POW camp, later going on to thrill audiences at La Scala, Vienna, and the Met. (2)

24. As a young man, this Neapolitan was so poor that he owned only one shirt. Once, at the beginning of his singing career, a photographer called on the tenor at home. The singer's shirt was soaking wet from having been washed, and the photography session was salvaged only when the rotund little man wrapped a bedsheet, toga-fashion, around his middle. In his peak years, this tenor had no trouble keeping himself in shirts. (1)

25. A Frenchman despite his Italian name, this young tenor has been praised for his work as Alfredo in *La Traviata*, Nemorino in *L'Elisir d'Amore*, and other roles. (3)

26. This tenor was pressed into service at the Met one night when Plácido Domingo felt ill and withdrew from a performance of

La Gioconda after the first act. The hapless chap strode onto the stage in Act II and sang an account of "Cielo e mar" that so displeased the audience that the worst incident of booing in the Metropolitan's history was touched off. (4)

27. This grade-A heldentenor's name suggests a Wagnerian hero on a tour of the Middle East! (1)

28. This tenor, a star in Italy, made his Metropolitan Opera debut on the same night that Mirella Freni made hers. What role did he sing? (3)

29. This very popular French tenor rarely sang outside his native land. His recordings include *Lakmé* with Sutherland and several Verdi and Puccini operas sung in French. (3)

30. This American tenor recorded Pelléas opposite the Mélisande of Elisabeth Soederstroem, and sang many leading tenor roles at the Metropolitan Opera during the 1960s. (3)

Tenor Michele Molese was a fixture at the New York City Opera in the 1960s and '70s. One night, however, opening a run of performances as Riccardo in *Un Ballo in Maschera*, Molese's high notes failed to impress critic Harold C. Schoenberg of *The New York Times.* Reviewing the performance, Schoenberg wrote that Molese's high Cs were inadequate. These are fighting words to a tenor. So, at the next performance, Molese belted out a particularly beefy high C in the second act, and then stopped singing long enough to say, very clearly, "That high C was for Harold C. Schoenberg." The audience tittered. City Opera Czar Julius Rudel fired Molese as soon as the final curtain descended, citing the tenor for unprofessional conduct. Critic Schoenberg, however, personally interceded with Rudel not to punish Molese and, several months later, he was allowed to return to the company.

31. A major Italian tenor of the 1950s, this artist occasionally sang at the Met and recorded many operas with such sopranos as Tebaldi, Callas, and Stella. (3)

32. This tenor from Binghamton, New York, began his career with the Tri-Cities Opera and, within a few years, was singing at the New York City Opera, the Met, Deutsche Oper (Berlin), and other important opera houses. (3)

33. This gentleman, a refugee from central Europe, liked to be billed as "the High C Tenor" and quarrelled with such prima donnas as Maria Callas and Zinka Milanov. (4)

34. Because he was not quite five feet tall, his operatic stage career was limited, but his gorgeous tenor voice brought him fame on radio, recordings, and in films. He died at thirty-nine in a displaced persons camp in Switzerland during World War II. (4)

35. This Mississippi-born tenor was a stalwart member of the Met and other American companies for nearly forty years. His repertoire ranged from *Faust* to *Ariadne auf Naxos,* and also included *Così Fan Tutte, Idomeneo,* and *Carmen.* (3)

Answers on page 314.

36. LICIA ALBANESE

1. Where was Mme. Albanese born? (3)
2. In what role did she make her Metropolitan debut? (2)
3. Name the opera that Albanese recorded in Italy, before her Met debut, with Beniamino Gigli? (1)
4. Which of the following roles in French opera was *not* in Mme. Albanese's repertoire?
   - a. Marguérite
   - b. Lakmé
   - c. Manon
   - d. Micaela (3)
5. How many complete operatic recordings did Licia Albanese make with Jan Peerce? For which label? (1)
6. With the operas of what composer is Albanese especially associated? (1)

7. Can you name the aria that Licia Albanese recorded in Russian? (3)

8. Albanese played a scene from *Otello* in a film with Mario Lanza. Name the film, the leading lady, the scene that Albanese and Lanza sang, and tell us, if you can, the bizarre ending for the operatic excerpt devised by the screenwriter. (4)

9. How many roles in Puccini operas did Albanese sing? Name them. (4)

10. What is the name of the organization founded by Licia Albanese to help young singers? (3)

Answers on page 315.

37. LUCINE AMARA

1. With what opera company did Amara score her first success? (4)

2. What was Miss Amara's nickname during her first years as a soprano? (3)

3. Can you name the conductor who guided Lucine Amara's career during its early years? (3)

4. Lucine Amara has sung in five opening-night performances at the Met. Give the years, and name the operas and roles she sang on those occasions. (4)

5. One of Miss Amara's most admired recordings is of an opera that she sang very often in the opera house, but in a role that she never performed except on that recording. Name the opera, the role Amara sang in the recording, and the role in that work for which she was noted in the theater. Who conducted this recording, and who were Miss Amara's colleagues? (1)

6. Name eight roles Lucine Amara recorded for the now-defunct Metropolitan Opera Record Club. (These discs are long out of print and are highly prized collector's items.) (4)

7. Miss Amara sang with Mario Lanza in what film? (2)

8. Lucine Amara is renowned for her ability to assume a role at a moment's notice. She has occasionally rescued a performance

by replacing an ailing soprano partway through an opera. One evening at the Met, the soprano had to go on in mid-scene, without benefit of an announcement. Identify the opera, the role, and the singer Amara replaced that night. (3)

9. Name five operas in which Lucine Amara has sung more than one role. (4)

10. Lucine Amara has sung more than 510 performances at the Metropolitan. She has also sung more than two hundred times with the Met on tour. Who is the only other soprano, also an American, who sang at the Met as often? (3)

11. Name the opera that Lucine Amara, Franco Corelli, and Tito Gobbi recorded together for EMI. (1)

12. One of Amara's greatest successes at the Met was in a Russian opera, singing in English. Name the opera and that production's leading baritone, tenor, mezzo, and bass. Who conducted this production, which had its premiere in 1957? (3)

Answers on page 315.

38. CECILIA BARTOLI

1. Where was Bartoli born? (1)

2. Bartoli's parents sang in the chorus of a major Italian opera company. Which one? (2)

3. Who has been Bartoli's principal teacher? (2)

4. Can you name the celebrated maestro—and star-maker—who invited Bartoli to appear at a major European music festival but died before the performance could take place? What was the music festival? (2)

5. Who are the two operatic composers whose works form the core of Bartoli's stage repertoire? (1)

6. Where did Bartoli have her American operatic debut? What role did she sing? When did this take place? (2)

7. In which of the following operas has Bartoli sung two roles?
   a. *Così Fan Tutte*
   b. *Il Barbiere di Siviglia*
   c. *La Cenerentola*
   d. *Il Turco in Italia* (2)

Dolora Zajick, a superb mezzo, was singing Amneris one afternoon at the Metropolitan when she noticed gasping and laughter from the audience during the opera's crucial Judgment Scene. What she didn't know was that one of the flaming torches hung from the flies behind her was spurting fiery blasts of alarming amplitude. Fearing a disaster, a company fireman, in full regalia, walked onto the stage carrying a hefty fire extinguisher, and in best Milton Berle manner, began spraying the wayward torch, indifferent to the long-suffering Amneris, pouring out her heart to the gods. Finally, the increasingly nervous Ms. Zajick managed to turn slightly to see what was going on. She must have been relieved to know that nothing she had been doing had so titillated the spectators. Of course, this mezzo was lucky that the intrepid firefighter arrived in time, or otherwise, she would have been the first artist ever to perform Amneris's Immolation Scene!

🌿 🌿 🌿

8. Name the first complete opera that Bartoli recorded. For which company did she make the recording? (4)
9. In what role did Cecilia Bartoli make her Metropolitan Opera debut? When did this take place? (2)
10. What was the name of the collection of vocal music for which Bartoli won the Grammy in 1994? What company released it? (3)
11. Although she is a mezzo-soprano, Bartoli has recorded several arias associated with the soprano voice. Can you name four of these pieces, all of which are available on Decca/London CDs? (2)
12. Do you know the name of the Wagnerian character that Bartoli sang, in German, early in her career? (4)

Answers on page 317.

39. KATHLEEN BATTLE

1. Where was Ms. Battle born? (3)
2. What did the soprano do for a living before becoming a professional singer? (3)
3. Can you identify the Broadway production that employed Kathleen Battle in 1975? In what capacity? (4)
4. Who is the musician who served as an informal mentor to Kathleen Battle, arranged her engagement by the Metropolitan Opera, and has often served as her accompanist during song recitals? (1)
5. What was Kathleen Battle's Met debut role? Also, who sang the title role that night? (3)
6. Battle and soprano Jessye Norman gave a concert together at Carnegie Hall, preserved on CDs and video. What kind of music was featured? Who conducted? (2)
7. With which of the following instrumentalists has Ms. Battle *not* made a recording?
    a. Jean-Pierre Rampal
    b. James Galway
    c. Winton Marsalis
    d. Christopher Parkening (2)
8. Battle canceled a concert with a world-famous musical ensemble at the last minute, forcing that group to cancel a concert for the first time in its more than a century of music-making. Please tell us the identity of this organization. (3)
9. In an article that began on the front page of *The New York Times*, a critic stated that Kathleen Battle was quite possibly the greatest exponent of a certain role in the history of that opera. Name the role, the opera, and the composer. (3)
10. Can you name the collection of lullabies and spirituals sung by Ms. Battle, backed by such jazz artists as Grover Washington, Jr., and Winton Marsalis, which Sony released in 1995? (2)
11. Which Mozart role is *not* in Battle's repertoire?
    a. Astrafiammante
    b. Pamina

c. Zerlina

d. Susanna (2)

12. Name the opera in which, at the Metropolitan, Battle and Dame Kiri Te Kanawa appeared as sisters. What role did Ms. Battle sing? (1)

13. What peculiar command has Battle issued to various colleagues, according to published reports? (4)

14. For what reason was Kathleen Battle fired from the Metropolitan Opera in 1994? What opera had she been scheduled to sing? Who replaced her? (3)

15. Can you identify three members of the Metropolitan Opera staff who testified against Ms. Battle in her unsuccessful arbitration hearings against the Met in 1995? (4)

Answers on page 317.

40. CARLO BERGONZI

1. What was Bergonzi's original voice type? (1)

2. In what role did Bergonzi make his operatic debut? (3)

3. Can you name the first two roles that Bergonzi recorded? For what label? (3)

4. What was Carlo Bergonzi's first important operatic engagement opposite Renata Tebaldi? Please name the opera, role, and city where the performance took place. (A recording is available.) (2)

5. Name the only role in a French opera that Bergonzi ever sang at the Met. (2)

6. Please identify the operatic composer with whose music Bergonzi is most closely associated. (1)

7. Do you know the name of the Italian city, also associated with the composer asked about in Question #6, where Bergonzi owns a hotel/restaurant? What is that establishment called? (3)

8. What rarely performed Puccini opera did Bergonzi sing and record in New York, in 1977? Who were his leading ladies? (2)

9. What opera did Bergonzi record with Maria Callas? (1)

10. Which of the following Verdi roles was *not* in Bergonzi's stage repertoire?
    a. Oronte
    b. Fenton
    c. Macduff
    d. Gustavo/Riccardo (2)

11. Please identify the two works by Verdi that Bergonzi recorded with Birgit Nilsson. (3)

12. Two "live" recordings document Bergonzi's work in a Gallic opera that he never committed to disc in the studio. One recording is in French, and the other is in Italian. What is the opera? (4)

13. Name the opera that Bergonzi recorded twice, once opposite Joan Sutherland, and once opposite Montserrat Caballé. (1)

14. Name Bergonzi's best-known comic role, which he broadcast from the Metropolitan opposite Roberta Peters and Renata Scotto. (2)

15. For what recording company did Bergonzi make an album comprising all of Verdi's tenor arias? (2)

16. Name the opera that Bergonzi and Zinka Milanov broadcast from the Met in 1960 (a recording survives) under rather tragic circumstances. What happened to cast a pall over the proceedings? (3)

17. Bergonzi sang Manrico in *Il Trovatore* in Moscow, in 1964, while on a tour with the La Scala company. Who sang Leonora, Azucena, and Di Luna in that performance (available as a CD)? (3)

18. Where and when did Bergonzi make his final appearance in a staged opera? Please identify the opera and the role. (4)

19. Who was the tenor whom Bergonzi replaced in the Decca/London recording of *La Gioconda* (opposite Renata Tebaldi) and in the EMI *La Forza del Destino* (opposite Martina Arroyo)? (2)

20. Name the opera that Bergonzi sang with Marilyn Horne at the Metropolitan Opera in 1970. Name two other important singers in the cast. (2)

*Answers on page **318**.*

41. MONTSERRAT CABALLÉ

1. Describe the unusual circumstances in which Caballé made her entrance into American operatic life. (3)
2. What was the soprano's childhood ambition? (3)
3. Critic Irving Kolodin, reviewing a Caballé performance as Desdemona that failed to impress him, made a devastating assessment of her abilities as an actress. What was his remark? (4)
4. Name the tenor to whom Caballé is married. (2)
5. Name two Italian operas that Caballé and her husband recorded together. (2)
6. Caballé "discovered" a young tenor during a 1970 performance of *Norma*. Who was he? (2)
7. Name the two operas in which Montserrat Caballé has appeared with Birgit Nilsson. (2)
8. Which three Richard Strauss heroines has Caballé sung? (2)
9. Where did Caballé sing her first Turandot? (4)
10. For what foible is Caballé notorious? (1)
11. When Caballé withdrew from *Anna Bolena* at this opera house at the very last moment (the houselights had gone down) a near-riot ensued. Where did this event take place? (3)
12. Which Rossini opera did Caballé record with José Carreras? (2)

Answers on page 319.

42. MARIA CALLAS

1. In what role did Callas have her first major success? Name the opera and its composer, and tell us the place and year of performance. (3)
2. Callas made her La Scala debut in 1950 as Aida, replacing which well-known artist? (3)
3. What was Callas's American debut role? Where and when was this performance? (4)
4. What was the name of Callas's little poodle? (4)

Several years ago, I attended a performance of Puccini's *Tosca* in which the title role was sung by a glamorous and justly renowned dramatic soprano from France. This lady, admired in many German and French roles, sang an overwhelmingly fine Tosca, certainly among the top four or five finest interpretations of that heroine in my experience. I went backstage that night to see the tenor, who was a friend of mine. However, when the Gallic diva swept by me in the corridor, I took her hand and gushed words to the effect that she had sung a truly great Tosca that night. The lady, proving to be as self-confident as she was talented, looked at me and, matter-of-factly, in a speaking voice that sounded something like a contrabass Maurice Chevalier, replied, "Well, when you have a great voice like I do, how can you help but be great?" *Zut alors!*

❀ ❀ ❀

5. Maria Callas's first American performance was preceded by the issuing of three complete operas on EMI/Angel that received much critical acclaim. Name the operas, her costars, and the conductors. (3)

6. How many roles did Maria Callas sing at the Met, and what were they? (3)

7. Callas and Jussi Bjoerling sang together only once. In what opera did they appear, and where did they sing it? (4)

8. What was Callas's final new role at La Scala? Who were her tenor and baritone colleagues that night? (2)

9. Name nine operas revived for Callas at La Scala. (4)

10. What opera was to have been staged for Callas at the Met when Rudolf Bing discharged her in a contract dispute? Name the artist who replaced Callas in that opera. (2)

11. Several of Callas's most famous operatic recordings were of roles she never actually performed in the theater. Name three of these roles. (2)

12. When Callas canceled a performance scheduled at the Edinburgh Festival, a little-known soprano replaced her and went on to become a major star. Who was the replacement, and what was the opera? (3)

13. What incident allegedly began the Callas-Tebaldi feud? (3)

14. How did Callas allegedly compare her voice to that of Tebaldi? (1)

15. Can you remember the name of Callas's husband? (1)

16. Callas sang only two comic roles. Name these roles, the operas and composers. (2)

17. In 1946, Edward Johnson, the general manager of the Metropolitan Opera, invited Callas to sing two roles at the Met. Callas refused the offer. What were the roles, and why did she decline them? (4)

18. Who was Maria Callas's costar on her final concert tour in 1973–74? (1)

19. Where and when did Callas's final public appearance take place? (4)

20. Identify the last staged opera in which Callas appeared. Tell us where and when this took place. (3)

21. Who was the conductor under whose guidance Callas shaped the early years of her career? Who was her principal voice teacher? (2)

22. What was Callas's only film? Who directed it? (3)

23. What were Callas's three Wagnerian roles? In what language did she sing them? (3)

24. A great figure in musical life and in Callas's own career died in 1974 a few hours before Callas's first New York performance in eight and a half years. Who was he? (3)

25. Name the only role Maria Callas ever broadcast live from the Met. Who was the baritone that afternoon, and why was Callas significant in his career? (4)

26. Callas had hoped to sing a performance of a Verdi opera under the baton of Arturo Toscanini. The maestro's failing health forced the project to be abandoned. What opera had been planned for this occasion? (4)

27. In what opera did Maria Callas, Giulietta Simionato, and Joan

Sutherland sing together? What role did each artist undertake, and in what opera house did this take place? Go ahead and tell us in what year did all this transpire. (4)

28. Callas caused an international scandal when, hours after canceling a *Norma* in mid-performance, she showed up at a party in Venice, hosted by an international socialite reputed to be in love with Callas. No, we're not talking about Onassis. Who threw the party? (3)

29. Broadway playwright Terrence McNally has written two plays in which Maria Callas figures prominently. Can you name them? (4)

30. In what Manhattan neighborhood did Maria Callas spend her childhood? (3)

Answers on page 320.

43. ENRICO CARUSO

1. Caruso was accorded the honor of being the first singer for whom a song was written especially for the purpose of making a recording. Name the composer and the title of the song. (2)

2. Eléazar in Jacques Halévy's *La Juive* was Caruso's final role at the Metropolitan Opera in 1920. In what role did the tenor make his Met debut, and in what year? (2)

3. Caruso recorded a patriotic song for the American war effort in World War I. What was it, and who wrote it? (3)

4. One night, a basso colleague of Caruso's found himself voiceless seconds before the cue for his aria. Whispering his problem to Caruso, the unfortunate artist was assured that Caruso would cover for him. What aria did Caruso perform? Of course, you may give us the name of the ailing bass. (4)

5. Caruso, at the height of his fame, was arrested in New York. Of what crime was he accused, and what was the outcome of the case? (3)

6. Puccini composed an outstanding tenor role with Caruso in mind for the world premiere. As it turned out, Caruso did

not appear in that opera's first performance but went on to sing the role with great success for the next two decades. Name the opera and the role. (2)

7. There was only one singer with whom Caruso had a long-standing disagreement that prevented the two from appearing together. Who was that singer, and what was the one duet the two artists recorded together? (2)

8. Caruso was a poor man's son, born in a poverty-stricken neighborhood in Naples, yet he often played royal or noble characters. Name six blue-blooded roles from Caruso's repertoire. (3)

9. What soprano, who often sang with the great tenor, was called by critics "Caruso in skirts"? (3)

10. What musical work composed by Sir Arthur Sullivan did Caruso record? In what language? (3)

11. Name two tenors whose publicists implied that each was "the American Caruso." (1)

12. What was the name of Caruso's Italian "common-law" wife, who abandoned the tenor, leaving an emotional wound from which, it has been claimed, he never fully recovered? (4)

13. Why did Caruso never record the aria "Nessun dorma"? (1)

14. What aria from Franchetti's opera *Germania* did Caruso record? (4)

15. Where was Caruso singing in December of 1920 when his throat began hemorrhaging during the performance? What opera was being performed? What role was Caruso singing? (1)

Answers on page 322.

44. FRANCO CORELLI

1. Where was Corelli born? (2)
2. With what celebrated tenor did Corelli study? (2)
3. Corelli sang in the La Scala premiere of what contemporary Russian opera? (4)

4. When Corelli canceled a performance of Maurizio in *Adriana Lecouvreur* at the Met, in 1968, who made a very successful surprise debut, replacing him on an hour's notice? (1)

5. There is an Italian film of *Tosca,* in which Corelli appears as Mario. Name the soprano heard on the soundtrack in the role of Tosca. Who acts that role on the screen? (3)

6. What three operas has Corelli recorded with Birgit Nilsson? (1)

7. Corelli and Renata Tebaldi were a powerful team when they sang together at the Metropolitan Opera. Name the five operas they sang together there. (3)

8. Corelli sang the tenor lead in a verismo opera at La Scala opposite Maria Callas in the title role. This is one of the few Callas performances at La Scala that has apparently not survived on tape. Name the opera. (4)

9. Corelli's wife is a former opera singer. What is her stage name? Name three opera recordings in which she is heard. (3)

10. Corelli once leapt from the stage of the Rome Opera into a box. Why? (4)

The following story about Birgit Nilsson and Franco Corelli has been told so many times that it has entered the realm of folklore, but it is so endearing that it bears telling again. During the Met's 1962 spring tour Nilsson and Corelli were singing in *Turandot.* After the second act, the tenor began to sulk, ostensibly because Nilsson had outsung him on a jointly held high note. Rudolf Bing, who dreaded having to inform a capacity audience that Corelli had left the theater, advised the tenor instead to bite Nilsson's lip during the final embrace. Corelli thought this a wonderful revenge and nipped the soprano when the magic moment arrived. Nilsson finished the performance but cabled Bing the next day to say: "Cannot continue tour. Have rabies."

11. Who is the music critic whom Corelli once threatened to punch in the nose? (4)
12. Corelli has sung in two operas by Handel. What are they? (4)
13. Name two operas that Corelli recorded in French. (2)
14. In his entire career, Franco Corelli sang only one complete performance of Donizetti's *Lucia di Lammermoor*. A week later he began a second performance of this opera but abandoned ship, as it were, after the first act. In each performance, the tenor was partnered by a different soprano. Both ladies are Americans. Who are they, and where did these performances take place? (3)
15. Which of the following roles, all Corelli favorites, has *not* been preserved on videotape:
    a. Don José
    b. Canio
    c. Calaf
    d. Don Alvaro (3)

Answers on page *323*.

45. MARIO DEL MONACO

1. In what role did Del Monaco make his professional debut? (4)
2. What was particularly notable about the performance of *Aida* that Del Monaco sang with Maria Callas in Mexico City in 1952? (2)
3. For which recording company did Del Monaco make his first recordings of arias? (3)
4. Name the sopranos who sang opposite Del Monaco in the complete commercially made recordings of the following operas:
   a. *Aida* (2)
   b. *Carmen* (3)
   c. *Fedora* (3)
   d. *Pagliacci* (both Decca/London recordings, please!) (4)
   e. *La Gioconda* (3)
   f. *Rigoletto* (2)

5. Name two French roles that Del Monaco sang with the Metropolitan Opera opposite Risë Stevens. (2)

6. Del Monaco sang at the La Scala premiere of what Berlioz opera? Name the role, his two leading ladies, and the language in which the opera was sung. (2)

7. Mario del Monaco sang two Wagnerian roles. What were they? (3)

8. Name two operas that Del Monaco recorded for Decca/London with soprano Elena Souliotis. (2)

9. Which opera did Mario del Monaco *not* broadcast from the Metropolitan opposite Zinka Milanov?
   a. *Andrea Chénier*
   b. *Otello*
   c. *Ernani*
   d. *Simon Boccanegra*

10. What other form of artistic expression did Mario del Monaco pursue in addition to singing? (3)

11. Do you know the two baritone arias Del Monaco often sang in recital appearances? Which one did he record for Decca/London? (3)

12. Two videotapes survive of Del Monaco singing the title role in *Andrea Chénier*. From what country does each originate, and who sings the role of Maddalena in each? (3)

13. Name the soprano whom Del Monaco, through some backstage politicking, manipulated into singing two performances of *Andrea Chénier* with him at La Scala, even though she had signed a contract to sing *Il Trovatore* with him instead. People rarely played such games successfully with this lady. (3)

14. Name the prima donna whom Del Monaco accused of kicking him in the shins backstage during a performance—a story that she publicly denied. (4)

15. Del Monaco's Otello, arguably his greatest role, has been preserved twice on videotape. Identify the artists who sing the roles of Desdemona and Iago with him in each performance. For good measure, identify the countries of origin of these two performances as well. (3)

Answers on page 324.

46. GIUSEPPE DI STEFANO

1. Name five operas that Di Stefano sang in performance with Maria Callas. (2)
2. Identify three operas that Di Stefano recorded with Callas but never sang on the stage with her. (2)
3. Name the operetta that Di Stefano sang first in Vienna, then on an international tour in the 1960s. What role did he sing? (4)
4. Di Stefano made only one commercial recording with Renata Tebaldi. What was it, and what unfortunate event occurred during the recording sessions? (4)
5. What is the nickname by which di Stefano is known to his friends? (2)
6. According to Di Stefano's American secretary, the late Devereux Danna, the tenor was offered a contract to star in a then-new Broadway musical. Di Stefano refused the contract. When the show was produced, a year or two later, it achieved much success, but the leading role had been rewritten for a baritone. Name the show, its composer, and its eventual star. (4)
7. Once, while singing the third act of *Carmen* at the Met, Di Stefano threw his Carmen to the ground with such force that the lady broke her arm. Who was the injured gypsy? (3)
8. Di Stefano took part in celebrated productions of *Fedora* and *Adriana Lecouvreur* at the Chicago Lyric Opera. Who were his principal colleagues in those productions? (3)
9. Name the roles in five French operas in Di Stefano's repertoire. (2)
10. Arturo Toscanini chose Di Stefano for one of his famous radio concerts with the NBC Symphony. Name the work that was performed, and identify the tenor's three colleagues. (This performance is still available on CD.) (2)
11. In what role (and when) did Di Stefano make his final Met appearance? (4)
12. Di Stefano sang Verdi's *Otello* once, in a performance that has

survived as a recording. Where and when did this *Otello* take place, and who were the soprano and baritone? (4)

13. Name the only role in a Bellini opera that Di Stefano recorded. (2)

14. Name the role in a Wagner opera that Di Stefano performed (in Italian) at La Scala. (3)

15. Di Stefano walked out after the first performance of the *La Traviata* production at La Scala directed by Luchino Visconti.

In a well-remembered incident that took place backstage at the Academy of Music in Philadelphia, tenor Giuseppe di Stefano demonstrated just how powerfully a star tenor could flex his muscles, even when the audience, singers, and conductor had not yet taken their places for the performance. Di Stefano, having completed dressing for a performance of Verdi's *Un Ballo in Maschera*, was leafing through the playbill shortly before the performance was to begin. An advertisement suddenly caught his eye, and the tenor became furious. He summoned the theater manager to his dressing room and declared that he would not walk onto the stage and begin to sing until the offending page was excised from every copy of the playbill. Knowing when he was licked, the poor manager had no choice but to accede to Di Stefano's demand, delaying the start of the opera by more than an hour. And just what, one might ask, was the terrible message contained on the doomed page? It was an ad from Angel Records, producer of most of Di Stefano's records, proclaiming that Franco Corelli, Angel's latest tenor acquisition, was the greatest tenor in the world! Di Stefano must have felt closer than usual to the character he sang that night, Riccardo—the king who is stabbed to death by his best friend.

In addition to a simmering quarrel with Visconti, the tenor had become angry with one of his colleagues. Who was the artist who infuriated Di Stefano? Bonus: What was the reason for their contretemps? (3)

Answers on page 325.

47. PLÁCIDO DOMINGO

1. Domingo spent the early part of his career as leading tenor of an opera company in a rather small country not famous for its opera. He sang his roles in the language of this nation. Do you know what country we're asking about and its language? (3)
2. In 1974, Domingo recorded the prison scene from Verdi's *Don Carlo*, singing the title role, on a special disc made by Deutsche Grammophon as a benefit for an anti-cancer crusade. Who sang the role of Rodrigo in that recording? (4)
3. Domingo's first operatic appearance in the United States coincided with the final appearance of a famous and beloved soprano. Please identify the opera and the soprano, the role Domingo sang, the year all this occurred, and the city where the performance took place. (4)
4. In what role did Domingo first attract critical attention in the United States? (3)
5. Domingo was invited to make his debut at La Scala at the suggestion of an American artist who turned down the role in question. Who recommended Domingo, and what was the role? (3)
6. When Domingo isn't singing in an opera house, he often appears in one in a different musical capacity. What is it? (1)
7. Name the five Wagnerian roles that Plácido Domingo has performed or recorded. (2)
8. One of Plácido Domingo's first professional engagements was a small role in the Mexico City production of an American musical comedy. Name the show. (3)
9. In what theater did Domingo sing his first performance of

Verdi's *Otello*? Name the conductor, soprano, baritone, and give the year when the performance took place. (3)

10. Which celebrated soprano once slapped Domingo across the face (during a performance) so hard that he required the services of a dentist? What opera were they performing, and where? (2)

11. Twenty-two years after the incident in #10 occurred, a baritone got "carried away" and punched Domingo so hard during a performance that he once again required a dentist's ministrations. Name the baritone and identify the opera being sung and the opera house where the mayhem took place. (2)

12. In October 1993, Domingo sang the title role of a Verdi opera in its Metropolitan Opera premiere. Name the opera. (2)

13. How many times, as of 1995, have Domingo and Luciano Pavarotti shared the stage on Opening Night at the Metropolitan Opera? (1)

14. In 1994, Domingo was named director of a prominent American opera company. Which one? (3)

15. With which American pop star did Domingo record a song entitled "Perhaps Love"? (1)

16. With which soprano did Domingo record an album of operatic duets including those from *Un Ballo in Maschera*, *Otello*, *Madama Butterfly*, and *Manon Lescaut*? (1)

17. With which prima donna listed below has Domingo *not* made a studio recording of a complete opera?
    a. Julia Migenes
    b. Maria Callas
    c. Aprile Millo
    d. Katia Ricciarelli (1)

18. What roles in operas by Richard Strauss has Domingo recorded? (2)

19. Domingo's "Christmas in Vienna" album combines the skills of Domingo, another stellar tenor, and a "pop diva." Please identify them. (3)

Answers on page 326.

48. MIRELLA FRENI

1. Where was Freni born? (2)
2. When Freni made her operatic debut, in 1955 as Micaela in *Carmen*, who sang Don José? (3)
3. In what opera, conducted by Von Karajan, did Freni make a lasting impression both at La Scala and the Vienna State Opera? (2)
4. In what year did Freni make her debut at the Metropolitan Opera? Who was her leading tenor that night? (3)
5. Freni has recorded the role of Micaela in *Carmen* three times. Please identify the labels for which she recorded the role, and the artists who sing the roles of Carmen, Don José, and Escamillo. (3)
6. During Freni's fourteen-year absence from the Metropolitan, she sang three performances of two roles at the Met, appearing with a guest company. What were the roles, what was the visiting troupe, and when did these performances take place? (4)
7. There is a commercial videotape of one opera performed by Freni at the San Francisco Opera. Identify the opera and name the leading tenor and bass. (2)
8. Name Mirella Freni's first and second husbands, and explain what they do for a living. (3)
9. Which two of the following operas has Mirella Freni *not* recorded commercially with Luciano Pavarotti?
   a. *Manon*
   b. *Tosca*
   c. *Pagliacci*
   d. *Otello*
   e. *L'Amico Fritz* (1)
10. Name the two Tchaikovsky roles that Freni has performed and recorded in Russian. (2)
11. At what opera house did Freni sing her first performance in the title role of *Adriana Lecouvreur*? (3)
12. In the 1970s, Freni recorded an album of duets with another

Italian soprano, perceived by some as a serious rival of Freni's. Who was she? (3)

13. In what role did Freni return to the Met, in 1983, after her lengthy absence? (3)

14. Name the opera closely identified with joint appearances by Freni and Franco Corelli, on stage and on a memorable recording. (2)

15. Where did Freni sing her first performances of Elisabetta in *Don Carlo*, Desdemona in *Otello*, and the title role in *Aida*? (3)

16. What two roles has Freni sung in *Falstaff*? (1)

17. Name the Handel opera recorded by Freni in the company of Dame Joan Sutherland. (4)

18. What roles did Freni perform at the Metropolitan Opera in the gala given to mark the twenty-fifth anniversary of her debut with that company? (4)

Answers on page 328.

49. TITO GOBBI

1. Which Italian theater was Gobbi's primary operatic home? (3)

2. Name three Wagnerian roles that Gobbi sang in Italian. (3)

3. Gobbi's brother-in-law was also a famous singer. The two men frequently appeared with one another in a pair of Verdi operas that threw them into adversary positions. Name Gobbi's brother-in-law, the operas in question, and the roles each man sang in them. (2)

4. According to the baritone's memoirs, a guest appearance he made at La Scala in a very difficult contemporary role was a great success, but one that so inflamed the jealousy of certain members of La Scala that Gobbi never felt really welcome at that Milanese theater again. Name the opera and role in question. (3)

5. During the 1964–65 opera season, Gobbi was asked to sing Baron Scarpia opposite two very famous Toscas who were re-

A redheaded diva from central Europe who has sung leading dramatic soprano roles in American and European opera houses since the 1970s has a reputation for hardline behavior that threatens to surpass her prowess as a singer. During the early days of supertitles, she threatened to walk out of a Chicago Lyric Opera performance of *Tosca*. The lady's wrath came about when the projected translation of Tosca's line after the murder of Baron Scarpia, "He is dead, now I forgive him," drew a laugh from the audience. Not used to snickering during her moments of high drama, the lady issued her ultimatum—"Choose between the titles and me!" —during the intermission. The diva won. Act III was performed with its heroine at her station but not a supertitle in sight.

🌿 🌿 🌿

turning to the operatic stage after prolonged absences. Name the sopranos and the opera companies involved. (1)

6. Gobbi, as were a number of the best singers of his generation, was nurtured in his early days as a singer by close proximity to what great Italian conductor? (3)

7. In later years, Gobbi became well known as a stage director. For which company did Gobbi stage his first opera? What was the opera? (4)

8. Gobbi appeared in Italian-made films of four famous operas. Name them. (4)

9. Name the well-known tenor who was Tito Gobbi's principal voice teacher. (4)

10. Gobbi and Maria Callas were closely identified with roles in an opera they sang together only twelve times. Since their performances were considered by many observers to have been all but perfect, it is generally but incorrectly assumed that they performed this opera with one another on a great many occasions. Name the opera. (1)

11. In addition to his work as a singer and stage director, Gobbi excelled in what other artistic pursuit? (4)

12. With what sopranos did Gobbi record the Puccini roles of Marcello, Sharpless, and Michele? (2)

13. Name the two Mozart roles that Gobbi sang. (2)

14. Tito Gobbi sang the title role in Verdi's *Falstaff* opposite Renata Tebaldi as Mistress Ford in three productions between 1958 and 1972. In what opera houses were audiences lucky enough to hear this famous pairing? (3)

15. What opera did Gobbi, Magda Olivero, and Mario del Monaco record together? (3)

*Answers on page **329**.*

50. ROBERT MERRILL

1. Where was Merrill born? (2)

2. To what other career than that of star baritone did Merrill give much consideration? (3)

3. Merrill made his Met debut in 1945 as Germont in *La Traviata*. Who was the Violetta that night? (4)

4. Merrill was chosen by Arturo Toscanini to sing in two radio broadcasts with the NBC Symphony. Please name the two operas that were performed and the years in which the broadcasts took place. (3)

5. Why did Rudolf Bing fire Merrill from the Metropolitan Opera in 1951? How did Merrill manage to get himself reinstated? (4)

6. Who was Merrill's first wife? (1)

7. Who was his second wife? (4)

8. Identify the tenor/baritone duets recorded by Merrill and Jussi Bjoerling in the early 1950s. (3)

9. Which Verdi baritone role is *not* in Merrill's repertoire?
   a. Amonasro
   b. Rigoletto
   c. Falstaff
   d. Count di Luna (2)

10. Merrill recorded the scores of two musicals for Decca/London. What were they? (4)

11. Merrill recorded Marcello in *La Bohème* on two occasions. Name the labels and the artists who are heard as Mimì, Musetta, and Rodolfo on each. Please name the conductors, too. (3)

12. What was the title of Merrill's first book of memoirs, published in 1966? (4)

13. In his memoirs, Rudolf Bing referred to Merrill as "first baritone in any company and second in ours only to . . ." and named another baritone. To whom was Bing referring? (3)

14. Name the soprano who once slapped Merrill across the face during a performance of *Aida*. Why did she smack the baritone? (4)

15. Name the two operas recorded together by Merrill and Joan Sutherland. (2)

Answers on page 330.

51. ZINKA MILANOV

1. What was Milanov's real surname? (4)

2. What two stipulations did the Metropolitan Opera's management make when they offered her her first contract? (4)

3. Name the two Verdi works that Milanov performed with Arturo Toscanini. (2)

4. Zinka Milanov's famous "live" recording of *Un Ballo in Maschera* from the Met made in 1940 costarred a great tenor. Name him. Can you name the four operas that Milanov recorded commercially with this artist? (2)

5. Which of the following roles did Milanov *not* sing at the Metropolitan Opera?
    a. Norma
    b. Minnie
    c. Desdemona
    d. Donna Anna (3)

6. What was the only Puccini role Milanov ever sang at the Met? How did this performance come about? (4)
7. What was Milanov's one excursion into the *bel canto* repertoire? (2)
8. Can you remember the name of the best-selling 1950s album of Milanov performing her Italian repertoire? (3)
9. What moment of Milanov's performances in *La Gioconda* was especially celebrated and eagerly anticipated by her fans? (2)
10. One of the rare evenings when Milanov's own singing was not the most breathlessly awaited component of the performance was a *Ballo in Maschera* heard on January 7, 1955. Why? (2)
11. Name the opera that Milanov and Franco Corelli, each making a rare London appearance, sang together in 1955. This performance is preserved on CD. (3)
12. Milanov, Leonard Warren, Mario del Monaco, and Cesare Siepi, under Dimitri Mitropoulos's baton, came together for a few performances of what was then (1956) a rarely performed Verdi opera at the Met. Name it, please. (2)

By the time Zinka Milanov arrived at the Metropolitan Opera, Arturo Toscanini had long since resigned from that company. However, he chose Milanov to sing in the Verdi *Requiem* in New York and London, and also invited her to sing in the famous 1944 War Bonds concert at Madison Square Garden. At that event, Milanov sang Gilda in the final act of *Rigoletto*, moments after the fall of Mussolini was announced. The diva and the maestro, it has been alleged, did not get along very well. Each artist, of course, had a huge ego. Milanov, as you may recall, was huge in other proportions as well. Supposedly, during a particularly tense moment, Toscanini raged at Milanov: "Madame, if you had as much in your head as you do in your—" and the maestro gestured to a particularly capacious portion of the soprano's anatomy—"you would be a great artist!"

A friend of mine once went to the opera intending to check out the qualifications of a young soprano singing her first performance of Maddalena in *Andrea Chénier*. Having splurged on an orchestra seat, this chap was quite annoyed when the woman behind him began singing along with the young singer, from her opening line on. By the time the new soprano on the stage and the unknown soprano behind him had finished the aria "La mamma morta," my friend could stand it no more. "Madame," he snapped as he turned around to chastise the obnoxious woman behind him. But then his jaw dropped as he recognized his tormentor, ". . . Milanov," he gasped at the formidable Zinka, herself a great Maddalena, of course, "What an honor to see you!"

(It is worth noting in passing, that the *Time* magazine opera critic reviewing that performance was sufficiently churlish as to headline his notice "Early Verdi, Late Milanov"! Frankly, I disagree.)

13. With what tenor did Milanov sing her final Met performance, in *Andrea Chénier* in 1966? (2)
14. Please identify the American university where Milanov taught voice for several years after her retirement from the operatic stage. (3)
15. Where and when did Zinka Milanov die? (3)

Answers on page 331.

52. JESSYE NORMAN

1. When and where was Ms. Norman born? (3)
2. Among her early stage triumphs, Jessye Norman counted this role in a Berlioz opera that she sang at Covent Garden in 1972. Can you identify the opera and role? (3)
3. What early Verdi work did Norman, in the company of José

Carreras and Fiorenza Cossotto, record in 1973? Which label released the album? (2)

4. Name the Mozart heroine that Ms. Norman recorded at a remarkably young age. (2)

5. In what role did Jessye Norman make her Metropolitan Opera debut, and when? (3)

6. How many Wagnerian roles has Ms. Norman sung at the Metropolitan, as of 1996? List them. (3)

7. What role was Ms. Norman scheduled to sing at the Tanglewood Music Festival in 1989, then canceled on short notice, although she recorded it elsewhere? (3)

8. What role in a Stravinsky opera has Ms. Norman appeared in and recorded? (4)

9. Who was Ms. Norman's tenor costar in Schoenberg's *Erwartung* at the Metropolitan Opera? (4)

10. Name the other famous soprano with whom Jessye Norman sang "A Concert of Spirituals" at Carnegie Hall. (1)

11. Name Ms. Norman's albums of show tunes and cabaret songs. (2)

12. What unexpected events affected the Metropolitan Opera premiere of Janáček's *The Makropoulos Case*, in which Jessye Norman sang the role of Emilia Marti, in January 1996?

Answers on page 332.

53. MAGDA OLIVERO

1. In what year did Magda Olivero make her professional debut? In what role? When did she make her U.S. debut? In what role and where? (4)

2. Who was Olivero's husband? (3)

3. What composer convinced Olivero to return to the stage in 1951, after a ten-year retirement, to appear in one of his operas? Can you name the opera? (2)

4. Can you tell us the titles of the two works that were the only complete operas Magda Olivero recorded in the studio? Who is the tenor in each recording? (2)

5. How did an illness of Renata Tebaldi's affect Olivero's career? (3)

6. Do you know what was Olivero's only Wagnerian role? (4)

7. Name the opera in which Magda Olivero made her Metropolitan Opera debut. When did this take place? (2)

8. One of Madame Olivero's La Scala triumphs in the 1970s was a non-Italian work in which she played a strong-willed older woman. Identify the opera and the artist who sang the title role. (4)

9. Name the opera in which Olivero toured the United States, in the company of Luciano Pavarotti, under the auspices of the Met. (3)

10. Which of the following operas was *not* in Olivero's repertoire?
    a. *Risurrezione*
    b. *Iris*
    c. *Pique Dame*
    d. *Otello*
    e. *La Wally* (3)

11. Can you think of a song from a Hollywood film that Olivero sang in concert, in Italian? (4)

12. In which western European country, not noted for its own operatic tradition, did Olivero sing quite often in the 1960s? (Many of these performances were recorded and are available on CD.) (2)

13. With which "school" of opera is Olivero most closely identified? (1)

14. In what role did Olivero make her debut at La Scala? When? Name the two famous women with whom Olivero shared the stage in that production. (4)

15. Where and when did Olivero first appear in *Der Rosenkavalier*? What role did she sing? (4)

16. Please identify the Tchaikovsky opera in which Olivero appeared with Boris Christoff and Ettore Bastianini. Where and when did this performance take place? (4)

17. In what opera did Magda Olivero make her San Francisco Opera debut? When did this occur? (3)

18. In how many operas by Franco Alfano did Olivero appear? Please identify the roles that she sang. (4)

According to an article in *Time* magazine, Leontyne Price
was readying herself backstage for her first *Aida* at La Scala
when, shortly before the curtain rose, a representative of the
company's makeup department stopped at her dressing room
to wish the soprano good luck. Momentarily forgetting herself, the visitor reminded the star to be careful lest her "Ethiopian" makeup start to run and soil her costume. Laughing
it off, the soprano shook her head and said, "Oh, sweetie,
you'd be surprised how well it stays on me!"

🐚 🐚 🐚

19. Please name the only role in a Donizetti opera sung by Ma-
    dame Olivero. (4)
20. Name the opera by Nino Rota in which Olivero appeared. (4)
21. In which Puccini opera did Olivero sing two different roles
    during her career? (3)
22. What was Olivero's only role in a Mozart opera? (3)
23. In what Verdi opera has Olivero sung two different roles? (3)
24. In Helsinki, in 1961, Magda Olivero sang one performance
    of an opera composed by a U.S. citizen. Please identify the
    opera, the composer, and the role she sang. (4)
25. In 1993, at more than eighty years of age, Olivero sang high-
    lights of one of her most famous roles in a public concert in
    Milan. What was the opera? (Yes, a recording exists of this
    event.) (2)

Answers on page 333.

54. LUCIANO PAVAROTTI

1. Where and when was Pavarotti born? (2)
2. A childhood friend of the tenor's grew up to become an internationally famous artist and sings with Pavarotti frequently.
   Please identify this artist. (1)

3. Pavarotti has a "good luck" role, which he prefers to sing when making a debut at an opera house. Name the role. (1)

4. Who was the soprano who was instrumental in establishing Pavarotti's international reputation? (2)

5. What did Pavarotti do for a living before he became a professional singer? (3)

6. What was Pavarotti's first complete operatic recording? (3)

7. Do you know which role can be said to have made Pavarotti a superstar in America? (2)

8. When Pavarotti sang *La Bohème* from the Metropolitan Opera House, televised "live" from the Met, who sang Mimì? (2)

9. From which opera company was Pavarotti unceremoniously fired because he canceled so many performances? (3)

10. Name the item Pavarotti advertised on American television. (2)

11. Where did Pavarotti sing his first performance of the title role in Verdi's *Otello*? (3)

12. In what city did Pavarotti's U.S. debut take place? What was his debut role? (3)

13. What was the name of Pavarotti's 1982 Hollywood film? What was the name of the love song that was supposed to have become the movie's biggest hit musical number? (2)

14. Which of the following parks was *not* the venue of a Pavarotti concert?

    a. Hyde Park
    b. Gorky Park
    c. Central Park
    d. Le Bois de Boulogne (2)

15. What was the nickname that attached itself to Pavarotti in the 1970s, even serving as the title of one of his albums? (2)

16. What is the first name of Pavarotti's former wife? (3)

17. Besides *Beatrice di Tenda*, list six complete operas that Pavarotti recorded with Joan Sutherland. (There are nine.) (3)

18. Which two of the following operas has Pavarotti *not* recorded commercially with Mirella Freni?

    a. *Madama Butterfly*
    b. *L'Amico Fritz*

    c. *I Puritani*
    d. *Luisa Miller*
    e. *Tosca* (3)

19. Pavarotti once did a "special" for ABC television in which he was seen in conversation with three "close friends," a TV star, a film star, and an athlete. Who were they? (4)
20. In which opera by Mozart has Pavarotti starred at the Met, Glyndebourne, and on a Decca/London recording? (2)
21. With which noted soprano did Pavarotti find himself feuding even though contractual obligations forced them to sing together for several seasons? (It should be noted that Pavarotti never publicly attacked the lady, even though she spoke ill of him to the media.) (4)

Answers on page 335.

55. LEONTYNE PRICE

1. Where was Miss Price born? (2)
2. What is her birth date? (3)
3. Before singing at the Metropolitan, Price sang four major operatic roles on NBC television. Name them. (4)
4. Where, and when, did Price make her operatic stage debut? (3)
5. Name three roles Price sang during her first Metropolitan season. (3)
6. In what role did Leontyne Price appear on Broadway? (1)
7. She sang at the inauguration of what U.S. president? (3)
8. What was the name of Price's late, beloved housekeeper? (4)
9. Who was Price's former husband? (3)
10. Leontyne Price sang three opening-night performances at the Metropolitan. Name the operas, her roles, and her costars. (3)
11. What complete operatic role has Price recorded three times? (2)
12. What was Price's first role in German, and where did she first sing it? (4)
13. Miss Price recorded a beautiful album of Christmas songs

Leontyne Price once related that, while browsing at Saks Fifth Avenue on a wintry afternoon, a shopper walked up to her, stared, and finally said, "You're Joan Sutherland." "Oh, no, I'm not," purred Miss Price. "I'm Beverly Sills!"

🌿 🌿 🌿

made in the early 1960s. Who is the conductor of that album? (3)

14. What was the first role Price sang at the new Metropolitan Opera *after* her opening-night Cleopatra? (4)
15. In what opera did Price appear in the former Soviet Union as a member of the visiting La Scala company? (2)
16. How many volumes were there in Miss Price's *Prima Donna* series of operatic recitals on L.P. on the RCA label? (3)
17. Price, Christa Ludwig, and Pavarotti sang a performance of *Il Trovatore* together in what European city? (4)
18. Leontyne Price recorded an album of show tunes for RCA. What was the title of the album, and who was her pianist? (3)
19. What was Price's final role at the Met? When did her last appearance there take place? (3)
20. The cast included Price, Giulietta Simionato, Franco Corelli, and Ettore Bastianini. The conductor was Von Karajan. It was the Salzburg Festival, 1962. What was the opera? (3)

Answers on page 336.

56. SAMUEL RAMEY

1. In what state was the American Ramey born? (2)
2. What did Ramey do before commencing his professional singing career? (4)
3. Please name the American opera company in which Ramey first attracted attention? (2)
4. In what role did Samuel Ramey make his debut at La Scala?

What happened during the performance that shook the entire cast? (3)

5. In what opera did Ramey makes his debut at the Metropolitan Opera? Who else appeared for the first time at the Met that night? (4)

6. Identify the opera that Ramey has sung at the Met in the company of Marilyn Horne and June Anderson. (2)

7. What is the title of Ramey's collection of songs from Broadway musicals? (3)

8. Which Verdi villain did Ramey portray with great success at the New York City Opera? This production represented the opera's first major staging in New York. (3)

9. At what opera house did Ramey take part in a telecast of Boito's *Mefistofele?* Who were the leading tenor and soprano that night? (2)

10. Name the rarely performed Verdi opera that Ramey recorded with José Carreras and Katia Ricciarelli. (10)

11. What major American opera company has consistently under-used Ramey? (1)

12. Which of the following roles has Ramey *not* recorded as of 1996?

  a. Olin Blitch
  b. Boris Godunov
  c. Philip II
  d. Baron Scarpia (2)

Answers on page ***337***.

57. LEONIE RYSANEK

1. In what city did Rysanek grow up? (3)

2. Name the diva who was Rysanek's early teacher and mentor. (4)

3. Name the conductor with whom Madame Rysanek was associated throughout much of her career, especially in the operas of Wagner and Richard Strauss. (2)

4. What was Leonie Rysanek's debut role at the Metropolitan Opera? How did she land the engagement? (2)

5. What was the vehicle for Rysanek's Met opening night in 1960? (2)

6. Which role in *Die Walküre* is associated with Leonie Rysanek? (1)

7. Rysanek recorded her *Walküre* role twice. Please tell us the conductor of each recording, and the company that released each version. (2)

8. For which Puccini role is Rysanek especially celebrated? (1)

9. Live performances by Madame Rysanek of the Puccini opera referred to in Question #8 exist in two languages. Name them. (2)

10. In which opera by Richard Strauss has Leonie Rysanek sung all three leading female roles? In which chronological order did she perform them? (3)

11. After several years of indifferent success at the Metropolitan (following her brilliant debut in 1959), Rysanek enjoyed a huge triumph weeks after the Met moved to Lincoln Center. The soprano interpreted an uncommonly difficult role in an opera that was receiving its local stage premiere. Name the opera, the role, and the conductor. (2)

12. Please list the seven Verdi heroines that Leonie Rysanek sang at the Metropolitan Opera during her thirty-eight-year career there. (2)

13. Can you name the two roles in operas by Leoš Janáček that Rysanek performed with distinction in the final decade of her career? (2)

14. For what vocal but extramusical touch is Rysanek noted? There are four splendid examples of this bit of operatic *shtick* that occur in works by Wagner and Richard Strauss. See if you can identify them! (3)

15. What was the final new role that Madame Rysanek added to her repertoire? (3)

Answers on page 337.

58. BEVERLY SILLS

1. What was the name of the radio serial in which Sills had a featured role? (3)
2. What role did Sills sing at her New York City Opera debut? When was it? (2)
3. What is the name of Sills's husband? (4)
4. In what opera did Sills achieve her first major triumph? (3)
5. Beverly Sills made her La Scala debut in 1969, replacing another artist in a rarely performed opera. Name the opera, the soprano whom Sills replaced, and the reason that other artist withdrew from the production. (2)
6. What are the three works that make up Donizetti's trilogy of operas dealing with queens of England, and what role has Sills sung in each? (1)
7. Name the bass from New Orleans who often costarred with Beverly Sills at the New York City Opera. (2)
8. How many roles did Sills perform during her five seasons with the Metropolitan Opera? Name them. (3)
9. Name the opera in which Beverly Sills and Joan Sutherland costarred. Where and when did this take place? Which role did each soprano sing? (4)
10. What was the first role Sills sang with the Metropolitan Opera company? (4)
11. Although Sills was acclaimed in such diverse operatic capitals as Milan, Naples, Paris, and Vienna, which is the one European city whose critics consistently rejected her? (3)
12. When Sills was named director of the New York City Opera in 1978, whom did she replace? (1)
13. Which two Donizetti operas did Sills telecast from the Wolf Trap Festival in Vienna, Virginia? (These are currently available as VHS tapes from VAI.) (2)
14. Which of the following works was *not* in Beverly Sills's stage repertoire?
   a. *Le Coq D'Or*
   b. *Il Trittico*

      c. *Les Contes d'Hoffmann*
      d. *Lakmé* (3)

15. With which baritone did Sills record an album of songs from old Broadway musicals? Name the album. (3)

Answers on page 338.

59. GIULIETTA SIMIONATO

1. In what Italian town was Simionato born? (4)
2. In 1936, Simionato made her La Scala debut singing tiny parts. In what year did she sing her first lead at La Scala? What was the role? (4)
3. Name the three operas that Simionato sang with Maria Callas in Mexico City, in the years between 1949 and 1952. (3)
4. Name the tenors who sang opposite Simionato in the following recordings:
      a. *Rigoletto* (Decca/London) (4)
      b. *L'Italiana in Algieri* (EMI) (4)
      c. *Aida* (Decca/London) (2)
      d. *La Favorita* (Decca/London) (4)
      e. *Il Barbiere di Siviglia* (Cetra) (3)
5. Simionato sang four roles at the Metropolitan Opera between 1959 and 1962, and another role on tour with the Met. Can you name them? (4)
6. With which U.S. opera company did Simionato spend the most time during her stay in America, singing such roles as Azucena, the Princess di Bouillon, and Mistress Quickly? (3)
7. Although she never recorded *Carmen* commercially, Simionato often sang the role in Europe, in both French and Italian. At least four complete live recordings exist of this fabulous artist's interpretation of Bizet's protagonist, two in French and two in Italian. Can you identify the tenor, theater of origin, and language of each? (4)
8. What was the opera that Simionato sang at La Scala in the company of such artists as Joan Sutherland, Franco Corelli,

Fiorenza Cossoto, and Ivo Vinco, in 1962. In what language was the opera sung? (3)

9. Most people would not be surprised to know that Simionato sang the roles of Cherubino in *Le Nozze di Figaro* and Dorabella in *Così Fan Tutte*, as they are usually assigned to mezzo-sopranos. What is surprising, however, is the fact that Simionato performed a long-suffering Mozart heroine usually undertaken by a lyric soprano. Which one? (3)

10. Among other examples of exotic repertoire performed by Simionato is this soubrette role in a romantic German opera. Can you guess what it is? (4)

11. Which of the following roles was *not* in Giulietta Simionato's repertoire?

    a. Mignon
    b. Lady Macbeth
    c. Arsace
    d. Fenena (2)

12. At which Italian opera house did Simionato head a young artists' program for a number of years after her retirement from singing in 1965? (2)

13. In 1995, a never previously published recording of Simionato singing a Bellini aria was made available by Decca in Europe. What is the name of the aria? (4)

14. What is the name of the film documentary in which Giulietta Simionato is interviewed in her capacity as a spokesperson for a very good musical "cause"? What is the charitable organization for which Simionato works? (4)

15. Simionato sang the role of Giovanna Seymour in *Anna Bolena* opposite two remarkable sopranos in Milan, in 1957. Recordings exist of both performances. Who sang the role of Anna in each? (3)

16. What was the first opera that Simionato broadcast from the Metropolitan? When did the performance take place? Who were the other three leading singers that day? (3)

Answers on page 339.

60. RISË STEVENS

1. Where was Miss Stevens born? (2)
2. To what country did she travel to gain operatic stage experience in the early days of her career? (3)
3. Stevens made a "double" debut at the Met. Can you explain this phenomenon? (3)
4. Name the three operas Risë Stevens often sang at the Met in the 1940s in the company of Ezio Pinza. (3)
5. What was the Hollywood film in which Miss Stevens costarred with Bing Crosby? What bearing did this movie have on her operatic career? (2)
6. What was Geraldine Farrar's famous comment about the career matter discussed in Question #5? (4)
7. For which of the following composers did Risë Stevens *not* have an affinity?

        a. Mozart
        b. Verdi
        c. Gluck
        d. Thomas (2)

8. Who directed Stevens in her 1952 Metropolitan Opera *Carmen*, arguably her most celebrated production? (3)
9. Carmen's death scene in that 1952 Met staging was rather special. Can you describe it? (It was televised.) (3)
10. With what enormously attractive tenor did Stevens sing Dalila in Saint-Saëns's opera at the Met and on tour? (1)
11. Stevens recorded scenes from *Samson et Dalila* with two stellar tenors and two noted conductors. Please name them. (3)
12. In 1964, Risë Stevens starred in the inaugural production of Richard Rodgers's Music Theatre of Lincoln Center. Name the show and Miss Stevens's leading man. (3)
13. In what opera did Miss Stevens make her debut at La Scala? (4)
14. Name the opera in which Miss Stevens sang at the Glyndebourne Festival in the early 1950s. What role did she sing? (This has been preserved on disc.) (1)

15. Risë Stevens, Lucine Amara, and Roberta Peters were the leading ladies in a notable production of this opera in 1955 at the Met (available on CD). What was the opera? (2)

16. In a classic TV appearance on TV's *Ed Sullivan Show*, Risë Stevens sang a rather foolish number with popular pianist Liberace. Can you describe it? (4)

17. After her retirement from the operatic stage, Miss Stevens served as a general manager for an opera company. Which one? (4)

18. Miss Stevens served as president of a college. Do you know which one? (3)

19. Risë Stevens is famous for a recipe for a favorite snack food. What is it? (3)

Answers on page 340.

61. TERESA STRATAS

1. How did Stratas come to the attention of the Metropolitan Opera management? (3)

2. In what role did Stratas make her debut at the Met? (4)

3. At what faraway opera house did Stratas score a success before she became a star in America? (4)

4. To which conductor was Stratas, at one point in her life, engaged? (4)

5. In what city was Stratas born? From what country did her parents emigrate? (3)

6. According to Stratas's recollections, when she sang in the basement of her home as a young child, what comprised her audience? (4)

7. With what famous singing actress did Stratas prepare the role of Jenny in Weill's *Mahagonny*? (3)

8. What foible does Stratas share with, among other sopranos, Montserrat Caballé? (2)

9. When the Metropolitan Opera played a short season in Paris in 1965, the company as a whole received disastrous reviews.

Only Stratas conquered the Parisian critics. Can you name the role that she sang? (3)

10. Stratas, Fritz Wunderlich, and Hermann Prey sang an exciting performance of an Italian opera in Munich, in 1965, preserved on CD. Name the opera. In what language was it sung? (3)

11. Although Stratas canceled a Metropolitan engagement in the standard, truncated version of this opera, she became the first soprano in the world to sing the completed, three-act version of the work. Name the opera and the location of the premiere of the finished version. (3)

12. Stratas filmed this opera in German and sang it at the Metropolitan in English. Please name the opera and identify its original language. (3)

13. Teresa Stratas once took several months off from her singing career to perform charitable work. With whom did she volunteer to work, and in what country? (3)

14. In 1989, Stratas had a stunning success at the Met in three separate roles sung in one evening. In spite of the rave reviews she received, she canceled four out of eight scheduled performances. Name the operas. (2)

15. What opera by Richard Strauss did Stratas sing in a German television production, available as a commercial videotape from Deutsche Grammophon? (2)

16. Name the opera that Stratas rarely sings in the opera house but whose film version won her much approval. Who directed it? (2)

17. Which of the following roles is *not* in Stratas's repertoire?
    a. Gretel
    b. Lisa (*Pique Dame*)
    c. Marie (*Wozzeck*)
    d. Manon
    e. The Composer (*Ariadne auf Naxos*) (3)

18. Name the two roles that Stratas sang at the Met on the opening night of the 1994–95 season. (3)

19. In 1991, Stratas scored a personal triumph, creating a leading role in a new opera. Name the opera, the composer, the librettist, and the opera house where this took place. (4)

Answers on page 342.

62. DAME JOAN SUTHERLAND

1. In what role did Joan Sutherland make her Covent Garden debut? (3)
2. Who was the designer/director of the production that catapulted Dame Joan into the realm of international opera? Name the opera as well. (3)
3. The first time she auditioned for the distinguished director of this most distinguished company, Sutherland was rejected. Who was the impresario with the inhumanly high standards? (3)
4. Name the two major singers whom Sutherland can justly be credited with discovering? (3)
5. After Sutherland's Italian debut, the local journalists coined a nickname for her. What is it? (1)
6. Dame Joan's coach first became her husband and then her conductor of choice. What is his name? (1)
7. What were three of the non-*bel canto* roles that Dame Joan sang at the Royal Opera in the years between her debut and her eventual superstardom? (4)
8. After years of singing tragic or, at least, long-suffering heroines, Sutherland had an enormous success as the charming, if boisterous, heroine of an *opera buffa* (comic opera). Name the role, the opera, the composer, and the tenor who costarred with her in both the London and first two Metropolitan Opera seasons of this work? (2)
9. American opera fans often request the Metropolitan to rebroadcast an intermission feature in which Sutherland exchanged shop talk and demonstrated technical terms in singing with another great soprano. Who is the other soprano? (2)
10. Before her husband took over the training of Sutherland's voice, a highly distinguished maestro helped the soprano prepare for several of her *bel canto* roles. Name him. (3)
11. What was Dame Joan's final new role at the Metropolitan Opera? (3)
12. What was the title of the television program on which Sutherland appeared, introducing opera to youngsters? (3)

13. Dame Joan once appeared in an opera at La Scala in what was a true opera lover's dream cast, including Franco Corelli, Giulietta Simionato, Fiorenza Cossotto, and Nicolai Ghiaurov. This performance has survived via CD. What was the opera performed that night? In what language was it sung? (3)

14. Name the nonoperatic film that Dame Joan made in Austria in 1994. Which respected actor is her costar? (4)

15. Which Mozart heroine did Sutherland sing at the Metropolitan? (3)

16. At which opera house, in the last decade of her career, did Sutherland explore such "new" repertoire as *Dialogues des Carmélites*, *Lakmé*, *Adriana Lecouvreur*, and *The Merry Widow*? (2)

17. At which opera house did Sutherland sing her first performance of Donizetti's *Lucrezia Borgia*? (3)

18. Who conducted Sutherland's first recordings of *La Sonnambula*, *Rigoletto*, *Lucia di Lammermoor*, and *La Traviata*? (3)

19. In Switzerland, where Sutherland and Bonynge own a home, one of their neighbors was the author of many wonderful plays and musicals. Dame Joan recorded a superb album of this artist's songs. Who was he? (3)

20. What was the vehicle for Sutherland's final performance at Covent Garden? (3)

Answers on page 343.

63. RENATA TEBALDI

1. A noted Italian composer and a celebrated Italian soprano were among the first to recognize Tebaldi's talent. Who were they? (4)

2. Tebaldi absented herself from La Scala during the late 1950s. During this time the soprano reigned as the public's favorite prima donna at the Met, while Maria Callas, who sang only sporadically in New York, was the *diva suprema* at La Scala. Tebaldi, however, returned to Milan in a tumultuously successful performance in 1959. Name the opera in which Renata

Tebaldi appeared. Who were her tenor and baritone co-stars? (3)

3. Where and when did Tebaldi's U.S. debut take place? (3)

4. Who was the tenor who sang opposite Tebaldi at both her American and Metropolitan debuts? What were his and Tebaldi's roles on those occasions? (3)

5. In 1958, Tebaldi sang the role of Mistress Alice Ford in a Chicago Lyric Opera production of Verdi's *Falstaff*. This was a truly "star-studded" event, and one that has been preserved as a CD. Who sang the following roles that night: Falstaff, Mistress Quickly, Meg Page, Nanetta, and Ford? Who was the conductor? (4)

6. Tebaldi has a favorite role in an opera that has never been fully admired by critics. Name the opera, the role, and its composer. (2)

7. Once, on American television, Tebaldi took part in an hour-long broadcast devoted to four reigning prima donnas. Who were the other three ladies on that wonderful broadcast (available on video)? (3)

8. Although she never sang German operas outside Italy or in their original language, Renata Tebaldi, in the first decade of her career, was greatly admired in three Wagnerian roles. Name them. (2)

Lucky opera groupies who got backstage after the Metropolitan Opera's 1968 opening-night *Adriana Lecouvreur* witnessed the public ending of the "feud" that allegedly existed between Renata Tebaldi (Adriana) and Maria Callas. Callas had attended the performance and had been brought backstage by Rudolf Bing. As the two prima donnas tearfully embraced, one of Tebaldi's fans was overheard to say, "Thank God! Now we can play our Callas records in the open!"

❋ ❋ ❋

9. In the last decade of her singing career, Tebaldi often shared the operatic and concert stage with this handsome tenor, with whom she made only one commercial recording. Name him. (2)

10. Tebaldi returned to sing in Italy in the autumn of 1967. She had not sung in her native land since 1962. What role did Tebaldi choose for her return, and in what opera house did the performance take place? (4)

11. Where did Tebaldi's final appearance take place? When was this performance given? (3)

12. What was the first song Tebaldi ever performed in a concert singing in English? (3)

13. Which of Tebaldi's commercial recordings was conducted by Fausto Cleva? (3)

14. Which of the following operas was the only one that Tebaldi did *not* broadcast from the Metropolitan Opera?
    a. *Mefistofele*
    b. *Andrea Chénier*
    c. *La Fanciulla del West*
    d. *Falstaff* (2)

15. Who was the pianist with whom Tebaldi recorded two superb discs of Italian and Spanish songs, now available as a CD from Myto? (3)

16. A videotape of a 1961 *Otello* from West Berlin has been made available from Legato. Tebaldi is the Desdemona. Who sings the roles of Otello and Iago? (3)

17. What was the only opera by Handel in Renata Tebaldi's repertoire? (3)

18. Which of Tebaldi's roles has been preserved on two different videos? Name the role and the tenor and baritone who sing with Tebaldi in each performance. (3)

19. From which two operas did Tebaldi record music for the mezzo characters, as well as the soprano roles? (3)

20. In January 1997, Decca/London surprised Tebaldi fans by publishing, as part of the long-awaited CD edition of the aria and song collection *Tebaldi Festival*, five arias that had been locked in the company vaults since 1968. These five great

scenes are from operas that Tebaldi never performed in public. Name the five arias, the conductor, and the orchestra heard in the sessions. (4)

21. What date was declared, in New York City, Renata Tebaldi Day? How did this come about? (4)

Answers on page 346.

64. DAME KIRI TE KANAWA

1. Where was Dame Kiri born? (2)
2. With which opera company did Dame Kiri make her U.S. debut? (3)
3. What role, sung in the city asked about in Question #2, catapulted Te Kanawa to fame? (3)
4. Can you name the film in which Kiri Te Kanawa is heard singing two arias by Puccini? Name the arias. (3)
5. Which of the following roles has Dame Kiri, as of 1996, never sung?
    a. The Queen of the Night
    b. Tosca
    c. The Countess Ceprano
    d. Arabella (3)
6. Name the Mozart opera that Kiri Te Kanawa and Samuel Ramey recorded together. (2)
7. Dame Kiri interviewed a great British soprano of the years between the wars for a TV documentary. Name the older soprano, and the program, which is available as a video. (4)
8. How did Dame Kiri publically celebrate her fiftieth birthday? (3)
9. After what career milestone was Te Kanawa made a Dame Commander of the British Empire by Queen Elizabeth II? (2)
10. Kiri Te Kanawa has recorded albums of theater music by three great American composers. Please identify them. (3)
11. What Israeli folk song did Dame Kiri record at the very beginning of her career? (3)

12. How did actor Jeremy Irons figure in Dame Kiri's recording career? (4)

Answers on page 346.

65. FREDERICA VON STADE

1. Who was the noted German soprano with whom Von Stade studied? (3)
2. In what role did Von Stade make her debut at the Metropolitan Opera? (4)
3. One of Frederica Von Stade's early roles at the Met was that of Wowkle, the Indian Squaw, in *La Fanciulla del West,* in 1970. Name the two sopranos who sang Minnie to Von Stade's Wowkle that season. (4)
4. Von Stade appeared at the San Francisco Opera in 1994 in a new opera based on an eighteenth-century novel and a more recent British play. Can you name it? (3)
5. Which of the following Mozart characters is *not* in Von Stade's repertoire?
   - a. Susanna
   - b. Zerlina
   - c. Idamante
   - d. Cherubino (2)
6. Who sings the title role in *Werther* opposite Frederica Von Stade's Charlotte on the Philips recording of Massenet's opera? (2)
7. When the La Scala company came to Washington, D.C., in 1976, as part of bicentennial celebrations, what role did Von Stade sing with that company? (4)
8. Von Stade reached large new audiences with recordings of a pair of famous Broadway musicals. Can you name them? (3)
9. Von Stade named her eldest daughter after one of the mezzo's favorite American songs, one that she has often sung in recital. What is the name of that song? (3)
10. With what role did Frederica Von Stade celebrate the twenty-fifth anniversary of her Metropolitan debut, in 1995?

11. Name the role in a Bellini opera usually sung by a soprano that Von Stade performed with success at the San Francisco Opera. (3)
12. What early opera did Von Stade sing during a special guest engagement at the New York City Opera? (4)

Answers on page 347.

66. THE THREE TENORS

Since their first joint appearance, the occasional collaboration of Luciano Pavarotti, Plácido Domingo, and José Carreras has become a phenomenon of immense proportions. Millions of compact discs, cassettes, videos and laser discs of these concerts have been sold. More than one billion people have watched their concerts on television.

1. Where did the first Three Tenors concert take place? When? (1)
2. Which of the Three Tenors is the eldest? (2)
3. Can you remember which tenor sang "Dein ist mein ganzes Herz" at the first Three Tenors concert? (2)
4. Name the tenor who had recovered from a potentially fatal illness shortly before the first Three Tenors concert. (2)
5. Name the recording company that issued the CDs, cassettes, and videos of the first Three Tenors concert. (1)
6. At that first concert, which Italian song did Pavarotti begin singing solo, before being joined by Domingo and Carreras? Do you recall the *bel canto* touch that Pavarotti, Domingo, and Carreras add to that *canzone*? (3)
7. Two songs from *West Side Story* were sung during the Rome concert. What were they, and who sang them? (3)
8. When and where did the second Three Tenors concert take place? (1)
9. Who conducted both concerts? (2)
10. Name the two great American entertainers who were honored by the tenors at their second concert. (2)
11. In a charmingly bizarre sequence, our three heroes joined forces to sing a samba. Can you provide the title of that piece? (2)

12. What was the estimated television audience, worldwide, for the second concert?
    a. 900 million
    b. 600 million
    c. 2 billion
    d. 1.4 billion (4)
13. At that second concert, which Verdi aria provided the grounds for a contest among the Tireless Trio? (1)
14. Name the participant in the second concert who sang the aria "Pourquoi me réveiller?" from *Werther* and had serious difficulty with that aria's rhythm. (2)
15. Who sang "Nessun Dorma" at the second concert? (2)
16. Please identify the recording firm that issued the CDs, cassettes, and videos of the second extravaganza. (2)
17. We don't think anyone who heard it could forget the rendition of another song from *West Side Story* at the second concert, this time sung by all three divi. What was the song? (2)
18. Great stars, apparently, can grant themselves leave to take a few liberties. Therefore, please name the Verdi piece for tenor, soprano, chorus, and orchestra that was transformed, at the second concert, into an ensemble for three tenors, chorus, and orchestra. (1)
19. What nonmusical event did each of the first two concerts celebrate? (2)
20. What was the top ticket price at the second Three Tenors concert?
    a. $1,000.00
    b. $750.00
    c. $1,250.00
    d. $500.00 (4)
21. Which member of the principal musical makeup of the Three Tenors changed in 1996, for the third tour? Who replaced him? (2)
22. Where in the United States was the only American concert on this tour played? (2)
23. In what way did TV coverage of the 1996 concert differ from that of the earlier concerts? (2)
24. Why was the American concert especially crucial for Pavarotti? (3)

Answers on page 347.

67. DEBUTS AT THE MET

Can you give the debut role for each famous Metropolitan Opera star listed here? For "extra credit" give the year of the debut, too.

1. Renata Tebaldi (2)
2. Leontyne Price (2)
3. Mario del Monaco (4)
4. Grace Bumbry (3)
5. Tito Gobbi (3)
6. Marian Anderson (2)
7. Robert Merrill (2)
8. Montserrat Caballé (3)
9. Cesare Siepi (4)
10. Giulietta Simionato (4)
11. Kirsten Flagstad (2)
12. Rosa Ponselle (3)
13. Birgit Nilsson (3)
14. Cornell MacNeil (4)
15. Joan Sutherland (3)
16. Maria Callas (2)
17. Franco Corelli (3)
18. Marcella Sembrich (4)
19. Beverly Sills (2)
20. Shirley Verrett (3)
21. Plácido Domingo (2)
22. Sherrill Milnes (3)
23. Renata Scotto (2)
24. Mirella Freni (2)
25. Luciano Pavarotti (1)
26. Aprile Millo (3)
27. Ezio Pinza (4)
28. Beniamino Gigli (4)
29. Roberto Alagna (3)
30. Enrico Caruso (2)

*Answers on page **348**.*

68. FAMOUS FIRSTS

Can you name the singers who created the following roles at the world premieres of these operas? If you can, give the place and year of the performance, too.

1. Abigaille in Verdi's *Nabucco*. (2)
2. Tosca in Puccini's *Tosca*. (3)
3. Otello in Verdi's *Otello*. (2)
4. Ariadne in Richard Strauss's *Ariadne auf Naxos*. (3)
5. Anne Truelove in Stravinsky's *The Rake's Progress*. (3)
6. Sophie in Richard Strauss's *Der Rosenkavalier*. (3)
7. Dick Johnson in Puccini's *La Fanciulla del West*. (2)

8. Cleopatra in Barber's *Antony and Cleopatra.* (1)
9. Canio in Leoncavallo's *Pagliacci.* (4)
10. Falstaff in Verdi's *Falstaff.* (3)
11. Mélisande in Debussy's *Pelléas et Mélisande.* (3)
12. Santuzza in Mascagni's *Cavalleria Rusticana.* (4)
13. Peter Grimes in Britten's *Peter Grimes.* (2)
14. The Old Prioress in Poulenc's *Dialogues des Carmélites.* (4)
15. Cecilia in Licinio Refice's *Cecilia.* (2)
16. Cio-Cio-San in Puccini's *Madama Butterfly.* (3)
17. Turandot in Puccini's *Turandot.* (3)
18. Norma in Bellini's *Norma.* (4)
19. Juana in Menotti's *La Loca.* (3)
20. Lulu at the world premiere of the complete, three-act version of Berg's *Lulu.* (3)
21. Figaro in Corigliano's *The Ghosts of Versailles.* (3)
22. Arabella in Richard Strauss's *Arabella.* (3)
23. Lavinia in Levy's *Mourning Becomes Electra.* (4)
24. Violetta in Verdi's *La Traviata.* (4)
25. Andrea Chénier in Giordano's *Andrea Chénier.* (4)
26. Esclarmonde in Massenet's *Esclarmonde.* (4)
27. Carmen in Bizet's *Carmen.* (4)
28. Parsifal in Wagner's *Parsifal.* (4)

Even the nicest of opera stars tends to be egocentric. Self-preservation is vital in the world of international opera, and it is useful for a singer to feel that he or she is indispensable. On the closing night at the old Met, a hasty decision was made: after the final scheduled number, the curtain was to rise and the entire company of soloists, chorus, and honored guests would lead the audience in "Auld Lang Syne." Informed of this, superdiva Birgit Nilsson frowned and shook her head. "Oh, no, we can't," she wailed. "I don't know the words!"

29. Anatol in Barber's *Vanessa*. (3)
30. Giuditta in Lehár's *Giuditta*. (4)

Answers on page 353.

69. THE YOUNGER GENERATION

See how many of today's brightest younger singers you can identify from the descriptions given here.

1. Admired for her singing of operas by Mozart and songs by Barber, this young soprano recorded a delightful collection of exotic show tunes and once fulfilled a Metropolitan Opera engagement as the cloistered Blanche in *Dialogues des Carmélites* while very obviously pregnant! (2)
2. This young baritone's Met debut as the Count in *Nozze* was hardly noticed. Now, however, he commands the stage as Rossini's Figaro, Mozart's Don Giovanni, and Britten's Billy Budd. He is also a formidable lieder singer and has championed American music. (2)
3. Acclaimed as a true heldentenor, this Canadian also excels in roles in operas by Puccini, Bizet, and Tchaikovsky. (2)
4. Of Greek-Italian roots, this young artist first made her mark internationally on a recording of a Donizetti *opera buffa*. (3)
5. One of the most impressive singers to emerge from Britain in years, this artist has sung Brünnhilde in Bayreuth and Rosalinde at the Metropolitan. (3)
6. An example of Franco-Italian cooperation, this tenor seems to be everywhere these days. (3)
7. A winner of the Marian Anderson Award, this singer includes Mozart, Beethoven, Purcell, Kern, and Arlen in her repertoire. (3)
8. Although his roots are in upstate New York, this fine tenor has sung Meyerbeer in Berlin and Verdi, Puccini, and Gounod at Lincoln Center. (2)
9. Well known for her *Trovatore* Leonora and Aida, this artist from upstate New York participated in the Metropolitan Opera premiere of Verdi's *Stiffelio* in 1993. (2)

Baritone Robert Merrill once recalled a performance of an opera during which he flubbed an important line, mangling several words. After the opera, Merrill encountered an elderly gentleman waiting for him at the stage door. The old fellow spoke with a heavy Italian accent. "Tell me, Mr. Merrill," the visitor inquired, "what part of Italy do you come from?" Sensing a possible confrontation, the Brooklyn-bred Merrill asked, "What part of Italy do *you* come from?" "I come from the south," answered the old man. "Well then," responded the baritone, "I come from the *north!*"

🌿 🌿 🌿

10. This fast-rising prima donna keeps her repertory firmly rooted in Rossini and Mozart and sings more concerts than operatic performances. Her recordings are all best-sellers. (1)

11. This coloratura from Korea has been charming audiences as Lucia, Gilda, and the Queen of the Night. She also sings French operetta arias. (2)

12. This imposing young gentleman from Wales has established himself, in fewer than five years, as an outstanding exponent of such roles as Mozart's Figaro and Leporello and is an admired interpreter of German and English art songs. (1)

13. A student of Franco Corelli, this handsome young tenor has been making a name for himself in Europe and America. (4)

14. This dark-voiced Russian first appeared outside her native land with the touring Kirov Opera but has since become a valued member of many companies in Europe and America. She has already recorded several discs of Russian songs. (3)

15. This young American received the Richard Tucker award and is the Metropolitan's most acclaimed Carmen in recent years. (3)

16. Still in his early thirties, this Russian baritone is as admired for his Verdi as for his Tchaikovsky and Rachmaninoff.

17. His first international accomplishment took place in Wales, and, in his Metropolitan Opera debut, he shared the stage with

a fabled artist of the last generation, in her farewell appearances. (1)

18. A linguist and a bright-voiced young soprano, this artist was chosen by Luciano Pavarotti to share the stage with him at a concert telecast all around the world and released commercially by Polygram. (3)

19. A charming artist from Washington, D.C., this soprano studied with Tebaldi and Bergonzi and attracted much favorable attention when she replaced the disgraced Kathleen Battle in *La Fille du Régiment* at the Met in 1994. (3)

20. This baritone, from a city associated more with baseball than with opera, has sung and broadcast a variety of roles from the Metropolitan Opera since his debut there, including Eugene Onegin (which he performed on short notice) and Pelléas, for which he received excellent critical reviews in 1995. His brother is a tenor. (3)

21. Another Russian finding success in the West, this baritone has staked his claim on the most important baritone roles in the Verdian canon and created the role of Stankar in the Met's 1993 premiere of *Stiffelio*. (3)

22. This strapping tenor sings Siegmund in the video of the Kupfner *Ring* cycle from Bayreuth and has recently been heard as Siegfried. (4)

23. This charming Scandinavian mezzo is the 1990s' most admired Octavian. (2)

24. Although she is from Long Island, this lyric soprano enjoyed much success in San Francisco before she was heard at the Met. In that theater, she has sung Adina, Gilda, and Susanna. Her debut recital disc is called *Positively Golden*. (3)

25. This American tenor has been heard in many operatic centers in operas by Mozart, Rossini, and Donizetti. In San Francisco, he partnered Kathleen Battle in *La Fille du Régiment*—and survived! (2)

26. A New Englander by birth, this soprano is one of the finest Cio-Cio-Sans in the world today. She also has charmed audiences as Mimì, Liù, Gilda, and Lodoletta. She took part in the first modern recording of the latter opera, as well as a rare

studio recording of Cilea's *L'Arlesiana*, and in 1995 recorded the first totally complete *Madama Butterfly*, comprising all the different versions of Puccini's opera, for Vox Records. (2)

Answers on page 354.

70. THEIR MARRIED NAMES

How many prima donnas, past and present, can you recognize by their "married names"?

1. Mrs. Peter Greenough. (2)
2. Mrs. Desmond Shaw. (3)
3. Mrs. William French. (4)
4. Mrs. Joseph Gimma. (4)
5. Mrs. Giovanni Battista Meneghini. (1)
6. Mrs. Richard Bonynge. (1)
7. Mrs. Ivo Vinco. (3)
8. Mrs. Walter Legge. (2)
9. The first Mrs. Robert Merrill. (2)
10. Mrs. Bernabé Martí. (2)
11. Mrs. George Cehanovsky. (4)
12. Mrs. Robert Sarnoff. (4)
13. Mrs. Paul-Émile Deiber. (4)
14. Mrs. Nicolai Ghiaurov. (1)
15. Mrs. Christoph von Dohnányi. (2)
16. Mrs. Lorenzo Anselmi. (3)
17. Mrs. Walter Surovy. (2)
18. Mrs. Wilfred Pelletier (4)

Answers on page 355.

71. OPERA STARS ON BROADWAY

Ever since Ezio Pinza conquered Broadway, singing in South Pacific, many opera singers have combined musical theater with operatic engagements. Listed below are some prominent opera singers who have also starred on Broadway. A list of their shows also appears. Match singers to shows. Some have appeared in more than one show. Break a leg!

1. Robert Weede (1)		a.	*Where's Charley?*
2. Cesare Siepi (4)		b.	*Man of La Mancha*
3. Robert Rounseville (3)		c.	*Shenandoah*
4. Risë Stevens (4)		d.	*Carmelina*
5. Giorgio Tozzi (4)		e.	*Porgy and Bess*
6. Eleanor Steber (4)		f.	*Milk and Honey*
7. William Warfield (2)		g.	*Candide*
8. Irra Petina (4)		h.	*The Yearling*
9. William Chapman (3)		i.	*I Remember Mama*
10. Mimi Benzell (3)		j.	*Bravo, Giovanni*
11. Helen Traubel (2)		k.	*Show Boat*
12. Ezio Pinza (besides *South Pacific*) (1)		l.	*The Most Happy Fella*
		m.	*Fiddler on the Roof*
13. Leontyne Price (1)		n.	*The Sound of Music*
14. Jan Peerce (2)		o.	*Annie*
15. Dolores Wilson (3)		p.	*Cry for Us All*
16. Teresa Stratas (3)		q.	*The King and I*
17. William Olvis (4)		r.	*Fanny*
18. Bruce Hubbard (3)		s.	*Pipe Dream*
19. Julia Migenes (3)		t.	*South Pacific*
20. Spiro Malas (3)		u.	*West Side Story*
21. Lawrence Tibbett (4)		v.	*Greenwillow*
22. Elaine Malbin (4)		w.	*Rags*
23. Ruth Kobart (4)		x.	*My Darlin' Aida*
24. Morley Meredith (4)		y.	*Christine*
		z.	*How to Succeed . . .*

Answers on page 355.

72. TINY FACTS ABOUT GREAT SINGERS

1. Name the American radio program on which both Beverly Sills and Maria Callas appeared as children. (2)

When Giacomo Puccini was a small boy, he studied the organ with an elderly priest in his native town of Lucca. The priest was, apparently, a disagreeable fellow. Puccini recalled that each time he played a wrong note, the priest would kick him viciously in the shin. Throughout his life, whenever Puccini heard a wrong note played or sung in the opera house, he jerked his leg violently, as if to avoid the blow.

🐚 🐚 🐚

2. How did Richard Tucker support himself before he scored as a tenor? (3)
3. What "bit" part did Fiorenza Cossotto record in an opera that starred Maria Callas and Giuseppe di Stefano? (3)
4. What prima donna is the mother of actor Nicholas Surovy? (3)
5. Piero Cappuccilli, the great Italian baritone, has sung only one performance at the Metropolitan. When did it take place, whom did Cappuccilli replace, and what was the role he sang? (3)
6. For what reason did Kirsten Flagstad receive undeserved bad publicity after the end of World War II? (1)
7. In what role and with which company did José Carreras make his American debut? (2)
8. Why was bass Boris Christoff prevented from making his American debut at the Met in 1950? (2)
9. Sherrill Milnes, prior to achieving fame as an operatic baritone, sang the television jingle for what popular brand of cigarette? (2)
10. Name the German opera that tenor Jan Peerce recorded twice. (2)
11. What were the two roles that Elisabeth Schwarzkopf sang at the Metropolitan Opera? (3)
12. Turn-of-the-century mezzo star Louise Homer was the aunt of what famous American composer? (3)

13. Birgit Nilsson has had a bitter feud with what celebrated conductor? (1)
14. Lily Pons once was married to a popular conductor. Who was he? (2)
15. Grace Moore was the mentor of what successful American soprano? (2)
16. Name the soprano who, nearly twenty years after her retirement from public performance, continues to record albums of jazz and show tunes. (2)
17. Shirley Verrett spent 1994 singing at Lincoln Center, but not at the Met or the City Opera. What was she doing? (3)
18. Who was the first African-American tenor to sing a leading role at the Metropolitan Opera? (3)
19. What tenor did Rudolf Bing call an "old boat" when he publically fired the gentleman, prior to the start of Bing's first season as General Manager of the Met? (3)
20. What mezzo-soprano created major roles in both of Samuel Barber's full-length operas, *Vanessa* and *Antony and Cleopatra*? (2)

Answers on page 356.

Few singers were more beloved in their time than was contralto Ernestine Schumann-Heink, whose career lasted from the turn of the century through the 1930s, when she ended her public life as a network radio star in the United States. She was a large woman, and one night during an orchestral concert, the dear lady had difficulty threading her way past the musicians and their music stands. One player, attempting to be helpful, whispered, "Madame, move sideways." Schumann-Heink snapped back, "With me there *is* no sideways!"

A beloved soprano and an equally admired tenor, at the time opera's most glamorous couple, exchanged some harsh words during the curtain calls after the second act of Ponchielli's *La Gioconda*. Each accused the other of upstaging during the act's finale. "Callas is a better Gioconda than you," shouted the tenor, certain that that remark would draw blood. Hardly batting a long eyelash, the diva retorted, "Tucker is a better *tenor* than you." They finished the opera amid an atmosphere reminiscent of the third act of *Who's Afraid of Virginia Woolf?* and didn't speak for weeks.

73. FAREWELLS AT THE MET

For each artist listed, give that individual's last role sung at the Metropolitan. Can you also give the year?

1. Kirsten Flagstad (3)
2. Zinka Milanov (3)
3. Enrico Caruso (1)
4. Leonard Warren (3)
5. Maria Callas (1)
6. Dorothy Kirsten (3)
7. Richard Tucker (3)
8. Lily Pons (2)
9. Renata Tebaldi (2)
10. Risë Stevens (2)
11. Maria Jeritza (4)
12. Giuseppe di Stefano (3)
13. Birgit Nilsson (3)
14. Elisabeth Schwarzkopf (3)
15. Jussi Bjoerling (4)
16. Beverly Sills (2)
17. Robert Merrill (3)
18. Geraldine Farrar (4)
19. Jan Peerce (3)
20. Eleanor Steber (2)
21. Régine Crespin (2)
22. Jon Vickers (2)
23. Licia Albanese (3)
24. Roberta Peters (3)
25. Elisabeth Soederstroem (4)
26. Anna Moffo (3)
27. Kathleen Battle (3)
28. Christa Ludwig (3)
29. Cesare Siepi (3)
30. Jarmila Novotna (4)

Answers on page 357.

III

Unforgettable Characters

74. TITLE ROLES

Give the names of the characters referred to by the titles of the following operas.

1. *Der Rosenkavalier* (2)
2. *Il Trovatore* (1)
3. *L'Amore dei Tre Re* (4)
4. *Die Walküre* (1)
5. *La Fanciulla del West* (3)
6. *Der Fliegende Holländer* (4)
7. *The Gypsy Baron* (4)
8. *The Merry Widow* (2)
9. *The Bartered Bride* (3)
10. *La Sonnambula* (2)
11. *La Rondine* (3)
12. *Il Barbiere di Siviglia* (1)
13. *La Favorita* (3)
14. *Pagliacci* (3)
15. *Die Fledermaus* (2)
16. *Die Frau ohne Schatten* (3)
17. *Il Pirata* (4)
18. *Lady Macbeth of Mtsensk* (3)
19. *The Saint of Bleecker Street* (4)
20. *L'Impresario* (4)

Answers on page **359**.

75. NOBLESSE OBLIGE

In many operas, the affairs of men are influenced by the wishes of royalty. Below is a list of kings, queens, and other noble men and women who appear in operas. Please name the opera and composer, and describe the influence each character has on the action. Please note that these people are not "title characters."

1. King Philip II (1)
2. Cleopatra (2)
3. Queen Elizabeth I (name two) (3)
4. Charles V (name two) (3)
5. Henry the Fowler (2)
6. Gustavus III (2)
7. Dmitri Ivanovich (2)
8. Jane Seymour (3)
9. Emperor Altoum (2)
10. Prince Shuisky (3)
11. Prince Orlofsky (1)
12. Duchess Federica (3)
13. Prince Gremin (3)
14. The Count of Saxony (3)
15. Duchess Elena (3)

Answers on page 359.

76. ELEVEN DONS AND A DONNA

All the characters asked about here have the Spanish sobriquet Don *added to their names—in most cases, they are not related to one another. Identify each character and the opera from which he or she comes.*

1. This Don, a bad guy, is foiled by a pistol packin' mamma who is determined to thwart his nefarious plans. (1)
2. This Don has a long list of lady loves but can't seem to score with anybody by the time we meet him. (1)
3. This Don is a head of state who loses his heart, and lots of jewelry, too, to an itinerant chanteuse. (3)
4. This Don is mean, and foolish enough to want to wed a girl who could practically be his granddaughter. (2)
5. The Don we seek here is an outcast in two nations. He survives a tragic love story to find glory in battle, but no peace in a monastery. (2)
6. This Don doesn't appear until the final scene of the opera, but his arrival helps to wrap up the plot. (2)
7. This Don is actually an alias used by a resourceful young fellow to explain the absence of another, less welcome Don. (1)
8. Do you recognize this Don, who sings a song about a dragoon from Alcala? (3)
9. This Don, a meddler, enlists a servant to intrigue against her employers. (2)

10. This Don, a notary, takes part in one of the most famous weddings in all opera. (2)
11. This unlucky Don kills his future father-in-law in a duel he did not wish to fight. (4)
12. This Donna can't help loving her man, although all she ever gets from him is trouble. (1)

Answers on page 362.

77. THREE GUYS NAMED DON CARLO

Giuseppe Verdi's operas feature no fewer than three leading characters named Don Carlo, one each in Ernani, La Forza del Destino, *and, not surprisingly,* Don Carlo. *These gentlemen were quite different from one another in terms of temperament, moral fiber, and fate. Can you tell them apart?*

1. Which Don Carlo is *not* a baritone? (1)
2. Which is a real villain? (1)
3. Do you know the Don Carlo who sings an aria entitled "Son Pereda, ricco d'onore"? (2)
4. Which Don Carlo is a disappointment to his dad? (2)
5. Who pardons his former enemy and restores to him the woman whom they both love? (3)
6. Which Don Carlo was the great baritone Leonard Warren singing the night he fell dead onstage at the Metropolitan Opera? (2)
7. Which Don Carlo sings three love duets with the woman he calls "mother"? (3)
8. Which Don Carlo abducts a woman from *one* of her own weddings? (3)
9. Which Don Carlo is marked for death by a very close relative? (1)
10. Can you tell us which Don Carlo is *not* based on a real, historical person? (2)
11. Which Don Carlo kills his own sister? (1)

12. Which Don Carlo meets a fate that no one, to this day, is completely certain about? (3)

13. Tell us which Don Carlo is praised by the entire cast, with one crucial exception, in an exciting ensemble that concludes the work's third act? (3)

14. Which Don Carlo was frequently performed over the years by Jussi Bjoerling, Richard Tucker, and Franco Corelli, but was never recorded commercially by those artists? (2)

15. Which Don Carlo takes part in a duet entitled "Io vengo a domandar grazia alla mia Regina"? (3)

16. Which Don Carlo is alive and well at the end of the opera? (2)

17. Which Don Carlo turns up under another name in one of the other operas discussed here? How is he known in that opera? What is his relationship to the Don Carlo in that opera? (3)

Answers on page 363.

78. THEIR MASTERS' VOICES

Operas often feature characters who own slaves or employ servants. Who is the servant of each character listed below? What voice part does he or she sing? In what opera do these characters appear?

1. Violetta Valery (2)
2. Sir John Falstaff (2)
3. Leonora di Vargas (3)
4. Selim (4)
5. Dr. Bartolo (in *Il Barbiere di Siviglia*) (3)
6. Medea (4)
7. Marquise de Birkenfeld (4)
8. Timur (3)
9. Rigoletto (3)
10. Sarastro (1)
11. Rocco (2)
12. Maria Stuarda (4)
13. Alice Ford (name four) (3)
14. Madame Larina (4)
15. Scarpia (1)
16. Elisabetta di Valois (3)
17. Desdemona (1)
18. Juliette (4)
19. Dido (4)
20. Countess Almaviva (1)

Answers on page 364.

79. SERVANTS, SLAVES, AND COMPANIONS

Identify the operas in which these servants or slaves appear. Who are their masters or mistresses, and how does each servant influence the outcome of the opera?

1. Annina (in an Italian opera) (1)
2. Mariandl (2)
3. Robin (3)
4. Aida (1)
5. Brangäne (2)
6. Adele (2)
7. Suzuki (1)
8. Bersi (3)
9. Carlo Gérard (2)
10. Curra (identify two maids named Curra) (3)
11. Despina (1)
12. Frantz (3)
13. David (1)
14. Monostatos (2)
15. Antonio (2)
16. Addie and Cal (4)
17. Leopold (2)
18. Charmian (4)
19. Dimitri (*not* in *Boris Godunov*) (4)
20. Billy Jackrabbit (2)

Answers on page 365.

80. DOCTOR, DOCTOR!

Operatic characters suffer more than their share of maladies and accidents—shootings, stabbings, poisonings, and wasting diseases, to name but a few. Here we have listed a number of operatic physicians. For each, kindly provide the name of his patient and the opera they appear in. Does the ailing character live or die?

1. Dr. Grenvil (2)
2. Dr. Miracle (3)
3. The unnamed Doctor in an American opera from the 1950s (3)
4. The unnamed doctor in a twentieth-century German opera (Note: This opera was composed before 1933.) (3)

5. The Surgeon in a nineteenth-century Italian opera, still a favorite with audiences (2)
6. Dr. Malatesta (1)
7. Dr. Javelinot (4)
8. A physician in a nineteenth-century Italian opera set in one of the British Isles (3)
9. Dr. Boroff (4)
10. Dr. Jesus (3)

Answers on page 368.

81. HOLY MEN AND WOMEN

Religious figures of all denominations appear in various operas. For each holy person listed, identify the opera he or she appears in, note his or her voice type, and summarize the influence the character has on the plot.

1. Zaccaria (3)
2. Varlaam (2)
3. High Priest of Dagon (3)
4. Ramfis (1)
5. Mme. de Croissy (3)
6. Cardinal Brogni (4)
7. High Priest of Baal (3)
8. The Bonze (2)
9. Athanaël (3)
10. Rangoni (3)
11. Frère Laurent (2)
12. John of Leyden (2)
13. Titurel (2)
14. Olin Blitch (3)
15. Abbé di Chazeuil (4)
16. Mme. Lidoine (3)
17. Baldassare (2)
18. The Grand Inquisitor (2)
19. Rabbi David (2)
20. Padre Guardiano (1)

Answers on page 369.

82. HI, MOM! HI, DAD!

Below are listed various operatic parents. Identify the child or children of each, and describe the parents' influence on the outcome of the operas involved.

1. Oroveso (2)
2. Peter and Gertrude (1)
3. Archibaldo (3)
4. La Cieca (2)
5. Mamma Lucia (1)
6. Marcellina (2)
7. Antonio (3)
8. Rocco (3)
9. Strominger (4)
10. Erda (1)
11. La Mère and Le Père (3)
12. Simon Boccanegra (2)
13. Marquise de Berkenfeld (3)
14. Mamm'Agata (4)
15. Azucena (1)
16. Stankar (4)
17. Alberich (2)
18. Veit Pogner (2)
19. Banco (2)
20. Madame Larina (3)
21. Cio-Cio-San (1)
22. Ford (2)
23. The Queen of the Night (1)
24. Siegmund (1)
25. Nabucco (3)

Answers on page 372.

83. FOUR GALS NAMED LEONORA

The following questions refer to a quartet of lovely lyric ladies who are similarly yclept. They are the heroines of Beethoven's Fidelio, *Verdi's* Il Trovatore *and* La Forza del Destino, *and Donizetti's* La Favorita. *We stipulate that, while Beethoven's Frau Florestan spells her name "Leonore" in the German text of that opera, she is Spanish and, in her own country, would spell her name with the "a" at the end.*

1. Identify the Leonora whose surname is Guzman. (3)
2. Which Leonora has a girl in love with her? (1)
3. Which Leonora is a lady-in-waiting to the Queen of Aragon? (2)
4. Which Leonora takes poison? (1)
5. Which Leonora was the title character of the first three versions of her opera? (1)

6. Which Leonora expires after singing a haunting trio with the opera's leading tenor and bass? (2) Name the trio. (2)

7. How many Leonoras are alive at the end of their operas? (2)

8. Which Leonora is frankly told by her lover that his mother always comes first? In which aria is she informed of this? (3)

9. Identify the sole mezzo among the four Leonoras. (2)

10. Marian Anderson recorded an aria sung by one of our Leonoras. Which one? What was the aria? (3)

11. Which Leonora digs a grave? (3)

12. Which Leonoras were often sung by Rosa Ponselle? (2)

13. Which Leonora did Maria Callas *not* sing? (3)

14. Which Leonora is rather unchivalrously judged to be unworthy of the man she loves? Why? (4)

15. Please tell us which two Leonoras are *not* loved by both the tenor and the baritone in their operas? (3)

16. Which Leonora is also portrayed in an opera by Paër? Name the opera. (4)

17. Name the Leonora who sings the aria "Pace, pace, mio Dio." (1)

18. Which Leonora's opera was originally composed to a French text? (3)

19. Which Leonora's self-sacrifice is totally ineffective? (2)

20. Two Leonoras have confidantes named Ines. Which two? (3)

21. Which Leonora does *not* hail from the Iberian peninsula? (4)

22. Which Leonora is the Countess di Sargasto? (4)

Answers on page 377.

84. WHAT'S MY LINE?

While many operatic characters are aristocrats with a great deal of money to burn, others must hold down jobs or, if they are lucky, run businesses. Below is a list of job titles. For each, name the operatic character of that profession, the opera, and the composer.

1. Actress in a repertory company (3)
2. Actress in a small traveling company (1)
3. Street singer (1)
4. Broom maker (2)
5. Birdcatcher (1)
6. Clown (name 3) (1)
7. Physician/matchmaker (1)
8. Rabbi (name two) (3)
9. Painter (name three) (2)
10. Valet (2)
11. Duenna (2)
12. Barmaid (3)
13. Soldiers (name five) (2)
14. Recruiting officer (name two) (3)
15. Schoolmistress (3)
16. Cigarette maker (1)
17. Stevedore (3)
18. Spy for the Inquisition (2)
19. Pig farmer (3)
20. Stage manager (3)

Answers on page 378.

85. DISGUISES

Operatic characters often conceal their identities in order to enter forbidden places or uncover treachery. Can you identify the characters whose disguises are described below? Name the opera and composer, too.

1. This chap pretends to be a pilgrim in order to be admitted to a palace where a wedding is about to be performed. The wedding doesn't come off quite as planned. (3)
2. Although he is a handsome nobleman, he dresses up as a drunken soldier in order to be with his beloved. (1)
3. He dresses up as a country girl in order to stay in a place from which he has been banished. His costume, however, does him little good. (2)
4. This noble lady costumes herself as a humble servant girl and finds true love in an unlikely place. (4)
5. These folks have a grudge against a certain fellow. They put on masks and are invited to a ball given by their enemy. At the ball, they accuse their host of unbecoming conduct. (1)
6. He dresses up as his own lawyer in order to trap the man who has dressed up as our hero. (1)

7. These fellows assume the most outlandish disguises in order to test the constancy of their fiancées. Ultimately, they wish they hadn't. (2)

8. He dresses up as a monk and follows his prey home from a town fair, then proposes an interesting exchange. (3)

9. Although she is a popular figure in society, this young lady pretends to be a Parisian *grisette* in order to enjoy a night on the town. (3)

10. In order to show off his power, this boastful fellow transforms himself into a small and loathsome creature, only to be promptly captured and robbed by the very one he sought to impress. (2)

11. A young woman disguises herself as a young man to protect what's left of her virtue while traveling but decides not to go anywhere except to heaven. (1)

12. A princeling transforms himself into a vendor of watermelons and eavesdrops on what local citizens have to say about his regime. (3)

Answers on page 380.

Basso Cesare Siepi was once asked by the Met's management to make a guest appearance in a gala New Year's Eve performance of *Die Fledermaus*, as the entertainment at Prince Orlofsky's ball. Evidently, Siepi wasn't familiar with the Strauss operetta, for, told that the "ball" would be hosted by mezzo Regina Resnik, Siepi did not seem to realize that Resnik would be playing a male, Prince Orlofsky. At the appointed moment Siepi strode onto the stage. He spotted Resnik at once but apparently failed to notice her false mustache and masculine attire. As the audience broke into laughter, he graciously bowed and kissed her hand.

86. ALIASES

Aliases and assumed identities are a staple of opera plots. Below is a list of false names assumed by opera characters. Can you identify each character by his or her real name, and tell why the alias was adopted in the first place? Name the opera and composer, too.

1. Lindoro (1)
2. Pereda (3)
3. Andrea (4)
4. Amelia Grimaldi (3)
5. Enzo Giordan (2)
6. The Wanderer (1)
7. Padre Raffaele (2)
8. Enrico (4)
9. Marquis Renard (2)
10. Tantris (1)
11. Mariandl (2)
12. Zdenko (3)
13. Signor Fontana (3)
14. Idia Legray (3)
15. Mlle. Olga (3)
16. Gualtier Maldé (1)
17. Sofronia (3)
18. Buoso Donati (3)

*Answers on page **380**.*

87. REALLY WEIRD NAMES

Even given the exotic settings of many operas, certain characters have highly unusual names. Identify each character listed here by opera and composer.

1. Clizia (4)
2. Lord Mountjoy (4)
3. Varvara (3)
4. Filka Morozor (4)
5. Serpetta (3)
6. Eudoxie (3)
7. Egberto (4)
8. Little Bat (3)
9. Osburgo (4)
10. Katiusha Mikailovna (3)
11. Squeak (3)
12. Wowkle (3)
13. Wurm (3)
14. Schigolch (4)
15. Vasek a.k.a. Wencel (3)
16. Mlle. Silberklang (3)
17. Giuseppe Hagenbach (3)
18. Yakuside (3)
19. Osaka (4)
20. Olga Sukarev (4)

*Answers on page **382**.*

88. TATTLETALES

Nobody likes a tattletale, but in opera, some of them get to sing wonderful music. Listed below are the names of operatic characters who spill the beans. For each, name the opera and composer. Whose trust is betrayed? What secret is revealed?

1. Tonio (2)
2. Tosca (1)
3. Fedora (4)
4. Valzacchi and Annina (2)
5. Amneris (1)
6. Desideria (4)

7. Iago (1)
8. Bardolph and Pistol (2)
9. Geronte di Ravoir (3)
10. Little Bat (4)
11. Mrs. Sedley (3)
12. Barbarina (3)

*Answers on page **382**.*

89. WHO WEARS THE PANTS?

One of opera's most exotic conventions is the travesti, *or trouser roles, in which a male character is played by a female. Guess the character, opera, and composer from the clues given below.*

1. This mischievous youth is constantly getting into scrapes. Even the threat of being shipped off to the army can't subdue him for very long. (1)
2. The queen's page, he is falsely accused of treason and is cruelly tortured. (3)
3. A crown prince, this character ascends the throne at the end of the opera, but history tells us that his reign was short. (2)
4. Too talkative for his own good, this foppish youth is tricked into betraying his master's disguise to an assassin. (2)
5. This young musician claims to live only for his art, but a pretty ankle (belonging to a bewitchingly high-voiced singer) turns his head. (2)
6. This foolish boy taunts his master's rival, provoking a tragic consequence. (3)

American tenor David Poleri, best known for creating the role of Michele in *The Saint of Bleecker Street*, once had trouble with a conductor while preparing a production of *Carmen* in Chicago. They could never agree on tempi, particularly in the opera's final scene. At the opening night, matters were no better than they had been during rehearsals. Finally, in a moment of immaturity that all but cost Poleri his American career, he stormed into the wings moments before the opera's climax, shouting to the maestro, "Finish it yourself," leaving the unlucky Carmen to improvise her own death—perhaps she stabbed herself with her fan! As for the tenor, he never worked steadily in the United States after that night!

7. Sent to woo in place of another, this young fellow immediately falls in love with the object of the other man's affection. (2)

8. This young stableboy remembers the name of his master's murderer. (4)

9. Flowers wither at his touch—until he finds the way to beat the devil. (2)

10. In this version of one of the greatest love stories of all time, the star-crossed hero is sung by a mezzo-soprano. (3)

11. A great lover's steadfast friend, this high-voiced chap helps sing the most famous tune in "his" opera. (2)

12. This jaded nobleman likes practical jokes and loves to launch young actresses' careers. (1)

13. This boy is a strolling singer and loves the neurotic title character of this opera. (3)

14. Virtually his only function in the opera is to announce to the work's heroine that he has learned to read. (4)

15. This youth is his father's pride and joy. How unfortunate that Daddy fears he has to sacrifice him to appease an angry deity. (3)

Answers on page 384.

90. IN-LAW TROUBLE

Tension between young marrieds and their "in-laws" is so pervasive that it is hardly surprising that these conflicted relationships are often the linchpins of operatic plots, both tragic and comic. A few such relationships are described below. Can you identify the characters and the operas in which they appear?

1. This fellow has such a fondness for his son-in-law that he takes a very dim view of his daughter's betrayal of her husband. Although his son-in-law is willing to forgive and forget, the old man is far more vengeful. (3)

2. Although we never actually meet this prospective mother-in-law, her presumably well-intentioned letter to her son, in which she praises the sweet and virginal qualities that she assumes her boy's intended embodies, causes problems. Since the lady comes up a bit short on the virginity question, she wisely leaves her callow lover and returns to her previous life, wayward but luxurious, with her old banker boyfriend. (3)

3. This haughty being disdains his son-in-law's social credentials, even though the young man is of royal rank. Father-in-law teaches his daughter's uppity husband the true meaning of "rock around the clock." (2)

4. This politically troubled gentleman's daughter wants to marry one of his many enemies, and Daddy isn't too pleased. While he finally is reconciled to his daughter's choice of spouses, an assassin sends him off to his reward. The dying dad lingers just long enough to appoint his new relation as his successor. (2)

5. This old gentleman has lost so many prospective sons-in-law to his daughter's bloodthirsty whims that he tries but fails to scare one last suitor away. (2)

6. This sharp-tongued lady so frightens the man her daughter longs to marry that the chap runs away from his responsibilities. The woman's revenge is twofold. (3)

7. This matriarch despises her husband's young bride, and wastes no opportunity to berate, insult, and humiliate her daughter-in-law. When the poor girl, who has been caught with a lover, drowns herself, the woman's only comment is to thank her neighbors for having pulled the corpse out of the icy depths. (3)

8. This father-in-law presumed that his daughter would marry the chap he had picked out for her. The young lady and her mother had other ideas, and took advantage of a midnight prank to accomplish a substitution. Daddy was a little put out at first, but soon gave the couple his blessing. (2)

9. This gent never liked or trusted his son's wife. In spite of his considerable handicaps, he catches the girl with her lover and takes it upon himself to punish her. (3)

10. This materialistic man is initially more concerned with his would-be son-in-law's social standing than with the man's appeal to his daughter. Once he recognizes what a lout the man is, though, he happily accepts his only child's own choice of husbands. (1)

11. This snobbish lady abruptly rejects the young man who loves her daughter, having set out to catch a duke for the girl. Fortunately, this basically kind mama relents and love is allowed to flourish. (2)

12. Not content to merely reject the young man his daughter loves for the most bigoted of reasons, he goads the boy cruelly and, when he is accidentally shot by the suitor, goes to his death cursing his daughter. (1)

Answers on page 385.

91. SINGLE PARENTS

Considering the frequency of seduction and betrayal, murder, and otherwise tragic death, it is no surprise that many operatic characters are left to raise children alone. For each single parent listed below, provide the name of the opera in which he or she appears and the name of his or her children (when possible). Did the kids turn out well?

1. Rocco (3)
2. Boris Godunov (2)
3. Madame Larissa (3)
4. Landgraf Hermann (3)
5. Teresa (4)
6. Sir Giorgio Walton (3)
7. Contessa di Coigny (3)
8. Nabucco (3)
9. Il Re d'Egitto (1)
10. Strominger (4)
11. Altoum (3)
12. Daland (3)
13. Marie (Hint: *not* a French opera.) (3)
14. Alberich (2)
15. Rosa Mamai (4)
16. Giorgio Germont (1)
17. Mamma Lucia (1)
18. Banco (3)
19. Mime (1)

Answers on page **386.**

92. HOME WRECKERS

Opera plots abound with illicit love affairs. Below are listed the names of some operatic home wreckers. Please identify the operas and composers, and the lovers or spouses the home wreckers betray. What is the outcome of the affair?

1. Luigi (3)
2. Werther (2)
3. Adalgisa (3)
4. Enzo Grimaldo (2)
5. Riccardo (1)
6. Roberto Devereux (3)
7. Alfred (2)
8. Percy (3)
9. Countess Geschwitz (3)
10. Drum Major (3)
11. Paolo da Verruchio (4)
12. Erda (1)

Answers on page **389.**

93. VILLAINS

Everyone loves a mean, low-down villain, especially if he or she boasts a beautiful voice. From the following descriptions, identify each of these gloriously unpleasant characters and the opera he or she appears in.

1. This villain is perfectly aware of the harm he does, and loudly proclaims that he has been created in the image of a cruel god. (2)

2. On the one hand, he presses his unwanted attentions on his boss's wife. On the other hand, he urges his boss to kill his wife when she is seen embracing yet another man. Furthermore, he has a glorious, rather philosophical aria to sing before the action begins. (1)

3. So desperate is he to possess the woman who has ignited his passion, he attempts to abduct her from the convent where she has taken refuge. His aria in that scene melts the heart. (2)

4. This tough cookie calls upon all the powers of darkness to give her the strength to carry out her evil plans. (3)

5. After singing an extraordinarily difficult aria, this sociopathic soprano takes her father prisoner and threatens the life of her sister and the man she once loved. (3)

6. Clearly as loathsome as his slimy father, he betrays his half-siblings and a good friend, in a vain attempt to get hold of something to which he has no right. (3)

7. This wily female knows a few good spells, and it's really not a good idea to invite her to one's wedding. (3)

8. Although she is intended to scare children, adults often find her amusing, and almost sympathetic. (2)

9. A figure of unmitigated evil, this character sets out to destroy an innocent man, for the pleasure of doing so. (4)

10. This manic bad guy appears in various disguises, including those of street singer and fisherman. His big aria comes early in the evening. (3)

11. This no-goodnik is foiled, to his utter humiliation, by no less than his intended victim's mate. (2)

12. Although his constant whining and complaining make him almost comically endearing, this little schemer is a mean-spirited spoiler, capable of murder. (3)

13. Another totally unlovable individual, this lout is consistently foiled in his attempts at evil-doing. He gets just what he deserves. (3)

14. A figure of towering evil, she despises mankind. Although in her own mind she is serving her superiors, no one can condone her wicked plans, and she is ultimately cast away. (3)
15. Although he is a murderer and a tyrant, this character's guilty conscience ultimately evokes pity from the audience. (2)
16. Although he doesn't hurt anybody, this backstabbing pest does his best to make trouble for the people whom he envies. (3)

Answers on page 391.

94. THREE GALS NAMED ELVIRA

Here is our salute to a trio of fascinating ladies from Ernani, Don Giovanni, *and* I Puritani.

1. Which Elvira makes her first appearance singing the aria "Ah, chi mi dissi mai"? (2)
2. Name the Elvira whose married life lasts just long enough for a trio to be sung. (2)
3. Which Elvira is abandoned at the altar, if for a higher but misunderstood purpose? (2)
4. Name the soprano who recorded one of the three Elviras complete, and only one aria from each of the other two roles. (3)
5. Identify the soprano who recorded two of the Elviras complete, but not a note from the third one. (3)
6. One of our Elviras goes mad. Which one? (2)
7. How many of the Elviras are left alone at the end of their operas? Which ones? Why? (2)
8. Which Elvira almost has to marry her uncle? (2)
9. Which Elvira is mocked in a famous aria sung by her ex-lover's servant? Name the aria. (1)
10. Which Elvira sings a scena beginning with the words "O rendetemi la speme, O lasciateme morir . . ."? (2)
11. Which Elvira is in love with a nobleman disguised as a bandit? (1)
12. Who is the American soprano who sang Elvira in *Ernani* on the stage but never recorded the part, and who recorded the

role of Donna Elvira in *Don Giovanni*, but rarely if ever sang that role in an opera house? (3)

13. Which Elvira has a doting uncle, a jealous suitor, and an impulsive fiancé? (2)
14. Which Elvira was often sung by Joan Sutherland? (1)
15. Name the Elvira who is loved passionately by three men. (2)

Answers on page 393.

95. GOOD DREAMS . . . BAD DREAMS

Identify the dreamers of the dreams described here. Name the opera, its composer, and state the relevance of the dream to the outcome of the opera.

1. He dreams of a terrible vengeance at the hands of the woman he has betrayed. (2)
2. In her dream, she views a horrible transformation to be undergone by her husband. (3)
3. This lady dreams of her own death at the hands of her children. (3)
4. She dreams of one who will defend her from false charges of witchcraft. (2)
5. She is frightened by a dream in which her closest relative is slain. (3)
6. This character dreams of a crime she has committed. (2)
7. A dream is reported that seems to implicate an adulterous couple. (1)
8. A dream that leads to a miracle terrifies the title character of this opera. (2)
9. A dream in which her lover is restored to her comforts this heroine. (3)
10. This account of a nightmare is not only a comic classic, but a highly detailed and lifelike description of this phenomenon. (4)
11. This man dreams that he has been changed into a donkey. (3)

12. This long-suffering maiden dreams . . . or perhaps actually sees . . . her dead lover greeting her from heaven. (3)

13. This young man recounts a beautiful dream to his lover moments before his life is shattered by the well-meant meddling of others. (2)

14. An old woman recounts a dream in which a long-dead person has returned from the "other side" to give instructions for finding a buried treasure. A delicious waltz ensues, prophesying an eventual happy ending. (4)

Answers on page 393.

96. LOCO EN EL COCO

Operatic mad scenes are often the musical and dramatic high points of the works they climax. Explain why the following characters go off their rockers, and identify the operas and composers.

1. Elvira (2)
2. Ophélie (2)
3. Lucia (1)
4. Nabucco (3)
5. Marguérite (1)
6. Peter Grimes (2)
7. Azucena (1)
8. Imogene (4)
9. Boris Godunov (1)
10. Juana (a.k.a. La Loca)
11. Anna Bolena (2)
12. Ah-Joe (4)

Answers on page 395.

97. SUICIDIO

Many operatic heroes and heroines take their own lives. Guess the identities of these poor souls from the following brief descriptions. Name the character, opera, and composer.

1. Her lover having just been killed in a natural disaster, this melancholy lady follows him to her own icy grave. (3)

2. Her only love rejects her as a faithless fiancée, and he prepares to travel onward in the hope of finding eternal love. Desperate

to prove her devotion, this girl offers her life as evidence of her loyalty. (1)

3. The villain holds the hero and his mother in his power. To free them, the heroine must declare her love for her enemy. Rather than live up to her promise, this lady chooses a fatal way out of her dilemma. (1)

4. Believing his humble sweetheart faithless, this titled chap poisons a carafe of water and drinks it, offering some to his unlucky beloved, who assures him—after it is too late—that she has never betrayed him. (3)

5. Responsible for two accidental deaths in a short period of time, this angry, misunderstood fellow is advised to end his own life. For once, he follows the advice. (3)

6. Determined to be united with her tenor in spite of all opposition, this maiden eludes her captors and reveals herself to him at the moment of his death. (1)

7. Having killed his faithless lover, this not-too-bright chap decides he can no longer cope, and wades out into a conveniently located sea to drown himself. (2)

8. In this first version of a familiar opera that had its ending changed, a boy finds his long-lost sweetheart, only to have her slain by their sworn enemy a few moments later. In despair, he jumps off a cliff to his death. (3)

9. Rather than reveal her hero's secret to a rival, this girl stabs herself for fear that torture might wring the secret from her lips. Her death was the final triumph of a beloved composer. (1)

10. This suicide is averted when the downcast lad with the rope in his hand is reminded of the magic powers he has in his own music. (2)

11. This neurotic soul who sings four soaring arias shoots himself with a pistol borrowed from his beloved's husband. (2)

12. By walking into a murderer's trap, this lovesick girl might be said to commit "passive" suicide. Her dying moments are spent with an adoring parent. (2)

13. Having seen all his earthly hopes destroyed by a malevolent ensign, this once-great individual stabs himself and dies kissing the corpse of the wife he has slain. (1)

A change in cast during a performance at the Metropolitan Opera is uncommon, and such a change during a broadcast of an opera is less common still. However, during the Met's 1995 radio broadcast of *Die Fledermaus*, Pamela Coburn, the soprano singing Rosalinde, felt sufficiently unwell after the second act to withdraw. She was replaced in the third act by Anne Evans. The audience in the opera house as well as radio listeners were informed of the change. To complicate matters in the theater, Miss Evans is several inches shorter than Miss Coburn, and the two ladies would never be taken as doubles for one another. This would perhaps have been more of a problem for those actually attending the performance than those listening to the radio, had it not been for the mischievous actor Dom DeLuise, who was appearing as Frosch, the wisecracking jailer. When Miss Evans made her entrance halfway through the act, DeLuise allowed himself an extravagant double-take, and then bellowed, for the benefit of home audiences, "Did you used to be an awful lot *taller?*"

❀ ❀ ❀

14. This youth stabs himself rather than obey his commander's orders to slay him. The shamed and shocked general promptly dispatches himself. (4)
15. "Death with honor" compels this most quintessentially operatic suicide, rarely performed to a dry eye. (1)

Answers on page 397.

98. MURDERS MOST FOUL

Operatic characters are often a bloodthirsty lot. See how many of these singing killers you can identify from the following descriptions. For each, name the opera and composer, too.

1. This lady combines chemistry with floristry in order to do in her romantic rival. Name her, her rival, the man they shared, and, of course, the method. (2)

2. This woman, denounced by all as a shameless, predatory hussy, stabs her rival to death in a moment of supreme defiance. What is her name, and what is the name of her victim? (4)

3. This man, in an event unseen but much discussed in the opera, shoots the villain who has seduced his wife. How is the dead man related to the opera's heroine? (3)

4. This ruler comes home from a hard day's debauchery, is greeted by his stepdaughter in surprisingly pleasant fashion, goes inside his palace, and there receives an unpleasant surprise. Name the king, his stepdaughter, and the "surprise." (1)

5. A hero has been betrayed by his paramour and humiliated by his enemies. Calling for aid from a friend on high, the man punishes the wicked and accepts his own doom in the bargain. Name the hero, the victims, and the method. (1)

6. A loyal friend jumps to the wrong conclusion and vows revenge. How does he get it and what happens to him? (2)

7. A famous and beautiful woman who loved to cook, and often felt the need to kill, combined hobbies at a dinner party in a beautiful Italian city. She finds out too late, of course, that she always hurts the ones she loves. Name the lady, the city, her intended victims, and her *unintended* one. (3)

8. Two big brothers argue over fee-splitting after a construction job. One kills the other. Who are they, what do they quarrel over, who kills whom, and then what happens? (2)

9. This wily fellow found that his dessert was none too good for him. Name the villainous Roman and describe his after-dinner surprise. (1)

10. The Scottish lass in question comes up with an effective, if tragic, way of annulling her marriage. What are the particulars? (2)

11. This man kills his mistress's brother in a duel, aided by a diabolical "friend." (1)

12. This lady believes that mushrooms add that special "something" to any meal or snack, and invites her father-in-law to help himself. (3)

13. This man frightens an old lady to death by brandishing a pistol. Mere death, however, can't stop the old girl from helping the cad into the afterworld. (3)

14. He catches a close relative making love to the woman he plans to wed, and stabs him to death before the horrified lady. This mysterious person goes into a decline, and soon perishes. (4)

15. She murders her husband because he protests that she is running away with her lover. (4)

Answers on page 399.

99. WIDOWS AND WIDOWERS

Because of the high rate of mortality among operatic characters, there are many widows and widowers to be found in opera libretti, some of whom are listed below. Identify each by opera. Briefly mention one or two significant characteristics. If the name of the departed spouse of a character is known, please include it.

1. Gutrune (2)
2. Elvira (the one who keeps planning weddings) (2)
3. Klytämnestra (3)
4. Lady Lucia Bucklaw (3)
5. Regina Giddons (4)
6. Enrichetta (4)
7. Serena (4)
8. Canio (10)
9. Frank Maurrant (4)
10. Macduff (2)
11. Loris Ipanoff (3)
12. The Thane of Cawdor (4)
13. Hanna Glawari (1)

Answers on page 401.

100. PRISONERS OF FATE

Guilty or not, many operatic folk are thrown into jail for one reason or another. Can you remember why the characters listed here were imprisoned? Describe each character's eventual fate, and name the opera and composer.

1. Piquillo (3)
2. Margherita (2)
3. Manon Lescaut (2)
4. Monterone (2)
5. Duchess Elena (4)
6. Don Carlo (the tenor) (2)
7. Angelotti (2)
8. Manon (2)
9. Eisenstein (2)
10. The Old Prisoner (4)
11. Don José (1)
12. Maria Stuarda (3)
13. The Carmelite nuns (3)
14. Billy Budd (2)
15. Peter the Honey Man (3)

*Answers on page **402**.*

101. CAPITAL PUNISHMENT

Many operatic characters face execution in the course of an opera. From the descriptions given here, name the character, the reason for his or her execution, the opera, and the composer.

1. This man loses his head, crying his beloved's name with his last breath. (2)
2. This fellow is shot even as his lover plots their escape and future joy. (1)
3. This man is beheaded, but not before he effects the death of the man who has ordered his execution. (3)
4. She is executed in the presence of her loyal followers, having lost a vicious power struggle. (3)
5. His beloved dead at his feet, this chap dies calling out a farewell to his mother. (1)

A salesman in an excellent classical record shop in Manhattan offered to help a customer who seemed a bit lost in the opera department. "I'm looking," said the shopper, "for a recording of Puccini's *Il Trovatore*." "I think you mean Verdi's *Il Trovatore*," said the clerk, trying to be helpful. "Gee," said the customer, "you mean Verdi wrote one, *too?*"

6. She dies for the crime of another but is glad enough to do so. (2)
7. These women go to their deaths calmly, singing a prayer. (2)
8. Although his death is not actually shown in the opera, it is foretold in the libretto and described in the novel on which the opera is based. The character's very last words would undoubtedly serve to convict him in any court. (2)
9. This nobleman is executed before the opera begins. He is survived by a fiery sister who is obsessed with avenging his death, as can be heard in her entrance aria. By the time she actually helps carry out an elaborate, bloody revenge, this lady no longer wishes to take part in the plot. But her second thoughts go unheeded and her former enemies are killed. (3)
10. He is beheaded, but the one who had wanted him killed is summarily executed very shortly thereafter because of her shocking behavior. (1)
11. He is executed, having fallen into a web of evil from which no one, not even his commander, can extricate him. (3)
12. She is executed on a trumped-up charge of treason at the moment when her treacherous spouse celebrates his next wedding. (3)
13. This highly respected man of God is executed by the forces of bigotry. He has, however, a wicked surprise for his chief tormentor. (3)
14. This austere farmer faces death rather than admit his membership in a nonexistent coven. (3)
15. Although a friend tries to save her from her fate by jumping backwards in time, the tragic member of two royal families gets it in the neck. (4)

*Answers on page **405**.*

102. FINAL REQUESTS

Some of opera's doomed characters are allowed to voice one last request before meeting their fate. For each character listed below, give the request. You won't, we are sure, forget to identify each opera and its composer. Bonus: Do they get their wishes?

1. Violetta (1)
2. Dick Johnson (3)
3. Mario (1)
4. Paolo Albiani (3)
5. Werther (3)
6. Amelia (in a nineteenth-century opera) (2)
7. Simon Boccanegra (2)
8. Anna Bolena (4)
9. Don Alvaro (2)
10. Desideria (4)
11. Mimì (1)
12. Turiddu (2)
13. Desdemona (3)
14. Pagano (4)
15. Mme. de Croissy (3)

Answers on page 407.

103. OPENING LINES

Below is a list of opening lines from operas. Identify the opera and its composer, and the character who sings these words, as well as the characters to whom they are addressed.

1. "Questo Mar Rosso mi ammollisce." (This Red Sea is freezing me.) (2)
2. "Della mia bella incognita borghese." (As I was saying about my anonymous little middle-class beauty.) (2)
3. "Una vela! Una vela!" (A sail! A sail!) (2)
4. "Popolo di Pekino, le legge è questa." (People of Peking, this is the law.) (1)
5. "All'erta, all'erta." (Be watchful.) (2)
6. "Wie schön ist die Prinzessin." (How lovely the Princess is.) (2)
7. "Buona notte, mia figlia, addio, diletta." (Good night, my daughter, farewell, beloved.) (3)
8. "Cinque . . . dieci . . ." (Five, ten . . .) (2)
9. "Zu Hilfe! Zu Hilfe!" (Help! Help!) (2)
10. "Rien!" (Nothing!) (3)
11. "Summertime, an' the livin' is easy." (2)
12. "Oh, just what I wanted. Thank you." (4)
13. "Glou, glou, glou . . . je suis le vin." (Glug, glug, glug . . . I am wine.) (3)

Verdi's *La Traviata* was considered very raunchy stuff when it was first heard in 1853. Clara Louise Kellogg, one of the first American opera stars, often sang *La Traviata* in an English translation. However, Kellogg sought to "protect" her audiences from the true miseries of a courtesan's life, and, therefore, when she thought that the English libretto was too steamy, she lapsed into the original Italian, and the "smut" went harmlessly over the heads of her American audiences.

❧ ❧ ❧

14. "Assez! assez!" (Enough! enough!) (4)
15. "From Alexandria, this is the news." (3)
16. "Ah, finalmente! . . . Nel terror mio stolto vedea ceffi di birro in ogni volto." (Ah, at last! In my stupid terror I saw spies wherever I looked.) (2)
17. "Sì, corre voce che L'Etiope ardisca sfidarci ancora." (Yes, the Ethiopians continue to defy us.) (1)
18. "Ma questa a una pazzia, Vuoi maritare tutti e, per colmo di sventura, io debbo shorsar la dote!" (But this is crazy! You want to marry off everybody, and what's more, I have to pay the dowry!) (4)
19. "No, signor mio, così non puo durare. I vostri amici Rodolfo e Marcello confiscano il 'stic trac'" (No, Sir, it can't go on this way, with your friends Rodolfo and Marcello taking over the backgammon boards.) (4)
20. "Hereinspaziert in die Menagerie. Ihr stolzen Herrn; Ihr Lebenslust'gen Frauen. Mitt heissen Wollust und mit kaltern Grauen, Die unbeseelte Kreatur zu Schauen." (Step right up, to the menagerie, haughty gentlemen and vivacious ladies, who with hot desire and cold shudders, come and see my soulless beasts.) (3)

Answers on page 409.

104. FAMOUS FIRST WORDS

Many operatic arias are introduced by recitatives, short, not always versified, lines that move the plot forward or set the scene for the aria—the "connective tissue" of the opera libretto. Below is a list of recitatives and aria cues. For each, identify the opera, its composer, the aria that follows it, and the character who sings the aria.

1. "Morir! Tremenda cosa!" (To die! A terrible thing!) (2)
2. "Qui Radames verrà!" (Radames will come here.) (1)
3. "E Susanna non vien!" (And Susanna doesn't come!) (2)
4. "Ti ringrazio, Sonora." (I thank you, Sonora.) (3)
5. "Quand je vous aimerai? Ma foi, je ne sais pas." (When will I love you? In faith, I do not know.) (1)
6. "Ancor non giunse!" (He is not here, yet!) (2)
7. "Son giunta! Grazie, o Dio!" (I am here! Thank God!) (3)
8. "Perché m'hai fatto segno di tacere?" (Why did you signal me to be quiet?) (3)
9. "Recitar! Mentre preso dal delirio." (To perform! While I tremble with delirium.) (1)
10. "Ecco: respiro appena." (You see: I scarcely breathe.) (3)
11. "Piangi, perché, perché? Ah, la fede ti manca! Senti." (Why are you crying? Ah, you lack faith! Listen.) (2)
12. "In quali eccessi" (In these excesses) (2)
13. "Sediziose voci, voci di guerra!" (Seditious, warlike voices!) (2)
14. "Ma perché mai discendere a tanta scortesia?" (But why be so rude and unkind?) (4)
15. "Vanne, lasciami; nè timor di me ti prenda." (Go away, leave me, don't fear for me.) (1)
16. "Teneste la promessa, la disfida ebbe luogo! Il barone fu ferito però migliora." (You have kept your promise. The duel took place. The baron was wounded but is recovering.) (2)
17. "Ah, più non vedrò la Regina!" (Ah, I shall never again see the queen!) (3)
18. "Allons! Il le faut! pour lui-même! Mon pauvre Chevalier!" (We must! For his own good! My poor Chevalier!) (3)

19. "O prêtres de Baal, Ou m'avez-vous conduite?" (O Priests of
    Baal, Whither have you brought me?) (4)
20. "Thy hand, Belinda! Darkness shades me,
    On thy bosom let me rest.
    More I would, but Death invades me.
    Death is now a welcome guest." (4)

Answers on page 411.

Tenor Barry Morell, who sang at the Metropolitan for more
than two decades, tells a wonderful story about Jussi Bjoerling. One night, when Jussi was singing Mario Cavaradossi
in *Tosca*, and Morell was the standby for that role, General
Manager Rudolf Bing invited the tenor to view the opera
from the Manager's parterre box. All was going smoothly
until the point in the second act when Bjoerling, as Mario,
was struck on the head by the singer playing Sciarrone and
dragged off to await execution. Bjoerling suffered from a
serious heart condition at that time, and Bing was aghast to
see the great tenor turn pale and go completely limp after
the fake blow to his head. "My God," muttered Bing to his
guest, "Bjoerling is having a heart attack. Let's go!" Bing
and Morell scurried backstage, afraid of what they thought
would await them. When the two men reached the wings,
the discovered the Swedish tenor, hale and hearty, cracking
jokes with the stagehands. Bjoerling looked up, surprised to
see Bing and the other tenor. "Jussi," gushed Bing, "you
looked terrible when they took you off the stage just now!
We thought you were in big trouble. What was the matter?"
"Oh, that," replied the suddenly modest Bjoerling, beaming,
who usually affected not to know a stage direction from a
character's motivation, "I was just *acting!*"

❀ ❀ ❀

105. DRAMATIC ENTRANCES

Below is a list of entrance lines of operatic characters. Identify the opera and its composer, the character who sings the line, and the person or persons being addressed.

1. "In questa reggia, or son mill'anni e mille, un grido disperato risuonò." (In this palace, thousands of years ago, a desperate cry rang out.) (1)
2. "Wes Herd dies ausch sei, hier muss ich rasten." (No matter whom this fireplace belongs to, I must rest here) (2)
3. "Me voici!" (Here I am!) (2)
4. "La sacra Iside consultasti?" (Have you consulted holy Isis?) (1)
5. "Flora, amici, la notte che resta d'altre gioie qui fate brillar." (Flora, my friends, the night remains for us to make merry.) (1)
6. "Madre adorata, vieni." (Come, beloved mother.) (3)
7. "Un'altra notte ancora senza vederlo!" (Yet another night without seeing him!) (3)
8. "Ho-jo-to-ho! Ho-jo-to-ho! Heiaha! Heiaha!" (War whoops) (1)
9. "Son io dinanzi al Re?" (Am I in the king's presence?) (3)
10. "Ohimè, di guerra fremere, l'atroce grido io sento." (Alas, I hear terrible cries of war.) (2)
11. "Wie du warst! Wie du bist!" (How you love! How you are!) (2)
12. "I am sick and sullen." (3)
13. "Non monsieur! je ne suis demoiselle, ni belle." (No, sir, I am not a lady, nor am I beautiful.) (2)
14. "Je viens célébrer la victoire de celui qui règne en mon coeur." (I come to celebrate the victory of he who reigns in my heart.) (3)
15. "Yes, I believe I shall love you." (4)
16. "Moi, je cherche un brigadier." (I'm looking for a corporal.) (1)

17. "Madama la Contessa?" (Yes, Countess?) (3)
18. "E suda e arrampica. Sbuffa, inciampica!" (I'm sweating and climbing, gasping and tripping!) (3)
19. "M'accordan di parlar? (Will you let me speak?) (3)
20. "Gott! Welch Dunkel hier!" (God, it's dark here!) (2)

Answers on page 413.

106. LOVE DUETS

Below are the titles or opening lines of some noted operatic love duets. Name the lovers, the opera and the composer for each.

1. "Pur ti riveggo" (To see you again) (2)
2. "O nuit d'amour" (O night of love) (2)
3. "Tu, tu, amore, tu" (You, you, beloved, you) (3)
4. "Veranno a te sull'aure i miei sospiri ardenti." (My ardent sighs will come to you on the breeze.) (3)
5. "Teco io sto." (I am here with you.) (3)
6. "Già nella notte densa s'estingue ogni clamore." (Now in the dark night every noise is stilled.) (1)
7. "Ist ein Traum." (This is a dream.) (2)
8. "Bimba, bimba, non piangere per gracchiar di ranocchi." (Sweetheart, sweetheart, do not weep about the croaking of a few frogs.) (1)
9. "Un dì, felice" (One happy day) (2)
10. "Decidi il mio destin." (Decide my fate.) (3)
11. "Va crudele, al Dio spietato." (Go cruel woman, share my blood.) (4)
12. "Principessa di morte! Principessa di gelo!" (Princess of death, Princess of ice!) (2)
13. "O soave fanciulla" (O lovely girl) (1)
14. "Il faut nous séparer." (We must part now.) (3)
15. "Heil dir, Sonne!" (Hail, o sun!) (1)
16. "O namenlose Freude!" (O nameless joy!) (3)
17. "Pace, pace, mio dolce tesoro." (Let's make peace, my beautiful treasure.) (3)

18. "Trinke, Liebchen, trinke schnell." (Drink, my darling, drink quickly.) (3)
19. "Vicino a te s'acqueta, l'irrequieta anima mia." (When I am near you, calm overtakes my rebellious spirit.) (3)
20. "Io vengo a domandar grazia alla mia Regina." (I have come to ask a favor of my queen.) (3)
21. "Perchè chiuso?" (Why was the door locked?) (1)
22. "Benvenuto, signore mio cognato." (Welcome, my brother-in-law.) (4)
23. "E il sol dell'anima" (Love is the flame) (2)
24. "Amaro sol per te m'era il morire." (Only because of you was death bitter to me.) (3)
25. "Deh! non turbare, con ree paure." (Ah, don't disturb yourself with guilty fear.) (3)
26. "Toi . . . vous!" (Thou . . . you!) (3)
27. "Ja, ihr seid es! Nein, du bist es!" (Yes, it's you! No, it is thou!) (4)

Answers on page 415.

107. CABALETTE

Bel canto, *the Italian expression for "beautiful song," lent its name to the Italian operas of the late eighteenth and nineteenth centuries which were characterized by limpid, often embellished melodies. This style of composition was followed to a greater or lesser extent by the great* bel canto *composers: Rossini, Donizetti, Bellini, and the young Verdi. The* bel canto *scena for a principal character consists of a longish, slow or moderately paced cavatina, in which the character expresses his mood or feelings—usually on the current status of his or her love life. The* cavatina *is followed by the* cabaletta, *an agitated, often brilliantly ornate final section of the aria that, generally, reflects a change of mood (sometimes, a message is transmitted to the protagonist). Listed below are titles of* cavatina *sections. For each, name the composer and opera, the character who sings the aria, and the title of the subsequent* cabaletta. *Finally, describe the dramatic context of the scene.*

1. "De'miei bollenti spiriti" (From my joyous spirits) (3)
2. "Quando le sere al placido" (When the evening is calm and silent) (3)
3. "Tacea la notte placida." (The peaceful night was silent.) (2)
4. "Casta Diva" (Chaste goddess) (2)
5. "Vieni! T'afretta!" (Come, hurry!) (3)
6. "Ah! non credea mirarti." (Ah! I didn't think I would see you.) (3)
7. "Ah fors'è lui che l'anima." (Ah, maybe he is the one I will love.) (1)
8. "Ah, si, ben mio" (Ah yes, my beloved.) (1)

Most people who have heard Jon Vickers sing the title role in Britten's *Peter Grimes* will agree that his portrayal of that tormented soul might be one of the finest operatic performances encountered in a lifetime of opera-going. Once in Paris, however, Vickers's performance was inadvertently sabotaged by the French chorus. That night, the audience was treated to the Canadian tenor's powerful interpretation of the gruff, inarticulate, sometimes brutal Grimes, and the orchestra sped the performance along during the storm that climaxes the act. Then Vickers, deeply in character, bellowed at the frightened, soaking-wet child who has just been brought in to be Grimes's apprentice to follow him out. The English soprano singing Ellen sweetly offered her line, "God bless you, my dear, Peter will take you home." Then, the linguistically impaired chorus, sounding as if it had stepped *en masse* out of an Inspector Clouseau movie, belted out the curtain line: "om . . . do you cull ZAT a om!" The large English-speaking portion of the audience was instantly convulsed with laughter, and at least one rather large American all but fell out of his box seat!

9. "Qui la voce sua soave." (Here I heard his sweet voice.) (3)
10. "Regnava nel silenzio." (Silence reigned here.) (3)
11. "Ernani, involami!" (Ernani, fly off with me!) (3)
12. "Vivi, ingrato, da lei accanto." (Live, ungrateful one, by her side.) (4)
13. "O, mio Fernando" (O, my Fernando) (4)
14. "Anch'io dischiuso un giorno." (Once I was kind and loving.) (3)
15. "Parmi veder le lagrime." (I can see her tears.) (2)

Answers on page 416.

108. "I AM WHAT I AM"

The following phrases are used by operatic characters to describe themselves. Name the character, the person or persons being addressed, the opera, and the composer.

1. "Io non sono che un critico." (I am only a critic.) (3)
2. "Io son l'umile ancella del Genio creator." (I am the humble handmaiden of creative genius.) (2)
3. "In povertà mia lieto scialo da gran signore . . . rime ed inni d'amore." (Happy in my poverty, I squander my poems like a gentleman of leisure.) (1)
4. "Son lo spirito che nega sempre tutto." (I am the spirit who negates everything, always.) (3)
5. "Somehow I could never believe that life was meant to be all dull and gray." (4)
6. "Io son la donna più lieta del Giappone." (I am the happiest woman in Japan.) (1)
7. "I do not ask to be believed, but I believe." (4)
8. "Ho il cor eccellente mi piace scherzare." (I'm good-hearted (but) I love to play tricks.) (3)
9. "Sono il factotum della città.") (I am the factotum of the whole city.) (2)

10. "Io rea non sono!" (I am not guilty!) (3)
11. "Sono un'ombra che t'aspetta." (I am a shadow that awaits you.) (3)
12. "Son tranquilla e lieta." (I am quiet and happy.) (2)
13. "La cosa bramata perseguo, me ne sazio e via la getto, volto a nuova esca." (I pursue the craved thing, sate myself and cast it away, and seek new bait.) (2)
14. "Non son più re, sono Dio!" (I am no longer king, I am God!) (3)
15. "Fuggo, fuggo, son vil!" (I am running away, I am a coward!) (2)
16. "Io non son che una povera fanciulla." (I'm only a poor girl.) (2)
17. "Siam pentiti e contriti." (We're repentant and contrite.) (4)
18. "Je ne suis que faiblesse et toute fragilité." (I am only weakness and fragility.) (2)
19. "Quando m'en vo soletta per la via, la gente soste e mira." (Whenever I go out, all the people stop to admire me.) (1)
20. "Io son dannata." (I am damned.) (2)
21. "Ah, maladetto io son!" (Ah, I am accursed!) (3)
22. "Una fanciulla povera son io, non ho sul volto luce di belta, regna tristezza sul destino mio." "I'm but a poor young maiden, no ray of beauty glows upon my face, and my future is filled with sadness." (4)

Answers on page 418.

109. FAMOUS LAST WORDS

From what operas do the following quotations, all exit lines or curtain lines, come? Name the opera, composer, the character who speaks, and briefly summarize the situation.

1. "Non ode più!" (She hears no more!) (2)
2. "Viva la morte! Insiem!" (Long live death! Together!) (2)
3. "Ah! La maledizione!" (Ah! The curse!) (1)

Once upon a time at a major American opera company, a soprano who often sang the title role in *Lucia di Lammermoor* had a simmering feud with a baritone often assigned to sing opposite her as Lucia's villainous brother, Enrico. This lady, who was a reasonably good singer and a powerful actress, had a large nose that no amount of makeup or hairstyling could successfully obscure. So, the spiteful baritone decided to call attention to the soprano's prominent feature by creating a "familial resemblance." With the aid of putty, he created an enormous nose for himself whenever they sang *Lucia* together. For some in the audience, this bit of infighting was the most memorable aspect of the opera.

🌿 🌿 🌿

4. "Tout est fini. . . . Noël! Noël!" (It's over. . . . Merry Christmas!) (3)
5. "Mio padre! . . . Ciel!" (My father! . . . Heaven!) (2)
6. "Notte d'orror!" (Night of horror!) (3)
7. "E spenta!" (She is dead!) (3)
8. "Cette bague autre fois tu me l'avais donnée—tiens!" (This ring you once gave me, take it!) (1)
9. "Ah, ma io ritorno a viver, o gioia!" (Ah, I am coming back to life, oh joy!) (1)
10. "Enrico, mi fai ribrezza!" (Enrico, you fill me with loathing!) (3)
11. "Maria!" (3)
12. "Madre, ah, madre, addio!" (Mother, oh mother, goodbye!) (1)
13. "Wer meines Speeres Spitze fürchtet, durchschreite das Feuer nie!" (Whoever fears the tip of my spear never shall pass through the fire!) (1)
14. "Ja . . . ja" (Yes . . . yes) (2)
15. "La commedia è finita!" (The comedy is finished!) (2)

16. "Now it is my turn to wait." (4)
17. "Seigneur, seigneur, pardonnez-nous!" (O God, forgive us!) (2)
18. "Orest! Orest!" (2)
19. "Gloria al Re!" (Glory to the King!) (2)
20. ". . . ancora un bacio . . ." (. . . and yet another kiss . . .) (2)
21. "Rattlesnake! Rattlesnake!" (2)
22. "Se stasera vi siete divertiti, concedetemi voi l'attenuante!" (If you have enjoyed yourself tonight, allow me your forgiveness!) (2)

Answers on page 419.

IV

And Then What Happens?
Opera Plots and Plotting

110. EXTRA! EXTRA! READ ALL ABOUT IT!

If there had been tabloid newspapers during the times in which various operas were set, their gory endings would have stimulated sensational headlines. Can you guess the operas that are referred to in these imaginary headlines?

1. SPY STRANGLES MA—SINGER KILLS SELF (2)
2. LONG-LOST BROTHER RETURNS—SIS DIES OF JOY (2)
3. QUADRUPLE MURDERS/SUICIDES ROCK ROME (1)
4. FUTURE RULER SLAYS GIRLFRIEND, RIVAL, SELF AS POP WATCHES (3)
5. KING ORDERS STEPDAUGHTER KILLED (1)
6. "I KILLED MY OWN BABY," SHRIEKS AGONIZED MOTHER (1)
7. POP'S MURDER ENDS HAPPY HONEYMOON FOR BRIDE (3)
8. WOULD-BE ROMANCER GETS DUMPED IN THE RIVER (2)
9. HUBBY FUMES, WIFE RUNS OFF WITH OWN BROTHER (1)
10. STRONG-MAN ACT BRINGS DOWN HOUSE (2)
11. CHIEF WITNESS SAYS, "I LIED"—TOO LATE TO SAVE CONDEMNED MAN (3)
12. TERRORISTS SLAY DOZENS AT WEDDING (3)
13. GENERAL STRANGLES WIFE, STABS SELF (1)
14. ROYAL WEDDING (FINALLY) PLANNED IN CAPITAL (3)
15. MIRACLE COMES TOO LATE TO SAVE PENITENT'S GIRL-FRIEND (2)
16. MAN, BOY MISSING—NEIGHBORS FEAR FOUL PLAY (3)
17. MONASTERY'S DOUBLE MURDER SHOCKS TOWN (2)
18. DUKE ESCAPES MURDER PLOT (1)
19. COUNT KILLED—MYSTERY WOMAN SOUGHT (3)

20. COMIC GOES NUTS—TWO DEAD (1)
21. ARMY SPY SCANDAL—ONE SURRENDERS, TWO ESCAPE (2)
22. EASTER PARTY ENDS IN TRAGEDY (2)
23. END OF WORLD PREDICTED (2)
24. "NO SEX, PLEASE, WE'RE BRITISH," QUIPS KING—WIFE DIES ANYWAY (2)
25. RIOT THREATENS HOLIDAY CELEBRATION (3)
26. CROWN PRINCE ASSASSINATED??? CHARGE COVER-UP (3)
27. FIANCÉ CRUSHED IN FREAK ACCIDENT, WOMAN KILLS SELF (4)
28. FIRE DESTROYS CELEB'S HOME—ARSON SUSPECTED (2)
29. SON AXES MOM, STEPDAD AFTER FAMILY QUARREL (2)
30. QUEEN EXECUTED AS KING REWEDS (3)
31. WOMAN STARVES TO DEATH NEAR BIG EASY (3)
32. OH, MARY! OFF WITH HER HEAD! (3)
33. BOY DIES—DID GHOSTS DO IT? (4)
34. "DEVIL MADE ME DO IT," SCREAMS GIRL WHO KILLED HER BABY (2)
35. LYNCHING AVERTED—POPULAR HANGOUT CLOSED (2)
36. FOREIGN PRINCESS TAKES POISON AFTER KILLING WOULD-BE IN-LAWS IN GOOF (4)

Answers on page 422.

111. THE RAIN IN SPAIN

Weather sometimes has a bearing on operatic plots. From the meteorological events described below, identify the opera, its composer, and the characters affected.

1. A raging thunderstorm provides a fitting background for this hostile encounter, often excised from a bel canto opera. (2)
2. Too much sun and too little water do in this glamorous heroine. (2)
3. Taking refuge in a stranger's home during a storm changes this fellow's entire life, and not necessarily for the better. (1)
4. It's so cold outside that this gentleman burns one of his own manuscripts in order to keep warm. (2)

5. Waiting outside her beloved's home, hoping to catch a glimpse of him, this poor woman freezes to death. (2)

6. A heat wave in the big city brings out the gossips, whose wagging tongues betray an adulterous neighbor. (3)

7. Traveling through Spain during a blizzard, this girl reaches her destination more dead than alive. (3)

8. A violent storm almost sinks this hero before he can make his first appearance. (2)

9. This short rainshower has little bearing on the story, but it does allow the composer of the opera to create a brief orchestral divertissement before bringing the plot to its happy ending. (2)

10. This poor tenor is not only tossed out into a snowstorm, he's shot as soon as the door is slammed behind him. (2)

11. A storm in which the wailing wind is suggested by humming choristers is part of the terrifying ambience of this opera's denouement. (2)

12. A furious gale traps virtually the entire cast of this opera in a tavern, as roads and bridges are washed away. (3)

13. A hurricane brings about the death of a hard-working fisherman, his crew, and his frantic wife, who rushes into the storm to find him. (3)

14. A storm in a northern sea drives a vessel off its course, leading to a strange, tragic adventure for its captain. (2)

15. Lightning and thunder punctuate a bizarre pact arrived at by two distinctly unpleasant characters, in a scene that invariably reduces contemporary audiences to helpless laughter. (3)

Answers on page 423.

112. LITTLE THINGS MEAN A LOT

Every opera fan knows that grandiose and supernatural props are often crucial to operatic plots—Wotan's spear, Alberich's Tarnhelm, Tamino's magic flute, and the like. However, common household items can influence the outcomes of operas, too. Below is a list of some of these simple objects. Name the opera (and its composer) in which the object is found, and explain its significance to the plot.

1. Four sheets of paper and some ink (2)
2. A little table (3)
3. A dime (4)
4. A boy's sweater (3)
5. A dinner knife (1)
6. An American flag (1)
7. A pair of earrings (2)
8. An injured garden plant (2)
9. A cup of coffee (4)
10. A handkerchief (1)
11. A lit match (3)
12. A rosary (2)
13. A chicken (3)
14. A last will and testament (3)
15. A discarded ring (1)
16. A bottle of Bordeaux (2)

Answers on page **424**.

113. HOT TIMES

Fires are often important operatic events. From the clues below, identify the opera, composer, and who or what gets burned by whom.

1. This ruler, himself governed by some shady religious figures, gathers all his enemies within his palace and has his own store of ammunition set on fire, thus incinerating his foes along with his friends. (4)
2. Setting his own ship on fire seems the only way to escape from his beloved's husband, so this hero puts his vessel to the torch, neatly accomplishing his exit and providing an exciting "curtain" for this scene of the opera. (2)
3. A folkdance around a campfire provides a rare, peaceful interlude in this opera that portrays passion, deceit, love, and violent jealousy. (2)
4. This fire punishes a couple who evoke the wrath of a primitive culture because they have been lovers. (2)
5. These poor souls are set on fire by local religious leaders and unwillingly provide entertainment of a cruel sort for a king and his court. (2)

There are many tales of operatic mayhem caused by props that were not in position or refused to work. A New York City Opera Violetta summoned Annina with a vocalized "ting-a-ling" when her bell was misplaced by the prop man. Caruso shot the Marquis of Calatrava with his fingers—shouting "Bang!"—to compensate for a gun that would not fire.

Murder weapons that don't work have caused more hysteria in operas than an army of Figaros attacking a regiment of Bartolos with shaving cream. There is the celebrated Tosca who aimed too low with her dinner knife, and Baron Scarpia thus met an embarrassing end, dying of a stab wound in his bottom. One corpulent Norma drew laughs from an audience when she ran to attack her children with a knife, showing the zeal with which one slices a ham during a midnight raid on the refrigerator. More recently, Luciano Pavarotti's Riccardo at the Met died of shock when Renato's gun misfired during a performance of *Un Ballo in Maschera*.

However, the ultimate death that didn't quite come off was the suicide of Renata Tebaldi's Tosca on New Year's Eve, 1969. Tebaldi ran up to the parapet and sang a suitably dramatic "Scarpia, avanti a Dio!" but didn't jump off the roof as she was supposed to. The soldiers, some of whom appeared rather confused, simply closed ranks around Renata as the curtain, mercifully, fell. Backstage, when asked about her new ending for *Tosca*, Tebaldi explained that the platform with the mattress that customarily awaits all Toscas had not been raised. "And if Rudolf Bing thinks I am going to jump fifty feet in the pitch dark just for him, he is crazy!"

6. These flames abruptly end the career of a famed party-giver and lover. They are the handiwork of an unexpected guest. (1)

7. This fire has been lit for the purpose of turning some guests into lunch. In a sudden turnabout, the hostess is cooked instead. (1)

8. If you burned the wrong victim in order to avenge a great injustice, you'd end up as cracked as what character in what opera? (1)

9. Probably the biggest bonfire of all time, this blaze takes care of just about everybody and expunges a world filled with guilt and lust. Only three creatures, apparently, survive. (2)

10. This question is about a fire that does *not* occur in an opera about a historical character who in all other accounts was burned at the stake, but here dies in battle. Who is the character and what is the opera? (3)

11. This notorious lady carries a candle in her hands as she performs one of the most astonishing "mad scenes" in all opera. (1)

12. The second act of this grand opera ends with a great city being put to the torch while its women kill themselves rather than allow themselves to be ravaged by the invading forces. (3)

13. The fire that is supposed to cook dinner for this heroine instead conjures up some strange manifestations from the spirit world. (3)

14. Lighting and then relighting a candle is the means by which a pair of lovers are brought together. (1)

15. Arguably the most famous forest fire in opera, these supernaturally powered flames protect a sleeping beauty from all but a true hero. (1)

*Answers on page **426**.*

114. HOLIDAYS

Certain opera plots are influenced by holidays. See how many of the special occasions listed below you can associate with an opera. Name the opera, the composer, and briefly outline the significance of the holiday in the operatic plot.

1. Christmas Eve (name four) (2)
2. Easter (2)
3. Midsummer Night (name two) (3)
4. All Hallow's Eve (3)
5. Viceroy's Birthday (4)
6. Passover (3)
7. Good Friday (1)
8. Carnival (name three) (3)
9. Feast of San Gennaro (4)
10. Feast of the Assumption (3)

Answers on page **428**.

115. WINE, PERSONS, AND SONG

Operatic plots are often affected by the actions of characters who drink more than is good for them or drink at the wrong time from the wrong glass. Below are a number of descriptions of liquor-related incidents in opera. Identify the characters, the opera, the composer, and note how the drink plays a role in the outcome of the opera.

1. This character makes his first entrance described by his neighbors as "cockeyed drunk," refuses to share his liquor with anyone else, then uses cocaine and commits a gruesome crime before the opera's first scene ends. (2)
2. She promises to meet him at her favorite night spot, where she will dance and drink her favorite wine with him *if* he does her a little favor. (1)
3. Whiling away the time between acts of a Mozart opera, this romantic fellow starts to sing about his amorous past. His friends ply him with drink until he loses track of the present, misses the end of Mozart's opera—and another chance at happiness. (2)
4. She invites some neighborhood rowdies to a party and serves poisoned wine. Overplaying her hand, the lady kills one guest too many. (3)
5. He offers her a glass of wine for fortitude. As she puts the glass aside, she finds a way out of a horrible dilemma. (1)
6. Taking a drink after a tiring journey, this heroic type is made to lose his memory, with earth-shattering results. (2)
7. Suffering the effects of a rough joke, he shivers as he sips his

sherry. The drink warms him up, as is demonstrated by a brilliant orchestral effect, but the wine dulls his senses and he is duped yet another time. (3)

8. This ardent man plies his sweetie with wine, hoping to remove all her scruples. All he gets for his trouble is a case of mistaken identity and spends the night not with her, but by himself in a drafty cell. (3)

9. Sharing a dinner laid out for two others, this shy maiden is encouraged by a houseguest to drink too much wine, with unfortunate results. (4)

10. While exchanging pleasantries and clinking glasses with a young guest at a dinner party, this girl begins to wonder if she should abandon her racy friends and settle down with one steady fellow. (1)

11. Lots of wine and a huge dinner convince an otherwise bright young woman to enter into a marriage of convenience—convenient, that is, for the groom. (3)

12. Believing it to be a potion, the more a certain lad drinks of a certain liquid, the closer he feels to success. (1)

13. His drinking is a town scandal and so affects his thinking that all he can do is shoot an otherwise decent fellow who seduces the drinker's sister. (4)

14. Having been fatally shot, this victim begs for water. All he gets from the loving wife who has just shot him is a glass of champagne. (3)

15. Not caring much for the local beverage, this wily old devil creates his own vintage. The townspeople show themselves to be a rather ungrateful lot. (3)

Answers on page 430.

116. SING IT WITH FLOWERS

Flowers are often important to the plots of operas. Try to identify the characters and operas from the following descriptions of blossom-scented operatic activity.

1. A young man has a bizarre spell placed upon him. Any flower that he touches will wilt. Who is the victim, who cast the spell, and how is that spell broken? (3)

2. This unhappy girl commits suicide by chewing a poisonous flower. Who is she, and why is she suicidal? (3)

3. These blossoms are spread by an ecstatic woman and her cynical servant. The heroine wishes to celebrate the presumed return of her husband. Things don't work out too well. Why? (1)

4. When this lady gives her corsage to a young man, inviting him to return it to her when it has faded, what is she really doing? (1)

5. These "few flowers" are shyly presented by a young girl to the young man with whom she is hopelessly in love. (3)

6. An animated, singing garden sounds like something out of Lewis Carroll—but it's not. What's going on? (2)

7. A swaggering guy ostentatiously presents these flowers to the girl who he believes is the prettiest in town but rudely snatches it back when he spies a girl he likes even better. (2)

8. This little posy changes hands three times in four acts and brings nothing but trouble. Who gives it to whom, and why? What kind of flowers are involved? (3)

9. This long-stemmed beauty is made of silver but smells like the real McCoy. Who gives it to whom, and why? (2)

10. In one of the most famous "entrances" in all opera, the prima donna walks onstage and after acknowledging her applause and perfunctorily kissing her tenor, she reverently places a bouquet at the altar of the chapel in which this all takes place. Name the character, the opera, the chapel, and the church in which it stands. (1)

11. This flower starts out in someone's teeth, ends up in someone's face, and finally becomes the subject of a great tenor aria. (1)

12. "Alas, the flowers that I create don't have a fragrance," laments this charming young girl to a young man she has just met. (1)

Answers on page 432.

117. CRIMES MAJOR AND MINOR

For each of the operas listed below, tell us the crimes committed in it, and identify the criminals and the victims.

1. *Boris Godunov* (2)
2. *Don Carlo* (3)
3. *Le Prophète* (4)
4. *Madama Butterfly* (1)
5. *La Gioconda* (2)
6. *Manon Lescaut* (2)
7. *Das Rheingold* (1)
8. *Simon Boccanegra* (3)
9. *Lulu* (4)
10. *Billy Budd* (4)
11. *Lucia di Lammermoor* (2)
12. *Die Fledermaus* (3)
13. *Lohengrin* (2)
14. *Porgy and Bess* (2)
15. *Don Pasquale* (15)
16. *Die Meistersinger* (2)
17. *I Lombardi* (4)

*Answers on page **433**.*

118. EAVESDROPPING

We've all been tempted to listen in on the conversations of others. Why should operatic characters be different? Here are summarized a number of operatic situations that involve eavesdropping. For each, name the opera, composer, and characters involved. Then, tell how each incident affects the opera's plot.

1. A girl listens in as her lover explains matters to a good friend, and she doesn't like what she hears. (1)
2. A silly musician overhears his master flirting with a servant and almost finds himself in trouble. (3)
3. A warrior manages to hear a crucial bit of enemy strategy, thanks to the wiles of a close relative. (1)
4. Eavesdropping on a carefully calculated conversation, this explosive personality draws the wrong conclusion, with disastrous results. (2)
5. After listening to a serenade intended for someone else, this hothead actually starts a full-scale, if funny, riot. (2)

6. Making a career of sticking their noses into the business of others, this couple tries to thwart a budding romance by tipping off an interested party. (3)

7. This worker overhears two higher-ups discussing a murder, and vows to save the intended victim. (3)

8. While listening to a supplicant's prayers, this fiendish entity finds new ways of driving his innocent victim to despair. (2)

9. This unpleasant chap discovers a married woman whom he loves making love to someone else. So, he runs to tell the indiscreet woman's husband the news. (2)

10. While two intriguers arrange a tryst for one of them, a quartet of lighthearted "show people" witness and comment on the folly of the others. (3)

*Answers on page **436**.*

119. HIDING PLACES

Below is a list of places in which, for whatever reasons, operatic characters hide. For each, identify the character who hides and what he or she is hiding from. Of course, name the opera and its composer as well.

1. A closet in a palace (2)
2. Behind a tree (2)
3. A well in a garden (1)
4. A loft (3)
5. A laundry basket (1)
6. Behind a gravestone (3)
7. A chapel (2)
8. Behind a partition (3)
9. Hidden in a crowd of sports fans (2)
10. A cave (2)
11. A trapdoor leading to a basement (14)
12. A closet in a private home (3)
13. A semitropical island (3)
14. Behind a screen (3)
15. Inside a "peace offering" (3)

*Answers on page **438**.*

120. INNS AND OUTS

Many operatic events take place in hostelries, some deluxe and others quite rustic. From the brief descriptions given here, please identify each inn by opera and composer, and name the characters who are enjoying the sometimes dubious hospitality. If the inn has a name, provide it, too.

1. A titled character picks up a local servant girl, takes her to a seedy inn and, while trying to bed her, lands himself in a lot of trouble. (1)
2. This inn is the place where a rascally seducer plots his escapades and, at times, comes to lick his wounds. (2)
3. This inn, located in the Iberian countryside, offers refuge to an unlikely group of pilgrims, camp-followers, and a pair of siblings in disguise. (2)
4. This inn has a fine view of the local river, a place where many of its guests end up! (2)
5. At this unnamed establishment on the road to an enticing city, a young woman captivates a young student and an elderly roué, who enlists the girl's own brother to help him seduce her. (3)
6. This unlikely but charming place serves its clientele as watering hole, post office, bank, and even Sunday School! (3)
7. This inn has a young hostess who takes great interest in a girl she spies in the bedroom of one of her guests. (4)
8. This tavern, with outdoor tables, is the scene where the proprietor's son is challenged to a duel by the husband of his lover. (1)
9. This tavern is situated offstage, but its existence allows an unhappy wife to entertain a suitor while her husband goes off for a drink. (2)
10. Three young girls, related to one another, run this pleasant Latin American bistro, a haven for street entertainers and incognito royalty, too. (2)
11. This is probably the most famous roadhouse in opera. On its

premises a popular siren is pursued by no fewer than three men in forty-five minutes. Name the lady and her suitors. (2)

12. The third act of this opera is set in the lobby of a mildly seedy hotel in which the heroine has allegedly been entertaining an illicit guest in her room. (3)

13. In a scene many opera-goers still haven't witnessed, a fallen woman for all seasons causes havoc during an evening of casino gambling at a fancy European hotel. (4)

14. A man sits drinking in a nightclub and discovers that the star singing attraction is his long-lost love. It's too late, however, to rekindle the sparks of love. (4)

Answers on page 440.

121. GIFTS

Operatic characters do their share of giving and receiving. Can you remember the gifts referred to below? As usual, name the opera and composer.

1. What does the Mikado give Cio-Cio-San's father? (1)
2. What token is given by Elvino to Amina? (4)
3. What does Arlecchino bring to Colombina? (3)
4. What does Arabella give to Mandryka? (3)
5. Name the present received by Manon from De Brétigny. (4)
6. What does Hans Sachs give to Beckmesser? (2)
7. What is given by La Cieca to Laura Adorno? (2)
8. What is the first present that Rodolfo buys for Mimì? (1)
9. What does Brünnhilde give to Sieglinde? (2)
10. Do you remember what Adriana Lecouvreur gives to Maurizio, and what he does with the gift? (3)
11. What does Michonnet give Adriana for her birthday? (3)
12. What does Prince Orlofsky give to Adele? (3)
13. What does Mario Cavaradossi give to his friend Angelotti? (1)
14. What does Ernani give to Silva? (3)
15. The ever-present Dapertutto offers aid to Hoffmann by giving the poet this item. What is it? (3)

16. What does Ford, disguised as Brook, give to Sir John? (3)
17. What do the Three Ladies give to Papageno, *after* he has been punished? (2)
18. What does Porgy bring to Lily, the wife of the Honey Man? (4)
19. What does Leonore give to Florestan? (2)
20. What does Joe bring to Minnie? (4)

*Answers on page **442**.*

122. MEMBERS OF THE WEDDING

Wedding celebrations or plans often figure prominently in opera. From the descriptions given below, identify the opera, its composer, and the characters being married, and assess their chances of marital bliss.

1. Although it is her wedding day and she dearly loves her husband-to-be, this bride arranges a rendezvous with an old admirer, to take place on her wedding night. (2)
2. The groom marries the bride after a rather brief courtship. It is a double wedding in which the groom's former fiancée marries the bride's brother. The ex-fiancée is bewildered and unhappy about the whole state of affairs, and she, her new husband, and another relative vow vengeance on this man who wronged her. (2)
3. This wedding celebration is interrupted when a passing gentleman forces his attentions on the bride. (1)
4. This couple's wedding night is spoiled because the bride reneges on a promise she had made. (2)
5. An act of political terrorism breaks up this wedding party. (3)
6. The bride stalls this ceremony because the beau she jilted isn't around for her to gloat over. (3)
7. This ardent couple share a brief, secret wedding ceremony that proves to be the calm before the storm. (3)
8. Soldiers rescue this reluctant bride whose past, when revealed, shocks her mother-in-law-to-be. (3)

9. The bride discovers, on the night before her wedding, that her fiancé is making love and telling state secrets to her hated rival. (2)

10. An eager bridegroom receives a terrible surprise when, as soon as the marriage contract is signed, his wife changes from demure maiden to raging hussy. (3)

11. Her wedding is halted because the groom has run off with an aging noblewoman. The abandoned bride suffers a tuneful nervous breakdown. (2)

12. As soon as she becomes engaged to the man she loves, this princess learns that she will have to marry her lover's mean old father, instead. (3)

13. This high-strung lassie shows that there are far worse things that can be done to a groom after that march down the aisle than stuffing cake into his face. (1)

The composer of a hugely successful musical play based on a famous horror story has been accused by many knowledgeable people of appropriating the music for the show's best-known tune from the score of *La Fanciulla del West*. In fact, the granddaughter of Puccini instigated a lawsuit against this gentleman alleging plagiarism. A couple of years after the musical in question was successfully transferred from London to Broadway, the composer, also known for a work about a Latin American dictator, stopped into a Manhattan record store and quickly located its opera department. Once there, he searched for, and discovered a recording of, what else? *La Fanciulla del West*. A clerk, whose eyes were as sharp as was his tongue, noticed this and remarked, in a voice loud enough to have been heard all the way to Broadway's Majestic Theatre, "Didn't he trash *Fanciulla last year?"

14. This bride is, to say the least, embarrassed, when something from her past is found frozen on her wedding morning. (3)
15. This bridegroom is told he has to pay a small sum for a divorce before he can "legally" marry the woman he loves. (3)
16. Her long-dreamt-of wedding has proceeded without a hitch until one of her relatives bluntly reminds her new husband that he owes him a major debt. (3)

*Answers on page **444**.*

123. STOP ALL THAT SINGING AND LET US DANCE!

The French formula for grand opera always included an interlude of ballet. Sometimes the ballet was used to further the plot, although it was often a divertissement presented for the entertainment of the characters in the opera, as well as for the audience. From the descriptions given here, identify the opera in which each ballet occurs. Incidentally, not all these works are French.

1. A tense situation between two rivals for a certain man's affections is temporarily interrupted when this ballet, in which the Judgment of Paris is depicted, is presented. The dancer playing Paris, knowing on which side his bread is buttered, presents his patroness with Paris's golden apple at the conclusion of the ballet. (3)
2. A political uprising is halted long enough for some skaters to frolic about the scene in a charming dance in which ice skating is simulated. (3)
3. A victory celebration is crowned by the appearance of a number of exotic dancers from the ranks of the conquered. (1)
4. A queen is paid tribute in this ballet, generally cut from a rather lengthy opera, in which the dancers portray pearl fishers. (Hint: This is *not* from an opera by Bizet!) (4)

5. A murder is announced shortly after this ballet (representing the metaphorical struggle between night and day) is performed for the assembled guests of a vengeful nobleman. (1)

6. In this ballet, the sensual delights of the netherworld are shown to this opera's protagonist in order to make him forget the pregnant girl he left behind. (2)

7. In this operatic account of a biblical event, a lusty crowd of pagans dances its way through an orgiastic ritual, unaware of the fate in store when Jehovah steps in. (1)

8. A lavish party is the scene for all kinds of amorous antics. These are interrupted when a ballet troupe arrives to waltz for all the guests. (3)

9. In a version of this opera not always performed, the delights of bacchanalian revels are graphically portrayed to the strains of some of the composer's headiest music. When the sung action begins, the hero "wants out," and one wonders why he wishes to leave. (2)

10. This solo dance is meant to be performed by the singer portraying the character who dances. It is not unknown, however, for the vocalist to withdraw in favor of a dancer when the dancing begins in this chilling scene that leads to the dramatic climax of the opera. (1)

11. Dancers portraying spirits of the departed, both happy and angry, try to bar this brave fellow from his sworn destination. (3)

12. A gavotte is interrupted by an angry demonstration of rebellious citizens. Once it has been, however temporarily, dispersed, the dancers, somewhat nervously, resume their activity. (3)

13. When this opera came to France, a ballet involving Gypsies had to be added to the third act. Nowadays, even in Paris, it is all but forgotten. Incidentally, it is the only balletic interlude by this composer to make use of music heard elsewhere in the opera. (3)

14. This lightweight balletic interlude comes during the fifth hour of this masterpiece which is more concerned with vocal than choreographic achievement. (2)

15. In the Parisian version of this intense Italian work, the "necessary" ballet comes at one of the opera's most dramatic moments, effectively cooling matters off. These days, it is only heard in concert, and not too often in that format, either. (3)

    *Answers on page **446**.*

124. GETTING THERE IS HALF THE FUN

Name the operas that feature the mode of transportation listed below. Name the character who avails himself or herself of this form of travel.

1. A barge (name characters from two different operas) (3)
2. A ship with blood-red sails (2)
3. A boat drawn by a fowl (1)
4. A cart driven by a ram (3)
5. A broomstick (2)
6. A goat cart (3)
7. A train (4)
8. A spaceship (4)
9. A bus (4)
10. The New York subway (3)
11. A fishing boat (3)
12. A warship (3)
13. Two feet for a very long walk (4)
14. A battered truck (4)
15. A sleigh (3)
16. Steerage class in a primitive ocean-crossing vessel (2)
17. Sometimes, but not always, a hot air balloon (3)
18. An elegant coach, if only briefly (1)
19. A cart drawn by a donkey (2)
20. A pair of horses (2)

*Answers on page **448**.*

125. FARAWAY PLACES

Name the operas that take place (at least in part) in the exotic locations listed on the following page. Don't forget the composer. He worked very hard so that you could have a good time!

1. India (3)
2. Bohemia (name two) (3)
3. Hell (1)
4. Venice (name at least three) (2)
5. Peru (3)
6. Palestine (1)
7. Gaul (2)
8. Mexico (name three) (3)
9. Lithuania (3)
10. Frankfurt (name three) (4)
11. Scotland (name two) (3)
12. Manhattan (name two) (3)
13. Brooklyn (4)
14. Colorado (4)
15. Salem, Massachusetts (3)
16. A mythical European country overrun by forces of repression (3)

*Answers on page **450**.*

126. CRUEL AND UNUSUAL

Opera plots abound with murders, suicides, and assorted torture and mayhem. While most lyric methods of dealing death blows are fairly straightforward—pistols, swords and the like—some characters meet their ends in remarkably imaginative fashion. What cruel and unusual punishments met the characters below? Name the operas, composers, and describe the circumstances.

1. Manfredo (4)
2. Rachel (3)
3. Cecilia (4)
4. Queen of the Night (2)
5. La Cieca (2)
6. Giuseppe Hagenbach (4)
7. Lisa (3)
8. Antonia (2)
9. Loris Ipanoff's brother, Valeriano (4)
10. Lakmé (2)
11. Glauce (3)
12. John of Leyden and Fidès (3)
13. Jokanaan (1)
14. Lulu and the Countess Geschwitz (3)
15. Hunding (2)
16. Miles (4)
17. Rebecca Nurse (4)

*Answers on page **451**.*

V

A Potpourri

127. OPENING NIGHTS

1. Gounod's *Faust* was the first opera to be performed at the Metropolitan Opera House. Who sang the role of Marguérite that night? (3)
2. What was the language of that first Met *Faust*? (2)
3. What was the first opera to be produced by the New York City Opera, and who sang the title role? (4)
4. How many important singers can you name who made Metropolitan Opera debuts on opening nights? Give their roles, too, if you can. (3)
5. What opera opened the Metropolitan Opera's first season at Lincoln Center? Give the names of the composer, librettist, designer, director, choreographer, and at least five singers. How about the conductor? (3)
6. What opera opened the first full season at the Chicago Lyric Opera? Who sang the title role? (4)
7. A famous operatic feud was ended moments after the opening night of the Met's 1968–69 season. Who sang, and who was feuding with whom? (3)
8. La Scala of Milan always opens on the same date. Coincidentally, this date has negative connotations for Americans. What is the date? (2)
9. Enrico Caruso sang every opening night at the Metropolitan Opera between 1903 and 1920—except one. To what artist did Caruso concede the honor, and what was the program? (4)
10. Do you recall the program with which the rebuilt La Scala opened after World War II? Can you name the conductor and at least three singers who took part in that concert? (4)

11. When, where, and why was Mahler's Second Symphony the opening-night attraction at one of the world's great opera houses? Who conducted? (3)

12. When this adored soprano opened the Met in 1961, the performance proved to be the only complete performance of this role she ever gave, although her career continued for another quarter century. Who is the artist? Name the opera and role. (3)

13. Name the first opera to be performed at the Bayreuth Festival. (4)

14. What was different about the world-premiere performance of Puccini's *Turandot*, compared to subsequent repetitions? (2)

Answers on page **454.**

128. OPERA HOUSES AROUND THE WORLD

What do you know about these famous opera houses and their history?

1. An Italian opera by an Austrian composer had its world premiere at this Eastern European opera house. Name the theater, the opera, and the composer. (2)

2. A soprano, famed more for her beautiful face than for her voice, managed this opera house for one season and nearly bankrupted the company. Name the soprano and the opera house. (3)

3. Now known as the Salle Favart, this theater, under another name, was the first to present one of the most popular operas of all time. Name the theater, the opera, and its composer. (2)

4. Which of Verdi's operas was his first work to be performed at La Scala? (3)

5. Puccini's *La Bohème* had its first performance at this Italian opera house in a city better known for its industrial output than for its artistic interests. This theater lay in ruins for years after World War II and reopened with a production of a rarely done work, staged by two famous singers. Name the opera

house, the work with which it reopened in 1971, and the singers-turned-directors who staged it. (4)

6. What opera house opened its doors with a French opera sung in Italian, and within a year switched to a policy of performing its entire repertory in German, a practice kept up for seven years? (3)

7. What Verdi opera was composed for the opera house in St. Petersburg, Russia? (2)

8. Who were the three codirectors who organized the Chicago Lyric Opera? (3)

9. This theater was the location of Renata Tebaldi's American debut. Name the opera house, the opera, the year of Tebaldi's debut, and her leading man at that performance. (3)

10. When Joan Sutherland made one of her earliest appearances at this theater, she was hardly noticed because of the brevity of her role and the presence of another fabulous soprano in that performance. Name the theater, opera, and prima donna of that evening. (2)

11. This tiny and beautiful opera house, in one of the playgrounds of Europe, was the scene of the first performance of a Puccini opera. Kindly name the house and the opera. (3)

12. What two major opera houses were destroyed by Allied bombing raids during World War II? Can you give the dates of the reopening of these rebuilt houses? (3)

13. This European opera house has created a famous production of a "standard repertory" opera that departs radically from the work's original libretto. Name the opera house and the opera, which is set in the country where this theater is found. (3)

14. Name the city that boasts the most-difficult-to-please group of opera buffs in the world. (1)

15. Giulio Gatti-Casazza managed what two great opera houses? (2)

16. This ancient outdoor amphitheater was the home of lavish summertime performances of *Aida*. Name the theater and give its location. (1)

17. What two Puccini operas had their premieres at La Scala? Name the leading sopranos and conductors of each perfor-

mance, and briefly describe how each work was received. (3)

18. *La Traviata* was created by Verdi for this house, but it was not initially a success. (3)

19. Rolf Liebermann, a quarter of a century ago, left one theater, which he had managed successfully for many years, in order to take on the challenge of restoring a fabled opera house to its former glory. From where was Liebermann lured, and where did he go? (4)

20. This annual summer music festival was the scene of Renata Scotto's first international success. Name the festival and the opera sung by Scotto, and describe the special circumstances surrounding her performance. (3)

21. Name the beautifully designed, whimsically named lyric theater that has been presenting opera each summer in upstate New York, alongside a nationally known sports attraction. What is the sports shrine? (3)

22. This house, a bus ride away from London's West End, was the birthplace of one of Britain's finest opera companies,

---

La Scala's *loggionisti,* the regulars who occupy the balconies night after night, are quick to pounce on an erring singer who loses control of a high note. Carlo Bergonzi, returning to La Scala as Radames after an absence of a few years, cracked the high B-flat at the end of "Celeste Aida" and was savagely booed. The diminutive master from Busseto did not lose his nerve and continued the performance with a Radames that ranked with his work fifteen years earlier. Bergonzi won a rare point from La Scala's *claque:* after a particularly beautiful phrase in the Nile Scene, an apologetic voice wafted down from the gallery, "Perdonateci, Carlo!" (Forgive us!)

and one of the world's greatest ballet troupes. For years, the D'Oyly Carte Opera Company held forth there. Name the theater and the opera and ballet companies it nurtured. (2)

23. This opera house, handsomely rebuilt after World War II, suffered a great fire some years later, and had to be rebuilt once more. (3)

24. This opera house, home to the likes of Caballé and Carreras, was almost totally destroyed by fire in the 1990s. (3)

25. One of the world's newest opera houses, this theater has kept going in the face of initially hostile assessments of its worth as a performing arts center. For many years its leading soprano was a local girl who had achieved fame and fortune all over the world. (1)

26. What Italian opera house burned to the ground just after it had undergone a long process of renovation in 1996? Name two famous Verdi operas that had their premieres there. Who was the nonoperatic star scheduled to be the first attraction at the newly redone opera house? (4)

Answers on page 456.

129. FROM PAGE TO STAGE

Here is a list of novels that have been adapted for opera. For each, name the opera, its composer, and the author of the original novel.

1. *Ivanhoe* (4)
2. *The Wings of the Dove* (4)
3. *Great Expectations* (4)
4. *Don Quixote* (2)
5. *The Gambler* (3)
6. *The Bride of Lammer-moor* (1)
7. *War and Peace* (2)
8. *L'Histoire de Manon Lescaut* (name 3) (2)
9. *The Postman Always Rings Twice* (4)
10. *The Turn of the Screw* (2)
11. *The Sorrows of Young Werther* (2)

Answers on page 458.

130. PLAY VERSUS OPERA

Match the literary work to the opera it inspired. Name the author of the original work and the composer of the opera.

1. *Much Ado About Nothing* (3)	a. *Lodoletta*
2. *Le Réveillon* (3)	b. *Mignon*
3. *Kabale und Liebe* (3)	c. *Peter Grimes*
4. *Le Roi S'Amuse* (1)	d. *Les Contes d'Hoffmann*
5. *Two Little Wooden Shoes* (4)	e. *Béatrice et Bénédict*
6. *Scènes de la Vie de Bohème* (name two) (1)	f. *La Traviata*
	g. *Rigoletto*
	h. *Die Fledermaus*
7. *La Dame aux Camélias* (1)	i. *Luisa Miller*
8. *The Borough* (3)	j. *La Bohème*
9. *Le Philtre* (2)	k. *L'Elisir d'Amore*
10. *Angelo, Tyran de Padoue* (name two) (3)	l. *La Gioconda*
	m. *Lulu*
11. *Wilhelm Meister* (3)	n. *Jenufa*
12. *Spring's Awakening* (3)	o. *Un Ballo in Maschera*
13. *Counsellor Crespel* (2)	p. *Il Giuramento*
14. *Her Foster Daughter* (4)	q. *La Forza del Destino*
15. *Don Alvaro o La Fuerza de Sino* (1)	

Answers on page 459.

131. LIBRETTISTS

Most of us can name the composers of our favorite operas, but can we readily recall those unsung (in a sense!) heroes who provided the words? Name the librettists for the following works:

1. *Aida* (3)
2. *La Bohème* (Puccini's) (2)
3. *Pagliacci* (2)
4. *La Gioconda* (4)
5. *Nabucco* (3)
6. *Andrea Chénier* (3)
7. *I Vespri Siciliani* (4)
8. *Così Fan Tutte* (1)
9. *Tannhäuser* (2)
10. *Carmen* (3)
11. *Turandot* (Puccini's) (3)
12. *Rigoletto* (2)
13. *Peter Grimes* (3)
14. *Francesca da Rimini* (Zandonai's) (3)
15. *Mefistofele* (2)
16. *Der Rosenkavalier* (1)
17. *Falstaff* (2)
18. *Salome* (3)
19. *Lucia di Lammermoor* (3)
20. *Eugene Onegin* (3)
21. *Der Freischütz* (4)
22. *Dialogues des Carmélites* (4)
23. *Tosca* (2)
24. *Faust* (3)
25. *Boris Godunov* (2)

Answers on page **460**.

In 1961, the Metropolitan Opera produced a revival of Flotow's *Martha* that was generally reviled by the critics and loathed by the public in spite of the fact that its cast included Victoria de los Angeles and Richard Tucker. Much of the disaster was attributed to the fact that the opera was sung in a truly lame English translation. One night, without warning, Tucker burst into the aria best known by its Italian translation, "M'apparì, tutto d'amor," in Italian. The audience cheered but Rudolf Bing was sufficiently angry to storm backstage and announce to the chuckling Tucker that he was fining him $100.00 for his naughtiness. Later on, the tenor was asked why he had performed the aria in Italian. With typical modesty, Tucker replied, "I wanted to let my fans hear how Caruso sounded!"

The city of Parma, Italy, is famous—perhaps notorious is more appropriate—for the hypercritical opera buffs who sit in judgment in the galleria and pounce on any and every mistake a singer might make. As recently as Christmas 1979, the booing and jeering sufficiently unnerved an experienced soprano that she canceled the final act of *La Traviata* rather than face the enraged audience. The best Parma story concerns a performance of *Pagliacci* that was given in the early 1950s. Halfway through the prelude, the baritone singing Tonio stepped through the curtain to sing the Prologue. Tonio's first words are "Si può?" (May I speak?) The audience, as one, roared, "No!" And there ended the shortest performance of *Pagliacci* ever attempted!

132. RECORD COLLECTORS I

1. Name the nine operas recorded by the Metropolitan Opera and released by Columbia Records between 1947 and 1954. Name principal singers and conductors. (3)
2. Who conducts the famous EMI *Tosca* with Maria Callas, Giuseppe di Stefano, and Tito Gobbi? (1)
3. Who are the two artists who share the role of Wotan in the Solti *Ring* cycle on Decca/London? In which operas do they each sing? (2)
4. Leontyne Price recorded the role of Leonora in *Il Trovatore* three times. Name her principal colleagues and the conductor on each recording. (2)
5. Name six operas recorded by the New York City Opera. (4)
6. A father-and-son team may be heard on the 1979 Decca/London recording of *Pagliacci*. Who are they, and what roles do they each sing? (3)
7. For what company were Caruso's first recordings made? (3)

8. There was a major cast change made only days before Arturo Toscanini entered studio 8-H of New York's RCA Building to conduct what became his final operatic broadcast and recording. For which role was there a hasty substitution? Who replaced whom? (2)

9. Magda Olivero recorded only two complete operas commercially (not including "pirates"). Name them, the roles she sang in each, and her principal colleagues in each. (3)

10. Dusolina Giannini, a famous soprano of the 1920s (and mother of the film star Gian Carlo Giannini), is best remembered as the protagonist in the first complete recording of what ever-popular Verdi opera? *Bonus:* What was her nationality? (4)

11. Who are the tenor partners of Kiri Te Kanawa in the following recordings:
    a. *Tosca* (Decca/London) (3)
    b. *La Rondine* (Sony) (2)
    c. *La Traviata* (Philips) (3)
    d. *Carmen* (Decca/London) (3)

12. What is José Carreras's first complete operatic recording? (4)

13. There is an exciting recording in German of highlights from Verdi's *La Forza del Destino* released by German EMI. Who are the Leonora, Alvaro, and Don Carlo on that disc? What is the German title of *La Forza*? (3)

14. What was the special memento found in the 1966 RCA release *Opening Nights at the Met*? (2)

15. Who sang the baritone and soprano leads in the first recording of Verdi's *Nabucco*? What label released this performance? (4)

16. Jussi Bjoerling's indisposition forced the cancellation of a recording of this opera midway through the sessions. Name the opera and Bjoerling's eventual replacement. (3)

17. Name six complete operatic roles recorded by Zinka Milanov. (2)

18. Why wasn't Maria Callas able to record a complete *La Traviata* for EMI in 1956? Did EMI ever get to release that opera with Callas? (2)

19. Who was the artist Birgit Nilsson replaced in the EMI recording of *La Fanciulla del West*? (1)

20. How many complete operas did Franco Corelli and Renata Tebaldi record together commercially? (2)

21. Name the artist who, on two separate occasions, recorded three leading roles in an opera in which such casting would be physically impossible in an actual performance. Name the opera and roles in question. (2)

22. Name two operatic recordings on which Renata Tebaldi, Birgit Nilsson, and Jussi Bjoerling appear together. (2)

23. What trick was played on the listener by the producers of the Flagstad/Suthaus/Furtwängler *Tristan und Isolde*? (3)

24. Pietro Mascagni conducted a 1940 recording of his opera *Cavalleria Rusticana*. Who sang the roles of Santuzza, Turridu, and Mamma Lucia? (2)

25. What was the first complete opera recorded by RCA in the United States? Name the leading soprano, mezzo, tenor, and baritone, and the conductor. In what year was the recording made? (3)

26. Decca/London once made the mistake of releasing an opera with an English-language narration dubbed over orchestral sections. Name the opera, and the artist who sang the title role. (4)

27. When Montserrat Caballé withdrew from a recording of *La Forza del Destino* for EMI, what soprano replaced her? (2)

28. Which label issued the first absolutely complete recording of Verdi's *Don Carlo*, sung in French? Name the artists who sing Don Carlo, Elisabeth, Philip II, Eboli, Rodrigo, and the Grand Inquisitor. Who conducts? At what opera house was the recording made? (2)

29. Name the diva who recorded Rosina's "Una voce poco fa" and Brünnhilde's "Immolation Scene" on the same aria recital. (3)

30. What role in *Il Barbiere di Siviglia* has Plácido Domingo recorded? What makes this bit of information interesting? (1)

Answers on page 461.

133. RUDOLF BING

The twenty-two years of Rudolf Bing's administration at the Metropolitan Opera were often marked by controversy but remain notable for much excitement and great singing. It may truly be said that Sir Rudolf presided over one of the most fabulous eras in the Met's history. His influence is much felt by current singers and management, and his wisdom and fabled wit are fondly remembered by all those privileged to know him.

1. What was Bing's principal operatic credit prior to coming to the Metropolitan? (3)
2. Whom did Bing replace as General Manager of the Met? (2)
3. Name the four important artists who made their debuts on Bing's first Met opening night. Also, name the opera and the roles sung by these four artists. (2)
4. What great soprano, whom the previous Met management had let go, did Bing reengage during his first Met season? (3)
5. One of the Bing regime's great triumphs was an idiomatic English version of *Die Fledermaus*. Who were the coauthors of that translation? (4)
6. What was the first work to be given its American premiere at the Met during the Bing years? (4)
7. Why did Bing dismiss Maria Callas from the Met? (2)
8. In one of the most bizarre nights of Sir Rudolf's time at the Metropolitan Opera, Birgit Nilsson sang her second Met Isolde opposite three Tristans—a different ailing colleague in each act. Name the three tenors! (4)
9. Very early on, Bing fired one noted tenor because the man balked at signing a contract by a specific date. Who was the tenor? (2)
10. Bing engaged the son of a great tenor, whom he had admired years earlier, for a comic role in an operetta revival. Name the guest artist, who was, incidentally, a noted stage and screen star. (2)
11. Which two operas were staged at the Met by Alfred Lunt during the Bing administration? (4)

12. Why did Sir Rudolf banish standees from the Met for one performance? (3)

13. Which renowned musician infuriated Bing on the occasion of the closing gala concert at the old Metropolitan Opera House, and why? (3)

14. Name three very important singers, an Eastern European, a Viennese, and an American, who did *not* appear at the Met during's Bing's regime. (3)

15. One of Bing's early seasons saw the farewell performance of Kirsten Flagstad. What was her final role at the Met? (2)

16. Bing allowed a famous Salome to sing one performance of Musetta in *La Bohème*. The night became legendary because of that lady's antics. Who was she? (1)

17. A famous soprano once listed Rudolf Bing as a "dependent" on her U.S. federal income tax return. Who was she? (2)

18. Name the then-unknown soprano who made her Met debut on three hours' notice during Bing's first season. Nineteen years old at the time, this lady became an authentic "overnight star" and remained at the Met for thirty-five years. (1)

19. What was the opera sung at the Met to mark the close of Bing's official tenure? (3)

20. Where did Bing go after leaving the Met? (3)

*Answers on page **464**.*

134. FAMOUS OPERATIC CONDUCTORS

Can you name the conductors from the clues provided?

1. He conducted the first performance at the Metropolitan Opera in 1883. (Hint: His brother sang the tenor lead that night.) (4)

2. One of his first professional musical assignments was playing second cello at the world premiere of Verdi's *Otello*. (1)

3. He was one of Verdi's favorite maestri. (4)

4. He "discovered" Maria Callas when she was an unknown singer struggling to make a career in Italy. (2)

Marilyn Horne once confided to a radio audience her method for getting balky conductors to employ tempi that suit her. Early in her career, Horne was singing Musetta in San Francisco. During rehearsals the mezzo found that her maestro was taking "Quando m'en vo soletta" at a frighteningly fast tempo. At the next rehearsal, Horne began her aria at breakneck speed. Down went the baton. "Oh, no, signorina," clucked the conductor. "You're singing much too fast. Let's try again, slowly." "I'm dreadfully sorry," purred the relieved Horne. For the rest of the engagement, this Musetta never had to worry that her waltz would be over too quickly!

❀ ❀ ❀

5. He conducted the opening night of the new Metropolitan Opera House. (3)
6. Wagner repaid him for brilliantly conducting his early operas by stealing his wife. (2)
7. She was the first woman to conduct an opera at the Met. (1)
8. Having been a cofounder of the Chicago Lyric Opera, he left with another member of that company's original triumvirate to create the Dallas Civic Opera. (3)
9. Shortly before his eightieth birthday, he conducted what has become a famous recorded performance of one of his own operas. (2)
10. Among this maestro's credits were flying his own airplane, creating his own music festival, reinterpreting many operas by Wagner, Verdi, Strauss, and Mozart, and molding the careers of such artists as René Kollo, Helga Dernesch, Anna Tomowa-Sintow, and flautist James Galway. (1)
11. This famous composer spent several years as a principal conductor at the Metropolitan Opera early in this century, leading the first Metropolitan performance of Giordano's *Fedora*. (2)

12. He conducted the first recording of *Der Ring des Nibelungen.* (2)

13. Once the director of the Bolshoi, this celebrated artist is also a fine cellist and married to one of the best singers ever to come from the former Soviet Union. (1)

14. Considered an heir to Toscanini, this brilliant young maestro, who left behind prized broadcast recordings of only a few operas and symphonic works, died in an airplane crash in 1956. (3)

15. This renowned specialist in Beethoven and Mozart fled the Nazis to America, conducting at the Met for several seasons before retiring to California. (2)

16. He celebrated his eighty-fifth birthday conducting *Die Frau ohne Schatten.* (3)

17. His specialty is the *bel canto* repertoire, and being married to a famous soprano undoubtedly helped his career. (1)

18. A master of the French repertoire, he had a concert hall in Montreal named for him. (3)

19. He conducted the first performance of the complete, three-act version of Berg's *Lulu.* (2)

20. Less than five years after his debut as a last-minute substitute in a very great theater, this conductor became music director of that company. (2)

21. This postwar musical director of La Scala, Milan, conducted the most famous *Tosca* recording of all time. The cast included Maria Callas, Giuseppe di Stefano, and Tito Gobbi. (3)

22. A close friend and great interpreter of Richard Strauss, this conductor and administrator lived the last years of his life tainted with the stigma of his pro-Nazi activities. (2)

23. As celebrated for his wit as for his abilities as a conductor, this beloved maestro enriched the Met's World War II years with his mastery of the French repertoire. His most famous operatic recording is a *La Bohème.* (2)

24. Famous for his Wagner, this conductor led a renowned *Ring* cycle at La Scala, shortly after the end of World War II. (1)

25. He brought international recognition to the once strictly regional New York City Opera. (2)

26. The former head of both the Royal Opera and the Chicago Symphony, he resigned under fire from his position as musical director of the Metropolitan Opera in 1974. (4)

27. Himself the son of a famous conductor, this gentleman has led unforgettable performances of such operas as *Tristan und Isolde, Otello, La Bohème, Der Rosenkavalier,* and *Die Fledermaus* in Europe and America. (1)

28. He was the first American ever to conduct at La Scala. (Can you name the opera, the year, and the prima donna?) (2)

29. An American conductor of great promise, he was killed in a freak boating accident in 1986. (4)

30. He directed the San Francisco Opera and conducted many of its performances for two decades after World War II. (2)

31. This outstanding Verdi conductor headed La Scala and the London Symphony Orchestra simultaneously for several years in the 1970s. (2)

32. This conductor heads the Santa Fe Opera and rarely conducts anywhere but there. (3)

33. This young American conductor heads the Opéra de Lyon, France, where he has made distinguished recordings of *Dialogues des Carmélites* and *Susannah.* (3)

34. Once, during a musicians' strike at La Scala, this conductor and head of that theater played the piano score of *La Traviata* from memory, allowing a performance of that work to take place despite the labor dispute. (2)

35. This American was named music director of the Paris Opéra in 1994. (2)

Answers on page 467.

135. THE NEW YORK CITY OPERA

1. What was the first performance by the New York City Opera? What was the company's original address? (4)

2. Whom did Erich Leinsdorf succeed as head of the New York City Opera? Who succeeded Leinsdorf? (4)

Late in his career, Arturo Toscanini was invited to dine at the home of a retired soprano, once the most beautiful and popular Carmen, Butterfly, and Zazà of the Met. Toscanini returned from the meal in one of his vilest rages. A friend innocently asked the maestro if he had enjoyed the dinner. "Damn that stupid woman!" ranted Toscanini. "For twenty-five years we slept together, and she still can't remember that I hate fish!"

🌿 🌿 🌿

3. What was the nonmusical significance of Camellia Williams's engagement to sing leading soprano roles at the New York City Opera? (3)
4. The baritone opposite whom Maria Callas sang Lady Macbeth at La Scala spent several seasons as a "utility" artist at the N.Y.C.O. Who was he? (3)
5. To what two U.S. cities did the N.Y.C.O. tour regularly in the 1960s and 1970s? (3)
6. Can you name the American soprano who triumphed at the N.Y.C.O. in such contemporary operas as *The Crucible* and was also a prized interpreter of Manon, Violetta, and Lucia? (3)
7. With what role at the N.Y.C.O. did Beverly Sills leap into the front ranks of American singers? Whom did Miss Sills, according to various accounts, force to be withdrawn from consideration for this role? (3)
8. Name the soon-to-be world-famous tenor who made his N.Y.C.O. debut in 1972. (Hint: He was *not* an American.) In what role did he make his debut? (1)
9. Birgit Nilsson sang exactly one performance with the N.Y.C.O. Can you describe the circumstances of her extraordinary debut? What role did she sing? Who was her tenor? (4)
10. Name the six Donizetti heroines that Beverly Sills sang at the N.Y.C.O. (4)

11. Who staged the legendary production of Boito's *Mefistofele* that starred Norman Treigle at the N.Y.C.O. in 1969? (4)

12. Phyllis Curtin and Norman Treigle scored a huge success in this opera by Carlisle Floyd that had its first N.Y.C.O. performance in 1957. The title, if you please. (2)

13. Please name the two roles Grace Bumbry sang at the N.Y.C.O. (2)

14. Maralin Niska scored the greatest success of her career in a multimedia production of this opera by a Czech composer. Name the opera, and tell us who staged this landmark version of a difficult and fascinating work. (3)

15. Which of the following operas did *not* have its world premiere at the N.Y.C.O.?
    a. *Regina*
    b. *Juana la Loca*
    c. *The Crucible*
    d. *Miss Havisham's Fire* (3)

16. A young baritone who was the N.Y.C.O's much-admired Rigoletto in the 1970s made his Metropolitan debut on short notice in *Pelléas et Mélisande* in 1972. For the next two decades he shuttled between the two companies. What is his name? (2)

17. Sherrill Milnes returned to the N.Y.C.O. after an absence of many years during which he was a leading baritone around the world, to sing this role, based on a Shakespearean character. Name the opera, role, and composer. (2)

18. Who directed many of the N.Y.C.O. productions associated with Beverly Sills, including *Manon, Roberto Devereux,* and *Lucia di Lammermoor*? (3)

19. Who, as manager of the N.Y.C.O., was responsible for engaging such artists as Beverly Sills, Plácido Domingo, Norman Treigle, Michele Molese, and many others? (1)

20. Name the soprano who, after two decades at the N.Y.C.O., was invited to sing Isolde at the Bayreuth Festival? (2)

21. Making his N.Y.C.O. debut in *Lucia di Lammermoor*, this tenor has gone on to sing leading roles in opera houses around the world. He is also admired for his recordings of historic Broadway musicals. Who is he? (1)

22. Can you name two operas that N.Y.C.O. revived in the 1990s, resetting them in Manhattan's "Little Italy"? They were televised nationally. (1)

23. What was soprano Dusolina Giannini's debut role at the N.Y.C.O.? (4)

24. What familiar opera did the N.Y.C.O. reset during the Spanish Civil War? In this bizarre edition of this work, the heroine was not only a sexy Gypsy girl, but a political operative. On which side of the conflict did she fight? (2)

Birgit Nilsson told friends that she had discovered an odd fact about her own singing. The longer she sang on a given evening, the more agile her enormous voice became. In fact, the soprano asserted, by the end of *Götterdämmerung*, in which she sang, as Brünnhilde, for nearly five hours, her voice was able to take on the additional demands of the Queen of the Night's second-act aria in *Die Zauberflöte*. To prove this, Madame Nilsson gathered a group of friends and fans around the piano in her dressing room after a Metropolitan performance of Wagner's epic, and proceeded to sing Mozart's fearsome aria in a manner that would have made every Met Queen of the Night then in residence tremble. The crowd in the dressing room was uproarious in its approval. The conductor of the evening was informed of Birgit's after-hours caper, but with his customary arrogance, dismissed it as a tall tale circulated by Nilsson's fans. Learning of this, Nilsson invited the maestro to visit her dressing room after her next *Götterdämmerung* with a piano score for *Die Zauberflöte*. So, accompanied by the suitably chastened conductor, Birgit Nilsson sang a repeat performance of her feat. When asked why she didn't add Mozart's villainess to her list of roles, the diva replied, "But I'd have to sing the aria too early in the evening for me to do it best!"

❀ ❀ ❀

25. Name the artist who succeeded Beverly Sills as the General Director of the N.Y.C.O., remaining in that post until his death in 1995. Weeks before his death, he conducted the N.Y.C.O.'s premiere of what important twentieth-century work? (2)

26. Who was named to replace the Music Director named in #25? (3)

Answers on page 468.

136. SATURDAY AFTERNOONS AT THE MET

So many Americans were first attracted to opera through the weekly live broadcasts from the Metropolitan Opera House that it is fitting to include a series of questions about these beloved programs.

1. Two great Wagnerian sopranos made unheralded debuts at the Metropolitan within six years of one another on Saturday broadcasts. They debuted in the same role. Who were they, and what role did they share? (3)

2. Maria Callas sang only one role broadcast from the Met. Name it. (3)

3. A famous singer was stricken with an acute (but fortunately not serious) illness while singing an aria during a broadcast. Who was the artist and what was the aria? What happened to the performance? (4)

4. A now-celebrated baritone flew to New York from Milan to replace a famous colleague who was forced to cancel a broadcast performance. Name the newcomer, the opera he sang, and the singer whose illness started the crisis. (4)

5. What was the first role that Dame Joan Sutherland broadcast from the Met? Who was her tenor? (3)

6. What was the first opera to be broadcast complete, live from the Met? When did this broadcast take place? (3)

7. Name the sponsor of the Met broadcasts. (1)

8. Who was the beloved soprano who shared hosting duties with Met commentator Milton Cross for several years during the 1940s? (3)

9. What was the first opera to be broadcast from the new Met at Lincoln Center? (2)

10. Jan Peerce, Zinka Milanov, and Richard Tucker were honored with broadcast ceremonies marking their twenty-fifth anniversaries at the Metropolitan Opera. What role did each sing at these commemorative performances? Identify the year of each anniversary. (4)

11. A broadcast performance of *Die Fledermaus* in 1995 underwent a major change of cast in mid-performance when one soprano canceled and another replaced her in the third act. Who canceled and who jumped into the performance? (3)

12. What was the only Met broadcast to be terminated after only three (of four) acts? Why? When did this occur? (3)

13. Elisabeth Schwarzkopf sang her only Metropolitan performance of this role on a broadcast. Name the role, the opera, and the year the performance took place. (3)

14. Who replaced Milton Cross as host of the Metropolitan Opera broadcasts? (1)

15. The broadcast of March 14, 1964, was significant because the prima donna was an artist returning to the Met after a year's absence brought on by a "vocal crisis." The return was, to say the least, victorious. Name the star, the opera, and the tenor. (3)

16. In what years did the first Met broadcasts of the following operas take place?
    a. *Dialogues des Carmélites*   f. *Die Frau ohne Schatten*
    b. *I Lombardi*   g. *Nabucco*
    c. *Eugene Onegin*   h. *The Queen of Spades*
    d. *Lulu*   i. *Luisa Miller*
    e. *Les Troyens*   j. *Wozzeck* (4)

17. In 1981, a scheduled broadcast of *Parsifal* had to be scrapped in the aftermath of a musicians' strike. A concert featuring a soprano and tenor was hastily put together. Who sang? Who conducted? (3)

18. Only once in the history of Met broadcasts was the opera to be performed changed because of the illness of one singer, for whom a substitute was not available. Name the opera that was

canceled, the one that replaced it, and the singer whose sore throat caused all the trouble. (4)

19. Name the only opera with music by Gian Carlo Menotti to be broadcast from the Met. In what year did this take place? (3)

20. Name four operas broadcast from the Met with Eileen Farrell singing the leading soprano roles. Give the years if you can. (4)

Answers on page 469.

137. OPERA ON THE SILVER SCREEN

The lyric theater has fascinated filmmakers since the early days of motion pictures. Test your knowledge about opera on film.

1. Name three silent versions of operas. (3)

2. A 1953 film of *Aida* featured Sophia Loren in the title role. Who sang Aida on the soundtrack? Can you name the other singers and the conductor? (4)

3. A nonoperatic treatment of *Salome* was born in the Hollywood of the mid-1940s. Although a few of the Wilde-Strauss plot devices were in evidence, much had been changed. What significant alterations of the story were there? (3)

4. Who starred in a nonmusical version of *Madama Butterfly* in a Hollywood film of the 1930s? (3)

5. In the film *Interrupted Melody*, a biography of soprano Marjorie Lawrence, another famous soprano did the singing for the movie's operatic sequences. Who was she? (2)

6. Everyone knows that Mario Lanza played and sang Enrico Caruso in the film *The Great Caruso*. Can you name the two well-known sopranos who sang with Lanza in the film? (3)

7. Years before he actually sang in the United States, a great tenor was introduced to American audiences in a film in which he sang one of his most famous roles. Name the tenor, the opera, and his soprano costar. (3)

8. Maria Callas appeared in one film. Although she did no sing-

During the intermission of an opera broadcast, a small group of singers was taking part in a round-table discussion about life on the operatic stage. A question was raised about the practice of canceling performances. One singer, a lady as much known for her claws as for her voice said, "Well, whenever I feel that I cannot do justice to the music, I will cancel." Her colleague, a baritone highly respected for incisive wit, responded, "Then, my dear Miss ————, you must have to cancel nearly every night!" The lady managed to swallow most of her outraged gasp, and the program continued.

ing, the film was a treatment of which of her signature operatic roles? (1)

9. Risë Stevens never got to make a film of her most famous operatic role, Carmen, but she did make several movies, and in one of them, she got to sing the "Habanera." Name the film and Stevens's costar, one of America's most popular singers. Bonus: What film did Stevens make with Nelson Eddy?

10. There is a beautiful film of an actual performance of *Der Rosenkavalier* from a major European festival. Do you know the names of the conductor, and the singers who portrayed the Marschallin, Octavian, and Baron Ochs in that performance? (2)

11. In the spring of 1982, American audiences were introduced to a virtually unknown American soprano by means of a French film in which she played an opera star. Shortly after the film opened, the soprano made her debut with the New York City Opera. Name the artist, the film in which she appeared, the aria she sang in the film, and her debut role at the N.Y.C.O. (4)

12. An American prima donna went to Paris to star in a film

version of one of her best roles, in 1935. Her leading man was a wonderful tenor. Name the lady, the opera, and the tenor. (4)

13. Who directed the 1986 film of *Otello* starring Plácido Domingo and Katia Ricciarelli, a film in which tremendous liberties were taken with the opera's score and libretto? (2)

14. Which of Jarmila Novotna's operatic roles did that lovely soprano re-create in a pre-World War II German film? (3)

15. What was Marilyn Horne's contribution to opera-related Hollywood films of the 1950s? (2)

16. A movie starring Cher made heavy use of music from *La Bohème*. What was the film? (1)

17. The multi-talented Teresa Stratas made a foray into film with this version of a role that she did not often sing onstage. Who were Miss Stratas's tenor and baritone colleagues? Who conducted? (2)

18. Who directed the 1979 film of *Don Giovanni?* Who sang the role of Zerlina in that film? (3)

19. What opera was filmed in 1983, with a cast headed by Julia Migenes and Plácido Domingo? Who conducted? (2)

20. In what film did Glenn Close portray a diva participating in a troubled production of *Tannhäuser?* Who dubbed the singing for Ms. Close? (3)

Answers on page 471.

138. OPERA ON TV

Opera has been brought to its widest audiences thanks to television. Although complete televised broadcasts of operas did not come into their own until the 1970s, there were a number of such telecasts in earlier years. How many of the telecasts mentioned here have you seen "live" or on videotape?

1. Which American network had its own opera company in the 1950s and 1960s? (2)

2. Renata Scotto, Alfredo Kraus, and Nicholai Ghiaurov broad-

In 1981, Luciano Pavarotti appeared in a dreadful Hollywood film called *Yes, Giorgio* that dealt in insipid fashion with an ill-fated romance between a doctor and an operatic tenor. Pavarotti's character was the self-proclaimed "greatest tenor in the world," but the film could easily have made the short list of the worst movies of the quarter-century. At a special screening arranged for "friendly" viewers, including artists, publicists, and music journalists, the viewers were anything but friendly. In a crucial scene, Giorgio (Pavarotti) storms out of a Metropolitan Opera rehearsal for Puccini's *Turandot* shouting, "I will *never* sing *Turandot* at the Met." (A promise kept, in fact, as of 1996, by Pavarotti.)* At this point, someone in the audience shouted out: "Get Corelli!" Everybody cheered. The movie opened anyway.

* In the spring of 1997, Pavarotti announced that he would add the role of Calaf in *Turandot* in the 1997–1998 season at the Metropolitan Opera.

✿ ✿ ✿

cast this opera together twice, in two different countries. Name the opera and the two countries. (3)

3. This popular television variety program presented, among other operatic highlights, the U.S. television debut of Maria Callas. Name the show, the operatic scene Callas performed, as well as her vocal costar and conductor. (3)

4. Callas's debut in this city was televised live only locally but was eventually released around the world as an EMI video. Name the opera house where this event took place, and the music that Callas performed. (2)

5. When this soprano starred in a "Live from the Met" performance, her detractors tried to disrupt the broadcast. Who was the diva and what was she singing? (4)

6. Luciano Pavarotti telecast *L'Elisir d' Amore* and *Un Ballo in Maschera* twice from the Met. Who were his soprano colleagues in each performance? (3)

7. A series of operas telecast from Japan in the early 1960s preserves the work of several fabled artists. For many years these have circulated throughout the world as videotapes. For each artist listed here, kindly name the opera(s) and role(s) he or she sang on these broadcasts.
   a. Giulietta Simionato (3)   d. Renata Tebaldi (2)
   b. Mario del Monaco (2)   e. Gabriella Tucci (3)
   c. Tito Gobbi (3)   f. Aldo Protti (4)

8. Name three operas with Beverly Sills telecast live from the New York City Opera in the 1970s. (3)

9. A telecast from the Mariensky Theatre in St. Petersburg has given us a splendid videotape and laser disc of Tchaikovsky's *Pique Dame.* In this performance, who sings the role of the Old Countess? (4)

10. For years, this weekly radio and television series showcased the talents of many great operatic performers. Name the show and the two songs heard at the opening and closing of each broadcast. Who composed those songs? (3)

11. An opera telecast internationally from Australia in 1994 was highly praised for its sets and costumes and the performance by its leading tenor. In fact, the performance was eventually released commercially by Decca/London. Name the opera, tell us the era into which it was reset, and the name of its leading tenor. (3)

12. Name the American tenor who walked out on his Metropolitan Opera career because the company's administration denied him telecasts of two of his best roles. What were the roles? (He returned to the Met several years later.) (4)

13. The farewell Met performance of one of its most brilliant sopranos was telecast live in January 1985. Who was the diva, and what was the role? (3)

Answers on page 473.

139. RECORD COLLECTORS II

1. This artist recorded the role of Kate Pinkerton in two EMI performances of *Madama Butterfly* made fifteen years apart—

first with Dal Monte and Gigli, later with De los Angeles and Di Stefano. Who is she? (4)

2. Please name four supporting roles recorded by Fiorenza Cossotto at the start of her career. (3)

3. Tullio Serafin's conducting of this recording caused a rift in his once-cordial relationship with Maria Callas. Name the opera and its stars, and state the reason for Callas's ire. (3)

4. Who are Tito Gobbi's soprano and tenor costars on his recording of *Il Tabarro*? Who conducts? (4)

5. José Carreras has recorded the role of Mario Cavaradossi in *Tosca* three times. Who are the artists who sing Tosca and Scarpia with Carreras on each recording? Who conducts each set, and on which labels do these recordings appear? (2)

6. The Metropolitan Opera recorded three complete operas for RCA. Identify the operas, their principal singers, and conductors. (3)

7. Soprano Antonietta Stella recorded three Verdi operas at La Scala for Deutsche Grammophon in the 1960s. What were they? Who were the tenors? (3)

8. Name three non-comic roles recorded by basso buffo Fernando Corena. (3)

9. For what reason did the 1970 Bolshoi recording of *Eugene Onegin* become a political embarrassment to the former Soviet Union? (4)

10. Name Maria Callas's only complete opera recording *not* sung in Italian. Identify the language, costars, and conductor. (1)

11. Who sings the title role in Renata Tebaldi's *first* recording of *Andrea Chénier*? (3)

12. Leonard Warren and Astrid Varnay recorded for RCA a duet from a Verdi opera they performed together in New York. Can you name the opera? (3)

13. Herva Nelli was a favorite of a very important conductor in the later years of his career. She performed and recorded five Verdi works under his direction. Name the conductor and the music in question. (1)

14. Birgit Nilsson sings Brünnhilde in two commercial recordings of the *Ring*. Who sings Wotan and Siegfried with her in each recording? (1)

15. Which three heroines of Offenbach operettas has Régine Crespin recorded? (2)

16. Who conducts these much-prized early operatic recordings starring Renata Tebaldi? They are *Otello, Aida, Tosca, La Bohème, Madama Butterfly,* and *Il Trovatore.* (2)

17. Giulietta Simionato sang the brief role of the Countess di Coigny on a recording of *Andrea Chénier.* Who sang the three leading roles on this recording, and who conducted? (3)

18. What was Luciano Pavarotti's first complete recording? Who were his soprano and mezzo colleagues? (Each received billing *above* Pavarotti's.) (2)

19. Who sang Calaf opposite Maria Callas's *Turandot* on the EMI label? (2)

20. Leontyne Price's first *Aida* recording was originally meant for another soprano who canceled because of illness. Whom did Price replace? (3)

21. Who sings the title role on the Virgin Records *Salome*? Whom did she replace? In what language is the opera sung on this recording? (3)

22. Name the Russian opera recorded by Kiri Te Kanawa and Thomas Hampson, sung in English. What company released this recording? (1)

23. In a contract dispute with Decca/London, the late tenor James McCracken held up the release of a new recording in a novel fashion. What was the opera, and what did McCracken do to make his point? (4)

24. Who conducts the 1995 Teldec recording of *Der Zigeunerbaron* in which forty-five minutes of music never before performed was restored to the score? (3)

25. Jon Vickers had a disagreement with maestro Georg Solti while recording an opera. As a result of this contretemps, the superb Canadian tenor and the brilliant Hungarian conductor never worked together again. What was the opera? (3)

26. What operatic duet did Ljuba Welitsch and Richard Tucker record for Columbia Records in New York? (3)

27. What complete opera recording features star turns by Maria Callas *and* Elisabeth Schwarzkopf? (1)

28. Who are the stars of an EMI German-language complete *Car-*

men never officially released in the United States in complete format, although highlights were available in the 1970s on LP? (3)

29. Who sings the role of the Italian Tenor on the complete recordings of *Der Rosenkavalier* listed below by conductor and label:

    a. Solti, Decca/London (1)
    b. Bernstein, Sony (2)
    c. De Waart, Philips (4)
    d. Karajan, EMI (3)
    e. Erich Kleiber, Decca/London (3)

30. Fedora Barbieri recorded the same role in a matter of weeks for two different record companies. Name the role, the opera, the conductors, and the labels. Incidentally, the executives at both companies were displeased by Mme. Barbieri's double-dealing, according to legend. (3)

Answers on page 474.

140. OLD VIENNA

See how much you can recall about those wonderful Viennese operettas that have been charming audiences around the world since the nineteenth century.

1. In what city does Lehár's *The Merry Widow* take place? (1)
2. In *The Gypsy Baron*, what is the secret that surrounds the heroine, Saffi? (3)
3. Who composed *Die Czárdásfürstin*? (2)
4. What country is meant by the title of Lehár's *The Land of Smiles*? (2)
5. In *The Merry Widow*, which character is in love with Valencienne? (2)
6. Also in *The Merry Widow*, who is Valencienne's husband? (3)
7. *Champagne Sec* was the title of a Broadway version of a well-known Viennese operetta. Name it. (2)

8. What is the name of the Viennese theater that specializes in operettas, and also performs opera sung in German? (2)

9. Returning to *The Merry Widow*, what is the name of the famous song for Hanna, early in Act II? (1)

10. For each of the following ten characters, name the operettas in which they appear and the composers. Can you identify the characters in brief?

    a. Prince Orlofsky (1)   f. Frosch (1)
    b. Mi (3)   g. Count Wittenburg (4)
    c. Giuditta (2)   h. Sonja (2)
    d. Sandor Barinkay (3)   i. Gabrielle (4)
    e. Loulou, Froufrou, Joujou (1) j. Bella Giretti (4)

11. Where does Prince Danilo, of *The Merry Widow*, like to spend his evenings? (1)

12. Which of Johann Strauss's operettas was created posthumously from his previously published music? (3)

13. Who composed *Two Hearts in ¾ Time?* (3)

14. Name the six operettas recorded by EMI in the 1950s that comprised that company's "Champagne Operetta Series." (3)

15. Which operetta heroine did soprano Hilde Gueden *not* record for Decca/London?

                    a. Rosalinde
                    b. Hanna Glawari
                    c. Saffi
                    d. Giuditta (3)

16. In *The Land of Smiles*, what makes Lisa decide to leave China and return to Vienna? (4)

17. In which Hollywood version of a Viennese favorite did Maurice Chevalier play the leading man? Who was his love interest in that film? (3)

18. From which operetta does the "Du and Du" waltz come? (1)

19. Name the fabled diva whose operatic farewell performance took place at Covent Garden in 1990, singing Rosalinde in *Die Fledermaus*. (1)

20. Can you name three Broadway musicals that have entered the repertoire of the Vienna Volksoper? (3)

21. For what tenor did Lehár compose *The Land of Smiles?* (2)

22. In the Decca/London "gala" *Die Fledermaus* recording, during the concert in Act II, what pieces were performed by the following artists: Renata Tebaldi, Birgit Nilsson, Jussi Bjoerling, Leontyne Price, Ljuba Welitsch, Giulietta Simionato, and Ettore Bastianini? (3)

23. What famous Met Salome was also a Metropolitan Rosalinde? (3)

24. Name the Italian composer about whom Lehár composed an operetta. (2)

25. Composer Emmerich Kalmán was of what nationality? Why was he forced to leave Europe? (2)

26. A famous and beautiful diva sang one Met *Fledermaus*, many years after her official retirement. Who? (4)

Answers on page 477.

141. THEY HAD SOME SONGS TO SING, O

Gilbert and Sullivan deserve a book of their own, but this brief quiz is included as a tribute to the importance of the G&S repertoire.

1. The first G & S opera was composed as a curtain-raiser for another work. Name this other piece, and the G & S work in question. (2)

2. Who was Richard D'Oyly Carte? (3)

3. For each of the characters listed here, identify the operetta in which they appear, and briefly describe him/her.

    a. Dick Deadeye (3)   i. Strephon (3)
    b. Rose Maybud (3)   j. Prince Hilarion (3)
    c. Colonel Fairfax (4)   k. Mad Margaret (4)
    d. Luiz (4)   l. Peep-bo (1)
    e. John Wellington Wells (4) m. The Lord Chancel-
    f. Jack Point (2)   lor (2)
    g. Cousin Hebe (2)   n. Josephine (1)
    h. Angelina (3)   o. Ruth (3)

4. What is Little Buttercup's real name? (4)

5. In *Iolanthe*, a reference is made to Captain Shaw. Who was

Captain Shaw, and in what song is the reference made? (4)

6. Name the London theater built for Gilbert and Sullivan's works. (1)

7. Which of Verdi's plots was a constant target of William S. Gilbert's satire? (2)

8. Name three other works by Sir Arthur Sullivan. (3)

9. Why did Queen Victoria knight Sullivan but not Gilbert? (4)

10. Which of the G & S operas almost had its world premiere in the United States? (3)

11. Which is the only G & S opera *not* to open with a chorus? How does it open? (2)

12. Which is the only Gilbert and Sullivan work in three acts? (1)

13. After a period of animosity that followed the composition of *The Gondoliers*, Gilbert & Sullivan collaborated on two more works, neither of which is frequently performed. Name them. (2)

14. Who was the principal comedian of the final years of the original D'Oyly Carte Opera Company? (1)

Jussi Bjoerling was such a wonderful singer that audiences forgave his less than dynamic acting and his occasional straying from the stage directions in the libretto. A *Manon Lescaut* that Bjoerling sang in the early 1950s was made memorable by his impromptu change in stage direction. Pleading fatigue, Bjoerling whispered to his "dying" soprano in Act IV that he would not go off and search for water as called for in the libretto. The obliging soprano wandered offstage herself and returned with the prop cup filled with water. More memorable still was a performance of *Tosca*, in which Bjoerling performed in spite of severe back pain. Not wishing to overexert himself, Bjoerling became the first Cavaradossi in the opera's history to die in front of a firing squad still standing!

15. For each song title listed here, name the operetta from which it comes and the character who sings it.
    a. "Braid the raven hair" (3)
    b. "Sorry her lot who loves too well" (2)
    c. "Never mind the why and wherefore" (2)
    d. "When I went to the bar as a very young man" (2)
    e. "The magnet and the silver churn" (4)
    f. "When Frederick was a little lad" (1)
    g. "When first my old, old love I knew" (2)
    h. "I stole the prince" (4)
    i. "I know a youth" (3)
    j. "I cannot tell what this love may be" (3)

16. Who was the only D'Oyly Carte star to re-create his most famous role in a Hollywood version of a G & S opera? Name the opera and the role. (2)

17. Which G & S character was modeled on Oscar Wilde? (3)

18. What are the subtitles of the following G & S operas?
    a. *H.M.S. Pinafore* (3)
    b. *The Pirates of Penzance* (3)
    c. *Iolanthe* (4)
    d. *The Mikado* (4)

19. What G & S operetta did Groucho Marx and Helen Traubel perform on American television in 1958? (3)

20. What G & S character is condemned to live in a pond, standing on her head, for twenty-five years? Why? (2)

21. In *The Mikado*, what does the expression "I shall get no yam for toko? mean? Who sings these words? (4)

22. What then brand-new invention is referred to in *H.M.S. Pinafore*, at the moment when Ralph Rackstraw is being taken to the dungeon for attempting to elope with Josephine? (3)

Answers on page 478.

142. SHAKESPEARE SUNG

The plays of William Shakespeare have inspired many operas. Some are quite faithful to the Bard, others less so. See if you can identify

the Shakespearean plays from the brief descriptions of the operatic ver-
sions found here. Please name the opera and its composer, too.

1. In this lyric version of a Shakespearean tragedy, the heroine dazzles the audience within minutes of her entrance by singing a charming, if anachronistic, waltz, which has no textual basis in the play. (3)

2. A history was combined with a comedy to produce an out- standing Italian opera. (1)

3. According to a famous letter, the composer of this opera based on a Shakespearean tragedy wanted his female protagonist to have an "ugly" voice—a requirement neatly fulfilled over the years at opera houses around the world. (2)

4. Shakespeare's own title for this play aptly summarized the plot. The title of its principal operatic treatment, however, salutes its two leads. (4)

5. In addition to providing part of the inspiration for a Verdi opera, this comedy has a once very popular German operatic incarnation. (3)

6. This play inspired superb incidental music, a ballet, and an opera by Britain's most celebrated twentieth-century com- poser. (3)

7. This Gallic edition of one of the Bard's seminal plays added a drinking song led by the title character and a relatively happy ending, at least as far as the protagonist is concerned. (3)

8. The composer of the music for three of Olivier's Shakespear- ean films also composed an opera based on this murky tragedy. (4)

9. Rossini and Verdi each composed an opera based on this play. Rossini's opera featured three roles for leading tenor. Verdi's was the more faithful adaptation and the better opera. (1)

10. Verdi tried but abandoned an opera based on this tragedy. The contemporary German composer Aribert Reimann suc- ceeded in having his completed work produced in Europe and America. (3)

11. Samuel Barber's opera based on this play failed to please at its first production, in spite of a brilliant cast. Neglected for a number of years, the composer revised it shortly before his

death, and it has occasionally been performed in the past decade. Bonus: Who starred in the leading soprano role when this
opera was telecast from the Lyric Opera of Chicago? (3)

12. Not long before this composer achieved his first fame, he composed this opera, an adaptation of one of Shakespeare's darker
comedies. (3)

*Answers on page **482**.*

143. OPERAS SET IN PARIS

*The City of Light might also be dubbed the City of Sound, as it has
served as the setting for many operas. From the brief descriptions given
here, please identify these operas and their composers. All of the operas
are set, at least in part, in Paris, but the composers are not all
Frenchmen.*

1. This perennial favorite, a story of young love and terminal
illness, is a veritable salute to the Left Bank. Having recently
reached its hundredth birthday, it shows no signs of fading
popularity. (1)

2. Set in and around a surreal vision of Paris, this challenging
work blends old and beloved personalities with new and distinctly different perspectives. (3)

3. This work has given opera-lovers a charming and fragile heroine, who has attracted such non-French singers as Victoria
de los Angeles, Beverly Sills, Bidù Sayão, and Mirella Freni to
portray her. (2)

4. This starkly realistic vision of Paris shows the grime beneath
the glamour, and the misery that lurks beneath the facades.
The Seine might as well be the river Styx in this grim, lurid
opera. (3)

5. Paris seems to close in on the protagonist of this short work,
as the reality of her private travail obscures the glitter of Paris
in the brilliant Art Deco era. (3)

6. A famous Parisian actress is the protagonist of this fragrant

work, and one of its acts is set in the Green Room of the Comédie-Française. (2)

7. Paris, in this opera, is described as a "populated desert" from which its central characters long to escape. (2)

8. Paris is the last destination of a poor soul who has trekked hundreds of miles in winter weather in order to join the man she loves. After singing the work's best-known aria, the heroine freezes to death, as her beloved sips champagne inside his house, oblivious of her presence. (4)

9. A Parisian demimondaine tries, but fails, to break away from her world of soirées and purchased love. In this case, however, no one suffers very deeply, and a dazzling soprano aria is sung. Some listeners have found this opera difficult to swallow. (2)

10. Paris in the time of the French Revolution is the scene of this melodic work that in some ways resembles an MGM epic, and requires the services of three golden-throated singers and a well-oiled guillotine. (1)

11. This opera shows Paris as only the natives know it, from sweat-shops to cafés and the lights of Montmartre. Four notable American divas have been associated with the title character. Few listeners are aware that the gorgeous aria that opens the work's third act was first composed as a song before the opera was conceived. Please name the aria, too. (2)

12. Outside of the *Ring* operas, few works for the lyric stage inspired sequels. One of the operas mentioned in this quiz, however, was followed by a sequel, named in honor of the leading tenor in the first work. It was a quick flop. Not even Caruso could keep it afloat. Name the opera and its "prequel." (4)

*Answers on page **482**.*

144. OPERA FOR THE BIRDS

Not surprisingly, since they are the most musical of animals, our feathered friends are frequently mentioned in opera. Sometimes they are crucial to the plot. Listed here are a number of operas, many quite familiar, in which birds figure. Your task will be to describe their significance in each work named.

1. *Siegfried* (1)
2. *Der Freischütz* (3)
3. *Lohengrin* (1)
4. *Parsifal* (2)
5. *Götterdämmerung* (3)
6. *Pagliacci* (two separate references, please) (3)
7. *Les Contes d'Hoffmann* (3)
8. *Gianni Schicchi* (4)
9. *La Rondine* (2)
10. *Die Frau ohne Schatten* (3)
11. *Carmen* (2)
12. *Die Zauberflöte* (1)
13. *Porgy and Bess* (3)
14. *Madama Butterfly* (1)
15. *Salome* (4)

Answers on page 483.

145. WOMEN'S WORLD

The questions below concern women who have influenced opera in another capacity than that of star soloist.

1. This lady ran a musical salon in nineteenth-century Milan, and was a close confidante of Giuseppe Verdi. What was her name? (3)
2. This scholarly Englishwoman has had a number of operas produced in recent years. She has chosen as subjects such varied material as the misadventures of a lovelorn monarch, a little-known Henry James novel, and an English classic. Who is she? (2)
3. For more than forty years, this dynamic broadcasting czarina ran the Metropolitan Opera broadcasts with a will of iron and the skill of a major general. Name her. (4)
4. Who was the first woman to conduct at the New York City Opera? (4)
5. The daughter of a great composer, she married another musical giant and shared his musical as well as ideological beliefs. Name her, and her father. (1)
6. Conductor/director Sarah Caldwell was the founder of what now defunct opera company? (3)

7. A female impresario was responsible for the U.S. debut of Maria Callas. Name the woman, and her company. (2)

8. A woman who conducts as well as produces opera has been responsible for important concert revivals of such operas as *L'Africaine, Katya Kabanova,* and *Tancredi* at New York's Carnegie Hall. Who is she, and what is the name of her company? (2)

9. This Englishwoman has directed many productions at Milan's La Scala and the Metropolitan Opera. Name her. (4)

10. This former actress who married a multimillionaire provided the impetus for the salvation of the Metropolitan Opera when that company faced financial ruin during the Great Depression. She was the founder of the Metropolitan Opera Guild. Name her. (2)

11. The daughter-in-law of a famous composer who died years before she was born, this woman ran a great music festival for many years but was barred from continuing in that capacity after World War II because of her unrepentant Nazi sympathies. Name her. Where was she born? (2)

12. This woman, a music critic for a major American daily, caused many an artist, as well as impresario, to tremble at her wrath. Who was she, and with which newspaper was she associated? (3)

13. This temperamental wife often made life difficult for her husband, a renowned composer. He paid tribute to his fiery spouse, who was, incidentally, a famous singer, by composing an opera that affectionately made fun of their conjugal life. Name the lady, her husband, and the opera. (3)

14. Although she had a brief but brilliant career as a soprano, this lady made her finest contribution to opera by loving and sustaining Giuseppe Verdi for half a century, first as an admirer of his music, later as mistress and wife. What was her name? (2)

15. This innocent girl's suicide caused a major scandal in the life of Giacomo Puccini, and almost cost the composer's wife a prison sentence. What was her name? (4)

16. Rudolf Bing invited this noted British director to enliven the-

atrical standards at the Met by directing productions of *Don Carlo* and *Aida* in the 1950s. (4)

17. This bass-voiced lady began her career as a singer, but ended it as a revered and sharp-tongued assistant conductor, voice coach, and intermission commentator at the Metropolitan Opera in the 1960s and 1970s. Name her. (4)

Answers on page 485.

146. OPERAS SET IN ITALY

Can you identify the operas described here, created by musicians from all over the globe, but set in Italy? Avanti!

1. This opera by a quintessentially Teutonic composer, is set in ancient Rome and rarely performed today. Its overture and one tenor aria are still occasionally heard. (3)

One of today's most glamorous and best-known sopranos was flying on the Concorde from Paris to New York, where she had a singing engagement. Although this lady is herself a mother, her patience with the children of strangers was limited. According to a bystander, this titled diva was seated in front of a young woman with an infant in her arms. This baby, like most, hated flying, and began crying before the jet took off and kept the wailing up for hours. Both the plane and the diva soon passed their points of no return. The soprano wheeled around in her seat and began berating the young mother in words and a tone of voice hardly consistent with a beloved Desdemona and Countess Almaviva. Finally the mother had heard enough. Recognizing her tormentor, the lady stood up and placed the child in the arms of the astonished diva. "You're the opera star," she snapped. "Why don't you just *sing* him to sleep?"

2. This comic opera celebrates the glories of the city of Dante. (2)

3. This opera uses the city of canals as background for a grim and emotionally fraught tale of obsession and doomed love. (Hint: For once, we don't mean *La Gioconda*!) (3)

4. This very popular opera is synonymous with the Eternal City. The woman who created the role of its heroine, however, was a Rumanian. (2)

5. Mozart set this scintillating work in Naples. It is not, however, a favorite in Italy. (3)

6. This merry work, not set to an Italian text, shows a lively, happy overview of the city that the opera in Question #3 paints in such somber colors. (3)

7. The name of this tragic heroine evokes one of Italy's most beautiful seacoast towns. This work is sometimes called "the Italian *Tristan*." (3)

8. Verdi vividly evoked Genoa and its coastal vista in this powerful opera of politics and love. (2)

9. Two Italian composers, each chiefly famous for one other work, created operas about a notorious Roman emperor. Name the character, the operas, and the pair of musicians. (3)

10. A minor northern Italian dukedom became, rather hastily, the setting for an evergreen lyric drama. Name the opera and the city. In what country was it originally set? (2)

11. Tuneful, colorful, and totally crazy, this "chestnut" offers yet another madcap tour of Venice. St. Mark's Square, the Grand Canal, and the Ca' d'Oro figure prominently in the libretto. Snobs hate it, opera buffs adore it. (1)

12. This Gallic treatment of a famous romance retains the Italian setting of the original source, although the names of some of the characters reflect the nationality of the composer and librettists. (2)

13. This opera brilliantly captures village life in a small Italian community, where the prospect of a night at the theater is deceptively festive. (1)

14. The first aria in this opera takes its name from the part of Italy in which the work is set. Name the aria and the opera. (2)

15. Although the title character is the Duchess of Ferrara, she creates trouble for herself by spending too much time with the wrong social set in Venice. (2)

16. This fascist-era work was set in Rome in the days when Christians were a persecuted minority. An incomparable artist created the title role in this work created for her by its composer. (3)

Answers on page 486.

147. OFF THE BEATEN PATH

The following questions deal with the exotica of operatic trivia.

1. Name a Polish opera. (3)
2. Name the Finnish bass who is noted for such diverse roles as Hagen, Baron Ochs, and Osmin. (2)
3. What was soprano Zinka Milanov's real name? (4)
4. To whom belong the last three solo voices ever heard onstage at the old Metropolitan Opera House? (3)
5. Who starred in the Hollywood film about an opera singer entitled *One Night of Love*? (2)
6. Which then-popular soprano openly denounced Luciano Pavarotti during a television broadcast? (2)
7. Who was the Wagnerian soprano who starred in a musical comedy by Rodgers and Hammerstein? Name the show, too. (3)
8. What was the first operatic "novelty" performed at the old Metropolitan Opera House in 1883? What was the first "standard" opera to be performed at the new Met in 1966? (3)
9. Mary Martin, prompted and harassed by Sir Noel Coward, once performed a hilarious rendition of a beloved aria on a classic TV show, "Together with Music" (available still as a CD). Name the aria. (4)
10. Ezio Pinza starred in a short-lived television situation comedy in the early 1950s. Do you recall its name? (4)

A wonderful Canadian tenor, internationally admired for his work in such roles as Peter Grimes and Otello, was singing Tristan in the American South. During Tristan's arduous third-act monologue, this singer, known for his temper, could no longer control his irritation at the audience's noisy display of respiratory ailments. In midphrase, he leapt from Tristan's deathbed, stalked to the footlights, and, shaking his fist at the audience, ordered them to "shut up your damned coughing!" Having vented his righteous anger, he stamped back to Tristan's cot and continued the scene.

🌿 🌿 🌿

11. What was the name of the self-styled artists' agent who sued Maria Callas, having her served with a subpoena as she stepped off the stage after a performance of Puccini's *Madama Butterfly* in Chicago? (4)
12. Who are three great sopranos born in Australia? (2)
13. What well-known French opera had its first performance in Vienna in a German translation? (3)
14. Who is the famous soprano who was a mere chorister in the 1937 Berlin recording of Mozart's *Die Zauberflöte*? (2)
15. Name two composers, celebrated in their own right, who created libretti for other composers to set. (3)
16. Who were Puccini's coauthors of the libretto for his *Manon Lescaut*? (None of them received billing on the libretto, by the way.) (4)
17. A soprano some consider to be the finest "Italian" soprano of the twentieth century was born in Connecticut. Who was she? (1)
18. Name an opera based on a motion picture script. (3)
19. Who was the operatic composer responsible for coaxing soprano Magda Olivero out of retirement in 1951? (2)

20. The daughter of the owner of Milan's Hotel Ritz, where Verdi died, was married to one of Verdi's successors as a composer of popular operas. Who was he? (3)

21. What was the German opera that was staged at the Vienna State Opera the night that Allied bombers practically destroyed that theater? (3)

22. Name two books written by the late Francis Robinson, for thirty-five years the principal raconteur (and assistant manager) of the Metropolitan Opera. (4)

23. What is the German opera whose most famous aria, sung by the tenor, is almost invariably sung in Italian, while its second most famous number, for soprano, is a German version of an English folksong? (1)

24. What was the name of the nineteenth-century social club that set the rules for performances at the Paris Opéra? (3)

25. Who are Ruben Ticker, Pincus Perlmutter, and Janet Angelovich? (3)

26. Soprano Dorothy Kirsten was the protégée of what very famous singer? (2)

27. Cesare Siepi appeared in two unsuccessful Broadway musical comedies. Coincidentally, the two characters he portrayed had the same occupation. Name the two shows and state the profession of Siepi's characters. (4)

28. Who were two opera singers who had foods named for them? What are the two dishes in question? (1)

29. Who was the Metropolitan star arrested on false charges of espionage, prompted by a jealous colleague, during World War II? (4)

30. Who was the first American ever to sing at the Bolshoi? What role did this artist perform? (3)

31. Name two composers who reorchestrated Mussorgsky's *Boris Godunov*. (2)

32. Name the artist who performed no fewer than seven roles in the world, London, and American premieres of Britten's *Death in Venice*, opposite the formidable Peter Pears, the opera's doomed protagonist. (3)

33. Name the British lady who was reputedly Puccini's mistress for many years. (4)

34. In which digital recording of *La Traviata* is the tenor singing the role of Alfredo Germont actually old enough to be the father of the baritone singing the role of Alfredo's dad, Giorgio Germont? (1)
35. Name the fabled diva who, in her great days, traveled in her own private railroad car. (2)

Answers on page 486.

148. DON'T BELIEVE EVERYTHING YOU READ I

See how well you do on this operatic "true or false" test!

1. *Carmen* was Bizet's first opera. (2)
2. Puccini adapted his opera *Tosca* from a play by Victorien Sardou. (2)
3. Two Verdian characters share the name Iago. Iago is, of course, the villain in *Otello*. However, in *Ernani* the title character has a henchman named Iago. (3)
4. Gustav Mahler conducted at the Metropolitan Opera for several years during the first decade of the twentieth century. (2)
5. In Verdi's *Il Trovatore*, Azucena's final revelation to Count di Luna is that she is the count's mother. (1)
6. Maria Callas was first introduced to American opera fans because of a film she made of *Medea*. (2)
7. In Verdi's *Falstaff*, the librettist Boito grafted a famous speech from Shakespeare's *Henry IV, Part I* onto the libretto he fashioned from the bard's *The Merry Wives of Windsor*. (3)
8. In Puccini's *Madama Butterfly*, the heroine is cursed for marrying a foreigner and renouncing her religion, by her father, a Buddhist priest. (1)
9. José Carreras was "discovered" by Joan Sutherland when he sang a small role in an opera in which she starred in London in 1970. (2)
10. Three composers who produced operas based on *Manon Lescaut* were Massenet, Puccini, and Leoni. (3)
11. Plácido Domingo sang for several seasons in Tel Aviv, relearning his roles in Hebrew. (2)

12. Ezio Pinza appeared in a Broadway musical with Ethel Merman. (3)

13. The recitatives in *Carmen* were composed not by Bizet, but by Ernest Guiraud, after Bizet's sudden death. (1)

14. Bruno Walter conducted the first performance at the rebuilt La Scala, after the damage done by Allied bombers had been repaired. (3)

15. The first opera ever televised "live" from the new Metropolitan Opera at Lincoln Center was Puccini's *La Bohème* starring Renata Scotto and Luciano Pavarotti. (2)

16. In *Götterdämmerung*, Siegfried is drugged and tricked into marrying Sieglinde. (2)

17. Beniamino Gigli died onstage at the Metropolitan during a performance of Verdi's *La Forza del Destino*. (3)

18. In Rossini's Cinderella opera, *La Cenerentola*, the heroine's wicked stepmother is named Giselda. (3)

19. The answers to the three riddles posed by Turandot to Calaf in Puccini's opera are, respectively: *Sangue* (blood), *Speranza* (hope), and Turandot herself. (2)

20. Richard Strauss and poet Hugo von Hofmannsthal collaborated on the following operas: *Elektra*, *Der Rosenkavalier*, and *Ariadne auf Naxos*. (2)

21. Richard Strauss's *Ariadne auf Naxos*, in its original format, was performed as part of a production of Molière's play *Le Médecin Malgré Lui*. (3)

22. Teresa Stratas deserves a place in any operatic book of world records for having sung such diverse roles as Gretel in Humperdinck's opera, and the title role of Berg's shocker *Lulu*. (1)

23. Beverly Sills is married to Julius Rudel, whom she replaced as general director of the New York City Opera in 1979. (2)

24. Puccini himself conducted his opera *La Fanciulla del West* on the occasion of its world premiere at the Met in December 1910. (3)

25. Tenor Joseph Schmidt would have enjoyed a greater career on the operatic stage had he not been so tall that he truly towered over every artist with whom he appeared. (4)

26. Tenor Jan Peerce was especially famous for his recording of the song "The Bluebird of Happiness." (3)

27. In *La Traviata*, the dying Violetta gives to Alfredo a letter with instructions that he show it to the girl whom he will someday marry. (2)
28. Baritone Robert Merrill once got into an argument (in the press) with the TV star Roseanne over the way she sang the National Anthem at a televised baseball game. (1)
29. The only two comic roles in Maria Callas's repertoire were Rosina in *Il Barbiere di Siviglia* and Adina in *L'Elisir d'Amore*. (3)
30. In the first version of Rossini's *Otello*, Desdemona convinced Otello of her innocence, and the opera ended with the reunited couple singing a love duet. (3)

Answers on page 489.

149. OPERATIC SCAVENGER HUNT

Can you supply the information called for by the following questions?

1. Name two soprano heroines who die of consumption. (1)
2. Name two soprano characters who kill themselves rather than let villainous baritone characters make love to them. (2)
3. Name a mezzo-soprano Gypsy who appears in a nineteenth-century opera who is *not* a "bad girl." (3)
4. Name four tenor characters in Italian operas who murder their wives or lovers. (Give the beloveds' names, too.) (3)
5. Name two Bellini heroines who have mad scenes but who regain their wits at the end of their respective operas. (3)
6. Who are three operatic fathers who are responsible for the deaths of their children? (Give the children's names, too.) (3)
7. How many villains can you name who are apprehended at the end of the works in which they appear? Who are the characters who catch them? Name at least five. (4)
8. Name three operas that have masked balls (excluding Verdi's *Un Ballo*, of course). (3)
9. Name two German operas based on Shakespearean plays, composed in the nineteenth century. (Name the plays, too.) (3)
10. Which American opera is based on a play by Chekhov? (4)

11. Who are two tenor characters who die shortly after leading drinking songs? (3)
12. Name at least three characters who are beheaded. (1)
13. Name two soprano characters who have happy marriages to bass characters. (Name the husbands and the operas, too.) (4)
14. Who are three operatic characters who kill their own brothers? (3)
15. Name three malevolent high priests. (2)
16. Name five baritone characters who are "good guys." (3)
17. Name five evil soprano characters. (3)
18. Name two operatic wives who strike their husbands. (4)
19. Who is an operatic doctor who ought to be sued for malpractice? (1)
20. Name five operas set in the United States. (2)
21. Name five operas by Mascagni excluding *Cavalleria Rusticana* and *L'Amico Fritz*. (3)
22. Name three operas based on plays by Eugène Scribe. (3)
23. Name three Verdi operas with libretti by Francesco Maria Piave. (3)
24. Name four German opera singers who fled Nazi Germany and settled in the United States. (3)
25. Name an opera whose heroine has four legs. (2)
26. Name an opera in which a mezzo character returns as a ghost. (2)
27. Name two operas in which women sing the roles of boys who, at some point, have to disguise themselves as young women. (2)

Answers on page 491.

150. DIRECTORS

How many of the following internationally known operatic stage directors can you identify from the brief descriptions given here?

1. Synonymous with large-scale productions of standard operas, this multitalented man had much to do with shaping the dra-

In his memoirs, Schuyler G. Chapin, whose brief, accidental
tenure as General Manager of the Metropolitan Opera
(1972–75) was not among that company's brightest eras,
was sufficiently indiscreet as to recount a conversation he
had with a great and much beloved soprano in the final years
of her career, in which he tactlessly suggested that the lady
become a mezzo-soprano. Not surprisingly, the insulted diva
left Chapin's office without a word, and never spoke to him
again. She never sang at the Met again, either, a situation
which infuriated her many fans. But Chapin received his
comeuppance, and not just by being abruptly fired from his
position while shepherding the Met through its first tour of
Japan. Not long after being sacked, Chapin was hospitalized
for ulcers in New York City. Someone on the hospital's staff
was a loyal fan of the artist whom Chapin had insulted. This
person, armed with a mean-looking hypodermic syringe, ma-
terialized at the patient's bedside in the dead of night and
administered a painful series of jabs in the name of some
medical necessity or other, and then growled to the by now
really frightened Chapin, "That's for what you did to
Madame———!"

❀ ❀ ❀

matic abilities of both Callas and Sutherland. He also directs
films and plays. (1)
2. This director is a product of the Actors Studio. His many
innovative productions at the New York City Opera intensi-
fied dramatic values and often stirred controversy. (2)
3. Many critics have accused this trendy director of the 1980s
and 1990s of distorting and desecrating operas by Mozart,
Handel, and Wagner. He once set the third act of *Tannhäuser*
at O'Hare Airport! (3)
4. This German has staged numerous productions of Wagner's

operas at the Bayreuth Festival in recent years, often creating striking stage pictures but infuriating people who prefer more literal, traditional mountings of opera. (3)

5. These brothers can be credited for rescuing one of Europe's greatest opera festivals from political ignominy after the Second World War. Their innovative, somewhat austere productions were copied all over the world. (1)

6. This German director, best known outside his own country as a film director, had his plans for a new *Die Zauberflöte* rudely canceled by the Metropolitan Opera several years ago, for reasons that have never been satisfactorily explained. (3)

7. This director can be credited with the staging for the first production of Corigliano and Hoffman's *The Ghosts of Versailles*. This 1991 production at the Metropolitan Opera was the most successful mounting of a new American work in decades. (4)

8. This young Briton with a biblical name has had his share of disasters at the Metropolitan Opera and elsewhere, but in his own country he is one of the most eagerly sought régisseurs to be found. His 1995 *Pique Dame* at the Met was a huge success. (3)

9. Straddling the worlds of spoken theater and opera, this notoriously crusty Englishman was responsible for such Metropolitan Opera successes as *Dialogues des Carmélites*, and such disasters as the 1976 *Aida*. For several years he served as one of a "troika" of artistic directors at the Met. (2)

10. A product of London's Royal National Theatre, this iconoclastic director mounted Royal Opera productions of *Salome* and *Carmen* that were created for one of his former wives. He also achieved notoriety through publication of his indiscreet diaries of his years at the RNT. (3)

11. The son of a favorite tenor, this artist stages bizarre productions in Europe, and lavish, more traditional ones in the United States. His *Fanciulla del West* at the Metropolitan is much admired. (2)

12. How many people compose, write their own libretti, and stage their own operas, and those of other composers, too? This man has been doing all this for more than half a century. (1)

13. This Broadway wunderkind came to opera in the fourth decade of his award-filled career. His productions are seen at all the "best" opera houses, including the Met, Chicago, the New York City Opera, and London's Royal Opera. (1)

14. An undisputed master of conducting, this larger-than-life figure began staging his own productions in the 1960s, and brought his *Ring* cycle to the Salzburg Festival. (1)

15. A Broadway and London theater luminary and an unforgettable, musical Captain Hook, this Australian native staged several operas at the Met during the Bing era, including *Il Barbiere di Siviglia, Le Nozze di Figaro, Les Contes d'Hoffmann, The Gypsy Baron,* and *La Périchole,* in which he also starred. (2)

16. This highly regarded Swede was poised to take over the reins of the Metropolitan Opera in 1972. He was going to direct *Carmen,* in a new production starring Marilyn Horne and James McCracken, conducted by Leonard Bernstein, when he was killed in an auto accident. Name him, and the director who, working from the dead man's notes, staged the *Carmen.* (3)

17. This actor-turned-régisseur has given Metropolitan audiences a popular *Ring* cycle and excellent productions of *Tosca, Tannhäuser,* and *Die Fledermaus.* (3)

18. This French director put his own, at times bizarre, imprint upon the operas of Mozart and Monteverdi. He died after a fall from an opera house stage, and took his plans for a new Metropolitan *Don Giovanni* with him. (3)

19. This onetime stage colleague of Dudley Moore is in demand around the world for innovative, sometimes silly, stagings of opera. His Metropolitan debut took place in 1995 with a production of *Pelléas et Mélisande.* (2)

20. Half of a famous acting team, he staged *Così Fan Tutte* in English at the Old Met, and *La Traviata* when the company moved to Lincoln Center. (3)

*Answers on page **494**.*

151. DON'T BELIEVE EVERYTHING
YOU READ II

True or false?

1. Verdi's first opera was *Nabucco*. (2)
2. The first singer to perform the title role in Puccini's *Turandot* was Rosina Storchio. (3)
3. Beethoven composed four overtures to his only opera, *Fidelio*. (2)
4. Renata Tebaldi recorded Cilea's *Adriana Lecouvreur* in 1946, with Arturo Toscanini conducting. (2)
5. Although Victoria de los Angeles recorded *Carmen* in 1959, she did not actually sing the title role onstage until she appeared in a production of Bizet's opera in Newark, New Jersey, in 1978. (2)
6. Tenor Carlo Bergonzi began his career as a baritone. (3)
7. Francesco Cilea, composer of *Adriana Lecouvreur* and *L'Arlesiana*, was a noted musicologist. (3)
8. Don Giovanni briefly allows Donna Elvira to think that he is coming back to her, but it is Elvira's maid who really interests him. (2)
9. Puccini once considered composing an opera about Marie Antoinette. (3)
10. In 1955, Leontyne Price became the first African-American artist to sing at the Metropolitan Opera. (2)
11. Alfredo Catalani, composer of *La Wally*, also composed an opera based on Murger's *Scènes de la Vie de Bohème*. Puccini stole the idea of the opera from the unfortunate Catalani. (2)
12. Sir Georg Solti spent several years as musical director of the Royal Opera House, Covent Garden. (3)
13. One of Verdi's principal librettists was Lorenzo da Ponte. (1)
14. On the first night of Rudolf Bing's regime at the Met, Cesare Siepi, Delia Rigal, Fedora Barbieri, and Lucine Amara all made their debuts in Verdi's *Don Carlo*. (3)
15. During Maria Callas's time at La Scala, the head of that opera company was Giovanni Battista Meneghini. (4)

16. Puccini once remarked that his favorite Tosca was Rosa Ponselle. (3)
17. The original cast of Carlisle Floyd's *Susannah*, as produced by the New York City Opera, included Norman Treigle as Blitch and Beverly Sills as Susannah. (3)
18. A vicious feud between Jan Peerce and Zinka Milanov made backstage at the Met a war zone whenever they appeared together in the 1950s. (2)
19. The great Italian mezzo-soprano Giulietta Simionato began her career at La Scala singing such minor roles as Mamma Lucia in Mascagni's *Cavalleria Rusticana*. (3)
20. Donizetti composed a revised version of his French opera comique *La Fille du Régiment* and called it *Die Regimentstochter*. (4)
21. Verdi composed *Aida* for Jenny Lind. (3)
22. Enrico Caruso sang the role of Dick Johnson in Puccini's *La Fanciulla del West* in that opera's world-premiere performance, at the Royal Opera, Covent Garden, London, in 1910. (1)
23. Verdi revised *I Lombardi* for production in Paris and retitled it *Aroldo*. (2)
24. Boris Christoff once had a real swordfight with tenor Franco Corelli during a performance of *Don Carlo* at the Rome Opera. (3)
25. Mezzo Rosalind Elias won an Emmy award for her televised performance of the Witch in *Hänsel und Gretel*. (3)
26. The aria known in English as "Hymn to the Moon" opens Mascagni's opera *Iris*. (3)
27. Maria Callas made her final appearance in a staged opera at the Paris Opéra in 1965. The role she sang was Tosca. (3)
28. Although Grace Moore was best known for singing Tosca and Mimì, her repertoire also included Louise in Charpentier's opera and Fiora in Montemezzi's *L'Amore dei Tre Re*, which she broadcast from the Met in the company of Ezio Pinza. (3)
29. Verdi revised his opera *Nabucco* twenty-five years after its premiere, adding to it the famous "Council Chamber Scene." (3)

30. As a child, Katia Ricciarelli was an entertainer on the Italian vaudeville circuit. Shades of *Gypsy!* (4)

Answers on page 494.

152. DON'T SING WITH YOUR MOUTH FULL

Food and eating can be very important matters in opera. From the brief descriptions given here, identify the opera, and the characters who are doing the eating.

1. A servant's terse announcement that dinner is ready briefly interrupts a spat between two beaux of a popular beauty. By the time the meal is finished, a bitter quarrel is raging. (1)
2. This surprising guest haughtily refuses the food of mortals. His host soon wishes the visitor hadn't come at all. (1)
3. Eating a bowl of pasta without commenting on the fact that his "intended" seems to be running away with another man is an absurd initiation rite in the society of "Papataci." (3)
4. A search for strawberries leads to near-disaster for this hardy pair. They just can't resist a nice piece of gingerbread. (2)
5. An opera begins with a woman ordering lobster and duck for someone else's dinner. By the end of the scene, she is consuming it, along with too much wine, herself. (4)
6. On her first date with a new boyfriend, this young lady orders ice cream. (2)
7. While everyone else enjoys supper, this romantic fellow slips off to dance with his host's daughter, who isn't the least bit interested in food. Do you know why she isn't hungry? (2)
8. This woman fusses over a roast chicken, but dinner is ruined anyway by an unexpected arrival. (2)
9. A bit of bread is secretly pressed into a condemned man's hand, giving him a frugal last meal. (3)
10. This irritable cleric hates dispensing soup to the "undeserving

poor" and, in a rage, spills the whole kettle on the ground, and is immediately scolded by his superior. (2)

11. When this poor woman suddenly finds she has hungry guests, she is ashamed to admit she has no refreshments to offer them. Fortunately, her neighbors bring plenty of nice things on which to snack. (3)

12. Before leaving on a blind date, this dutiful young woman serves dinner to her younger siblings. (3)

13. A young girl in an austere career choice greedily devours some fresh fruit, then offers some to her colleagues. (4)

14. A basket of food, intended to help someone in need, becomes an important clue for an enemy. (2)

15. "My poor little supper has been interrupted," kvetches this savvy villain to his unwilling guest. (1)

16. This character rings down the curtain by inviting the entire company to dine at the expense of the work's protagonist. (3)

17. A shrewd restaurateur cadges an extra crab from a street vendor with the aplomb of a born con artist. (3)

18. A rogue learns the hard way that sitting down to another man's dinner can lead to unpleasant consequences. (2)

Answers on page 496.

153. OUT IN THE COLD

Below are groups of four—titles of operas, names of characters, singers, or companies. Three items in each group share a common characteristic. Select the one item that is different from the others and explain why.

1. Eboli, Fenena, Amneris, Federica. (3)
2. *Le Nozze di Figaro, Suor Angelica, Turandot, Das Rheingold.* (two possibilities) (4)

3. *Norma, I Puritani, Il Pirata, La Sonnambula.* (4)
4. Ernani, the Duke of Mantua, Enzo Grimaldo, Chevalier des Grieux. (2)
5. Carmen, Mignon, Dalila, Preziosilla (two possibilities). (4)
6. Scarpia, Adriana, Luisa Miller, Gennaro. (3)
7. Mimì, Maddalena di Coigny, Leonora di Vargas, Violetta. (4)
8. The Metropolitan Opera, the Royal Opera House, La Scala, Paris Opéra. (3)
9. *Falstaff, Don Carlo, Un Ballo in Maschera, Il Trovatore* (two possibilities). (4)
10. Mary Garden, Grace Moore, Patrice Munsel, Dorothy Kirsten (two possibilities). (4)
11. *Linda di Chamounix, Parisina d'Este, Emilia di Liverpool, Elisabetta, Regina d'Inghilterra.* (4)
12. Leporello, Mariandl, Despina, Figaro (two possibilities). (3)
13. *Don Giovanni, Mitridate, Le Nozze di Figaro, Così Fan Tutte.* (2)
14. Agnes Baltsa, Nicola Moscona, Maria Callas, Nicola Zaccaria. (3)
15. Luciano Pavarotti, Plácido Domingo, José Carreras, Alfredo Kraus (two possibilities). (1)
16. *Vanessa, Susannah, The Ballad of Baby Doe, Regina.* (2)
17. *Lohengrin, Götterdämmerung, Parsifal, Der Fliegende Holländer* (2 possibilities). (3)
18. Emmy Destinn, Dorothy Kirsten, Barbara Daniels, Renata Tebaldi. (3)
19. Gilda Cruz-Romo, Leontyne Price, Martina Arroyo, Aprile Millo. (3)
20. Bruno Walter, Herbert von Karajan, Franz Allers, George Szell. (1)

Answers on page 498.

154. RECORD COLLECTORS III

1. What was the first opera to be recorded in the digital process? Name the label, conductor, and principal singers. (3)
2. Fiorenza Cossotto, known primarily for her Verdi, *bel canto*, and *verismo*, recorded a Mozart role in a delightful performance of a great comedy. Name the role, opera, conductor, and Cossotto's colleagues. (1)
3. Name five sopranos who have recorded *The Merry Widow* in English. (3)
4. Who sings Pollione opposite Callas's Norma in the soprano's first recording of the Bellini opera? (2)
5. When in 1949 Boris Christoff recorded the death of Boris Godunov for the first time, what soon-to-be-famous soprano sang the brief lines of the czar's little boy? (4)
6. Who sings the title role of Spontini's *La Vestale* in the Cetra recording? (3)
7. What is the only complete opera recorded commercially by Anita Cerquetti, the brilliantly gifted soprano whose career ended after only fourteen seasons before the public? Who are her colleagues on this set? (2)
8. Who are the two artists who have recorded all three leading soprano roles in Puccini's *Il Trittico*? (2)
9. Soprano Ilva Ligabue recorded a Verdi heroine two and a half times. Name the role, opera, and the labels for which she recorded it. Name the conductors. (3)
10. Tenor Jon Vickers has recorded Florestan in *Fidelio* on two occasions. Who were the sopranos and conductors on each set? (2)
11. Soprano Martina Arroyo recorded Elena in Verdi's *I Vespri Siciliani* for RCA as a last-minute replacement for an ailing colleague. Whom did she replace? (3)
12. Name the soprano who has recorded both Mimì and Musetta on complete recordings of *La Bohème*. (2)
13. Elisabeth Schwarzkopf recorded scenes from a major opera by Richard Strauss, providing that work with its first LP in-

carnation, however abridged. Identify the opera, the role Schwarzkopf sang, and her baritone colleague. (4)

14. Name the three operatic roles recorded by Anna Moffo for EMI. Who sang the leading tenor roles opposite her on these sets? (2)

15. One of Maria Callas's complete operatic recordings was not released for several years after it was made, until Callas could be persuaded to allow its distribution. Name it. (3)

16. Who was the extraordinately gifted producer of the first stereophonic recording of the *Ring*? (2)

17. A famous interpreter of Salome sings a cameo role on a beloved recording of another Strauss opera. Name the soprano, the role, the conductor, and the label of the performance. (2)

18. What were the last two Verdi operas to receive complete commercial recordings? (4)

19. Licia Albanese, Patrice Munsel, Giuseppe di Stefano, and Leonard Warren are all heard on an early LP recording of highlights from a very popular opera. The recording is long out of print. Name the opera. (4)

20. Who sings the title role on the only stereo version of Thomas's *Mignon*? For what label was this recorded? (3)

21. Who sings the role of Figaro opposite Cecilia Bartoli on Ms. Bartoli's Decca/London recording of *Il Barbiere di Siviglia*? (2)

22. Name ten operas of which there exist "live recordings" in which Leyla Gencer sings the leading soprano role. (4)

23. For which label has Thomas Hampson recorded the title role in *Don Giovanni*? (2)

24. Who is the first mezzo-soprano to record the role of Isolde in Wagner's music drama? Name the Tristan, conductor, and label. (2)

25. In Jussi Bjoerling's famous RCA recording of collected operatic arias, in what language does he sing Lensky's Aria from *Eugene Onegin*? (3)

Answers on page 500.

155. RECORD COLLECTORS IV

1. Name two roles in operas by Rossini recorded by Jennifer Larmore for Teldec records. (3)

2. Roberto Alagna and Tiziana Fabbricini sing the leads in a Sony recording of a popular opera that is available as a video and an audio production. Who is the conductor? Where was the opera recorded? (3)

3. Name the opera recorded in the 1980s by Joan Sutherland and Luciano Pavarotti that, as of 1996, has still not been released by Decca/London. (4)

4. Bryn Terfel sings the role of Angelotti in a recording of *Tosca* made shortly before he achieved major recognition as a singer. Identify his soprano, tenor, and baritone colleagues. Who conducts the recording, and what label released it? (3)

5. Catherine Malfitano has recorded Salome in Strauss's opera twice, once on video and once on audio. Identify the artists who sing Jokanaan and Herodias on each. Name the conductors. (3)

6. Name the opera that Plácido Domingo and Jessye Norman recorded together under James Levine's baton. What label released it? (2)

7. List four Russian operas recorded at the Kirov (Mariensky) opera in St. Petersburg and released in the United States by Philips. (3)

8. A composite recording of *Tristan und Isolde* made up of acetates made at Covent Garden before World War II was issued by EMI in 1992. Name the artists who sing Tristan and Isolde and the two superb conductors whose work was "morphed" by the engineers. (3)

9. Sir Georg Solti, at the age of eighty-three, conducted a Verdi opera for the first time in his career at Covent Garden in 1994. Name the opera, the leading artists, and the label that released the album. (2)

10. Name three operatic recordings in which tenor Richard Leech sings a leading role. (2)

11. Identify the rarely performed opera by Rossini recorded by Renée Fleming and released by Sony. Where was this album made? (3)

12. A recently discovered recording of a 1951 *Giovanna d'Arco* performance with Renata Tebaldi in the title role was released in 1995 by Legato. Who is the tenor singing the role of Carlo? (4)

13. Which of the following was *not* a recording by Maria Callas released since 1983?
    a. "Non mi dir"
    b. "Je dis que rien ne m'épouvante"
    c. "Pur ti riveggo, mia dolce Aida" (with Franco Corelli)
    d. "Ah, perfido!" (live from Paris) (4)

14. A recording of the world-premiere of an opera by Benjamin Britten was released for the first time ever in 1994 by the VAI label, forty years after the performance took place. Please name the opera and the artist who sang the title role. (4)

15. A nineteenth-century French opera had to wait until 1995 to receive its first complete recording from a major label, and then two different performances were released within a period of one month. Name the opera, composer, labels, and the soprano, mezzo, tenor, and baritone leads on each set, as well as the conductors of the two recordings. (3)

16. Please identify the soprano who sings opposite Luciano Pavarotti in his 1994 recording of Verdi's *Il Trovatore*. (4)

17. Which label boasts the "Prima Voce" series in its catalogue? Name ten historical male singers and ten historical female singers who have individual CDs devoted to them. Also, list three opera houses that have discs devoted to them on this label. (4)

18. In 1996, London records issued an album of Mozart arias featuring soprano Renée Fleming. The album has a rather odd title. What is it? (4)

19. Who sings Roméo and who sings Juliette on the RCA recording of Gounod's opera released in 1996? (2)

20. Who is the subject of the "La Divina" series of aria collections issued by EMI? (1)

21. Name the recording label that has recently made more than twenty French, Italian, and German operas, all sung in their original languages and recorded in Prague. All are available on DDD CDs, at very low prices. (3)

22. Who conducts soprano Sumi Jo's London CD *Carnival*, a collection of French coloratura arias from operas that are now mostly out of vogue? Name the soprano rumored to have admitted to being a little jealous of the success of this recording. (3)

23. An English-language recording of *Eugene Onegin* was released by EMI in 1994. Who sings the baritone and soprano leads on that set? (2)

24. A famous/notorious dramatic soprano of the 1960s and 1970s sings a brief but telling mezzo-soprano role on a recording of a tragic Italian opera released in 1993. Name the lady, the opera, the label on which it appears, and the soprano who is the opera's prima donna. (3)

25. Who is the woman who stars on a CD called *The Men in My Life*? Who are the men, and which label released the album? (3)

26. Name the work in which Plácido Domingo both sings the leading tenor role *and* conducts. What label released this recording? (3)

27. Who emerged as Maria Callas's successor, in terms of recordings of Bellini's *Norma* for EMI in 1995? (3)

28. An opera by Philip Glass based on a film by Jean Cocteau received a widely hailed recording in 1995. Name the opera and the label that issued the recording. (4)

29. Several years ago, London Records began issuing recordings of music by German composers whose works were banned during the Nazi era. Please name the series, and list at least four operas included therein. (4)

Answers on page 502.

156. ULTIMATE, ULTIMATE WAGNER

1. How many solo parts are there in *Der Ring des Nibelungen*? (4)
2. List, in order of appearance, every character in the *Ring*. (Note: Do not list characters again that appear in more than one section.) (4)

Answers on page 504.

My cat, Fedora, patiently endures the opera constantly playing on the stereo in my apartment, and even puts up with my singing along. But one night, as I was declaiming Violetta's spoken fragments in the last act of *La Traviata*, and reached her final delirious lines as she expires, Fedora stopped what she was doing, shot across the room, and leapt into my arms, licking my face. She has responded this way to Violetta ever since, in front of friends and even her veterinarian, and to no other opera. One night after Fedora performed this trick several times, I looked deep into her feline eyes and murmured, "I suppose in your last life you were a great Violetta, right?" She met my gaze. Fedora was born in 1981, four years after one of the great Violettas of all time had passed away. What a great joke of karma if Maria Callas had been reincarnated as a cat in a Tebaldi household!

157. OPERA PIX: A PHOTO QUIZ

Answers on pages 505–507

ABOVE: 1. One of these gentlemen is a world-famous tenor, now retired. Identify him. Can you identify the obscure chap standing with him? (3)

ABOVE: 2. These two stars often sang together. What opera have they just finished here, and where did the performance take place? (2)

RIGHT: 3. This soprano, shown in one of her best roles, created a sensation when she made her La Scala debut in this opera. Her Metropolitan debut, made in the company of a certain Mr. Pavarotti, was in a work by Verdi. Identify the artist, and name the vehicle for her Met debut. (4)

ABOVE: 4. If this tenor seems pensive, perhaps he is contemplating his future. Identify the artist, and the person who designed the set on which he is standing. (2)

LEFT: 5. "Hey, Mama, I want to *axe* you something!" Identify the lady, and the role she is singing. (2)

RIGHT: 6. If there were an opera based on *Yes, Minister,* this might be it. Identify the singer, the role, and the opera. (3)

BELOW: 7. It's difficult to imagine that this lady would ever have a bad hair day, but . . . Can you identify the artist and the role that she is singing? (2)

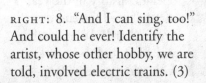

RIGHT: 8. "And I can sing, too!" And could he ever! Identify the artist, whose other hobby, we are told, involved electric trains. (3)

9. Not since Rembrandt painted Aristotle admiring a bust of Homer has such a moment been captured pictorially. Name the lady, and the subject of the drawing that she is holding. (4)

RIGHT: 10. The lady seen with jazz great Mabel Mercer is a soprano whose own blue notes are as fabulous as her celestial high notes and incomparable low notes. Who is she? (1)

11. The soprano and stage director shown here made operatic history in the years that followed the end of World War II. Who are they, and where did they work with one another? (3)

RIGHT: 12. Now a peerless character singer, this lady was once described as the "Jayne Mansfield of the Metropolitan Opera." Name her, and identify the role for which she is costumed. (3)

BELOW: 13. It is hard to believe that this diminutive artist could create such a ruckus offstage. Name her, and the role for which she has disguised herself as a boy. (2)

BELOW RIGHT: 14. In 1994, this prima donna joined the line of Lina Cavalieri, Renata Tebaldi, Licia Albanese, Montserrat Caballé, and Renata Scotto and sang this heroine at the Met. Can you identify the lady and the character? (2)

ABOVE: 15. The lady shown here played several male roles, as well as temptresses, and once "romanced" Beverly Sills while wearing a false mustache. Who is she, and whom is she portraying here? (2)

BELOW: 16. This lady's performance as Amneris is, quite simply, the finest I've ever heard. Who is she? (2)

LEFT: 17. These are two great stars of a faraway company, here dressed for a very popular opera not native to their country of origin. Name this pair, and the opera in question. By the way, this couple is related to one another. How? (4)

ABOVE: 18. Maybe it was something she ate. Tell us who the lady is, and what role she is performing. (1)

LEFT: 19. Known in America mostly for her Wagner and Strauss, this soprano also sings operas by Italian composers. What is her name? Can you guess the role for which she is costumed? (3)

RIGHT: 20. We concede that
the role is Carmen. Who is the
singer? (2)

BELOW: 21. For more than two
decades, this tenor owned the role
for which he is costumed here.
Kindly identify the artist and the
opera. (2)

RIGHT: 22. Since this artist's very
recent retirement, no one has come
forward to replace her in her repertoire. One lives in hope…Who
is she? Whom is she portraying
here? (3)

LEFT: 23. If this photo tells a story, it is that great artists travel in threes. Who are they? (1)

RIGHT: 24. Although the 18th and 19th centuries provide this diva with most of her roles, she has, on occasion, sung something more contemporary. Identify this gifted native of Pennsylvania. (2)

25. Luciano Pavarotti is seen here in a role which he premiered on the stage of the Metropolitan Opera. Name the role, opera, and the year the Met gave its premiere. (3)

RIGHT: 26. Although the artist is shown here in a melancholy mood, the opera being performed is comic and charming. Who is the soprano, and what opera is being done? (2)

ABOVE: 27. These three smiling individuals have each commanded attention from the stage of New York's Metropolitan Opera, albeit in different capacities. Identify each person and describe his or her function at the Met. What occasion brought them together for this photo? (3)

RIGHT: 28. Charming, affable, and wholesome, this singer still manages to portray a horde of evil, despicable villains, including the one pictured here. Identify the singer, and the opera and role in which he appears here. (3)

LEFT: 29. This couple often appear together. Name them, and the opera and roles they are singing. (1)

BELOW: 30. Still another Carmen who hasn't spent a great deal of time in Spain. Name her, if you will. (3)

LEFT: 31. He was the first, and hardly the last, to feel the sting of Rudolf Bing at the Met. Name this all-time great tenor, and list five roles with which he was associated. (2)

32. Some people called her "La Stupenda." Judging from this picture, she might have been called "La Serena" too. Now, they call this lady a dame. Who is she? (1)

33. West Virginia's gift to Mozart. Samuel Barber gave her a couple of gifts, too. Who is she, and what were Barber's "presents" to her? (3)

RIGHT: 34. Just a few of the roles that these tenors shared over the years were Werther, Alfredo, Edgardo, and Boito's Faust. Who are they? (2)

ABOVE: 35. This gentleman could often be found at La Scala or at the Chicago Lyric. His Met career, however, consisted of a one-night stand. Who is he, and for what role is he dressed? (3)

RIGHT: 36. Wherever she sang, the lady on the right always made the sun shine at night. The role she is costumed for here was not one that she sang often. Name the lady, and the role. (3)

BELOW: 38. All we are going to tell you about the character shown here is that she is not the Girl of the Golden West! Identify the artist, and name the character she is singing in this 1995 photograph. (3)

ABOVE: 37. The character shown here rarely smiles. The artist shown here rarely smiled (in public) either. Name the singer and the character. (3)

39. This was a signature role of the lady seen here, and one that is preserved on a memorable recording. Give us the facts, please! (1)

40. Even grand dames were young once. Please identify this very special diva. (4)

LEFT: 41. Why is the lady smiling? If you sang at the Metropolitan Opera for more than forty years, you'd be smiling, too. Who is she? (2)

RIGHT: 42. Don't you love backstage visitors? If they greet you in Parma, you must be doing something right! Name the actual occupant of the dressing room, and this most welcome visitor. Guess what opera had been performed? (2)

43. (By popular demand!) What is the name of Madame Tebaldi's little poodle? (3)

44. What is the name of Madame Tebaldi's not-so-little fan? (4)

THE *Answers*

❈ ❈ ❈

I

The Operas and Their Composers

1. AMERICAN OPERA

1. Gian Carlo Menotti was born in Italy but became an American citizen and currently resides in Scotland. Menotti's *Amahl and the Night Visitors*, commissioned by the National Broadcasting Company, was the first opera to have its inaugural performance on television.

2. Callas declined the invitation to sing the title role in Samuel Barber's *Vanessa*. The honor was given to Eleanor Steber after Sena Jurinac, who had agreed to sing the role, canceled a few weeks before the January 15, 1958, premiere. Miss Steber enjoyed one of the greatest successes of her long and notable career.

3. Sills starred in the New York City Opera premiere and many subsequent revivals of Douglas Moore's *The Ballad of Baby Doe* based on a true story: the love affair of one-time silver magnate Horace Tabor, and the money-chasing Baby Doe. Perceived by many as being merely a fortune hunter, Baby Doe, who survived into the 1930s, was truly devoted to Tabor, nursed him through his final illness and, after his death, lost touch with reality in an almost *bel canto*-esque way.

4. Blitzstein's opera in progress was based on the case of Sacco and Vanzetti.

5. Beeson's *Lizzie Borden* does not, unfortunately, feature a chorus of "Lizzie Borden took an axe . . ."

6. Miller's *The Crucible* was adapted into a melodious and dramatically powerful opera by Robert Ward.

7. The work, of course, is *Porgy and Bess*. George Gershwin composed the music, while the libretto was written by Ira

Gershwin and DuBose Hayward. Three stars of the original production were Todd Duncan (Porgy), Anne Brown (Bess), and John W. Bubbles (Sportin' Life). In 1952, soprano Leontyne Price received international acclaim in a revival of the work, in which she sang Bess opposite the Porgy of William Warfield (whom she subsequently married and divorced). The production played on Broadway and toured Europe and the Soviet Union. *Porgy and Bess* had its Metropolitan Opera premiere in 1985.

8. Hanson's opera, now largely forgotten, is *Merry Mount.*

9. Traubel debuted in the May 2, 1937, premiere of *The Man Without a Country,* composed by Walter Damrosch, based on the story by E. E. Hale.

10. Eugene O'Neill's *Mourning Becomes Electra* was the basis for Marvin David Levy's 1967 opera of the same name. Its world premiere as the second American opera to be created during the Met's inaugural season at Lincoln Center served as the vehicle for Evelyn Lear's Met debut.

11. Powers sang Madame Flora (also called Baba) in *The Medium* by Menotti.

12. A crucial tenor-soprano duet, accompanied by the IRT, is found in Menotti's *The Saint of Bleecker Street.*

13. Gertrude Stein's *The Mother of Us All* was set to music by Virgil Thomson. The "Mother" in question is Susan B. Anthony.

14. *Susannah,* by Carlisle Floyd, is a version of the story of *Susannah and the Elders,* set in the rural South. It was first performed at Florida State University, Tallahassee, in 1955. Phyllis Curtin (Susannah) and Norman Treigle (Olin Blitch) were the two stars of the New York City Opera's production in 1957. The opera's first commercial recording was made in France in 1994.

15. *Miss Havisham's Fire,* by Dominick Argento, is based on material taken from *Great Expectations. A Christmas Carol,* by Gregory Sandow, is adapted from Dickens's perennial Yuletide favorite.

16. The opera is *The Voyage.* It had its world premiere at the

Metropolitan Opera on October 12, 1992—the 500th anniversary of the day Columbus arrived on the shores of what for him was the New World.

17. *The Tender Land* is Copland's only opera.

18. Marc Blitzstein's *Regina* is based on Lillian Hellman's *The Little Foxes*. The role of Regina was created in the opera by Jane Pickens. Soprano Brenda Lewis created the role of Birdie, Regina's unhappy sister-in-law, in the original production of the opera on Broadway. Miss Lewis subsequently sang the title role in the New York City Opera production that was recorded by Columbia.

19. Tibbett sang Emperor Jones in Louis Gruenberg's opera based on the Eugene O'Neill play, and the title role in Deems Taylor's *Peter Ibbetson*.

20. William Hoffman.

21. *Le Nozze di Figaro* is closely related to *The Ghosts of Versailles*, which is partially based on the third play in Beaumarchais's Figaro trilogy, *La Mère Coupable*.

22. Teresa Stratas and Marilyn Horne scored major triumphs in *Ghosts*.

23. The opera is *Summer and Smoke*, based on Tennessee Williams's play of that name. Alma, unforgettably etched on stage and screen by Geraldine Page, was sung by Mary Beth Piel at the New York City Opera.

24. The work is *Sweeney Todd*. The role is that of Mrs. Lovett.

2. ENGLISH OPERA

1. Henry Purcell is considered the first English composer of opera. His two best-known operas are *Dido and Aeneas* and *The Fairy Queen*. A third Purcell opera is *King Arthur*.

2. Britten's *The Turn of the Screw* is based upon Henry James's novel of the same name.

3. Paul Bunyan.

4. *The Midsummer Marriage.*

5. Thea Musgrave is Britain's best-known living woman com-

poser. Two of her operas are *Mary, Queen of Scots* and *A Christmas Carol.*

6. The Sadler's Wells Opera metamorphosed into the English National Opera.

7. The Welsh National Opera.

8. Sir Peter Pears.

9. One learns in that opera's prologue that Grimes's first apprentice died of dehydration when Grimes's fishing boat was stalled in a becalmed sea.

10. Theodor Uppman.

11. The Royal Ballet.

12. The English National Opera.

13. George Frederic Handel.

14. Benjamin Britten composed *Gloriana* for Her Majesty's coronation. The opera deals with the new queen's namesake, Elizabeth I.

15. South-African-born Marie Collier replaced Callas as Tosca, an assignment that boosted her career, which was sadly cut short by Collier's death in 1971.

16. Shuard was a celebrated Turandot.

17. 2. Margaret Price has not, as of 1996, achieved "Damehood."

18. Tadzio, the young boy to whom the opera's protagonist is fatally attracted, is a mute role played by a dancer.

19. The London Coliseum.

20. Francesco Paolo Tosti and Franco Leoni were Italian composers living in London at the turn of this century. Leoni's best known opera was *L'Oracolo*, once a vehicle for Antonio Scotti and later recorded by Tito Gobbi and Joan Sutherland. Leoni's other operas, now quite forgotten, include *Raggio di Luna, Rip van Winkle, Ib and Little Cristina, Trigana, Francesca da Rimini,* and *La Terra del Sogno.*

21. Alberto Remedios.

22. Bryn Terfel.

23. Britten composed the title role in *Peter Grimes*, Vere in *Billy Budd*, Aschenbach in *Death in Venice*, and Quint in *The Turn of the Screw* for Peter Pears.

24. Glyndebourne Festival.

25. a. Frederick Delius
     b. Ralph Vaughn Williams
     c. William Walton
     d. Benjamin Britten
26. *A Village Romeo and Juliet.*

3. FRENCH OPERA

1. Two of Thomas's operas are *Mignon* and *Hamlet.*
2. Verdi composed *Les Vêpres Siciliennes* and *Don Carlos* for the Paris Opera. He borrowed much of the music from *I Lombardi* and reset it to a new libretto entitled *Jérusalem* that was first produced at the Paris Opéra. This stepchild among Verdi's operas was refitted into an Italian version, *Gerusalemme.* Neither the French nor the Italian edition of this work has attained much popularity.
3. The librettists for *Carmen* were Henri Meilhac and Ludovic Halévy. They based their work upon the novella by Prosper Mérimée.
4. Le Théâtre des Italiens.
5. Poulenc's *Dialogues des Carmélites,* Massenet's *Thérèse,* Giordano's *Andrea Chénier,* and John Eaton's recent American opera *Danton and Robespierre.*
6. The first Mélisande was Mary Garden.
7. a. Zuniga, in Bizet's *Carmen,* is the officer who is one of Don José's principal rivals for Carmen's affection.
    b. Spalanzani, in Offenbach's *Les Contes d'Hoffmann,* is the inventor whose creation, Olympia, captures Hoffmann's heart.
    c. Philine, in Thomas's *Mignon,* is the flighty actress who is not terribly kind to the heroine.
    d. Siebel, in Gounod's *Faust,* is the youth who adores Marguérite.
    e. Blanche is the heroine of Poulenc's *Dialogues des Carmélites.*

    f. Charlotte is the already promised object of Werther's melancholy passion in Massenet's *Werther*.

    g. De Brétigny is the officer who becomes Manon's protector after Des Grieux has been spirited away in Massenet's *Manon*.

    h. Schlémil is the unfortunate admirer of Giulietta in *Les Contes d'Hoffmann*. He loses his shadow to Giulietta and his life in a duel with Hoffmann.

    i. Mercédès is Carmen's fortune-telling friend in Bizet's *Carmen*.

    j. Rachel is the foster daughter of Eléazar in Halévy's *La Juive*.

    k. Leïla is the heroine of Bizet's opera *Les Pêcheurs de Perles*.

    l. Cassandre is the prophetess daughter of the Trojan King Priam in Berlioz's *Les Troyens*.

    m. Athanaël is the sex-crazed monk who attempts to reform a courtesan in Massenet's *Thaïs*.

    n. Abimelech is the Hebrew-hater whom Samson kills early on in Saint-Saëns's *Samson et Dalila*.

    o. Nicklausse is Hoffmann's devoted companion in Offenbach's *Les Contes d'Hoffmann*.

8. *Louise*, and its sequel, *Julien*.

9. Camille Saint-Saëns composed *Henri VIII*.

10. The world premiere took place at La Scala, Milan, in January 1957.

11. Sibyl Sanderson.

12. Aix-en-Provence and Orange.

13. Debussy was working on *La Chute de la Maison Usher*. The long-lost manuscript was given its first performance in 1979 at the Juilliard School of Music.

14. *La Périchole*, *La Vie Parisienne*, and *La Grande-Duchesse de Gérolstein*.

15. *Le Coq d'Or* is a Russian opera by Nikolai Rimsky-Korsakov. The other operas are, respectively, the work of Édouard Lalo, Giacomo Meyerbeer, and Jules Massenet.

16. Wilfred Pelletier was a renowned Canadian conductor.

17. The old Comique is now known as the Salle Favart.

18. Hoffmann's loves are: Olympia, the doll; Giulietta, the courtesan; Antonia, the young girl; and Stella, the prima donna.

19. a. Sung by the title character in Massenet's *Werther.*

    b. Sung by Olympia in Offenbach's *Les Contes d'Hoffmann.*

    c. Sung by the newly blinded Samson in Saint-Saëns's *Samson et Dalila.*

    d. Sung by Micaela in Bizet's *Carmen.*

    e. Sung by the title character in Thomas's *Mignon.*

    f. Sung by Marguérite in Gounod's *Faust.*

    g. Sung by Valentin in Gounod's *Faust.*

    h. Sung by Chimène in Massenet's *Le Cid.*

    i. Sung by Rodrigue in Massenet's *Le Cid.*

    j. Sung by the title character in Massenet's *Cendrillon.*

    k. Sung by Marguérite in Berlioz's *La Damnation de Faust.*

    l. Sung by the title character in Rossini's *Guillaume Tell.*

    m. Sung by Des Grieux in Massenet's *Manon.*

    n. Sung by the title character in Offenbach's comic opera *La Périchole.*

    o. This is otherwise known as Lakmé's "Bell Song" in Léo Delibes's *Lakmé.*

20. *Les Martyrs* is a French opera by Donizetti. Its Italian version, *Poliuto,* was a 1960 La Scala vehicle for Maria Callas, Franco Corelli, and Ettore Bastianini.

21. The new home is known as the Opéra-Bastille, a spanking-new, rather ugly auditorium on the site of the pre-Revolutionary prison. A branch of Fouquet's has opened near the Bastille, and the surrounding neighborhood is picturesque, if hardly as elegant as the Boulevard des Italiens. The "old" Paris Opéra, known as the Palais Garnier, is the present home of the Paris Opera Ballet. Rumors are flying that the two companies will switch home bases, bringing Paris opera back where it belongs.

22. James Conlon.

23. The duet is "Dôme épais" from Delibes's *Lakmé.* The piece is sung by Lakmé (soprano) and her confidante, Mallika. British Airways borrowed the duet for its ad campaign in the 1990s.

24. The Opéra Châtelet performs at the hoary Théâtre de Châtelet.
25. Denise Duval.

4. GERMAN OPERA

1. Two of Lortzing's operas are *Zar und Zimmermann* and *Der Wildschütz*. Another is *Undine*.
2. Otto Nicolai composed this opera, based on Shakespeare's *The Merry Wives of Windsor*.
3. *Margarete* is the German title for Frenchman Charles Gounod's *Faust*. This opera has always been popular in Germany, but Germans took exception to the excessively sentimental and unintellectual qualities of the adaptations and therefore renamed the opera after Faust's unlucky mistress in order to distinguish it from Goethe's play.
4. Beethoven's *Fidelio* had its premiere at Vienna's Theater an der Wien on November 20, 1805.
5. Ernestine Schumann-Heink's supposed immolation took place at the Metropolitan Opera.
6. Georg Büchner wrote the play *Woyzeck*. The spelling of Berg's opera is different because of a typographical error in his edition of the play.
7. Wozzeck's tormentors are the Captain, the Doctor, and the Drum Major. The Captain degrades and badgers Wozzeck, the Doctor subjects him to weird experiments, and the Drum Major not only steals Marie, Wozzeck's common-law wife, from him, but brutally attacks the poor man as well.
8. *Martha*. Its popular tenor aria is best known in its Italian translation, "M'appari tutt'amor," as it was recorded by Enrico Caruso.
9. Max and Agathe are the lovers in Carl Maria von Weber's *Der Freischütz*.
10. This aria is from Carl Maria von Weber's *Oberon*. More commonly known as "Ocean, thou mighty monster," Maria Cal-

las's EMI rendition of this piece is the only aria she recorded in English.

11. Friedrich Cerha, a musicologist and expert in Berg's music, completed the third act of *Lulu.*

12. Berg's widow claimed that Berg had communicated with her from beyond the grave. In his visits, the composer allegedly told his wife not to allow anyone to tamper with his notes. Frau Berg's death made her objections academic, and Cerha reported no visitations from ghosts, friendly or otherwise, during his work on Berg's score.

13. The completed *Lulu* premiered at the Paris Opéra in February 1979. Pierre Boulez conducted, and Teresa Stratas sang Lulu.

14. Sir Rudolf Bing, General Manager of the Metropolitan Opera from 1950 to 1972, performed the role of the whip-cracking trainer of the young lord in the 1973 production.

15. The opera is *Lear,* the composer is Aribert Reimann, and the artist who created the title role is Dietrich Fischer-Dieskau.

16. The Deutsche Oper, the Staatsoper and the Komische Oper.

17. Siegfried Wagner was the composer of such operas as *Schwarzschwanenreich, Die Bärenhäuter,* and *Banadietrich.*

18. 1. Kienzl
    2. Weber
    3. Von Einem
    4. Korngold
    5. Krenek

5. ITALIAN OPERA

1. *Il Barbiere di Siviglia* and *L'Italiana in Algeri.*
2. *Il Duca d'Alba.*
3. Mayr was Donizetti's mentor.
4. Ponchielli (composer of *La Gioconda*) was the teacher of Giacomo Puccini.
5. The elder Verdi ran a humble inn and general store in the village of Le Roncole.

6. Catalani's two best-known operas are *La Wally* (for whose heroine Toscanini named a daughter) and *Loreley*.

7. *Il Giuramento* shares its source, Victor Hugo's *Angelo, Tyran de Padoue*, with Ponchielli's *La Gioconda*.

8. Riccardo Zandonai's *Francesca da Rimini*.

9. The composer was Fr. Licinio Refice, the opera was *Cecilia*, and the diva was Claudia Muzio.

10. a. Arrigo Boito's *Mefistofele*, sung by Faust.
    b. Giuseppe Verdi's *Luisa Miller*, sung by Rodolfo.
    c. Pietro Mascagni's *L'Amico Fritz*, sung by Suzel.
    d. Amilcare Ponchielli's *La Gioconda*, sung by La Cieca.
    e. Mascagni's *Cavalleria Rusticana*, sung by Alfio.
    f. Gaetano Donizetti's *L'Elisir d'Amore*, sung by Nemorino.
    g. Vincenzo Bellini's *La Sonnambula*, sung by Amina.
    h. Umberto Giordano's *Andrea Chénier*, sung by Carlo Gérard.
    i. Gioacchino Rossini's *L'Italiana in Algeri*, sung by Isabella.
    j. Riccardo Zandonai's *Francesca da Rimini*, sung by Francesca.

11. The censors rejected *Un Ballo in Maschera* as it originally stood because it involved the assassination of a European monarch.

12. a. Giordano's *Andrea Chénier*
    b. Verdi's *Macbeth*
    c. Mascagni's *Cavalleria Rusticana*
    d. Bellini's *Norma*
    e. Verdi's *Nabucco* (This, the chorus of Hebrew slaves, is practically the second national anthem of Italy.)

13. a. Gaetano Donizetti
    b. Umberto Giordano
    c. Giuseppe Verdi
    d. Donizetti
    e. Pietro Mascagni
    f. Riccardo Zandonai
    g. Vincenzo Bellini
    h. Amilcare Ponchielli
    i. Both Mascagni and Arrigo Boito wrote operas based on the exploits of the Emperor Nero of Rome.

j. Wolfgang Amadeus Mozart

k. Giacomo Puccini

l. Gioacchino Rossini

m. Joseph Haydn

n. Mascagni

o. Gian Carlo Menotti (This opera was composed to an Italian libretto before Menotti immigrated to the United States.)

p. Verdi

q. Antonio Vivaldi

14. Shakespeare's *King Lear.*

15. Rome's Teatro dell'Opera.

16. The Verdi d'Oro.

17. d. *Aida* had its world premiere in Cairo.

18. The Baths of Caracalla.

19. La Scala.

20. Antonio Ghiringhelli.

21. a. Venice

b. Naples

c. Palermo

22. La Scala.

23. Casa Ricordi.

24. Callas and Di Stefano codirected a production of Verdi's *I Vespri Siciliani* at Turin's rebuilt Teatro Regio.

25. Parma.

6. RUSSIAN OPERA

1. Mussorgsky wrote the libretto and the music for *Boris Godunov.*

2. Nikolai Rimsky-Korsakov and Dmitri Shostakovich each reorchestrated *Boris Godunov.* For many years Rimsky-Korsakov's version was the most frequently performed, as he brightened the austere orchestral palette of the original version. Shostakovich's edition of *Boris* is occasionally performed. In 1974 the Metropolitan began performing *Boris* in the four-act edi-

tion orchestrated by the composer. Many other companies are now using this version, too. In 1994–95 the Chicago Lyric Opera presented the first version of *Boris,* which does not have the "Polish" act with the character of Marina. Even the Russian companies are now beginning to perform Mussorgsky's own orchestration.

3. Both operas are based on poems by Pushkin.

4. a. The show is *Kismet.*
   b. *Kismet's* score was taken, in large part, from the Polovtsian Dances.
   c. The Broadway team of Robert Wright and George Forrest created *Kismet.*
   d. The hit song is "Stranger in Paradise."
   e. Richard Kiley, better known for his work in *Man of La Mancha,* sang "Stranger" in the original Broadway production, but Tony Bennett made the hit record.

5. Tatyana, the sensitive young heroine of *Eugene Onegin,* sends a declaration of love to Onegin, whom she has only just met. The cynical Onegin rejects Tatyana's proffered love. Years later, at a ball in Moscow, Onegin again meets Tatyana, now married to Prince Gremin. Onegin suddenly realizes that he has always loved Tatyana. Singing in the same melody as that of Tatyana's Letter Scene, he begs her to leave Gremin. Tatyana acknowledges her love for Onegin but refuses to desert her husband, leaving Onegin in despair.

6. *War and Peace's* American premiere took place not in an opera house but on television as part of the old NBC Opera Company series.

7. The Bolshoi's U.S. debut, at the Metropolitan Opera House in June 1975, was a performance of *Boris Godunov.* Evgeni Nesterenko sang Boris, Vladimir Atlantov sang Dmitri, and Elena Obraztsova sang Marina.

8. Bolshoi soprano Galina Vishnevskaya was the first Soviet soprano to appear at the Met. She made her debut as Aida in 1960, singing that role and the title role in *Madama Butterfly* in Russian while her colleagues sang in Italian. In 1975, after Vishnevskaya and her husband, Mstislav Rostropovich, had

left the Soviet Union, the soprano returned to the Met for one performance of *Tosca*, this time singing in Italian.

9. The first version of *Boris Godunov* had no love interest and no sizable role for a woman. Mussorgsky amended this by adding the "Polish act," in which the pretender Dmitri dallies with a Polish princess, Marina, whom the Jesuits have persuaded to seduce Dmitri into bringing Roman Catholicism to Russia. The role of Marina contains a solo aria, a duet with a bass, Rangoni (a Jesuit priest), and a duet with the leading tenor, Dmitri.

10. Dostoevsky's *The Gambler.*

11. *The Czarevitch* is a Viennese operetta by Franz Lehár. *The Czar's Bride* is an opera by Rimsky-Korsakov; *A Life for the Czar* is an opera by Mikhail Glinka.

12. Lisa's first suitor is the baritone Prince Yeletsky, who, unlike Hermann, has a beautiful and romantic aria to sing.

13. a. Dmitri Hvorostovsky is a young baritone from Siberia who has been successful around the world in both Russian and Italian operatic roles, especially Eugene Onegin, Yeletsky, and Giorgio Germont.

   b. Irina Archipova is an outstanding veteran mezzo-soprano who sang with the Bolshoi and Kirov Operas, and made guest appearances in major theaters throughout Europe and America. Her Met debut was in March 1997, as Filipyevna in *Eugene Onegin.*

   c. Tamara Milashkina is a soprano who was active with the Bolshoi in the 1960s and 1970s, well known for her Tchaikovsky heroines.

   d. Fyodor Chaliapin was the charismatic Russian bass who, singing during the first three decades of the twentieth century, popularized the opera *Boris Godunov* in Europe and America. He was also famous for his Mephisto and Don Quichotte.

   e. Maria Guleghina is a Russian soprano who has been increasingly active in the West in recent years. Her U.S. roles have included Tosca and Maddalena.

14. a. Tchaikovsky
    b. Mussorgsky

   c. Glinka
   d. Rachmaninoff
   e. Rimsky-Korsakov
15. The Kirov Opera, formerly the Mariensky Opera, has resumed its original identity. It is situated in Leningrad, which is once again known as St. Petersburg.

7. *AIDA*

1. Phthà.
2. Amneris tells Aida that Radames has been killed in the war between Egypt and Ethiopia. When Aida becomes distressed, Amneris cries out that she has been lying, and Radames is really alive. Aida is overjoyed, and Amneris immediately pounces upon her rival for Radames' heart.
3. Teresa Stolz was the first Aida. Although the truth has never been established, Stolz is believed to have been Verdi's mistress for many years, in spite of his apparent devotion to his wife, Giuseppina Strepponi.
4. *Aida* originally began with a full overture. While preparing the Italian premiere of the opera, Verdi discarded that piece in favor of the brief prelude heard ever since. Recordings of the overture by Toscanini and Claudio Abbado exist.
5. In the score of *Aida*, Verdi instructs the tenor to sing the high B-flat that ends the aria *ppp* or very, very softly. Since many tenors won't and most can't take that note on anything less than a *fortissimo*, Verdi sanctioned that change, provided that the tenor repeat the last three words, "vicino al sol," one octave lower, quietly. Richard Tucker opted for the alternate ending on the famous Toscanini recording of the opera. More recently, Plácido Domingo has performed this version, too.
6. Sophia Loren acted the part of Aida, while Renata Tebaldi did the singing.
7. Radames plans to take his men through the gorge of Napata (in Italian, Le gole di Nápata).
8. The cast of the RCA video and recording included Herva Nelli

(Aida), Eva Gustavson (Amneris), Richard Tucker (Radames), Giuseppe Valdengo (Amonasro), and Teresa Stich-Randall (the Priestess).

9. Callas, singing Aida in 1951, interpolated a high E-flat at the very end of the Triumphal Scene. The audience went wild. Legend has it that Callas sang the high note as a way of annoying tenor Kurt Baum, who sang Radames. Baum, it is said, had been unkind to Maria. In any event, the audience was thrilled. Reengaged for *Aida* the following year, Callas again sang the high E-flat, this time joined by tenor Mario del Monaco. Recordings of both performances survive.

10. Antonio Ghislanzoni.

11. Leontyne Price.

12. Radames accuses Amneris of having killed Aida, one of the few nasty things that the Egyptian princess hasn't done!

8. *CARMEN*

1. A letter, a little money to add to his pay, "and yet another thing worth more than money and which a good son will surely value higher," a kiss given to Micaela by José's mother to be passed on to him.

2. The women quarrel after Carmen insults her colleague, who has recently acquired a donkey. Carmen tells the woman that she should have bought a broom to ride on instead.

3. Manuelita.

4. *Les Pêcheurs de Perles* was composed first, in 1863. *Carmen*, composed in 1875, turned out to be Bizet's final work, as he died three months after the opera's first performance.

5. The directors of the Opéra-Comique were afraid that their middle-class subscribers would be offended by a heroine who not only got herself murdered but actually smoked on stage. It was these timid souls who insisted on the invention of Micaela, the sweet, virtuous hometown sweetheart of Don José, to act as a foil to the unwholesome Carmen.

6. El Dancairo is the boss. In the Opéra-Comique version of

Carmen he is constantly reprimanding his loquacious subordinate, El Remendado.

7. Ernest Guiraud, the New Orleans-born friend of Bizet, composed music for the recitatives that replaced *Carmen*'s spoken dialogue when the work was performed at the Vienna opera. The recitatives truncated the spoken words but transformed *Carmen* into a "grand opera." For the first century following *Carmen*'s appearance, the recitatives were part of the standard version of the opera, but recently major international theaters have restored the original spoken dialogue.

8. Escamillo lets José live, saying that his business is to slaughter beef, not men. José repays his generosity by attacking Escamillo after he has turned his back.

9. Early critics claimed Bizet had imitated Wagner in *Carmen*, mentioning use of the "fate motif" that punctuates Carmen's various adventures.

10. Geraldine Farrar, the most celebrated Carmen of the first two decades of this century, first sang the role of Micaela.

11. Tyrone Guthrie.

12. De los Angeles sang *Carmen* with the New Jersey State Opera and the New York City Opera.

13. b. Leonard Warren.

14. Micaela is searching for Don José to bring him the news that his mother is dying and wishes to see and forgive him before she breathes her last.

15. First, it was a silent film and thus depended upon Farrar's beauty and abilities as an actress for her to score her points. Second, the film was based upon Mérimée's novella, not the opera, because the Bizet work was still under copyright. Therefore, many details of the plot are quite different from the story known by opera fans.

9. *CAVALLERIA RUSTICANA*

1. Santuzza has been excommunicated because of her affair with Turiddu and because, one supposes, she has become pregnant with Turiddu's baby.

2. Gemma Bellincioni.
3. Turiddu is once again in love with his old flame, Lola, who, unfortunately for all concerned, has become the wife of Alfio, the village carter.
4. Alfio says that he is afraid that the beverage would turn to poison in his breast.
5. Turiddu asks Lucia to bless him, as she did when he went off to be a soldier. Then he begs his mother to pray for him. Finally, he makes her promise that, in case he should not return, she will be like a mother to Santuzza.
6. "A te, la mala Pasqua, spergiuro!" (An evil Easter to you, betrayer!) As Turiddu is murdered by Alfio a short time later, Santuzza's curse is fulfilled in no uncertain terms!
7. Zinka Milanov.
8. Jussi Bjoerling recorded the role of Turiddu in both instances.
9. Giovanni Verga.
10. Grace Bumbry and Franco Corelli.

10. *LES CONTES D'HOFFMANN*

1. The opera is based on short stories by E. T. A. Hoffmann.
2. The libretto was written by Michel Carré and Jules Barbier, who based their work on their successful stage adaptation of Hoffmann's tales.
3. The Paris Opéra-Comique.
4. The villains are Lindorf, Coppélius, Dapertutto, and Dr. Miracle.
5. a. Dapertutto
   b. Coppélius
   c. Giulietta and Nicklausse
   d. Hoffmann
   e. Antonia
6. Giulietta magically ensnares Schlémil's shadow.
7. Hoffmann, as he himself puts it, takes from Schlémil the key to Giulietta's house, and Schlémil's life.
8. Giulietta snatches Hoffmann's reflection.

9. Antonia.
10. Spalanzani.
11. Giulietta, in this version, dies after drinking poison intended for Hoffmann. This ending for the scene is taken from the play mentioned in Question #2.
12. Fritz Oeser.
13. Richard Tucker sang Hoffmann; Canadian-born George London sang the four villains; Roberta Peters sang Olympia; Risë Stevens sang Giulietta; Lucine Amara sang Antonia. Pierre Monteux conducted. Note: At the broadcast performance used on the recording, London was replaced by French baritone Martial Singher.
14. Domingo has recorded Hoffmann twice. Joan Sutherland sings all four heroines in Domingo's Decca/London set. In the performance he recorded for DG, the soprano who sings each heroine is Edita Gruberova.
15. a. Jon Vickers.

11. *DON GIOVANNI*

1. Il Dissoluto Punito.
2. Lorenzo da Ponte.
3. Leporello is trying to keep the coast clear while Don Giovanni attempts to rape Donna Anna.
4. Donna Elvira.
5. a. Zerlina
   b. Don Ottavio
   c. Donna Anna
   d. Don Giovanni and Zerlina
   e. Masetto
6. The minuet.
7. Donna Anna, Don Ottavio, and Donna Elvira.
8. d. Hermann Prey.
9. Price recorded Donna Elvira on a LP set released first by RCA and subsequently by Decca/London. Birgit Nilsson sings

Donna Anna on that recording. The CD version was issued in 1996.

10. Don Giovanni refuses the command of the Statue of the Commendatore to repent of his licentious ways.

11. Donna Anna.

12. Callas recorded Donna Anna's "Non mi dir" as a "test" for EMI. It was released after her death. In the early 1960s, Callas recorded Donna Elvira's "Mi tradi."

12. *L'ELISIR D'AMORE*

1. The story of Tristan and Isolde.

2. "Quanto è bella, quanto è cara."

3. Belcore compares himself to Paris, who won the heart of Helen of Troy in the Greek myth.

4. Enrico Caruso.

5. The price is a single scudo.

6. Nemorino has partaken of Dr. Dulcamara's phony elixir of love. Dulcamara, in order to make a clean getaway, has warned Nemorino that the magic potion will not work until twenty-four hours have passed. Thus, when Belcore and Adina decide to marry the next day, the gullible Nemorino doesn't become alarmed. However, when Adina agrees to marry the sergeant that evening, poor Nemorino becomes frightened that Adina will first marry Belcore and then discover the next day that she loves Nemorino.

7. The comic duet is "La Nina Gondoliera e il Senator Tredenti."

8. a. Jussi Bjoerling.

9. The girls pay court to Nemorino because they have heard that the simple boy has just inherited a fortune from his late uncle. No one has informed Nemorino of this good news, so he attributes his sudden popularity to the effects of the elixir that he has been drinking in copious quantities.

10. Nemorino.

11. "Una furtiva lagrima" is followed by Adina's aria "Prendi, per me sei libero."

12. Sutherland's Adina is loved by Luciano Pavarotti's Nemorino. Freni sang opposite Nicolai Gedda. The lovely Carteri is courted by Luigi Alva.

13. d. Ezio Pinza.

13. *FAUST*

1. Gounod added Valentin's aria in the second act for the first London performance of *Faust*. The French text begins with the words "Avant de quitter ces lieux/sol natal de mes aïeux," but the original, English text began: "Even the bravest heart may swell/ at the moment of farewell . . ."

2. Faust wants pleasure, youth, and young women.

3. a. Méphistophélès
   b. Marguérite
   c. Faust
   d. The chorus (This is the Soldiers' Chorus.)
   e. Marguérite

4. The brothers De Reszke often shared the stage in *Faust*. Tenor Jean sang the title role, bass Édouard was Mephisto.

5. The Metropolitan Opera.

6. Peter Brook, in 1953. Mephisto sported a top hat and a red-lined cape.

7. Dame Marthe Schwerlein.

8. Victoria de los Angeles, Nicolai Gedda, and Boris Christoff recorded two *Fausts*, each time conducted by André Cluytens. Aside from some changes in the supporting cast, the main difference between the two sets is that the first, released by RCA, was recorded monaurally, and the second, released by EMI (after a complicated corporate split from RCA), was recorded in stereophonic sound.

9. The *Faust* ballet music has occasionally been attributed to Franz Liszt.

10. Geraldine Farrar and Marcel Journet.
11. c. Jussi Bjoerling.
12. Boris Christoff, Nicolai Ghiaurov, Cesare Siepi, Norman Treigle, Samuel Ramey, Ezio Pinza, and Feodor Chaliapin, among others, have been admired in both diabolical roles.
13. Marguérite, Faust, and Méphistophélès.
14. Renata Tebaldi, Mirella Freni, Montserrat Caballé, and Magda Olivero have sung both Marguérite and Margherita.
15. The first scene of Act IV is often cut. In this scene, Marguérite, abandoned by Faust and carrying his child, sits forlornly at her spinning wheel as her former friends are heard offstage, mocking her. The ever-faithful Siebel joins Marguérite after her aria, "Il ne reviendrà plus" and pledges his friendship to her. In the next scene, however, Siebel greets the returning Valentin with the news of Marguérite's plight, which makes things even worse.
16. Frank Corsaro. Marguérite was hanged, not escorted to heaven by angels.
17. d. Patrice Munsel.
18. Act II, a.k.a., the Kermesse Scene, ends with a brilliant waltz, a dance that did not exist in medieval times.

14. *MADAMA BUTTERFLY*

1. The short story on which Belasco based his play was written by John Luther Long (1861–1927).
2. Under the terms of Pinkerton's lease, the agreement is to run for 999 years but is cancelable on one month's notice. The latter point is identical to the "escape clause" of Pinkerton's marriage contract.
3. Butterfly shows him a jar of rouge. With an unparalleled show of hypocrisy, Pinkerton registers displeasure, and the compliant bride throws the rouge away.
4. At the moment of Butterfly's first entrance, a solo violin quotes Musetta's Waltz from *La Bohème*. The anti-Puccini claque that had smuggled itself into the theater seized upon this detail as

a reason for one of the many noisy demonstrations that wrecked the first night.

5. This recording, made by RCA but ceded years later to EMI, starred Toti dal Monte as Butterfly and Beniamino Gigli as Pinkerton.

6. Pinkerton promises that he will return to his bride "when the robins return," meaning, one assumes, the following spring. Since three springs have passed before Sharpless visits Butterfly to attempt to break the news of Pinkerton's remarriage and imminent arrival, Butterfly asks him if, in America, the robins nest less frequently than in Japan. Sharpless is embarrassed and teaches Butterfly a new English word when he disclaims all knowledge of ornithology.

7. The opera is set in Nagasaki.

8. First, Puccini divided the two scenes of the original second act into two separate acts. This gave fidgety members of the audience a break. Second, the composer removed an aria in Act I from Pinkerton's role but made amends by adding the show-stopping "Addio, fiorito asil" for the tenor to sing in Act III. Third, Puccini omitted the brief solo role of Butterfly's mother from the first act—the character still appears, but since she has no solo lines to sing, the role is almost always assigned to a chorus member. Fourth, Puccini further shortened the first-act wedding scene by excising a vignette during which Butterfly's Uncle Yakuside gets very drunk. Puccini made many small cuts and changes throughout the opera, especially concerning Pinkerton, who is much more crude and boorish in the original than the later edition of *Madama Butterfly*. Perhaps most important, Puccini created a new main theme for the love duet for Butterfly and Pinkerton, one with a more sumptuous melody than the first version. If you listen closely to the intermezzo played before Act III, you can hear remnants of the original love theme. This change also affects "Butterfly's Entrance" and the "Flower Duet."

Since the first edition of this book, a number of opera companies have experimented with the original version of the opera. I personally prefer the later version. It simply "plays better."

9. The sopranos are Renata Tebaldi, Victoria de los Angeles, Renata Scotto, and Mirella Freni. Tebaldi's two Pinkertons are Giuseppe Campora and Carlo Bergonzi; De los Angeles sings with Giuseppe di Stefano and Jussi Bjoerling; Scotto's pair of Pinkertons are Carlo Bergonzi and Plácido Domingo. Freni sings with Luciano Pavarotti and José Carreras.
10. Butterfly is wooed by the wealthy Prince Yamadori.
11. Enrico Caruso.
12. Butterfly demands that Sharpless leave her house when he urges her to forget Pinkerton and marry her rich suitor, Prince Yamadori.
13. Maria Spacagna, for Vox Records, in 1995.
14. Callas sang Butterfly in Chicago at the Chicago Lyric Opera. Giuseppe di Stefano was Pinkerton that night. After the performance, the diva was served with a subpoena she had been trying to avoid for weeks, concerning a lawsuit by a former agent.
15. Tucker recorded the opera for Columbia and RCA. The sopranos were Eleanor Steber and Leontyne Price, respectively.

15. VERDI'S *OTELLO*

1. Giulio Ricordi.
2. Verdi insisted on the right to withdraw *Otello* from production at La Scala right up through the dress rehearsal.
3. Rossini.
4. Shakespeare's first act is omitted in Boito's libretto for Verdi's *Otello*.
5. a. Otello
   b. Iago
   c. Desdemona
   d. Emilia
6. Act IV.
7. Ramón Vinay.
8. Renata Tebaldi, 1955 and 1958, and Victoria de los Angeles, 1958.
9. The Venetian ambassadors are shocked when Otello, wracked

by jealousy, hurls Desdemona to the ground and curses her.

10. The fact that Cassio is in possession of the handkerchief that Otello had given Desdemona convinces the Moor that his wife has been unfaithful. The credulous Otello has no idea that Iago placed the hankie in Cassio's lodgings.

11. Sergei Leiferkus.

12. Bastianini was replaced by Aldo Protti in Herbert von Karajan's Decca/London recording of *Otello*.

13. Giovanni Martinelli.

14. Callas recorded Desdemona's Willow Song and Ave Maria for EMI but never performed Desdemona on stage or in concert.

15. In Karajan's film, Jon Vickers sang Otello, Mirella Freni portrayed Desdemona, and Peter Glossop was the Iago. Karajan cut the children's serenade to Desdemona in the opera's second act, and cut a lengthy portion of the ensemble that climaxes the third act.

16. In his earlier career as a comprimario tenor at the Metropolitan Opera, McCracken sang the small role of Roderigo.

17. Both Caruso and Bjoerling recorded the duet from Act II, "Sì, pel ciel." Caruso sang the duet with Titta Ruffo, and Bjoerling was partnered by Robert Merrill.

18. Freni sang the first-act love duet at the Met's Centennial Gala in 1983, and the entire, staged third act in the gala celebrating the Met's twenty-fifth season at Lincoln Center, in September 1991. Plácido Domingo sang Otello on both occasions. In the 1991 gala, Justino Díaz sang Iago and James Levine conducted.

19. b. Beverly Sills.

20. Iago.

16. *PAGLIACCI*

1. Originally, Tonio speaks the final line. Once, however, a tenor singing Canio usurped the line, and it has remained a tenor property ever since. However, in his film of *Pagliacci*, Von Karajan gave the line back to Tonio.

2. The famous last line is "La commedia è finita!"
3. Leoncavallo based *Pagliacci* on an actual case tried in the court of the composer's magistrate father.
4. Silvio.
5. Tonio counsels Canio to calm down, predicting (correctly, as it turns out) that Nedda's lover will attend the evening's performance by Canio's troupe and reveal himself.
6. Plácido Domingo.
7. Mario del Monaco was Canio; Ettore Bastianini sang Tonio. Collectors of live operatic performances should seek out this recording.
8. a. Maria Callas.
9. "Si può?" (May I speak?)

17. *DER RING DES NIBELUNGEN*

1. Alberich must renounce love.
2. They are worried because Wotan has promised the goddess Freia to the two giants, Fasolt and Fafner, who have built Valhalla for the gods.
3. Freia's special talent is caring for the tree that produces magic apples that keep the gods eternally youthful. Without Freia and her fruit, the gods will grow ancient immediately.
4. Alberich makes himself invisible by means of the Tarnhelm, a magical cap of loosely woven chain mail that allows its wearer to assume any shape (or lack thereof) that he chooses.
5. Valhalla.
6. In the Solti *Ring*, Flagstad sings Fricka in *Das Rheingold*.
7. Loge helps Wotan trump the unsavory little baritone. Loge wheedles Alberich into transforming himself into a tiny mouse and then the demigod traps him, rendering Alberich powerless. Thus Wotan and Loge wrest the gold away from Alberich.
8. According to the libretto of *Die Walküre*, Fricka travels in a cart drawn by a ram.
9. Siegmund is honored when Brünnhilde describes to him the hero's welcome that will await him in Valhalla, but he refuses

to consider going there unless Sieglinde goes with him, which, as things turn out, is out of the question.

10. Initially, Wotan wants to put Brünnhilde asleep on her rock, to be awakened by the kiss of the first man who happens by. After much pleading from his daughter, Wotan agrees to surround Brünnhilde with magic fire, which only a brave, heroic type could penetrate.

11. Before Brünnhilde leaves Sieglinde, she tells her that she, Sieglinde, will bear Siegmund's child, and Brünnhilde gives her the pieces of Siegmund's sword, Nothung, which was shattered by Wotan and Hunding.

12. Unlike its three sister musical dramas, *Siegfried* has some moments of humor and a happy ending. Siegfried and Brünnhilde live happily ever after until the first act of *Götterdämmerung*.

13. The magic of the blood enables Siegfried to understand the language of the Forest Bird, which leads him to the hidden Tarnhelm and helps him divine the real meaning behind Mime's deceitful words.

14. Siegfried kills Mime because the Forest Bird has told him that the dwarf who has reared him will now try to kill him in order to have the cursed ring for himself.

15. Siegfried learns of Brünnhilde's existence from the Forest Bird.

16. The Wanderer, who appears in *Siegfried*, is actually Wotan, who has come down from Valhalla to enter the human drama that has overtaken the ring, once the plaything of gods, giants, and dwarves.

17. Between *Das Rheingold* and *Siegfried*, or, to be exact, *Das Rheingold* and *Die Walküre*, Wotan and Erda have produced a litter of Valkyries, warrior maidens who serve Wotan & Co.

18. The Norns, daughters of the surprisingly prolific Erda, are spinning the rope of fate. The rope breaks, which means that the world, as the *Ring* characters know it, will soon end.

19. Siegfried's Rhine Journey.

20. Waltraute visits her sister Brünnhilde in a vain attempt to get the ring of the Nibelungen, which, in spite of its jinxed history, Siegfried has given to Brünnhilde as a wedding ring.

21. The *Ring* libretti were sketched backward because Wagner

originally contemplated doing one opera—more or less *Göt-terdämmerung*. Then, mired in mythology, he realized that a first opera, giving background, would be necessary. Hence came the idea for *Der Junge Siegfried*. Ultimately, he conceived the grand tetralogy as we know it today.

22. Wagner wrote his own libretti.

23. Hagen, who has been conspiring evilly throughout *Götterdäm-merung*, has drugged Siegfried into forgetfulness, and has had him marry Hagen's half-sister, Gutrune. Now, as a ruse for gaining possession of the ring, Hagen gives Siegfried a drink that will bring back his memory. Siegfried soon begins expounding upon his love for Brünnhilde, and Hagen stabs him in the back for "treachery."

24. Brünnhilde's horse, which she calls for in order to ride into the flames of Siegfried's pyre at the climax of the Immolation Scene, is called Grane.

25. Five orchestral highlights would include the Entrance of the Gods into Valhalla, the Ride of the Valkyries, Forest Murmers, Siegfried's Rhine Journey, and Siegfried's Funeral March.

26. Andrew Porter, the South African–born musicologist, wrote the excellent new English version of the *Ring*.

27. Fricka is angry at Siegmund because Fricka is the goddess of marriage, and Siegmund has not only broken up Hunding's home, but has also committed incest.

28. Wotan is Siegmund's father.

29. Brünnhilde is a half sister to Siegmund and Sieglinde.

30. Brünnhilde is actually Siegfried's aunt.

31. Her first words are "Heil dir, Sonne" (Hail to thee, O Sun).

32. Seing his very first woman, Siegfried exclaims, "Das ist kein Mann!" (That's *not* a man!)

33. *Götterdämmerung* is the only *Ring* opera that uses a chorus, and an all-male one at that. The men are used in the Act II sequence known as Hagen's Gathering of His Vassals.

34. The "neo-Bayreuth" style of spare, symbolic sets and subdued lighting was developed by Wieland Wagner, a grandson of the composer, who ran the Bayreuth Festival from 1951 until his death in 1966.

35. Birgit Nilsson, Kirsten Flagstad, Régine Crespin, Astrid Varnay, and Helen Traubel all sang Brünnhilde and Sieglinde. Of these five, only Crespin did not go on to sing the *Siegfried* and *Götterdämmerung* Brünnhildes.

36. Helen Traubel, a great singer on anyone's list, was an especially prized Brünnhilde during the war years when Flagstad and various other European artists were unavailable.

37. Pierre Boulez.

38. Von Karajan first staged his own *Ring* at the Salzburg Easter Festival. The Metropolitan Opera bought his concept, but von Karajan personally directed only *Das Rheingold* and *Die Walküre* in New York.

39. Rita Hunter is the British Wagnerian who has sung the *Ring* in two languages. Hunter was Birgit Nilsson's "cover" when the Metropolitan produced *Götterdämmerung* in 1974. Days before the premiere, Nilsson broke her shoulder when, in a freak accident, part of the set collapsed under her during a rehearsal. Nilsson managed the premiere but withdrew from the nationwide broadcast a few days later. Although millions were disappointed by the cancellation, Hunter did a fine job of substituting. In the 1990s, Rita Hunter has sung frequently in Australia.

40. Nilsson and Caballé sang a "joint" *Walküre* at Barcelona's Teatro Liceo. Richard Cassilly was the fortunate tenor.

41. Callas sang Brünnhilde at the Teatro La Fenice, Venice, with Tullio Serafin conducting.

42. Toscanini's soloists in *Walküre*, Act I, scene 3, and the *Die Götterdämmerung* Dawn duet were Helen Traubel and Lauritz Melchior.

43. In the von Karajan *Ring* recording, Dietrich Fischer-Dieskau sings the *Rheingold* Wotan, while Thomas Stewart is heard in *Die Walküre* and as the *Siegfried* Wanderer.

44. Von Karajan's two Brünnhildes are Régine Crespin in *Die Walküre* (interestingly, Crespin doubles as Sieglinde in Solti's *Walküre*), and Helga Dernesch, a onetime Karajan protégée currently a distinguished singer of character roles, in the two subsequent operas.

45. Dame Joan Sutherland may be heard as the Forest Bird in Solti's *Siegfried*.

46. The Met's Brünnhilde in the 1950s was Margaret Harshaw.

47. Astrid Varnay, Swedish-born but reared in the United States, enjoyed a series of triumphs at Bayreuth during the 1950s, including her Brünnhilde under the baton of Hans Knapperts-busch, a performance still available on CD.

48. The curse pronounced on the ring by the dwarf Alberich, who is understandably bitter because Wotan has stolen it from him, is that it will bring death to all who own it until it is returned to the Rhinemaidens.

49. Wilhelm Furtwängler conducted, and Kirsten Flagstad sang Brünnhilde. This is the only complete *Ring* cycle featuring Flagstad that is available to record collectors.

18. *RIGOLETTO*

1. Monterone curses the jester Rigoletto for having mocked him about his daughter's seduction by the Duke of Mantua.

2. Count Ceprano is Rigoletto's neighbor. This becomes important at the end of the first act, when Rigoletto suddenly appears as the Mantuan courtiers are preparing to abduct Gilda, the jester's daughter. They tell Rigoletto that they are planning to kidnap the Countess Ceprano, and he believes them.

3. Sparafucile charges ten scudi to murder a commoner and twenty scudi to bump off a nobleman.

4. These words precede Gilda's second-act aria, "Tutte le feste al tempio."

5. The censors were horrified by several aspects of the libretto for *Rigoletto*. In the opera's original French setting, the libretto depicted a plot to murder a sitting monarch, François I. This was unacceptable to representatives of a much-hated royal government. For this reason the setting was changed to Mantua and François became a fictional duke. Also, the character of Rigoletto, a deformed, malevolent court jester, was considered too raunchy for respectable folks to stomach, even if he did

have a tender, fatherly side. Verdi won on that score, as Rigoletto himself was not altered to please the faint-hearted censors.

6. In Victor Hugo's play, *Le Roi S'Amuse* (on which Verdi based his opera), the jester was named Triboulet. Verdi therefore called him Tribuletto.

7. Marullo.

8. Rigoletto and Gilda are interrupted by the appearance of Count Monterone, on his way to prison. The Count bemoans the fact that his curse on the Duke has not taken effect. Rigoletto, despite the fact that Monterone has cursed him, too, vows to fulfill the curse on the Duke.

9. "La donna è mobile" is sung three times in Act III. The Duke sings it upon his arrival at Sparafucile's inn, then repeats it as he falls asleep waiting for Maddalena to appear in his room. The Duke reprises the aria a final time as he takes leave of Maddalena. Rigoletto, dragging the sack in which he believes the Duke's dead body has been placed toward the river, hears the Duke's voice and realizes that he has been duped.

10. Verdi uses the chorus to wordlessly imitate the wind in the storm that occurs in the last act, as Gilda prepares to enter Sparafucile's inn. She and the audience know that she will be murdered in place of the evil Duke whom she loves.

11. Francesco Maria Piave.

12. After the Duke of Mantua concludes his aria "Parmi veder le lagrime," in which he bemoans Gilda's abduction, he learns that his high-spirited courtiers have brought the girl to his own bedchamber. He then launches into the cabaletta, "Possente amor."

13. This wonderful performance of *Rigoletto* was given at the Metropolitan Opera House.

14. Jonathan Miller staged this travesty of *Rigoletto* for the English National Opera.

15. d. Dobbs, a Metropolitan Gilda of the 1950s, did not record the opera.

16. A handkerchief.

17. When Sutherland sang Gilda at the Met, Sparafucile needed a male assistant costumed similarly to the assassin, to help carry

the sack with Gilda inside it. The two men placed the heavy parcel on the stage floor, where Rigoletto could gloat over it.

19. *DER ROSENKAVALIER*

1. The Marschallin often refers to Octavian as Quinquin, while he calls her Bichette.
2. Ochs auf Lerchenau.
3. Leopold is Ochs's bumptious valet and confidant. Ochs implies to the Marschallin that Leopold is Ochs's illegitimate son. In the Act III farce staged to embarrass Ochs, Annina, pretending that Ochs is her long-lost husband and father of a large brood of urchins, calls him "Leopold."
4. She tries to assuage Octavian's hurt feelings by saying that he may ride alongside her carriage at the end of the day. Of course, by the end of that day, Octavian will have fallen blindly in love with Sophie, and the Marschallin will sadly relinquish him to the younger woman.
5. She calls for her little servant to take the silver rose to Octavian, who will act on behalf of Ochs by presenting the rose to Sophie.
6. At first, Ochs seems a little bit put out, but then he encourages Octavian to make love to Sophie, to "break her in" for Ochs. This horrifies Sophie and so offends Octavian that he challenges Ochs to a duel.
7. The irate Faninal, who wishes to marry off his daughter to a titled person, even if he is as boorish as Ochs, tells Sophie that if she doesn't marry the baron, he will place her in a convent.
8. The Marschallin is sung by Elisabeth Schwarzkopf; Octavian by Sena Jurinac; Sophie by Anneliese Rothenberger; Ochs by Otto Edelmann. The conductor is Herbert von Karajan.
9. The Marschallin is sung by Lotte Lehmann; Octavian by Maria Olszewska; Sophie by Elisabeth Schumann (re-creating her world-premiere performance); Ochs by Richard Mayr. The conductor is Robert Heger.
10. Annina has brought Ochs the *billet-doux* from "Mariandl"

(Octavian dressed as the Marschallin's maid) setting up a tryst, and Ochs, while overjoyed by this development, is so stingy that he does not tip her. This makes Annina more eager than ever to undo Ochs.

11. The Marschallin tells Ochs that his supposed marriage to Sophie will never happen. Then, when Ochs starts to make allusions to the Marschallin's affair with Octavian, the Marschallin firmly tells Ochs to put the entire matter out of his mind and to go home and never refer to the incident again. Sophie, who chatters nervously as Octavian presents her to the Marschallin, is advised not to talk so much. The Marschallin assures Sophie that she is so pretty she need not bother with making so much conversation.

12. Mohammed is sent back to look for Sophie's fallen handkerchief, which he finds as the curtain falls.

13. Lotte Lehmann.

14. Erich Kleiber and his son, Carlos Kleiber.

15. Welitsch sings Marianne, Sophie's duenna.

20. *TOSCA*

1. The play, *La Tosca*, was written by Victorien Sardou, and Sarah Bernhardt had one of her greatest successes touring in the title role.

2. Puccini had a penchant for stealing the ideas and wives of other men. He became enamored of *La Tosca*, but the rights were owned by Alfredo Franchetti. Ricordi, guessing that a Puccini *Tosca* would be a bigger success than one by Franchetti, went with Puccini to visit the unfortunate Franchetti. Together, the two convinced the lesser composer that the play was too violent for successful transition to opera. Franchetti agreed to relinquish his option, and Puccini immediately snapped it up.

3. The unwitting model for Mario's religious artwork is La Marchesa d'Attavanti, Angelotti's sister, who does not herself appear in the opera, but is significant to the plot for several

reasons. Her frequent visits to church are meant to conceal her real purpose—arranging her brother's escape. The Marchesa leaves a key to her family's private chapel, as well as some women's clothing with which Angelotti can disguise himself. Also, the Marchesa is vital to the plot because she provides, by virtue of her beauty, the bait with which Scarpia triggers Tosca's jealousy. Scarpia produces a fan left behind by the fleeing Angelotti and suggests to Tosca that the Marchesa herself had dropped it, fleeing with Tosca's lover, Mario.

4. Angelotti escapes from the Castel Sant' Angelo, a notoriously grim and brutally administered prison.

5. Tosca returns to the church to give Mario the bad news that she has been summoned to sing for Queen Caroline of Rome, to celebrate the supposed defeat of Napoleon. Scarpia, at the church to investigate Angelotti's escape from prison, seizes the opportunity to poison Tosca's mind against her lover and to use her as an unwitting spy, hoping that she will lead him to Angelotti, Mario's friend.

6. Puccini eventually came to dislike Tosca's Act II aria, "Vissi d'arte." He felt that the introspective prayer held back the action and cooled the suspense.

7. Scarpia asks which road Tosca would like to travel, and she replies, "The shortest." Scarpia suggests Civitavecchia, the major highway leading from Rome, and Tosca approves.

8. In an early production of *Tosca* in Vienna, soprano Maria Jeritza, who came to be Puccini's favorite Tosca, tripped while dodging Scarpia's attentions, and found herself face down on the floor as her cue to sing the aria drew near. Therefore, the beautiful Jeritza sang the aria from that extraordinary position and has been emulated by many Toscas since.

9. The premiere performance was plagued by undercurrents of political unrest and professional jealousy on the part of the composer's rivals. Although no bombs were tossed inside the opera house, the opening scene was interrupted when sounds of fracas in the foyer reached the auditorium. Angry latecomers were being refused entry, and their shouts so unnerved the conductor, Leopoldo Mugnone, that he stopped the perfor-

mance and barricaded himself in his dressing room until he was assured by the management that no saboteurs were present, at which time the performance resumed.

10. The music for the offstage cantata in the second act was composed by Puccini's father. The elder Puccini, a locally famous organist and composer, died when Puccini was a young child. He studied his father's compositions and conferred immortality on this piece by making use of it in *Tosca*.

11. Both are from 1961. One is from Tokyo, where Tebaldi's partners include Gianni Poggi as Mario and Giuseppe Taddei as Scarpia. The second is from Stuttgart, and the Mario is Eugene Tobin, while Scarpia is sung by George London.

12. Two complete performances of Act II survive. The first is from the gala evening in which Callas made her debut at the Paris Opéra. Albert Lance is Mario, while Tito Gobbi is Scarpia. The second video dates from 1964, from Covent Garden. Renato Cioni sings Mario, and Gobbi is once again Scarpia.

13. Catherine Malfitano sang Tosca; Plácido Domingo sang Mario. Scarpia was sung by Ruggero Raimondi. The conductor was Zubin Mehta. Giuseppe Patroni Griffi directed. WEA issued the videodisc and VHS tape. The CD was finally released in 1996.

14. Claudia Muzio.

21. *TRISTAN UND ISOLDE*

1. Some of the love music from *Tristan und Isolde* was "tested" by Wagner in his Wesendonck Songs.

2. She is angry because Tristan has courted her under false pretenses, winning her love not for himself but for his sovereign, King Marke of Cornwall.

3. Munich.

4. Brangäne substitutes a love potion for the death potion that Isolde has commanded her to prepare for herself and Tristan.

5. This section is called Isolde's Narrative and Curse.

6. Having shared the love potion with Tristan, Isolde is now

hopelessly smitten with the young knight, and the prospect of marriage with the elderly Marke seems even less attractive than it had previously.

7. Melot is another knight in King Marke's service and, like Tristan, is rumored to be an illegitimate son of the king. Melot first suspects that Tristan and Isolde are lovers, and later catches the pair together. Tristan allows Melot to wound him mortally in their brief duel at the end of the opera's second act.

8. a. Rysanek never sang Isolde, although she was often invited to undertake the role.

9. Karl Liebl.

10. The EMI *Tristan* conducted by Wilhelm Furtwängler starred Kirsten Flagstad as Isolde and featured Blanche Thebom as Brangäne. Recorded in the 1950s, the sessions found the aging Flagstad nervous about attacking the high Cs in the second act. Walter Legge, the producer of the recording, proposed that his wife, soprano Elisabeth Schwarzkopf, sing those notes. All concerned were sworn to secrecy, but the story soon became public knowledge, much to Flagstad's annoyance. Listen carefully to the performance and you will be able to detect the inserted high Cs.

11. Isolde.

12. Brangäne.

13. Edwin MacArthur.

14. On Nilsson's Decca/London *Tristan* recording, Regina Resnik sings Brangäne. On the Deutsche Grammophon recording, Brangäne is sung by Christa Ludwig.

15. Tristan.

22. *LA TRAVIATA*

1. *La Traviata* was given its first performance on March 6, 1853, at the Teatro La Fenice in Venice.

2. Two reasons for the opera's initially cool reception were that the audience was surprised and displeased by the contemporary

settings and costumes (for years afterward the opera was given in eighteenth-century costumes) and by the fact that the obese soprano singing Violetta was a most unlikely consumptive.

3. Baron Douphol.

4. The party guests include Douphol, Flora, the Marquis d'Obigny, Gastone, Alfredo, and Dr. Grenvil.

5. This aria is sung by the temporarily joyous Alfredo in Act II.

6. Papa Germont wants to break up Violetta and Alfredo because the scandal of Alfredo's living with a courtesan threatens the marriage plans of Alfredo's sister and her seemingly snobbish fiancé.

7. Germont figures out Alfredo's plans when he finds the invitation to Flora's party, which Alfredo has read and thrown to the ground in despair.

8. Germont sings "Di sprezzo degno sé stesso rende chi pùr nell'ira la donna offende" (He who, even in anger, insults a woman, is worthy only of contempt). These words are surprising since Germont's own first words to Violetta accuse her of "ruining" his son.

9. Maria Callas sang Violetta, Giuseppe di Stefano sang Alfredo, and Ettore Bastianini sang Germont. The production was designed and staged by Luchino Visconti, and conducted by Carlo Maria Giulini.

10. Toscanini's cast included Licia Albanese as Violetta, Jan Peerce as Alfredo, and Robert Merrill as Germont.

11. Violetta's outburst occurs shortly after Alfredo returns to her. Although she wishes to leave with him, she finds that she is not strong enough even to dress herself.

12. Violetta's last delirious words are: "Ah! Ma io ritorno a viver! O gioia!" (But I am returning to life! Oh joy!).

13. Merrill recorded *La Traviata* twice for RCA and once for Decca/London. For RCA, the baritone's colleagues were first Albanese and Peerce, later Anna Moffo and Richard Tucker. For Decca/London, Merrill was in the distinguished company of Joan Sutherland and Carlo Bergonzi.

14. c. Franco Corelli.

23. I'VE HEARD THAT BEFORE

1. In the final scene of Mozart's *Don Giovanni*, Don Giovanni is giving a party. A stage band entertains, playing tunes from two non-Mozartean operas, allowing Leporello to make a few topical allusions. Finally, the band strikes up Mozart's own "Non più andrai" from *Le Nozze di Figaro*. Leporello, recognizing the tune, quips, "I've heard that one too often!"

2. In Puccini's *Il Tabarro* the barge-bound Giorgetta and her stevedore lover, Luigi, listen to a song vendor hawk a song about the love of Mimí and Rodolfo. Sure enough, in *Il Tabarro*'s one humorous moment, the orchestra briefly plays "Sì, mi chiamono Mimì" from *La Bohème*.

3. In the prologue to Offenbach's opera, Hoffmann and his friend Nicklausse arrive at Luther's tavern after an act of *Don Giovanni*. Nicklausse sees that his subservient attitude toward Hoffmann, and the latter's condescension toward him, make him into a nineteenth-century Leporello. Therefore, Nicklausse sings a few bars of Leporello's "Notte e giorno faticar."

4. In the third act of *Die Meistersinger von Nürnberg*, Wagner slips the famous "Tristan chord" into the scene in which Sachs realizes that he must help Walther win Eva's hand. As the music echoes Wagner's tragic work, Sachs alludes to the story of King Marke, Tristan, and Isolde to his young friends.

5. In the first act of *Madama Butterfly*, at the point of Cio-Cio-San's first entrance, Puccini quotes Musetta's Waltz from *La Bohème*. It is totally unmotivated and probably was an unconscious quote by the composer.

6–7–8. We'll take the three megamusicals sometimes called pop operas together. In *Phantom*, the composer, Andrew Lloyd Webber, quotes the waltz from the first act of Puccini's *La Fanciulla del West* in the song "All I Want from You." In *Cats*, Lloyd Webber heavily borrows from "Un bel dì" from *Madama Butterfly* in the song "Memories." In *Les Misérables*, the composer, Schonberg, uses the tune of "Le Roi de Thulé" from *Faust* as the basis for "Castle in the Clouds" and the Humming

Chorus from *Madama Butterfly* in "Bring Him Home." There is no dramatic reason for these quotations. At its most innocent, the practice might be called naive imitation. Taken more seriously, the word *plagiarism* does come to mind.

24. WAGNER I

1. Wagner's first opera, more or less neglected in his own day and in our own, was *Die Feen*, which had its American premiere in a concert performance by the New York City Opera on February 24, 1982.
2. Wagner's first wife was Minna.
3. The critic was Eduard Hanslick. Wagner mercilessly caricatured Hanslick in the character of Beckmesser, the comic villain in *Die Meistersinger von Nürnberg*.
4. The first version of *Tannhäuser* is known as the Dresden version. The revision is called the Paris version. The principal difference is that in the Paris version, the bacchanal that opens the opera (the Venusburg Scene) is expanded to accommodate the ballet that was *de riguer* at the Paris Opéra during the nineteenth century. Also, the orchestral coloration is more sensual and the character of Venus is more fully developed than in the Dresden version.
5. King Ludwig II of Bavaria was a staunch supporter and financial "angel" of Wagner.
6. Wagner's second wife was Cosima Liszt von Bülow, the illegitimate daughter of Franz Liszt. When Wagner met her, she was married to the conductor Hans von Bülow, an early champion of Wagner's music.
7. Mathilde Wesendonck was a close friend of Wagner's. She wrote the poems that Wagner set to music in his Wesendonck Lieder.
8. Themes from *Tristan und Isolde*'s love music are heard in the Wesendonck Lieder.
9. George Bernard Shaw was the writer, and the book is *The Perfect Wagnerite*.

10. The several Wagnerian operas that treat this theme include *Die Walküre*, in which Wotan is forced by pressure from his wife Fricka to allow his son Siegmund to die at Hunding's hands. In *Götterdämmerung* the evil dwarf Alberich appears to his son, the equally hideous Hagen, to urge him to recapture the ring. In *Tristan und Isolde*, King Marke's feelings toward Tristan are, initially, those of a father for a son, and, indeed, it has often been argued that Tristan actually *is* Marke's son. Finally, Lohengrin, one learns, has been consecrated to a life as a Knight of the Holy Grail by his father, Parsifal (*Lohengrin*).

11. Wagner learned about the legend of the Flying Dutchman while on a miserable, storm-wracked ocean voyage, during which the sailors recounted the tale to the composer.

12. Rysanek has been particularly well received as Senta in *Der Fliegende Holländer* and as Sieglinde in *Die Walküre*. She is also known for her performances as Elsa in *Lohengrin* and as Elisabeth in *Tannhäuser*. Early in her career, Rysanek was heard as Gutrune in *Götterdämmerung*, and, in the 1980s, she became a formidable Ortrud in *Lohengrin*.

13. The composer was Engelbert Humperdinck, best known for his *Hänsel und Gretel*. The few bars that Humperdinck composed for *Parsifal* were never performed. They were discarded before the premiere because the stage machinery had been improved to the point where the scene change could be accomplished before Wagner's own music ended.

14. Wagner composed the *Siegfried Idyll*, a tone poem made up of themes from the *Ring*, as a present for Cosima upon the birth of their son Siegfried.

15. a. Melot is the aide to King Marke in *Tristan und Isolde*. He fatally wounds Tristan in a duel after Marke and his retainers have discovered Tristan and Isolde making love.

    b. Henry is the king in *Lohengrin*.

    c. Wolfram is the noble friend of both Tannhäuser and Elisabeth in *Tannhäuser*. Based on a real medieval poet, Wolfram sings the famous Evening Star aria.

    d. Erik is the huntsman who loves Senta in *Der Fliegende*

Holländer. His inopportune appearance at the wedding of Senta to the Dutchman indirectly causes Senta's death.

e. Fafner is the crueler of the two giants in *Das Rheingold.* He and his brother Fasolt have built Valhalla for the gods. The two giants quarrel over possession of the ring of the Nibelung, included as part of the ransom for Freia, the goddess whom the two giants were promised as payment for their work. Fafner kills Fasolt and takes the ring for himself.

f. Mary is the older woman who keeps a watchful eye on Senta and the other young girls in *Der Fliegende Holländer.*

g. Pogner is one of the Mastersingers in Wagner's only comedy, *Die Meistersinger von Nürnberg.* He offers his daughter, Eva, in marriage to the winner of the Mastersingers' song contest. Fortunately, the young man to whom Eva has lost her heart, Walther von Stolzing, wins!

h. Waltraute is one of Brünnhilde's sister Valkyries. Her role in *Die Walküre* is brief, but in *Götterdämmerung* Waltraute makes a crucial appearance in Act I when she urges Brünnhilde to return the ring that Siegfried has given her to its rightful owners, the Rhinemaidens.

i. Woglinde is a Rhinemaiden. She appears in *Das Rheingold* and *Götterdämmerung.*

j. Brangäne is Isolde's servant in *Tristan und Isolde.* Brangäne complicates matters when, although Isolde has called for a death potion for her and Tristan to imbibe, the well-meaning Brangäne substitutes a love potion.

16. a. These words are cried out by Parsifal as he breaks away from Kundry's attempt to seduce him. His realization of Amfortas's terrible suffering prevents him from falling into Klingsor's power. (*Parsifal*)

b. With these words Lohengrin begins his revelation of who he is and why has he come to Brabant. (*Lohengrin*)

c. These rapturous words are sung by Sieglinde to her newly discovered twin brother Siegmund as they prepare to leave Hunding's hut. (*Die Walküre*)

d. These are the first words uttered by the Dutchman as he

steps ashore for the first time in seven years. (*Der Fliegende Holländer*)

e. These are the opening words of Isolde's Liebestod. (*Tristan und Isolde*)

f. These nonsensical words are cooed by the Rhinemaidens as they frolic about in the deceptively tranquil opening of *Das Rheingold.*

g. These are the first words of Elisabeth's entrance aria in *Tannhäuser.*

h. Tristan sings these words to Isolde as part of their love duet. (*Tristan und Isolde*)

i. These words open Adriano's aria in *Rienzi.*

j. These hostile words are addressed by Fricka to Wotan in *Die Walküre.*

17. Klingsor was not "pure" like the other knights and, in his desperation, castrated himself in a futile attempt to root out his sexual obsessions (which leads one to wonder why Klingsor is sung by a *baritone*).

18. Kundry, we learn in her scene with Parsifal, was a contemporary of Christ. She laughed at Him on His way to the Cross, and was condemned by God to wander incessantly in a kind of living Hell.

19. *Parsifal.*

20. The composer died in Venice in 1883.

21. Kirsten Flagstad (1935) and Astrid Varnay (1941).

22. *Tannhäuser*, in which Nilsson sang both Venus and Elisabeth.

23. *Parsifal.*

24. Lohengrin arrives in Brabant in a boat drawn by a swan. In the final scene, after the swan has been transformed back into the missing Prince Gottfried, Lohengrin's boat is drawn by a somewhat oversized dove.

25. a. Senta jumps off a cliff. (*Der Fliegende Holländer*)

b. Telramund is slain by Lohengrin in a brief fight in Lohengrin and Elsa's bridal suite. (*Lohengrin*)

c. Hunding is slain by a wave of Wotan's hand. (*Die Walküre*)

d. Mime is slain by Siegfried, who runs him through with Nothung. (*Siegfried*)

e. Fasolt is beaten to death by his brother Fafner. (*Das Rheingold*)

25. WAGNER II

1. Tenor René Kollo.
2. Soprano Lillian Nordica.
3. Siepi's only Wagnerian role was Gurnemanz in *Parsifal*, which he sang with great success at the Met in 1970.
4. Tristan is served by the fiercely loyal if not terribly bright Kurwenal.
5. Tristan originally introduced himself to Isolde, when he came to claim her as King Marke's bride, as "Tantris."
6. Herzelaide is Parsifal's mother, as Kundry tells us. However, she does not make an appearance in the opera.
7. Price never sang a full Wagnerian role, although she was announced for Elsa at the Boston Symphony's Tanglewood Festival in 1965. She withdrew and was replaced by Lucine Amara at the performance and in the subsequent recording.
8. Anna Russell delighted audiences for years with her satirical monologues on Wagner, especially on the *Ring*.
9. Arturo Toscanini.
10. In the third act of *Die Meistersinger von Nürnberg*, the elderly Sachs realizes that, although he loves Eva, he cannot hope to compete for her love against Walther, and he alludes to the legend of Tristan as the orchestra echoes King Marke's monologue from Wagner's *Tristan*.
11. The Mastersingers include: Hans Sachs, Veit Pogner, Kunz Vogelgesang, Konrad Nachtigall, Sixtus Beckmesser, Fritz Kothner, Balthasar Zorn, Ulrich Eisslinger, Augustin Moser, Hermann Ortel, Hans Schwarz, and Hans Foltz.
12. Only *Die Meistersinger* is "naturalistic." There are no spells, potions, gods, or miracles.
13. Reginald Goodall.
14. Melba, misunderstanding a comment made by Jean de Reszke, who had suggested that she sing the Forest Bird in *Siegfried*,

insisted on attempting Brünnhilde in that opera. One disastrous performance at the Metropolitan taught Melba to stay away from Wagner.

15. Grace Bumbry was the first black artist to sing at the Bayreuth Festival (1961). She sang Venus in *Tannhäuser*. The press created the nickname.

16. Gwyneth Jones.

17. The Liebestod from *Tristan und Isolde*.

18. Hitler misappropriated Wagner's music during the Third Reich. It is hardly surprising that the many Israelis who are Holocaust survivors derive no pleasure from Wagner's music. Although the ban is moral, rather than legal, no opera by Wagner has ever been produced in Israel.

26. MOZART

1. Mozart's first opera was *La Finta Semplice*, composed when he was eleven.

2. Fiordiligi and Dorabella are sisters.

3. a. From *Don Giovanni*, this is sung by Don Ottavio.
   b. This is Papageno's famous song from *Die Zauberflöte*.
   c. This angry arioso is sung by Count Almaviva in *Le Nozze di Figaro*.
   d. This romanza belongs to Ferrando in *Così Fan Tutte*.
   e. This little duet is sung toward the end of *Le Nozze di Figaro* by Figaro and Susanna.
   f. This charming piece is a duet for Pamina and Papageno in *Die Zauberflöte*.

4. a. *La Clemenza di Tito*
   b. *Idomeneo*
   c. *Le Nozze di Figaro*
   d. *Don Giovanni*
   e. *Die Zauberflöte* (Astrafiammante is the Queen of the Night's other name.)
   f. *Così Fan Tutte*

5. Milanov's one Mozart role was Donna Anna in *Don Giovanni*.

6. *Le Nozze di Figaro* and *Don Giovanni* were first performed in Prague.

7. *Der Schauspieldirektor* (*The Impresario*).

8. "Dalla sua pace" and "Non mi dir."

9. Clemens Krauss was better known for his Richard Strauss then for his Mozart.

10. *Der Rosenkavalier* was intended as a salute to *Le Nozze di Figaro*, while *Die Frau ohne Schatten* was a tribute to *Die Zauberflöte*.

11. Don Ottavio proposes to the still grieving Donna Anna. She agrees to marry him after another year of mourning for her slain father. Donna Elvira announces that she will retire to a convent. Masetto and Zerlina simply declare that they are going home to supper, while Leporello says that he is heading for the inn, hoping to find a new, better master.

12. Sarastro sentences Monostatos to a sound thrashing for his wickedness.

13. Constanze in *The Abduction from the Seraglio* is a gallant portrait of Frau Mozart.

14. Feodor Chaliapin was not known for singing Mozart.

15. Callas occasionally sang Constanze's "Martern aller Arten" in Italian as "Tutte le torture."

16. Joseph Losey directed the film version of *Don Giovanni* released in 1979. Loren Maazel conducted. Don Giovanni was sung by Ruggero Raimondi; Donna Anna was sung by Edda Moser; Elvira was sung by Kiri Te Kanawa, while Teresa Berganza portrayed Zerlina.

17. Lunt staged an unforgettable *Così Fan Tutte* at the Metropolitan in 1951. From then on, this opera has been a frequent adornment of the Met's stage. Richard Tucker sang Ferrando.

18. Bergman changed Pamina's lineage, making her not only the Queen of the Night's daughter, but Sarastro's as well, thus more clearly motivating Sarastro's removal of the girl from her mother's clutches.

19. The Glyndebourne Festival in England and Austria's Salzburg Festival were initially best known for their Mozart performances. More recently the repertories of both festivals have broadened considerably.

20. Cherubino's love song is "Voi che sapete."
21. *Mitridate, Rè di Ponto.*
22. Da Ponte created the libretti for *Don Giovanni, Così Fan Tutte,* and *Le Nozze di Figaro.*
23. Freemasonry is the moral basis for *Die Zauberflöte.*
24. *La Clemenza di Tito.*
25. Chagall's 1967 settings and costumes for the Metropolitan Opera's *Die Zauberflöte* are ranked among the painter's finest achievements.
26. Peter Sellars directed monstrous productions of *Don Giovanni, Così Fan Tutte,* and *Le Nozze di Figaro.*
27. Thomas Hampson.
28. Ljuba Welitsch.
29. The opera is *Die Zauberflöte.* In the 1964 EMI recording, Schwarzkopf sang the First Lady, Janowitz sang Pamina, and Popp was the Queen of the Night.
30. The play is *Man and Superman.* Act III is often referred to as "Don Juan in Hell."

27. PUCCINI RARITIES

1. Giacomo Puccini was born in Lucca, Italy, on December 22, 1858.
2. Barry Morell.
3. Rosa Raisa.
4. Torre del Lago, Italy.
5. Blanche Bates starred as Cio-Cio-San in the Broadway and London companies of *Madame Butterfly,* a play by David Belasco, based on a story by John Luther Long.
6. Puccini stole the idea of an operatic setting of Henri Murger's novel, *Scènes de la Vie de Bohème* from Ruggiero Leoncavallo, the composer of *Pagliacci.* Leoncavallo's *Bohème* was produced nearly two years after Puccini's opera, but even the presence of Caruso in the cast (as Marcello) could not prevent the opera from being overshadowed by the all but perfect Puccini version. In 1996, Jonathan Larson "borrowed" Puccini's plot for his musical *Rent.*

7. *La Fanciulla del West* and the three works that form *Il Trittico: Il Tabarro, Suor Angelica,* and *Gianni Schicchi* were given their first performances at the Met.

8. Puccini paid this compliment to Enrico Caruso. As Puccini began the audition, Caruso responded to the composer's question "Who are you?" by quoting, in song, a line from Rodolfo's aria "Che gelida manina": "Chi son? Sono un poeta." (Who am I? I am a poet.)

9. The original cast of *La Fanciulla del West*, which had its world premiere in December 1910, at the Metropolitan, included Emmy Destinn as Minnie, Enrico Caruso as Johnson, and Pasquale Amato as Rance. Arturo Toscanini conducted.

10. The libretti for *La Bohème, Tosca,* and *Madama Butterfly* were written by Giuseppe Giacosa and Luigi Illica.

11. The fiftieth-anniversary *La Bohème* was performed in New York City on February 3 and 10, 1946, in Studio 8-H of the RCA Building, and broadcast over the NBC network to commemorate the first performance of that work on February 1, 1896. The cast included the following artists: Rodolfo was sung by Jan Peerce; Mimì was sung by Licia Albanese; Marcello was sung by Francesco Valentino; Musetta was sung by Anne McKnight; Colline was sung by Nicola Moscona; Schaunard was sung by George Cehanovsky; Alcindoro/Benoit were sung by Salvatore Baccaloni. The conductor was Arturo Toscanini, who had conducted at the work's premiere at the Teatro Regio, Turin. The anniversary performance is still available on RCA CDs.

12. Hungarian playwright Ferenc Molnár turned down Puccini's bid for the rights to the play *Liliom*, saying that he wanted the popular drama to be remembered as a play by Molnár, *not* an opera by Puccini. A generation later, Molnár's mind was changed by a bid from Richard Rodgers and Oscar Hammerstein, who transformed *Liliom* into the musical play *Carousel*.

13. Tebaldi sang her only staged *Fanciulla*s at the Met, in February 1970. Sándor Kónya was the tenor who portrayed Dick Johnson in those performances. Franco Corelli had been promised in that role, but scheduling changes forced him to withdraw from the cast.

14. Puccini's *Il Trittico* was influenced by Dante. The structure of the work paralleled that of Dante's *Divine Comedy*. "Inferno," "Purgatorio," and "Paradiso" are suggested by the tragic *Il Tabarro*, the sad but touching *Suor Angelica*, and the wryly comic, triumphant *Gianni Schicchi*. Moreover, the libretto for *Schicchi* was inspired by a minor reference in the "Inferno": Dante placed Schicchi, a lawyer who impersonated a dead man in order to change the corpse's will, in Hell, making reference to a scandal that had shocked twelfth-century Florence.

15. In *La Fanciulla del West*, Sheriff Jack Rance, the baritone, slugs Dick Johnson, the tenor hero.

28. EARLY VERDI

1. The title character in *Stiffelio* was not received with sympathy by audiences in a country where cuckolded husbands were traditionally objects of scorn.
2. *I Lombardi*.
3. The victim is the title character in *Attila*.
4. *Oberto*.
5. *Alzira*.
6. *Aroldo*.
7. *Un Giorno di Regno*.
8. *Nabucco* is best known for the chorus of the Hebrew slaves, "Va, pensiero, sull'ali dorate," and Abigaille's aria "Anch'io dischiuso un giorno."
9. *La Battaglia di Legnano*.
10. *I Due Foscari*.
11. *Ernani*.
12. *Il Corsaro*.

29. VERDI I

1. Verdi was born in the Italian village of Le Roncole.
2. Antonio Barezzi.
3. Verdi's first operas were composed during an era of great po-

litical turbulence in the then-disunited Italian peninsula. Admirers of Verdi who were also political activists discovered that the name Verdi was an anagram for "Vittorio Emanuele, Re d'Italia." The future king was supported by many reform-minded people, including Verdi. Political censorship was strict and free speech did not exist. Therefore, many of those who dreamed of a united Italy saluted their cause, as well as their country's greatest composer, by shouting "Viva Verdi" wherever his operas were presented, and writing the slogan upon every wall they could find.

4. Verdi composed *Don Carlo*, *Les Vêpres Siciliennes*, and *Jérusalem* (a revised version of *I Lombardi*) to French libretti for performances at the Paris Opéra.

5. *I Masnadieri*.

6. Sant'Agata.

7. The author of the libretto's revisions was Arrigo Boito. The principal addition to the score was the council chamber scene (Act I, scene 2), from which the ensemble beginning "Plebe! Patrizi!" is considered by many to be the opera's most brilliant moment.

8. The *Requiem* was composed in honor of Alessandro Manzoni, the nineteenth-century Italian novelist and patriot, whose most famous work is *I Promessi Sposi*.

9. Francesco Maria Piave. He provided texts for several other Verdi operas, including *La Traviata* and the first version of *Simon Boccanegra*.

10. "Stornello," "In solitaria stanza," and "Lo spazzacamino."

11. Arturo Toscanini.

12. "Va, pensiero, sull'ali dorate" from *Nabucco*.

13. In *Nabucco*, the role of Abigaille was first sung by soprano Giuseppina Strepponi, who became Verdi's second wife.

14. Baritone Victor Maurel.

15. *The Hymn of Nations*, as adapted by Toscanini, was played by the NBC Symphony Orchestra, with Jan Peerce as the tenor soloist.

16. Verdi passed up *La Tosca* because he thought himself too old to compose a new opera.

17. He died at the Hotel Ritz in Milan.

18. Casa Verdi, the Verdi home for elderly musicians, in Milan, was established by Verdi's estate.

19. The mythical opera is *Rocester*; *Oberto*, in all likelihood, is the opera that it became.

20. c. Elisabeth Rethberg.

30. VERDI II

1. Giselda is the heroine of *I Lombardi*; Federica is Luisa's rival in *Luisa Miller*; Fenena is the younger, better-natured sister of Abigaille in *Nabucco*; Odabella plots her Hun enemy's death in *Attila*.

2. "La mia letizia infondere" is heard in *I Lombardi*, and is sung by the tenor hero, Oronte.

3. Silva offers Ernani a cup of poison or a dagger. Ernani chooses the dagger.

4. The libretto of *Nabucco* was written by the poet Temistocle Solera.

5. The soprano aria "La luce langue" in Act II of *Macbeth* is much better known than "Trionferai," which it replaced when Verdi revised the opera.

6. Verdi's *Il Corsaro* is based on Byron's poetic drama *The Corsair*.

7. Poland.

8. The aria "Me pellegrina ed orfano" was intended for Cordelia in *King Lear* but was given to Leonora in *La Forza del Destino*.

9. The song "In solitaria stanza," changed and expanded, later became Leonora's "Tacea la notte placida" in *Il Trovatore*.

10. a. Amelia is actually the long-lost daughter of the title character in *Simon Boccanegra*.

    b. Abigaille is the daughter (revealed eventually as the foster daughter) of the title character in *Nabucco*.

    c. Nannetta is the Verdi/Boito transfiguration of Anne Page in Shakespeare's *The Merry Wives of Windsor*. In the play, Anne is the daughter of Meg Page and Master Page. In

Verdi's *Falstaff*, Master Page has been eliminated, and Nannetta is the daughter of Master Ford and his wife, Alice.

d. Gilda is the daughter of the title character in *Rigoletto*.

e. Leonora is the ill-starred daughter of the Marquis di Calatrava in *La Forza del Destino*.

11. *Otello* contains Verdi's only true "drunk scene." Iago and Roderigo make Cassio tipsy in Act I, in order to disgrace him in the Moor's eyes.

12. Shakespeare's *Henry V*, which contains an account of the death of Sir John Falstaff, was not a source for Verdi's final opera. The Honor Monologue was lifted from *Henry IV, Part 1;* Schiller's *Die Räuber* became *I Masnadieri;* and the Duke of Rivas's *La Fuerza del Sino* became *La Forza del Destino*.

13. *La Traviata*.

14. Oronte in *I Lombardi*, Banco in *Macbeth*, and Charles V in *Don Carlo* all return from the next world. Poor Banco, however, returns with nothing to sing.

15. Mirella Freni began her association with Verdi's *Falstaff* by singing the role of Nannetta. Recently, the ageless Miss Freni has added the role of Alice Ford, Nannetta's mother, to her list of opera house triumphs.

16. d. Rodrigo, in *Don Carlo*, is a noble soul.

17. The opera was *La Traviata*. The stars were Anna Moffo, Bruno Prevedi, and Robert Merrill.

18. The duet was "Pur ti riveggo" from *Aida*. EMI recorded Callas partnered by Franco Corelli.

19. Joan of Arc is the only saint Verdi portrayed in an opera, *Giovanna d'Arco*. Most accounts have Joan burned at the stake by the English forces. Verdi and Schiller allow the Warrior Maid to be wounded in battle, revived long enough to sing in the opera's strenuous finale, and then die as the curtain falls.

20. *La Forza del Destino*.

II

Opera Stars and Supernovas

31. BARITONES

1. Leonard Warren fell dead onstage at the Metropolitan Opera on the night of March 4, 1960, midway through the aria "Urna fatale" in *La Forza del Destino*. The baritone had apparently suffered a stroke.
2. Robert Merrill.
3. Tito Gobbi.
4. Ettore Bastianini.
5. Victor Maurel.
6. Lawrence Tibbett.
7. Cornell MacNeil. The fracas occurred during a performance of Verdi's *Un Ballo in Maschera*. The claque booed the soprano, unjustly, in MacNeil's opinion. As a protest, he quit the opera midway.
8. Walter Berry (once married to Christa Ludwig).
9. John Reardon (*DO-RE-MI* in 1960).
10. Antonio Scotti.
11. Piero Cappuccilli.
12. Sherrill Milnes.
13. Robert Weede (*The Most Happy Fella*).
14. Gino Bechi in *La Traviata*.
15. Sir Geraint Evans.
16. George London.
17. Robert McFerrin.
18. Eberhard Wächter.
19. Renato Capecchi.
20. Dietrich Fischer-Dieskau.
21. Sesto Bruscantini (once married to Sena Jurinac).

22. Gabriel Bacquier.
23. Richard Stilwell.
24. George Cehanovsky (married to Elisabeth Rethberg).
25. Cyril Ritchard, straight from his famous characterization of Captain Hook in the musical version of *Peter Pan* that had starred Mary Martin, staged Offenbach's *La Périchole* at the Metropolitan Opera and cast himself as the lecherous, if sentimental, Peruvian viceroy, Don Andres.
26. Thomas Hampson.
27. Simon Estes.
28. Dimitri Hvorostovsky.
29. Vladimir Chernov.
30. John Charles Thomas.

32. BASSES

1. Boris Christoff.
2. Norman Treigle.
3. Salvatore Baccaloni.
4. Gottlob Frick.
5. Ezio Pinza.
6. Bonaldo Giaiotti.
7. Jerome Hines.
8. Nicolai Ghiaurov, who, you may recall, is married to Mirella Freni.
9. Tancredi Pasero.
10. Justino Díaz.
11. Pol Plançon.
12. James Morris.
13. Fyodor Chaliapin.
14. Fernando Corena.
15. Nicola Rossi-Lemeni.
16. Giorgio Tozzi.
17. Kurt Moll.
18. Martti Talvela.
19. Matti Salminen.
20. Ruggero Raimondi.

21. Hans Hotter. Stepping off an airplane at Heathrow, the bass was delighted to see a newspaper headline reading "Hotter in London," mistaking an newstory about a bit of unseasonable weather for a discussion of his return to British musical life!
22. Italo Tajo.
23. Ezio Flagello (his brother was the composer Nicholas Flagello).
24. Plinio Clabassi.
25. Donald Gramm.
26. Paul Robeson.

33. MEZZOS

1. Risë Stevens.
2. Elena Obraztsova.
3. Giulietta Simionato.
4. Minnie Hauk.
5. Ernestine Schumann-Heink.
6. Louise Homer.
7. Fiorenza Cossotto.
8. Frederica Von Stade.
9. Ebe Stignani.
10. Shirley Verrett.
11. Regina Resnik.
12. Christa Ludwig.
13. Irina Arkhipova.
14. Cloe Elmo.
15. Gladys Swarthout.
16. Fedora Barbieri.
17. Rosalind Elias.
18. Teresa Berganza.
19. Marilyn Horne.

34. SOPRANOS

1. Kirsten Flagstad.
2. Geraldine Farrar.
3. Leontyne Price.
4. Eleanor Steber (*Vanessa*).
5. Victoria de los Angeles.
6. Lotte Lehmann.
7. Renata Tebaldi.
8. Zinka Milanov.
9. Anna Moffo.
10. Joan Sutherland.
11. Shirley Verrett.
12. Elisabeth Schwarzkopf.
13. Lillian Nordica.
14. Lucine Amara.
15. Birgit Nilsson.
16. Montserrat Caballé.
17. Leonie Rysanek.
18. Rosa Ponselle.
19. Grace Moore.
20. Maria Callas.

21. Beverly Sills.
22. Mado Robin.
23. Renata Scotto.
24. Luisa Tetrazzini.
25. Anna Russell.
26. Teresa Stratas.
27. Reri Grist.
28. Sharon Sweet.
29. Hildegard Behrens.
30. Anita Cerquetti.
31. Maria Spacagna.
32. Leyla Gencer.
33. Roberta Peters.
34. Dorothy Kirsten.
35. Patricia Brooks.
36. Mirella Freni.
37. Rosanna Carteri.
38. Rose Bampton.
39. Maria Caniglia.
40. Licia Albanese.
41. Gabriella Tucci.
42. Martina Arroyo.
43. Ina del Campo.
44. Régine Crespin.
45. Maria Pellegrini.
46. Mary Garden.
47. Ghena Dimitrova.
48. Lisa Della Casa.
49. Lucrezia Bori.
50. Jessye Norman.

35. TENORS

1. Franco Corelli.
2. Plácido Domingo.
3. Ramón Vinay.
4. Lauritz Melchior (and Lily Pons).
5. Richard Tucker and Jan Peerce.
6. Giovanni Martinelli (sang the emperor in *Turandot* in Seattle in 1963).
7. Richard Tauber.
8. Mario Lanza.
9. Michele Molese (at the New York City Opera, during a performance of *Un Ballo in Maschera* in 1974).
10. Leo Slezak.
11. Jussi Bjoerling.
12. Robert Rounseville.
13. Mario del Monaco.
14. Luciano Pavarotti.
15. Beniamino Gigli sang the role of Turiddu in the 1941 recording of Pietro Mascagni's *Cavalleria Rusticana.*
16. Jan Kiepura.
17. Jon Vickers.
18. Nicolai Gedda.
19. John McCormack.
20. Carlo Bergonzi.
21. Alfredo Kraus (born in the Canary Islands).
22. James McCracken.
23. Giuseppe di Stefano.
24. Enrico Caruso.
25. Roberto Alagna.

26. Carlo Bini.
27. Siegfried Jerusalem.
28. Gianni Raimondi (as Rodolfo in *La Bohème*).
29. Alain Vanzo.
30. George Shirley.
31. Gianni Poggi.
32. Richard Leech.
33. Kurt Baum.
34. Joseph Schmidt.
35. John Alexander.

36. LICIA ALBANESE

1. Albanese was born in Bari, Italy.
2. The title role in *Madama Butterfly*.
3. Puccini's *La Bohème*.
4. b. Albanese never sang Lakmé.
5. Albanese recorded Puccini's *La Bohème*, Verdi's *La Traviata*, and Bizet's *Carmen* (singing Micaela) with Peerce under RCA's auspices. The two Italian operas were the Toscanini broadcast performances.
6. Puccini.
7. Albanese recorded the Letter Scene from Tchaikovsky's *Eugene Onegin* in the original Russian.
8. Licia Albanese had a "guest" role in *Serenade*, which starred Lanza and Joan Fontaine. Albanese played a diva singing Desdemona opposite Lanza's Otello. In the film, Lanza is in love with Joan Fontaine. During the third-act confrontation of Desdemona by Otello, Lanza's character notices that Fontaine has left her box seat. Therefore, Lanza storms off the stage, leaving Albanese to fend for herself until the curtain can be rung down. Trust us, it's the best moment in the whole movie!
9. Albanese's Puccini roles included Manon Lescaut, Mimì, Tosca, Cio-Cio-San, Magda, Lauretta, and Liù.
10. The Puccini Foundation.

37. LUCINE AMARA

1. The San Francisco Opera.
2. In San Francisco, the soprano was known as "the Cinderella

soprano" because she rose from chorister to featured artist within one year.

3. The conductor whose early faith in Amara was borne out was Pierre Monteux.

4. Amara's five Met openings were: 1950—*Don Carlo* (Celestial Voice); 1951—*Aida* (Priestess); 1955—*Les Contes d'Hoffmann* (Antonia); 1957—*Eugene Onegin* (Tatyana); and 1971—*Don Carlo* (Celestial Voice). The 1971 performance was a special favor to the retiring Rudolf Bing, who invited four members of his first *Don Carlo* opening-night cast to re-create their roles on the occasion of Bing's final opening night. The other artists were Robert Merrill, Cesare Siepi, and Jerome Hines.

5. The opera was Puccini's *La Bohème*. Amara, one of the best Mimìs of her generation, undertook the role of Musetta in the RCA performance (now available on EMI/Angel) made in New York in 1955. Jussi Bjoerling sang Rodolfo, Victoria de los Angeles portrayed Mimì. Robert Merrill was the Marcello, and Giorgio Tozzi, Fernando Corena, and John Reardon filled out the cast. Sir Thomas Beecham conducted.

6. The roles include Micaela in *Carmen*, the title role in *Aida*, Tatyana in *Eugene Onegin*, the Countess in *Le Nozze di Figaro*, Pamina in *The Magic Flute*, Antonia in *Les Contes d'Hoffmann*, Mimì in *La Bohème*, and Nedda in *Pagliacci*. Pamina, Tatyana, and Antonia, incidentally, were recorded in English.

7. *The Great Caruso* (1950).

8. In 1975, Amara literally jumped into *La Forza del Destino*, replacing the ailing Martina Arroyo in the role of Leonora, midway through the Convent Scene.

9. *La Bohème* (Mimì and Musetta); *Aida* (Priestess and Aida); *Turandot* (Liù and Turandot); *Carmen* (Frasquita and Micaela); *Die Zauberflöte* (First Lady and Pamina).

10. Geraldine Farrar sang 517 performances at the Met.

11. *Pagliacci*.

12. The opera was Tchaikovsky's *Eugene Onegin*. In addition to Amara as Tatyana, the cast included George London (Onegin), Richard Tucker (Lenski), Rosalind Elias (Olga), and Giorgio Tozzi (Gremin). Dimitri Mitropoulos conducted.

38. CECILIA BARTOLI

1. Rome.
2. The Teatro dell'Opera, Rome.
3. Bartoli's mother, Silvana Bazzoni.
4. Herbert von Karajan; the Salzburg Festival.
5. Rossini and Mozart.
6. Bartoli's first U.S. stage role was that of Rosina in Rossini's *Il Barbiere di Siviglia*, at the Houston Grand Opera, in 1993.
7. a. In *Così Fan Tutte*, Bartoli has sung Dorabella and Despina.
8. Her first complete operatic recording was Rossini's *Il Barbiere di Siviglia* for Decca/London.
9. Bartoli's Met debut, on February 8, 1996, was as Despina in *Così Fan Tutte*.
10. *The Impatient Lover*, a Decca/London release.
11. "Bel raggio lusinghier" from Rossini's *Semiramide*, Pamira's prayer from Rossini's *L'Assedio di Corinto*, "Come scoglio" from Mozart's *Così Fan Tutte*, and "Mi tradi" from *Don Giovanni*. All are generally considered to be soprano arias.
12. Magdalene in *Die Meistersinger von Nürmberg*.

39. KATHLEEN BATTLE

1. Cincinnati, Ohio.
2. She was a schoolteacher.
3. Ms. Battle served as Carmen Balthrop's understudy in the title role of Joplin's *Treemonisha* when the Houston Grand Opera's production of that work played Broadway in 1975.
4. James Levine.
5. Battle's Met debut was in the role of the Shepherd in *Tannhäuser* in 1977. James McCracken sang Tannhäuser that night.
6. The two divas sang spirituals. The conductor was James Levine.
7. b. James Galway.
8. The Vienna Philharmonic Orchestra.

9. The opera was Richard Strauss's *Der Rosenkavalier*, in which Kathleen Battle sang the role of Sophie.

10. *So Many Stars.*

11. a. Astrafiammante, the Queen of the Night, in *Die Zauberflöte.*

12. The opera was Richard Strauss's *Arabella*. Battle sang the role of Zdenka.

13. The soprano has told various colleagues not to look at her mouth while she is singing!

14. Ms. Battle was fired for what the Metropolitan's management called "unprofessional conduct," which apparently involved deviation from rehearsal schedules and squabbles with the conductor and her onstage colleagues, especially Rosalind Elias. The opera being rehearsed was Donizetti's *La Fille du Régiment*, and Battle was replaced in the role of Marie by Harolyn Blackwell.

15. The three witnesses against Ms. Battle were mezzo Rosalind Elias, tenor Frank Lopardo, and assistant conductor Jane Klavitor. Ms. Battle offered no defense and the dispute was arbitrated in the favor of the Metropolitan Opera.

40. CARLO BERGONZI

1. Bergonzi started out as a baritone.

2. Figaro in Rossini's *Il Barbiere di Siviglia.*

3. Gabriele Adorno in *Simon Boccanegra* and Canio in *Pagliacci*, for Cetra.

4. In 1951, Bergonzi costarred with Tebaldi in a landmark revival of Verdi's *Giovanna d'Arco* at the Teatro La Fenice in Venice. Bergonzi sang the role of Carlo opposite Tebaldi's Joan of Arc.

5. Don José in *Carmen.*

6. Verdi.

7. Busseto; Bergonzi's hostelry is called "I Due Foscari."

8. The opera was Puccini's *Edgar*, with the Opera Orchestra of New York. Renata Scotto sang Fidelia, and Gwendolyn Kil-

lebrew was heard as Tigrana. Eve Queler conducted. (The recording is available on the Sony label.)

9. *Tosca*, in 1964.
10. b. Fenton.
11. Verdi's *Un Ballo in Maschera* and *Messa da Requiem*.
12. Massenet's *Werther*.
13. *La Traviata*.
14. Nemorino in *L'Elisir d'Amore*.
15. Philips.
16. The opera was *Simon Boccanegra*. Leonard Warren, slated to sing the title role, had died two weeks earlier. He was replaced in the broadcast by Frank Guarrera.
17. Gabriella Tucci sang Leonora, Giulietta Simionato sang Azucena, and Piero Cappuccilli was the Count di Luna.
18. Bergonzi's official farewell to the operatic stage was in the role of Nemorino in *L'Elisir d'Amore* in Baltimore, in April 1993.
19. Franco Corelli.
20. The opera was *Norma*, in which Horne made her Met debut as Adalgisa. Joan Sutherland sang Norma, and Cesare Siepi was the Oroveso.

41. MONTSERRAT CABALLÉ

1. Caballé was virtually unknown in the United States when she made her debut with the American Opera Society in New York, singing the title role in Donizetti's *Lucrezia Borgia* as a last-minute replacement for Marilyn Horne.
2. Caballé has stated in interviews that, as a young child, she dreamed of becoming a ballet dancer.
3. Kolodin described the soprano's Desdemona as having been so dull that Otello probably strangled her out of sheer boredom.
4. Caballé's husband is the now-retired tenor Bernabé Martí.
5. Caballé and Martí recorded *Il Pirata* (EMI) and *Madama Butterfly* (Decca/London) together.
6. Caballé's "discovery" was a twenty-four-year-old tenor named

José Carreras who sang with her at the Teatro Liceo in Barcelona.

7. Caballé was Liù to Nilsson's Turandot at the Metropolitan, and Sieglinde to Nilsson's *Walküre* Brünnhilde at the Teatro Liceo in Barcelona.

8. The Marschallin in *Der Rosenkavalier* and the titles roles in *Salome* and *Ariadne auf Naxos.*

9. At La Scala in 1976. Although scheduled to sing in the opening performance of that production, the soprano caused a scandal when she canceled her appearance moments before the second act (in which Turandot makes her first singing appearance) began.

10. Caballé is notorious for her many "sudden" indispositions. A British writer for *Opera* magazine once quipped that "Mme. Caballé has gone into semiretirement, and thus will be available for only a few cancelations each season."

11. La Scala.

12. *Elisabetta d'Inghilterra.*

42. MARIA CALLAS

1. Ponchielli's *La Gioconda* at the Verona Arena in 1947.

2. Renata Tebaldi.

3. The title role in *Madama Butterfly* in Chicago, in 1955.

4. Toy.

5. Bellini's *I Puritani* with Giuseppe di Stefano, Rolando Panerai, and Nicola Rossi-Lemeni, conducted by Tullio Serafin; Donizetti's *Lucia di Lammermoor* with Giuseppe di Stefano and Tito Gobbi, conducted by Serafin; and Puccini's *Tosca*, with Di Stefano and Gobbi, conducted by Victor de Sabata.

6. There were four roles: Norma, Lucia, Tosca, and Violetta (*La Traviata*).

7. Callas and Bjoerling appeared together in a Chicago Lyric Opera production of *Il Trovatore.*

8. Paolina in Donizetti's *Poliuto*, with Franco Corelli and Ettore Bastianini.

9. Cherubini's *Medea*; Donizetti's *Anna Bolena* and *Poliuto*; Bellini's *I Puritani*, *Il Pirata*, and *La Sonnambula*; Gluck's *Alceste*, Spontini's *La Vestale*, and Verdi's *Macbeth*.

10. Verdi's *Macbeth*. Callas was replaced by Leonie Rysanek.

11. Carmen, Mimì in *La Bohème*, Nedda in *Pagliacci*, and the title role in *Manon Lescaut*.

12. Callas was replaced by Renata Scotto in the role of Amina in Bellini's *La Sonnambula*.

13. Both singers were appearing at a benefit concert at the Teatro Municipal in Rio de Janeiro. Supposedly, the two artists agreed not to give any encores, but Tebaldi received a prolonged ovation and therefore decided to sing an encore, after all.

14. "It is like comparing champagne to cognac. No—to Coca-Cola."

15. Giovanni Battista Meneghini.

16. Rosina in *Il Barbiere di Siviglia* and Fiorilla in *Il Turco in Italia*, both by Rossini.

17. The title roles in *Fidelio* and *Madama Butterfly*. Callas did not want to sing *Fidelio* in English and feared she was too heavy to sing Cio-Cio-San on stage.

18. Giuseppe di Stefano.

19. Tokyo, Japan, in 1974.

20. *Norma*, in Paris, in July of 1965.

21. Tullio Serafin; Elvira de Hildago.

22. *Medea*, directed by Pier Paolo Pasolini. (This was a dramatic version, not the Cherubini opera.)

23. Isolde, Brünnhilde in *Die Walküre*, and Kundry in *Parsifal*. She sang them in Italian.

24. Impresario Sol Hurok, Callas's own concert manager, died suddenly on the afternoon of March 5, 1974, only a few hours before Callas and Di Stefano were to appear at Carnegie Hall, marking the soprano's first New York appearance since 1965.

25. The title role in *Lucia di Lammermoor*. Baritone Enzo Sordello, singing the role of Enrico, offended Callas by holding the last note in their duet longer than Callas. She complained to the management, which promptly sacked Sordello.

26. Verdi's *Macbeth*.
27. *Aida*, at Covent Garden, in 1953. Callas sang Aida, Simionato sang Amneris, and Sutherland sang the Priestess. Legato has issued a recently discovered transcription of this performance on CD.
28. Elsa Maxwell.
29. *The Lisbon Traviata* and *Master Class*.
30. Washington Heights.

43. ENRICO CARUSO

1. Ruggiero Leoncavallo, composer of *Pagliacci*, penned "La Mattinata" especially for Caruso to record.
2. Caruso made his Met debut as the Duke of Mantua in Verdi's *Rigoletto* in 1903.
3. "Over There" by George M. Cohan in 1917.
4. "Vecchia zimarra" (the Cloak Aria) from Puccini's *La Bohème*. The bass was Andrés de Segurola.
5. Caruso was arrested in 1908 at the monkey house in New York's Central Park Zoo after a woman complained that he had pinched her. The case never came to trial, as the woman disappeared. Caruso's friends worried that the adverse publicity would hurt the tenor's American career, but the opposite was true, and Caruso was given a warm reception at the Metropolitan when he sang his first performance after the incident.
6. The opera was *Tosca* and the role was Mario Cavaradossi.
7. Baritone Tita Ruffo and Caruso were not on good terms. Their recording of the duet "Sì, pel ciel marmoreo giuro!" from *Otello* makes one wish that they had worked together more often.
8. The Duke of Mantua in *Rigoletto*; Riccardo in *Un Ballo in Maschera*; Enzo in *La Gioconda*; Ferrando in *La Favorita*; and Chevalier des Grieux in both *Manon* and *Manon Lescaut*.
9. Rosa Ponselle.
10. *The Lost Chord*, in English.
11. Richard Tucker and Mario Lanza.

12. Ada Giachetti.
13. The aria, from *Turandot,* was written after Caruso's death in 1921.
14. "Studenti uniti."
15. Caruso was singing with the Metropolitan Opera on a visit to the Academy of Music, in Brooklyn. He was singing the role of Nemorino in *L'Elisir d'Amore.*

44. FRANCO CORELLI

1. Ancona, Italy, a small and picturesque city not far from Venice.
2. He studied with the late Giacomo Lauri-Volpi.
3. Pierre in Prokofiev's *War and Peace.*
4. Plácido Domingo.
5. Corelli starred in a film of *Tosca.* His on-screen Tosca was Franca Duval, while Tosca's voice was that of Maria Caniglia.
6. *Tosca, Aida,* and *Turandot.*
7. *La Bohème, Tosca, Andrea Chénier, La Gioconda,* and *Adriana Lecouvreur.*
8. Corelli's lost verismo outing with Callas was Giordano's *Fedora.*
9. Corelli's wife, Loretta, sang under the name Loretta di Lelio. She can be heard on the Cetra recordings of *Aida,* in which she sings the role of the Priestess, and *La Favorita,* as Ines. She is also heard on the EMI *Don Carlo* led by Gabriele Santini.
10. Corelli's stunt was intended to silence a member of the audience who had booed him.
11. Corelli announced violent intentions against Alan Rich, critic for the old *New York Herald Tribune* and *New York* magazine.
12. Corelli's atypical ventures into Handel operas included *Giulio Cesare* and *Hercule.*
13. *Carmen* (twice) and *Faust.* A third is *Roméo et Juliette.*
14. The ladies were Roberta Peters and Gail Robinson, in per-

formances that took place a week apart at the Met in 1971.
15. a. Don José.

45. MARIO DEL MONACO

1. Pinkerton in *Madama Butterfly*.
2. That evening, Callas and Del Monaco took unwritten high
   E-flats at the climax of the finale to Act II, scene 2 of Verdi's
   opera. Fortunately, this performance has survived on disc.
3. EMI.
4. a. Renata Tebaldi
   b. Joan Sutherland sang the soprano role of Micaela. Mezzo
      Regina Resnik sang Carmen.
   c. Magda Olivero
   d. Clara Petrella (mono) and Gabriella Tucci (stereo)
   e. Anita Cerquetti
   f. Hilde Gueden
5. Don José in *Carmen* and Samson in *Samson et Dalila*.
6. The opera was *Les Troyens*. Del Monaco sang Anée, Nell Ran-
   kin sang Cassandre, and Giulietta Simionato sang Didon. Berlioz's opera was sung in an Italian translation. A complete tape
   survives, and VAI has issued a CD of highlights from the
   performance.
7. Siegmund in *Die Walküre* and the title role of *Lohengrin*.
8. *Cavalleria Rusticana* and *Norma*.
9. b. *Otello*.
10. Del Monaco was a painter in his spare time.
11. Del Monaco enjoyed singing the "Largo" from *Il Barbiere di
    Siviglia* and the "Prologo" from *Pagliacci*. He recorded the
    latter for Decca/London, although it is not currently available.
    "Live" recordings exist of the "Largo."
12. One is from Japan, where Del Monaco was joined by Renata
    Tebaldi. In this performance, the tenor stumbles as he runs
    off to the guillotine. The second video is from Italy, and the
    Maddalena is Antonietta Stella.
13. Maria Callas.

14. Not surprisingly, the answer once again is Maria Callas.
15. One *Otello* is from Italy, and Desdemona is sung by Rosanna Carteri while Iago is sung by Renato Capecchi. The other video is from Japan, with Gabriella Tucci singing Desdemona and Tito Gobbi portraying Iago.

46. GIUSEPPE DI STEFANO

1. Among the operas that Di Stefano and Callas performed together were *Tosca, La Traviata, Rigoletto, Un Ballo in Maschera, I Puritani,* and *Lucia di Lammermoor.*
2. *La Bohème, Manon Lescaut,* and *Pagliacci.*
3. Di Stefano sang a production of Lehár's *Land of Smiles,* at the Vienna Volksoper, and then on a tour that included Canada and the United States, in 1967–68. His role was that of Prince Sou-Chong. Some years later, Di Stefano returned to the Volksoper to sing the title role in another Lehár operetta, *The Czarevitch.* Recordings were made of highlights from both operas. As of 1996, neither is available in the United States, although copies of *The Czarevitch* may be found in some stores.
4. Di Stefano and Tebaldi, along with Cesare Siepi and Maestro Tullio Serafin, began to record Boito's *Mefistofele* for Decca/ London. The tenor was not at his best vocally and left the project after recording the opera's first two acts and the epilogue. The recording was remade with Mario del Monaco singing Faust. The outtakes with Di Stefano, some of which are glorious, lay in Decca's vaults for more than a decade until they were used as "Highlights from *Mefistofele*" on a 1972 LP. Only Di Stefano's solo arias from this session are in print in 1996.
5. "Pippo."
6. The show was *The Most Happy Fella,* the composer Frank Loesser, and the star Robert Weede.
7. Risë Stevens.
8. Renata Tebaldi sang both *Adriana Lecouvreur* and *Fedora* with

Di Stefano in Chicago. For the Cilea opera, they were joined by Giulietta Simionato and Tito Gobbi in what is certainly the most lavishly cast *Adriana Lecouvreur* in that work's history.

9. Five of Di Stefano's French roles were Don José in *Carmen*, the title role in *Faust*, Des Grieux in *Manon*, the title role in *Werther*, and the title role in *Les Contes d'Hoffmann*.

10. Di Stefano sang the tenor part in Verdi's *Requiem*. His colleagues were soprano Herva Nelli, mezzo Fedora Barbieri, and bass Cesare Siepi.

11. His final appearance at the Met was in 1965, singing Offenbach's Hoffmann.

12. The *Otello* was performed in San Jose, California, in 1965. Marcella Pobbé was Desdemona, and Tito Gobbi sang Iago.

13. Arturo in *I Puritani*.

14. The title role in *Rienzi*.

15. The offending artist was Maria Callas. Di Stefano became infuriated when the diva told him that only she would take a curtain call after the final act. Di Stefano, according to the proverbial unimpeachable source, replied, "Okay, Maria, don't worry, you can have the bows to yourself. As for me, I am leaving the stage, I am leaving La Scala, I am leaving my house, and, in fact, I am leaving Milan!" He did all of those things. Fortunately for all of us, they eventually made up!

47. PLÁCIDO DOMINGO

1. Domingo sang several seasons at the Tel Aviv opera in Israel. He sang many roles in Hebrew.

2. Domingo, temporarily making himself sound like a baritone, sang both Rodrigo and Don Carlo in that recorded excerpt.

3. In 1961, Domingo appeared with the Fort Worth (Texas) Opera singing Arturo in *Lucia di Lammermoor*. Lucia that night was sung by Lily Pons.

4. Domingo scored his first really important success singing the title role in Ginastera's *Don Rodrigo* at the New York City Opera in 1966.

5. Domingo was offered his La Scala contract for the title role in Verdi's *Ernani* at the suggestion of Richard Tucker, who was unable to accept that engagement.

6. Domingo is also a gifted operatic conductor.

7. Domingo has sung the title roles in *Tannhäuser*, *Lohengrin*, and *Parsifal*, as well as Siegmund in *Die Walküre* and Walther in *Die Meistersinger von Nürnberg*. He has indicated that the role of Tristan is a possibility for the future.

8. Domingo appeared as one of Doolittle's barroom companions in the first Mexican production of *My Fair Lady* (*Mi Bella Dama*). He can be heard singing "With a Little Bit of Luck" (in Spanish) on the original cast album of that production.

9. Domingo sang his first *Otello* at the Hamburg Opera in September 1975. James Levine conducted, and the cast included Katia Ricciarelli as Desdemona and Sherrill Milnes as Iago.

10. At the first New York City Opera performance of Donizetti's *Roberto Devereux*, in September 1970, soprano Beverly Sills, as Queen Elizabeth I, got so carried away that the slap she dealt Domingo, who sang Devereux, loosened some dental work. The slap, of course, was in the script.

11. This time, it was baritone Sherrill Milnes who slugged Domingo. The opera was Puccini's *La Fanciulla del West*, at the Metropolitan. Domingo was singing Dick Johnson and Milnes was portraying Jack Rance. This punch was scripted, too.

12. *Stiffelio*.

13. Three times. In 1991, there was a gala to commemorate the twenty-fifth anniversary of the inauguration of the "new" Metropolitan Opera at Lincoln Center. Domingo was heard in the third act of *Otello* while Pavarotti sang Act III of *Rigoletto*. They also sang "O Mimì, tu più non torni" from *La Bohème*. In 1993, Domingo was heard in Act I of *Die Walküre*, Pavarotti in Act I of *Otello*, and the two shared the stage in Act III of *Il Trovatore*—Domingo sang "Ah sì, ben mio" and Pavarotti attacked "Di quella pira." In 1994, Domingo and Teresa Stratas were heard in Puccini's *Il Tabarro*, paired with Pavarotti singing his first fully staged *Pagliacci*.

14. Washington, D.C., Opera.

15. John Denver.

16. Leontyne Price.
17. b. Callas.
18. The Italian tenor in *Der Rosenkavalier* and the Emperor in *Die Frau ohne Schatten.*
19. José Carreras and Diana Ross.

48. MIRELLA FRENI

1. Modena, Italy.
2. Beniamino Gigli.
3. Freni's breakthrough success at both La Scala and the Vienna State Opera was as Mimì in Puccini's *La Bohème*, as designed and staged by Franco Zeffirelli and conducted by Herbert von Karajan.
4. Freni's Met debut was accomplished in September 1965. Once again, the vehicle was *La Bohème*. Her tenor was Gianni Raimondi, also making his Metropolitan debut.
5. Freni's first complete *Carmen* was for RCA. Leontyne Price sang Carmen, Franco Corelli was Don José, and Robert Merrill sang Escamillo. This was released in 1964. The next *Carmen* to utilize Freni was the EMI edition published in 1970, on which Grace Bumbry, Jon Vickers, and Kostas Paskalis may be heard as Carmen, Don José, and Escamillo, respectively. The soprano's most recent *Carmen*, released in 1990, was recorded by Philips. Jessye Norman is the Carmen, Neil Shicoff is the José, and Simon Estes sings Escamillo.
6. The roles were Susanna in *Le Nozze di Figaro* (once) and Marguérite in *Faust* (twice). The visiting company was the Paris Opéra, during an American visit honoring the 1976 Bicentennial.
7. The opera is Puccini's *La Bohème*. The leading tenor is Luciano Pavarotti, and the bass is Nicolai Ghiaurov.
8. Freni's first husband was conductor Leone Magiera. Her second and current husband is the legendary basso Nicolai Ghiaurov.
9. a. *Manon*; and d. *Otello.*

10. Tatyana in *Eugene Onegin* and Lisa in *Pique Dame*.
11. La Scala.
12. Renata Scotto.
13. Elisabetta in *Don Carlo*.
14. Gounod's *Roméo et Juliette*.
15. The Salzburg Festival.
16. Nannetta and Alice Ford.
17. *Alcina*.
18. She sang Marguérite in the Garden Scene from *Faust*, Elisabetta in the Cabinet Scene from *Don Carlo*, and Cio-Cio-San in the third act of *Madama Butterfly*, her only stage appearance in this role. Freni was flanked by Nicolai Ghiaurov and Alfredo Kraus, also celebrating twenty-fifth anniversaries at the Met.

49. TITO GOBBI

1. The Rome Opera.
2. The Herald in *Lohengrin*, and the Watchman and Pogner in *Die Meistersinger von Nürnberg*.
3. Gobbi's brother-in-law was Bulgarian bass Boris Christoff, who was married to Gobbi's wife's sister. The two men were renowned for their recorded work in Verdi's *Simon Boccanegra* and *Don Carlo*. In *Don Carlo*, Gobbi and Christoff performed the roles of Rodrigo and King Philip, respectively, while in *Boccanegra*, Gobbi sang the title role and Christoff sang Fiesco.
4. Gobbi's performance of the title role in Berg's *Wozzeck* in a guest engagement at La Scala was a success with the critics, but it did not endear Gobbi to that theater's backstage circles.
5. Gobbi sang Scarpia opposite Renata Tebaldi's Tosca at the Metropolitan Opera in New York in 1964, and opposite Maria Callas at Covent Garden in 1964 and at the Met in 1965.
6. Gobbi was one of Tullio Serafin's protégés, a select group of singers that included, among others, Rosa Ponselle, Maria Callas, Renata Tebaldi, and Joan Sutherland.
7. Gobbi's first credit as a stage director was Verdi's *Simon Boc-*

canegra. Curiously, although London's Royal Opera was the first company to invite Gobbi to stage an opera, the baritone received Chicago's invitation shortly thereafter, and the American production predated the British engagement by several months.

8. Gobbi appeared in film versions of *Il Barbiere di Siviglia*, *L'Elisir d'Amore*, *Rigoletto*, and *Pagliacci*. The *Pagliacci* film is notable in that Gobbi played both baritone roles, Tonio and Silvio. The on-screen Nedda is Gina Lollobrigida (dubbed by Onelia Fineschi).

9. Gobbi first studied with tenor Giulio Crimi.

10. *Tosca.*

11. Gobbi was a highly regarded painter.

12. These three Puccini roles were recorded with Renata Scotto (*La Bohème*, DG), Victoria de los Angeles (*Madama Butterfly*, EMI), and Margaret Mas (*Il Tabarro*, EMI).

13. Don Giovanni, and Count Almaviva in *Le Nozze di Figaro*.

14. San Carlo (Naples) 1958, Chicago Lyric Opera, 1958, and the Metropolitan Opera, 1972.

15. Giordano's *Fedora.*

50. ROBERT MERRILL

1. Brooklyn, New York.

2. Merrill had ideas about becoming a professional baseball player, but his love for singing was stronger than the lure of the ballpark. In later years, Merrill often sang the national anthem at New York Yankees games.

3. Licia Albanese.

4. The operas Merrill sang under Toscanini's baton were *La Traviata* in 1946 and *Un Ballo in Maschera* in 1954.

5. Bing fired Merrill because the uppity young baritone skipped the Met's spring tour in order to appear in a truly awful film entitled *Aaron Slick from Punkin Crick*. After months of begging, Merrill was reinstated by Bing after he publicly apolo-

gized for his arrogant behavior in the pages of *The New York Times* and *The Herald Tribune.*

6. Soprano Roberta Peters.
7. Pianist Marion Machno.
8. The duets included "Dio, che nell'alma infondere" from *Don Carlo*, "O Mimì, tu più non torni" from *La Bohème*, "Solenne in quest'ora" from *La Forza del Destino*, "Au fond du temple saint" from *Les Pêcheurs de Perles*, and "Si, pel ciel" from *Otello.*
9. c. Merrill never sang Falstaff.
10. *Kismet* and *Fiddler on the Roof.*
11. Merrill's first *Bohème* was for RCA, later released by EMI. Victoria de los Angeles sang Mimì, Lucine Amara portrayed Musetta, Jussi Bjoerling was Rodolfo, and Sir Thomas Beecham conducted. The second *Bohème*, also for RCA, and still available on that label, matched Merrill with Anna Moffo as Mimì, Mary Costa as Musetta, and Richard Tucker as Rodolfo. Erich Leinsdorf was the conductor.
12. *Once More from the Beginning.*
13. Leonard Warren.
14. The diva was Zinka Milanov, who smacked the baritone because he had garlic on his breath.
15. *Lucia di Lammermoor* and *La Traviata.*

51. ZINKA MILANOV

1. The soprano was born Zinka Kunc.
2. The Metropolitan's management required Milanov to relearn her Verdian repertoire in Italian (she had been singing in German and her native Croatian) and to lose twenty pounds. Milanov complied.
3. Milanov sang the *Requiem* and the third act of *Rigoletto* with Toscanini.
4. The tenor was Jussi Bjoerling. Milanov and Bjoerling recorded *Aida*, *Il Trovatore*, *Cavalleria Rusticana* and *Tosca* for RCA.
5. b. Minnie in *La Fanciulla del West.*

6. Milanov sang Tosca at the Metropolitan. One day, Renata Tebaldi, scheduled to sing *Aida*, had to cancel because of illness. Milanov, who vehemently refused to "cover" other singers, agreed to sing when Rudolf Bing changed the opera to *Tosca* in her honor. The critics, summoned for the occasion, were generous to the soprano, who, after all, managed the feat of singing *Tosca* at the Met for the first time, without benefit of rehearsal.

7. The title role in Bellini's *Norma*.

8. The album was called *Milanov Sings*.

9. In Act I of *La Gioconda*, Milanov, exiting into Saint Mark's Cathedral, floated a B-flat pianissimo on the final note of the phrase "Enzo adorato, ah come t'amo" that to many listeners seemed like entry into heaven without having to die first. If you listen to the commercial recording of Milanov's *Gioconda* (RCA or London LPs, or available as a Decca/London CD set), or any of the several Metropolitan broadcast *Gioconda*s that still circulate, you'll understand!

10. If Milanov's performance attracted secondary interest that evening, it was because Marian Anderson made her debut in the role of Ulrica, an honor that ought to have been bestowed upon the contralto thirty years earlier.

11. *Tosca*.

12. *Ernani*.

13. Richard Tucker.

14. The University of Indiana.

15. Milanov died in New York City in May of 1989.

52. JESSYE NORMAN

1. Norman was born in Augusta, Georgia, on September 15, 1945.

2. Cassandre in Berlioz's *Les Troyens*.

3. The opera was *Un Giorno di Regno*. The recording firm was Philips.

4. The Countess in Mozart's *Le Nozze di Figaro*.

5. Norman made her Metropolitan Opera debut as Cassandre and Didon in *Les Troyens,* in 1983.
6. As of 1996, Jessye Norman's Wagnerian roles at the Metropolitan Opera include Elisabeth in *Tannhaüser,* Sieglinde in *Die Walküre,* and Kundry in *Parsifal.*
7. The role was Carmen in Bizet's opera.
8. Jocasta in *Oedipus Rex.*
9. This was a trick question. Schoenberg's work is a monodrama.
10. Kathleen Battle.
11. *With a Song in My Heart* and *Lucky to be Me* from Philips.
12. At the scheduled premiere, January 5, 1996, Richard Versalle, the tenor singing the role of Vitek, suffered a fatal heart attack onstage at the Met, moments after the curtain went up on the opera's first act. The performance was canceled in the wake of this tragedy before Norman made her first entrance. Incredibly, the opera's next scheduled performance, the following Monday, had to be canceled because of a snowstorm that was nicknamed "The Blizzard of '96." On Thursday, January 11, the first performance of Janáček's opera at the Met, finally took place, in an atmosphere of nervousness on both sides of the curtain.

53. MAGDA OLIVERO

1. Magda Olivero made her professional debut on December 2, 1932, in Torino, singing Nino Cattozzo's *I Misteri Dolorosi.* She made her American debut thirty-three years later in Dallas, Texas, singing the title role in Cherubini's *Medea.*
2. Aldo Busch.
3. The composer was Francesco Cilèa, who persuaded Olivero to sing the title role in his *Adriana Lecouvreur* again.
4. The operas were Puccini's *Turandot* and Giordano's *Fedora.* Olivero, singing Liù in *Turandot,* was partnered by Francesco Merli. Her Fedora was paired with the Loris of Mario del Monaco.
5. When Tebaldi canceled a series of *Adrianas* in Naples, in

1958, she was replaced by Olivero. This *Adriana*, broadcast and made available first on LP and later on CD, galvanized Olivero's career. After years of singing in secondary theaters with an occasional date in Milan or Rome, the soprano was, from this point on, in demand in every opera house in Italy and many in other nations, too.

6. Elsa in *Lohengrin.*
7. *Tosca*, in April 1975, forty-two years after her operatic debut.
8. The work was Janáček's *Jenufa*, sung in Italian. Olivero sang Kostelnicka. Grace Bumbry sang the title role.
9. *Tosca.*
10. d. Olivero never sang Desdemona. She once stated in an interview that she felt the role lacked sufficient dramatic range for her interpretive powers.
11. Olivero liked to sing "Love Is a Many-Splendored Thing" as "Si, quell'amor e splendida." A recording exists.
12. The Netherlands.
13. Magda Olivero exemplifies the verismo style of Italian opera.
14. The opera was *Nabucco*, on January 18, 1934. Olivero sang the tiny role of Anna, Gina Cigna sang Abigaille, and Ebe Stignani sang Fenena. One might have called the opera *Three Saints in Four Acts!*
15. Olivero sang Sophie in *Der Rosenkavalier*, in Italian in Torino in 1935.
16. The opera was the rarely done *Mazeppa*, at the Florence May Festival in 1954.
17. *Tosca*, in November 1978.
18. Magda Olivero appeared in four operas by Franco Alfano, apart from Puccini's *Turandot*, which Alfano completed. The final scene of that opera, which Alfano reconstructed from Puccini's notes, does not include music for Liù, the character that Olivero portrayed. The Alfano operas, each followed by the role that Olivero performed are: *Cyrano de Bergerac* (Rossana), *La Leggenda di Sakuntala* (Aniusa and Sakuntala), *Risurrezione* (Katiusha), and *L'Ultimo Lord* (Freddie).
19. The only Donizetti opera in which Olivero ever appeared was *La Favorita*, in which she sang the role of Ines.

20. Olivero sang in Rota's *Il Cappello di Paglia di Firenze*, singing the role of La Baronessa.
21. In *Suor Angelica*, Olivero sang both Suor Genovieffa and the title role.
22. Zerlina in *Don Giovanni*.
23. In *Falstaff*, Olivero has sung both Nannetta and Alice Ford.
24. The opera was Menotti's *The Medium*, in which she sang the title role, Madame Flora.
25. *Adriana Lecouvreur*.

54. LUCIANO PAVAROTTI

1. He was born on October 12, 1934, in Modena Italy.
2. Soprano Mirella Freni.
3. Rodolfo in Puccini's *La Bohème*.
4. Joan Sutherland.
5. He taught physical education in a boys' school.
6. *Beatrice di Tenda* for Decca/London.
7. Tonio in Donizetti's *La Fille du Régiment*, which he sang in February 1972. Tonio's aria, "Pour mon âme," with its nine high Cs, electrified the audience when Pavarotti sang it, and his career skyrocketed after that.
8. Renata Scotto.
9. The Chicago Lyric Opera.
10. The American Express Card.
11. At the Philadelphia Academy of Music in a concert performance with the Philadelphia Orchestra.
12. Miami, Florida, singing Edgardo in *Lucia di Lammermoor*.
13. *Yes, Giorgio*; "If We Were in Love."
14. b. Gorky Park
15. "King of the High Cs."
16. Adua.
17. *Rigoletto, La Traviata, Lucia di Lammermoor, Maria Stuarda, Il Trovatore, La Sonnambula, I Puritani, La Fille du Régiment, L' Elisir d' Amore*.
18. c. *I Puritani* and d. *Luisa Miller*.

19. Richard Thomas, Jacqueline Bisset, and John McEnroe.
20. *Idomeneo.*
21. Renata Scotto.

55. LEONTYNE PRICE

1. Laurel, Mississippi.
2. February 10, 1927.
3. Tosca; Mme. Lidoine in Poulenc's *Dialogues des Carmélites*; Pamina in *Die Zauberflöte*; and Donna Anna in *Don Giovanni.*
4. In San Francisco in 1957, as Tosca.
5. Leonora in *Il Trovatore,* Liù in *Turandot,* and the title role in *Madama Butterfly.*
6. Bess in Gershwin's *Porgy and Bess* in 1952.
7. Price sang at Lyndon B. Johnson's inauguration in 1965.
8. Lulu Shoemaker.
9. Baritone William Warfield.
10. Puccini's *La Fanciulla del West* (1961), singing Minnie, with Richard Tucker and Anselmo Colzani; Barber's *Antony and Cleopatra* (1966—opening night of the new Met at Lincoln Center), singing Cleopatra, with Justino Díaz, Jess Thomas, and Rosalind Elias; the title role in Verdi's *Aida* (1969) with Tucker, Irene Dalis, and Robert Merrill.
11. Leonora in Verdi's *Il Trovatore.*
12. The title role in Richard Strauss's *Ariadne auf Naxos* in San Francisco in 1977.
13. Herbert von Karajan.
14. Amelia in Verdi's *Un Ballo in Maschera.*
15. In 1963 Price sang the title role in Verdi's *Aida* with the La Scala company in Moscow.
16. Five.
17. Vienna.
18. *Right as the Rain*; André Previn.
19. Aida, in January of 1985.
20. *Il Trovatore.*

56. SAMUEL RAMEY

1. Kansas.
2. Ramey worked for a New York City publishing house before becoming a professional singer.
3. The New York City Opera.
4. Ramey made his La Scala debut as King Philip II in Verdi's *Don Carlo*. Also in the cast that night was Luciano Pavarotti, singing his first performance of the opera's title role. Pavarotti missed a crucial musical entrance and had high-note problems. The audience roundly booed the tenor and the new production of the opera. Ramey, however, scored a personal triumph.
5. Handel's *Rinaldo*. Also debuting that night was conductor Raymond Leppard.
6. Rossini's *Semiramide*.
7. *So in Love*.
8. Attila in Verdi's opera.
9. The San Francisco Opera. Plácido Domingo and Eva Marton were Ramey's co-stars.
10. *I Due Foscari*.
11. The Metropolitan Opera.
12. b. Ramey has not yet recorded the title role in *Boris*, although a live performance from Europe is available.

57. LEONIE RYSANEK

1. Vienna, Austria.
2. Maria Cebotari.
3. Karl Böhm.
4. The role was Lady Macbeth in Verdi's *Macbeth*. Rysanek was hastily invited to sing the role after Rudolf Bing abruptly dismissed Maria Callas after a dispute over scheduling.
5. Rysanek sang Abigaille in the first (and only) Metropolitan Opera production of Verdi's *Nabucco*, which had its premiere on Opening Night, 1960.
6. Sieglinde.

7. Wilhelm Furtwängler conducted Rysanek's EMI recording of *Die Walküre*, and Karl Böhm conducted her Philips recording of the opera.

8. Rysanek is a celebrated, if somewhat controversial, Tosca. She has been cheered and booed in this role over the years, often at the same performance!

9. Rysanek's Tosca can be sampled in both Italian and German.

10. Rysanek has sung all three leading female roles in Strauss's *Elektra*. First, Rysanek triumphed as Chrysothemis, later she was heard in the title role, and, in the closing years of her career, Rysanek sang Klytämnestra with much success.

11. In October of 1966, Rysanek enjoyed a spectacular success singing the title role (the Empress) in Richard Strauss's *Die Frau ohne Schatten*. Karl Böhm conducted.

12. Lady Macbeth, Aida, Leonora (in *Forza*), Abigaille, Amelia (in *Ballo*), Elisabetta, and Desdemona.

13. Kabanicha in *Katya Kabanova* and Kostelnicka in *Jenufa*.

14. Leonie Rysanek is famous for her passionate, wordless shrieking at key, dramatic moments. Four unforgettable examples occurred when Rysanek, as Sieglinde in *Die Walküre*, glimpsed Siegmund pulling Wotan's sword out of its niche in the tree; in the third act of *Die Frau ohne Schatten* when the Empress refuses to drink the bloody water that will give her the shadow that had belonged to the Dyer's Wife; the twin shrieks at the beginning of *Parsifal*'s second act, when Kundry realizes that she is, once again, in Klingsor's power; and in the second act of *Der Fliegende Holländer* when Senta turns and sees the Dutchman in her home. There are other examples, as well, that you may remember with pleasure.

15. The Old Countess in Tchaikovsky's *Pique Dame*, which served as her farewell to the operatic stage, at the Metropolitan Opera, in January of 1996.

58. BEVERLY SILLS

1. *Our Gal Sunday* was a radio serial that dealt with the ups and downs of a poor girl from an American mining town who

married a rich fellow. Sills's role was that of an orphaned child.

2. Rosalinde in *Die Fledermaus*, 1955.
3. Peter B. Greenough, financier and former publisher of the Cleveland *Plain Dealer*.
4. Handel's *Giulio Cesare* at the New York City Opera in 1966.
5. In Rossini's *L'Assedio di Corinto*, Sills replaced Renata Scotto, who withdrew because she was pregnant.
6. *Roberto Devereux, Maria Stuarda,* and *Anna Bolena.* Sills sang Queen Elizabeth I in *Devereux*, and the title characters in the other two operas.
7. Norman Treigle.
8. She sang five roles, Pamira in *L'Assedio di Corinto*; Violetta in *La Traviata*; the title roles in *Lucia di Lammermoor* and *Thaïs*, and Norina in *Don Pasquale*.
9. Sills and Sutherland costarred in *Die Fledermaus* in San Diego, California, in September 1980. This was Sills's last staged operatic appearance before her official retirement from singing in October 1980. Sutherland was heard as Rosalinde, while Sills sang the role of Adele.
10. Although Sills's debut at the Metropolitan Opera House took place in April 1975, when she sang Pamira in *L'Assedio di Corinto*, she sang one concert performance of Donna Anna in *Don Giovanni* with the Metropolitan Opera Company at Lewisohn Stadium (in Manhattan) in July 1966 (*before* her City Opera triumph as Cleopatra in *Giulio Cesare*).
11. Sills always had a hard time with the critics in London.
12. Julius Rudel.
13. *Roberto Devereux* and *La Fille du Régimemt* (the latter sung in English).
14. d. *Lakmé.*
15. Sherrill Milnes joined Sills in an album of old show tunes entitled *The Fireman's Bride.*

59. GIULIETTA SIMIONATO

1. Forlì.
2. Hänsel in Humperdinck's opera in 1942.

3. *Aida, Il Trovatore,* and *Norma.*
4. a. Mario del Monaco
   b. Cesare Valletti
   c. Carlo Bergonzi
   d. Gianni Poggi
   e. Luigi Infantino
5. Simionato appeared at the Met as Azucena in *Il Trovatore,* Amneris in *Aida,* Rosina in *Il Barbiere di Siviglia,* and Santuzza in *Cavalleria Rusticana.* On tour with the Met, Simionato was heard as Dalila in Saint-Saëns's *Samson et Dalila.*
6. The Chicago Lyric Opera.
7. In French: with Giuseppe di Stefano at La Scala, and with Nicolai Gedda at the Vienna State Opera. In Italian: with Franco Corelli at the Verona Arena, and with Mario del Monaco in Tokyo.
8. Meyerbeer's *Gli Ugonotti* (*Les Huguenots*) in Italian.
9. Donna Elvira in *Don Giovanni.*
10. Ännchen in *Der Freischütz.*
11. b. Lady Macbeth.
12. La Scala.
13. "Casta Diva" from *Norma.*
14. The film was *Tosca's Kiss,* a documentary about the Casa Verdi, the home for elderly musicians that Verdi founded in his will. Simionato has been active for many years as a patroness of this organization.
15. Maria Callas and Leyla Gencer.
16. The opera was *Il Trovatore,* in February 1960. The cast included Antonietta Stella as Leonora, Carlo Bergonzi as Manrico, and Ettore Bastianini as Count di Luna.

60. RISË STEVENS

1. The Bronx, New York.
2. Czechoslovakia.
3. Miss Stevens's first appearance with the Metropolitan Opera Company was in the title role of Thomas's *Mignon* on one of

the company's famous Tuesday evening visits to the Academy of Music, in Philadelphia, on December 17, 1938. Two days later, the mezzo made her first appearance on the stage of the Metropolitan Opera, in the title role of *Der Rosenkavalier*.

4. *Mignon, Boris Godunov*, and *La Gioconda*.

5. The film was *Going My Way*. In it, Miss Stevens, playing a young opera singer, performed the Habanera from *Carmen*, a role which she had not yet sung in an opera house. Public delight with her appearance in the Bizet excerpt led to numerous requests by fans that Stevens sing the role "for real."

6. The acerbic Farrar sniffed at Stevens's Hollywood triumph. The great Carmen of the previous generation snapped, "In *my* day, one became a famous Carmen by actually *singing* the role!"

7. b. Verdi.

8. Sir Tyrone Guthrie.

9. In that *Carmen*, the fourth act was set not outside the corrida, as described in the libretto, but in a reception hall where a pre-event party has been given for Escamillo, Carmen, and their friends. It is in this room that the final confrontation between Carmen and José took place. The murder was quite realistic. Carmen screamed, struggled, and, in a desperate bid to stay on her feet, clutched at a wine-colored drapery for support. She ultimately collapsed under the drapery as the crowd emerged from the bullring. This vivid scene, viewed nearly forty years ago in my first visit to the Met, has stayed with me ever since, countless other *Carmen* performances notwithstanding.

10. Mario del Monaco.

11. Risë Stevens recorded an "abridged" *Samson* with Mario del Monaco, for which the conductor was Fausto Cleva. She also recorded scenes from the opera with Jan Peerce, with Leopold Stokowski conducting.

12. *The King and I*, with Darren McGavin.

13. Mortari's *La Figlia del Diavolo* (a world premiere).

14. Cherubino in *Le Nozze di Figaro*.

15. *Les Contes d'Hoffmann*.

16. They performed, to the tune of the Habanera, a silly chanson about a cement-mixer.
17. Miss Stevens served as co-general manager (with Michael Manuel) of the Metropolitan Opera National Company, a very worthy venture for which the funding expired after only two seasons.
18. She was president of Mannes College of Music in the late 1970s.
19. Risë Stevens's fudge was a hot-selling item at the Metropolitan Opera gift shop for many years.

61. TERESA STRATAS

1. Stratas won the 1959 Metropolitan Opera Auditions of the Air.
2. Poussette in *Manon*.
3. The Bolshoi.
4. Zubin Mehta.
5. Toronto. Her parents had moved to Canada from Greece.
6. Stratas once recalled performing in the basement of her family's home to a group of apparently culture-craving rats!
7. Stratas worked on the role of Jenny with Lotte Lenya, the widow of the *Mahagonny*'s composer, Kurt Weill, and the creator of Jenny at the opera's world premiere.
8. As did Caballé, Stratas has canceled an incredible number of performances and engagements during her long career.
9. Stratas sang Cherubino in *Le Nozze di Figaro*, disarming the chauvinistic French press and audiences.
10. The opera was *La Traviata*, sung in Italian—all three of these artists had been known to sing and record Italian operas in German during the 1960s.
11. The opera was Berg's *Lulu*. Stratas sang the first performance of the completed *Lulu* in Paris in 1979 and appeared a year later in the Metropolitan premiere of the three-act *Lulu*.
12. The opera is Smetana's *The Bartered Bride*, and its original language is Czech.

13. Stratas worked with her namesake, Mother Teresa, in India.
14. Stratas triumphed in all three operas of Puccini's *Il Trittico*, singing Giorgetta in *Il Tabarro*, the title role in *Suor Angelica*, and Lauretta in *Gianni Schicchi*.
15. Stratas sang the title role in *Salome* in this superb video production.
16. *La Traviata*; Franco Zeffirelli.
17. c. Stratas has not sung Marie in *Wozzeck*, although she'd undoubtedly be stunning in the role.
18. Giorgetta in *Il Tabarro* and Nedda in *Pagliacci*. We'd probably better mention that Plácido Domingo sang Luigi in *Il Tabarro* and Juan Pons sang Michele. In *Pagliacci*, Luciano Pavarotti sang Canio and the versatile Pons sang Tonio.
19. Stratas had another major success as Marie Antoinette in *The Ghosts of Versailles*, composed by John Corigliano, with William Hoffman the librettist. The Metropolitan Opera hosted the world premiere, only the third such occasion since moving to Lincoln Center.

62. DAME JOAN SUTHERLAND

1. The First Lady in *Die Zauberflöte*.
2. Franco Zeffirelli created a new production of *Lucia di Lammermoor* for Sutherland in 1958 at the Royal Opera House, Covent Garden.
3. The first time Rudolf Bing heard Sutherland sing, he was not sufficiently impressed to offer her a Metropolitan contract.
4. Marilyn Horne and Luciano Pavarotti. Horne was a young, unknown mezzo when Sutherland heard her and began requesting her as a colleague in operatic and concert appearances. Sutherland's helping hand culminated in Horne's 1970 Metropolitan Opera debut as Adalgisa to Sutherland's Norma in Bellini's opera. Pavarotti, also unknown, auditioned for Sutherland, who was casting her tour of Australia in 1965. Pavarotti, having proven himself to the diva, was eventually

recommended by Sutherland to the Royal Opera and Decca/
London records. The rest of his story is well known.

5. La Stupenda.
6. Richard Bonynge.
7. Sutherland performed Desdemona in Verdi's *Otello*, Eva in
   Die Meistersinger von Nürnberg, and Amelia in *Un Ballo in
   Maschera*, among others.
8. Her comedy hit was in the title role of Donizetti's *La Fille du
   Régiment*, in which she and Pavarotti starred in London and
   New York.
9. Birgit Nilsson.
10. Tullio Serafin.
11. Leonora in *Il Trovatore*, in 1987.
12. *Who's Afraid of Opera?*
13. The opera was Meyerbeer's *Les Huguenots*, sung in Italian as
    Gli Ugonotti.
14. *On Our Selection*. The costar is John Mortimor.
15. Donna Anna in *Don Giovanni*.
16. Sydney (Australia) Opera House.
17. The Royal Opera, Covent Garden.
18. Silvio Varviso conducted *La Sonnambula*. The other three
    operas were conducted by Sir John Pritchard.
19. Noel Coward.
20. *Die Fledermaus*.

63. RENATA TEBALDI

1. Riccardo Zandonai (composer of *Francesca da Rimini*) and
   Carmen Melis.
2. Tebaldi returned to La Scala singing the title role in *Tosca*.
   Giuseppe di Stefano sang Cavaradossi that night, joined by
   Tito Gobbi as Scarpia.
3. The San Francisco Opera in 1950.
4. Mario del Monaco sang Radames to Tebaldi's Aida in San
   Francisco in 1950. Five years later, Del Monaco's Otello wel-

comed Tebaldi's Desdemona to the stage of the Metropolitan Opera.

5. Tebaldi's colleagues in that wonderful *Falstaff* included Tito Gobbi as Falstaff, Giulietta Simionato as Quickly, Anna Maria Canali as Meg, Anna Moffo as Nannetta, and Cornell Mac-Neil as Ford. Tullio Serafin conducted.

6. Tebaldi's favorite role has always been the title role in Cilea's *Adriana Lecouvreur.*

7. The other three sopranos in that unforgettable 1967 *Bell Telephone Hour* were Birgit Nilsson, Joan Sutherland, and Leontyne Price.

8. Eva in *Die Meistersinger von Nürnberg*, Elisabeth in *Tannhäuser*, and Elsa in *Lohengrin*. (Although no recording of her Eva has ever turned up, Tebaldi's Elisabeth and Elsa were put on vinyl, and, in "highlight" form, on CD.)

9. Franco Corelli.

10. Tebaldi sang the title role in Ponchielli's *La Gioconda*, an opera that she had first sung at the Metropolitan in 1966. The opera was performed at the Teatro San Carlo in Naples. A tape of that performance survives.

11. Renata Tebaldi's final public performance was a recital given at La Scala, Milan, on May 22, 1976.

12. "If I Loved You" from Rodgers and Hammerstein's *Carousel.*

13. *La Wally.*

14. a. *Mefistofele.*

15. Giorgio Favoretti.

16. Hans Beirer was Otello, and William Dooley sang Iago.

17. *Giulio Cesare*, in which Tebaldi sang Cleopatra.

18. Tosca. One video is from Japan, where Gianni Poggi sang Mario Cavaradossi, and Giusepe Taddei sang Scarpia. The other is from Stuttgart, where Eugene Tobin sang Mario and George London sang Scarpia. Both performances took place in 1961.

19. Tebaldi recorded mezzo-tenor duets from *La Gioconda* and *Aida* with Franco Corelli for Decca/London.

20. Decca/London issued a quintet of operatic scenes from the *bel canto* repertoire and Verdi roles not otherwise associated with

Renata Tebaldi. These include: Abigaille's *scena* "Anch'io dischiuso un giorno" from Verdi's *Nabucco*; "Casta diva" from
Bellini's *Norma*, "Ah, non credea mirarti" from Bellini's *La
Sonnambula*, "Qui la voce" from Bellini's *I Puritani*, and,
from the realm of the Verdian mezzo-soprano, "O don fatale"
from *Don Carlo*. Maestro Fausto Cleva conducts the orchestra
of the Monte Carlo Opera.

21. Tebaldi returned to New York City for a week in December
1995, after twenty years away from the city that had been for
many years her second home. The diva's visit was filled with
book-signings (a new biography, *The Voice of an Angel* by
Carlamaria Casanova, translated by Connie DeCaro, had been
published), parties in her honor, and a triumphant appearance
in the audience at the Met. A fan of the soprano's, who knew
Mayor Rudolph Giuliani, asked the Mayor about a ceremony
in Tebaldi's honor. The Mayor, himself an admirer of Renata's, agreed, and thus, December 11, 1995, was proclaimed as
"Renata Tebaldi Day," complete with a ceremony at City
Hall.

64. DAME KIRI TE KANAWA

1. New Zealand (on March 6, 1944).
2. The Santa Fe Opera.
3. The Countess in Mozart's *Le Nozze di Figaro*.
4. In the film *A Room with a View*, Dame Kiri may be heard
   singing "Chi il bel sogno di Doretta" and "O mio babbino
   caro."
5. a. She has not sung the Queen, nor, would one think, is she
   likely to do so in the future. This highly demanding coloratura
   role would seem to lie beyond Dame Kiri's *fach*.
6. *Le Nozze di Figaro*.
7. Dame Kiri interviewed Dame Eva Turner in the documentary
   Tosca: I Live for Art.
8. She celebrated with a gala concert at London's Royal Albert

Hall, which was televised and subsequently released for home video.

9. This honor was given to Te Kanawa in 1982, after she had sung at the wedding of Britain's Prince Charles and Princess Diana. In light of that couple's divorce, one hopes that the soprano will be allowed to retain her damehood!
10. Jerome Kern, George Gershwin, and Cole Porter.
11. "Hava Nagila."
12. Irons played Henry Higgins in a concert version of *My Fair Lady* in which Dame Kiri sang Eliza. Televised in the United Kingdom, the performance inspired a "cast album" and was issued for home video.

65. FREDERICA VON STADE

1. Lotte Lehmann.
2. The First Boy in *Die Zauberflöte*.
3. Renata Tebaldi and Dorothy Kirsten.
4. *Dangerous Liaisons*.
5. a. Susanna.
6. José Carreras.
7. The title role in Rossini's *La Cenerentola*.
8. *Show Boat* and *The Sound of Music*.
9. "Jennie Rebecca."
10. Mélisande in Debussy's *Pelléas et Mélisande*.
11. Amina in *La Sonnambula*.
12. Monteverdi's *Il Ritorno d'Ulisse in Patria*.

66. THE THREE TENORS

1. Rome, Italy, in July 1990.
2. Luciano Pavarotti is the eldest of the three tenors.
3. Domingo.
4. José Carreras had recently recovered from leukemia.
5. Polygram Records.

6. They sang "O Sole Mio," adding trills to the refrain.
7. "Maria" was sung by Domingo, and "Tonight" was sung by Carreras.
8. Los Angeles, in July 1994.
9. Zubin Mehta.
10. Frank Sinatra and Gene Kelly.
11. "Brasil."
12. d. 1.4 billion.
13. "La donna è mobile."
14. Pavarotti.
15. Pavarotti.
16. WEA Atlantic.
17. "America."
18. The "Brindisi" from *La Traviata*.
19. Each concert celebrated the final game of the World Cup Soccer tournament.
20. a. $1,000.00.
21. Conductor Zubin Mehta was replaced by James Levine.
22. Giants Stadium in Rutherford, New Jersey.
23. The first two concerts were broadcast internationally. The third concert was a Pay-Per-View cable television event.
24. Pavarotti had endured a troubled 1995–96 season. The tenor was plagued by poor health that forced him to cancel a number of performances. Those that he actually sang had not been unalloyed triumphs. Rumors concerning Pavarotti's personal life had been aired in the media. Many people wondered if Pavarotti would undertake the Three Tenor tour. Not only did Pavarotti appear as scheduled, but he was, by all accounts, in excellent form.

67. DEBUTS AT THE MET

1. Tebaldi's debut was as Desdemona on January 31, 1955. Her costars were Mario del Monaco and Leonard Warren, with whom she sang on many occasions in the years to come.
2. Price's Met debut, as Leonora in *Il Trovatore*, in January 1961,

capped a career that had taken her to the opera houses of San Francisco, Chicago, Vienna, and Salzburg.

3. Del Monaco's debut was a one-night stand as Des Grieux in Puccini's *Manon Lescaut* in 1949. Del Monaco sang many roles at the Met over the next twelve years until he left the Met in a huff, claiming that Franco Corelli had been given the new production of Puccini's *Turandot* that Rudolf Bing had allegedly promised to Del Monaco.

4. Bumbry's debut, as Eboli in Verdi's *Don Carlo* in 1965, was the first of many occasions on which the St. Louis–born mezzo would sing the Verdi mezzo roles of Eboli, Amneris, and Azucena until, in the mid-1970s, she became a soprano.

5. Gobbi's debut, on January 13, 1956, was a great success with the public. The role was Scarpia. Unfortunately for the New York public, Gobbi and the Met's Bing never really felt comfortable with one another, and the baritone's Metropolitan engagements were sporadic. Also, although the public and press were ecstatic about Gobbi's performance, the baritone related in his memoirs that Bing was furious that Gobbi changed a bit of the Met's staging. Years later, Gobbi staged a *Tosca* revival at the Met.

6. Marian Anderson made her Met debut as Ulrica in Verdi's *Un Ballo in Maschera* on January 7, 1955.

7. Merrill's debut in 1945, as Giorgio Germont in *La Traviata*, found the inexperienced and—to judge from his memoirs—nervous baritone singing opposite Licia Albanese. Throughout Merrill's thirty-year Met career, he frequently forgot some of Germont's words!

8. Caballé's Met debut, a one-night stand at the old Met during its final season in 1965, was in the role of Marguérite in *Faust*. She was not in spectacular voice that night, and the occasion is best remembered by many for the debut of another artist (see Question #22) and for conductor Georges Prêtre's being jostled by a latecomer in the first row!

9. Siepi's first night at the Met was as Philip II in *Don Carlo* in 1950. Several other artists made debuts that night, as did General Manager Rudolf Bing. Siepi was a replacement for the Bulgarian bass Boris Christoff, who had visa problems.

10. Although a star in Europe since the 1940s, Giulietta Simionato made her Metropolitan debut in 1959, singing Azucena in *Il Trovatore* on opening night, sharing the stage with Antonietta Stella, Carlo Bergonzi, and Leonard Warren.

11. Flagstad's debut, as Sieglinde in *Die Walküre*, on a broadcast matinee in 1935, was an unheralded triumph. Toscanini, long feuding with the Met, listened to her voice and telephoned the Met, demanding to be told everything there was to know about Flagstad!

12. Ponselle's Met debut in 1918 was opposite Caruso in the Met premiere of *La Forza del Destino*, singing Leonora. Ponselle, a lifelong victim of before-the-performance nervousness, swore to friends she nearly fainted when the curtain rose on the first act.

13. Birgit Nilsson's Metropolitan debut, as Isolde in 1959, was reviewed on the front page of *The New York Times*. What else is there to say?

14. MacNeil flew to New York from an engagement in Milan, to substitute for an ailing Robert Merrill, making his debut on the broadcast of Verdi's *Rigoletto*, singing the title role on less than a day's notice, with no rehearsal, in March 1959. MacNeil became a stalwart member of the company for the next quarter of a century.

15. Joan Sutherland made her Met debut in the title role of *Lucia di Lammermoor*, at a special Sunday performance in November 1961.

16. Maria Callas's Met debut in the title role of *Norma* in 1956 on opening night was, curiously, anticlimactic. By all accounts, including her own, she was not in best form that night. Moreover, the public was wary of her because of a hostile article that appeared in *Time* magazine the week of her debut. The audience reaction was cordial, but Callas's difficulties with Bing and the men in her life conspired to make her visits to New York all too few.

17. Franco Corelli made his Metropolitan debut as Manrico, sharing the evening with Leontyne Price in that unforgettable 1961 *Il Trovatore*. Corelli and Price sang memorable perfor-

mances of *La Forza del Destino, Ernani, Aida,* and *Tosca* together at the Metropolitan.

18. The legendary Marcella Sembrich made her Met debut on the third night of the very first Met season, 1883–84, in the title role of *Lucia di Lammermoor.* The extraordinarily versatile Polish soprano sang at the Met through the first decade of the twentieth century.

19. Sills made her Met debut as Pamira in *L'Assedio di Corinto* in 1975, only five years before her retirement from singing. Technically, Sills's Met debut had occurred nine years earlier, when the soprano sang the role of Donna Anna in *Don Giovanni* with the Met in a summer concert in Manhattan's Lewisohn Stadium. The diva insists in her memoirs that a debut at the Met means singing within the four walls of the opera house. Sills's first appearance *inside* the Met attracted international attention, and she received an ovation of several minutes' duration when she stepped onto the stage for the first time. Her debut was an emotional occasion for the girl from Brooklyn and thousands of her fans.

20. Verrett's Met debut, as Carmen, took place in 1968. Reports of a fracas with her tenor, Jon Vickers, at the dress rehearsal had the fans on edge, but the performance went smoothly, and Verrett and Vickers remain good friends.

21. Domingo's Met debut, in 1968, was as Maurizio to the Adriana Lecouvreur of Renata Tebaldi. Domingo was signed to sing that role a week later, but Franco Corelli's sudden indisposition led to Domingo's first Met appearance being made on an hour's notice. Several months later, Domingo replaced Corelli in a new production of *Il Trovatore,* when Corelli returned to Italy to be with his critically ill father. A few years later, Corelli returned Domingo's "favor" by replacing him, on equally short notice, in two Met performances of *Ernani.*

22. Sherrill Milnes's Met debut, as Valentin in *Faust* in 1965, was shared with that of Montserrat Caballé. Milnes stole the show from the Spanish diva with his thunderously applauded "Avant de quitter ces lieux" and his powerful rendering of Valentin's death scene.

23. Renata Scotto made her Met debut in 1965 in the title role of *Madama Butterfly*, a part that suited her well and that she sang frequently for the next twenty years.

24. Mirella Freni made her Met debut the night before Scotto's bow, as Mimì in *La Bohème*, in 1965. Freni captivated the New York public, but personal considerations kept her away from the company between 1969 and 1983. Once returned to her still-adoring Met public, Freni sang there regularly for the next thirteen years and seems to have no plans to retire.

25. Luciano Pavarotti made his Met debut as Rodolfo in *La Bohème*, during a flu epidemic in 1968. He canceled several of his own Met appearances that season because of the flu, and he sang at the Met only sporadically until his great triumph with Joan Sutherland in *La Fille du Régiment*. The popular tenor has returned to Lincoln Center virtually every season since then.

26. Aprile Millo made her Met debut in 1983, replacing Anna Tomowa-Simtow on short notice as Amelia in *Simon Boccanegra*. For the next few seasons Millo was principally a "cover" artist but was elevated to "prima donna" status in 1989, when she opened the Met season singing *Aida*. Since then, she has sung many Verdi heroines at the Met.

27. Ezio Pinza made his Metropolitan Opera debut in 1926 as the High Priest in Spontini's *La Vestale*, an opera otherwise planned as a vehicle for Rosa Ponselle. Pinza remained at the Met for twenty-two seasons, reigning as Boris, Don Giovanni, Mozart's Figaro, and Méphistophélès, before starring on Broadway, Hollywood, and TV.

28. Beniamino Gigli debuted at the Met in the role of Faust in Boito's *Mefistofele* in November 1920. By a sad coincidence, Gigli's debut took place a few weeks before Enrico Caruso sang at the Met for the last time. Gigli left the Met a dozen years later, during the Great Depression. He is said to have been the only artist who refused to take a pay cut of 10 percent while the Met suffered through the financial crisis that nearly destroyed it.

29. Tenor Roberto Alagna made his Metropolitan Opera debut as

Rodolfo in Puccini's *La Bohème*, on April 14, 1996. The French-born tenor was victimized by excessive publicity in which, at the age of thirty-two, he was hailed as the equal of Pavarotti, Domingo and Carreras. Worse still, Alagna sang his first performance while suffering from a bad cold. The evening went badly and many reviews were unkind. Alagna redeemed himself with the New York public the following fall, were he distinguished himself in *L'Elisir d'Amore* and *Rigoletto.*

30. Caruso made his Met as the Duke of Mantua in *Rigoletto* in 1903. In the history of the Met, he was probably the single most important member of the company.

68. FAMOUS FIRSTS

1. Giuseppina Strepponi, who would eventually become Verdi's wife, sang Abigaille in the world premiere of *Nabucco* at La Scala, in 1842.
2. Hariclea Darclée, at the Rome Opera in 1900.
3. Francesco Tamagno, at La Scala in 1887.
4. Maria Jeritza in Dresden in 1913.
5. Elisabeth Schwarzkopf, in Venice in 1951.
6. Elisabeth Schumann, in Dresden in 1910.
7. Enrico Caruso, at the Metropolitan Opera in 1910.
8. Leontyne Price, on the first opening night of the New Met at Lincoln Center, in 1966.
9. Francesco Tamagno, in Milan, in 1892.
10. The great French baritone Victor Maurel, at La Scala in 1893. It was Verdi's final opera.
11. Mary Garden, at the Paris Opéra in 1902.
12. Gemma Bellincioni, in 1890 at the Rome Opera. It was Mascagni's first and most successful opera.
13. Peter Pears, at Covent Garden in 1945.
14. Gianna Pederzini (in Italian, surprisingly), at La Scala in 1955.
15. Claudia Muzio, deeply attached to the Jesuit priest Refice, who had composed *Cecilia*, sang in the opera's first performance in Rome, in 1934.

16. Cio-Cio-San, or Madama Butterfly, was first sung by Rosina Storchio when Puccini's opera had its disastrous premiere at La Scala in 1904.

17. La Scala wasn't favored with another Puccini premiere after the *Butterfly* debacle until the posthumous first performance of *Turandot* in 1926. Rosa Raisa sang the title role.

18. Giulia Grisi, in 1831 at La Scala.

19. Beverly Sills, at the San Diego Opera in 1979.

20. Teresa Stratas, at the Paris Opéra in 1980.

21. Gino Quilico, at the Metropolitan Opera in 1991.

22. Soprano Viorica Ursuleac, in 1933, in Dresden.

23. Evelyn Lear, making her Metropolitan Opera debut, in 1967.

24. Fanny Salvini-Donatelli, whose first name emphasized her silhouette, was the first Violetta, at Venice's Teatro La Fenice, 1853.

25. Giuseppe Borgatti was the first tenor fortunate enough to sing Chénier's four stirring arias and two thrilling love duets, at La Scala, in 1896.

26. Sibyl Sanderson, the beautiful American soprano who died young, and was reputed to have been one of Massenet's mistresses, created the role of Esclarmonde, with the Paris Opéra-Comique, at the Théâtre du Châtelet, in 1889.

27. Marie Célestine Galli-Marié, at the Paris Opéra-Comique, in 1875.

28. Hermann Winkelmann, at Bayreuth in 1882.

29. Nicolai Gedda, at the Met, in 1958.

30. The first Giuditta was the superbly gifted Jarmila Novotna, in Vienna in 1934.

69. THE YOUNGER GENERATION

1. Dawn Upshaw.
2. Thomas Hampson.
3. Ben Heppner.
4. Eva Mei.
5. Anne Evans.
6. Roberto Alagna.
7. Sylvia McNair.
8. Richard Leech.
9. Sharon Sweet.
10. Cecilia Bartoli.
11. Sumi Jo.
12. Bryn Terfel.

13. Fabio Armiliato.
14. Olga Borodina.
15. Denyse Graves.
16. Dmitri Hvorostovsky.
17. Dmitri Hvorostovsky
made his Met debut as
Yeletski in Tchaikovsky's
Pique Dame, sharing the
stage with the peerless
Leonie Rysanek, who was
making her final Met ap-
pearances in the role of
the Old Countess.
18. Nuccia Focile.
19. Harolyn Blackwell.
20. Dwayne Croft.
21. Vladimir Chernov.
22. Poul Elming.
23. Anne Sophie von Otter.
24. Ruth Ann Swenson.
25. Frank Lopardo.
26. Maria Spacagna.

70. THEIR MARRIED NAMES

1. Beverly Sills.
2. Dame Kiri Te Kanawa.
3. Dorothy Kirsten.
4. Licia Albanese.
5. Maria Callas.
6. Dame Joan Sutherland.
7. Fiorenza Cossotto.
8. Elisabeth Schwarzkopf.
9. Roberta Peters.
10. Montserrat Caballé.
11. Elisabeth Rethberg.
12. Anna Moffo.
13. Christa Ludwig.
14. Mirella Freni.
15. Anja Silja.
16. Renata Scotto.
17. Risë Stevens.
18. Rose Bampton.

71. OPERA STARS ON BROADWAY

1. f, l, p
2. d, j
3. b, g
4. q
5. l, t
6. a, n
7. e, k
8. g
9. c, v
10. f
11. s
12. r
13. e (Price met her former
husband, William War-
field, when she played
Bess to his Porgy in 1952)
14. m
15. i, h, m, o
16. w
17. g, x

18. k	22. x
19. m	23. z
20. l	24. y
21. r	

72. TINY FACTS ABOUT GREAT SINGERS

1. Callas and Sills (separately) appeared as contestants on the Major Bowes program, the forerunner of the *Ted Mack Amateur Hour.*

2. Tucker had a silk-lining business in Manhattan.

3. Cossotto performed the Madrigal Singer in the Callas/Di Stefano recording of Puccini's *Manon Lescaut* for EMI.

4. Risë Stevens.

5. Piero Cappuccilli appeared as Germont *père* in one Met *La Traviata* in 1960, replacing Leonard Warren, who had died a few weeks earlier.

6. Flagstad ran into trouble because of her husband's association with the hated pro-Nazi government in their native Norway. Flagstad spent the war years at home by her husband's side, and, while she never sang for the Nazis, rumors to the contrary caused her much difficulty.

7. Carreras's debut came in 1972 when he sang Pinkerton in *Madama Butterfly* with the New York City Opera.

8. Christoff, by virtue of his Bulgarian passport, was not granted a visa to enter the United States, then in the throes of anticommunist hysteria.

9. Marlboro.

10. *Fidelio.*

11. The Marschallin in *Der Rosenkavalier* and Donna Elvira in *Don Giovanni.*

12. Samuel Barber.

13. Nilsson feuded with Herbert von Karajan, who tried to have her removed from the cast of his proposed Metropolitan Opera *Ring* cycle.

14. André Kostelanetz.

15. Dorothy Kirsten.
16. Eileen Farrell.
17. Verrett appeared as Nettie in the revival of *Coraviel* at the Vivien Beaumont Theatre.
18. George Shirley.
19. Lauritz Melchior.
20. Rosalind Elias.

73. FAREWELLS AT THE MET

1. Alceste in Gluck's *Alceste*, 1952.
2. Maddalena in *Andrea Chénier*, 1966.
3. Eléazar in *La Juive*, 1920.
4. Don Carlo in *La Forza del Destino*. (Warren died during the performance on March 4, 1960. His last complete role at the Met, sung three days earlier, was the title role in *Simon Boccanegra*.)
5. Tosca, 1965.
6. Her official farewell was as Tosca, in 1975. Her last appearance, however, was as Mimì in *La Bohème*, in 1977.
7. Canio in *Pagliacci*, 1974.
8. Lucia di Lammermoor, 1960.
9. Desdemona in Verdi's *Otello*, 1973.
10. Carmen, 1962.
11. Rosalinde in *Die Fledermaus*, 1951.
12. Hoffmann in *Les Contes d'Hoffmann*, 1965.
13. The Dyer's Wife in *Die Frau ohne Schatten*, 1981. She also sang Isolde's Narrative and Curse from *Tristan und Isolde* and a Swedish folksong at the Met's Centennial Gala on October 22, 1983. She later sang Brünnhilde's "Ho-jo-to-ho!" at the Gala celebrating the 25th anniversary of James Levine's Met debut, in April 1996.
14. Donna Elvira in *Don Giovanni*, 1966.
15. Gounod's *Faust*, 1960.
16. Norina in *Don Pasquale*, 1979.
17. Baron Scarpia in *Tosca*, 1975.

18. Title role in *Zazà*, 1920.
19. Don Ottavio in *Don Giovanni*, 1967.
20. Minnie in *La Fanciulla del West*, 1966.
21. Old Prioress in *Dialogues des Carmélites*, 1986.
22. Samson in *Samson et Dalila*, 1987.
23. Cio-Cio-San in *Madama Butterfly*, 1965 (Also sang "Un bel dì" at Closing Gala at the old Met, April 16, 1966.)
24. Gilda in *Rigoletto*, 1985.
25. The Marschallin in *Der Rosenkavalier*, 1986.
26. Nedda in *Pagliacci*, 1974.
27. Pamina in *Die Zauberflöte*, 1994.
28. Fricka in *Die Walküre*, 1993.
29. Gurnemanz in *Parsifal*, 1973.
30. Orlofsky in *Die Fledermaus*, 1956.

III

Unforgettable Characters

74. TITLE ROLES

1. Octavian, Count Rofrano
2. Manrico
3. Fiora
4. Brünnhilde
5. Minnie
6. Philip Vanderdecken
7. Sandor Barinkay
8. Hanna Glawari
9. Marenka
10. Amina
11. Magda
12. Figaro
13. Leonora de Guzman
14. Canio, Nedda, Tonio, and Beppe
15. Dr. Falke
16. The Empress (We never learn the lady's actual name!)
17. Gualtiero
18. Katerina Ismailova
19. Annina
20. Franz a.k.a. Frank

75. NOBLESSE OBLIGE

1. King Philip II, in Verdi's *Don Carlo*, sets the opera's conflict in motion by marrying Elisabetta de Valois, his son Carlo's betrothed.

2. Cleopatra, in Handel's *Giulio Cesare*, provides the love interest for the Roman invader of Egypt. Cleopatra beguiles Caesar with her beauty, charm, and coloratura, and thus Caesar remains in Egypt, fighting Cleopatra's battles against her rivals for the Egyptian throne.

3. Good Queen Bess is painted anything but kindly in Donizetti's *Roberto Devereux* and *Maria Stuarda*. In the first work, Elizabeth allows Devereux, whom she loves, to be executed for

alleged treason, although she is more annoyed by his infidelity. In *Maria Stuarda*, Elizabeth has her unlucky cousin, Mary of Scotland, imprisoned at Fotheringay, and eventually has her beheaded.

4. Charles V, in Verdi's *Ernani*, is just plain Don Carlo for the first three of *Ernani*'s four acts. In those early scenes, he pursues Elvira, who loves the dashing bandit Ernani but is betrothed to her elderly guardian—and uncle!—Silva. Carlo abducts Elvira, and Ernani enlists Silva's aid in freeing her, pledging his own life to Silva's command. Carlo, when crowned Holy Roman Emperor, modestly bestows Elvira on the man she loves, but Silva has other ideas that spoil the wedding—but that's another story.

   In Verdi's *Don Carlo*, Charles V, Philip II's father, is supposedly dead and buried when the action begins, but his ghost, in the guise of a friar, haunts the Cloister of St. Just, and rescues Carlo from the Inquisition at the end.

5. Henry the Fowler, the King in Wagner's *Lohengrin*, is led by the evil Telramund (and the latter's witchy spouse, Ortrud) to think that Elsa, his ward, has murdered her brother, the heir to the throne. Actually, Ortrud has turned the lad into a swan—an industrious fowl who lands a temporary job as Lohengrin's chauffeur. Henry is an ineffectual type who seems given more to oratory than action. Henry does, however, arrange the trial by combat that brings Lohengrin to Brabant to act as Elsa's defender.

6. Gustavus III is the hero of the original libretto of Verdi's *Un Ballo in Maschera*. Local censors, worried about the effect of the plot in strife-torn Italy, refused to allow an opera dealing with the assassination of a European monarch, so the original Swedish locale was changed to the rather incongruous Boston of the Puritan era. Nowadays, many opera houses set *Un Ballo in Maschera* in Sweden, where the tale of Gustavus, the liberal, charming monarch who carries on a platonic but unwise affair with Amelia, the wife of his best friend, Count Anckerström, unfolds. When Anckerström realizes that his wife is the king's beloved, the once-loyal courtier joins the conspiracy and assassinates the king, who pardons all his foes as he dies.

7. Dmitri is the son of Ivan the Terrible, whom regent Boris Godunov has had murdered even before Mussorgsky's *Boris Godunov* begins. The tenor lead in Boris, however, is the monk Grigori, who masquerades as Dmitri in order to lead a revolt against Czar Boris. Dmitri, aided by Poland, wins, and Boris dies of a guilty conscience. The Pretender's triumph is limited, however, as history records that he was executed by still another group of insurgents three days after taking the throne.

8. Jane (Giovanna) Seymour is crowned King Henry VIII's third queen offstage, during the final scene of Donizetti's *Anna Bolena*. In the action of the opera, Seymour is portrayed as a sweet girl who, against her will, is wooed by the king and who, through no design of her own, is one of the reasons for Anne Boleyn's downfall and execution.

9. Emperor Altoum is the father of Puccini's Princess Turandot. Although the old man reigns in theory, his man-hating daughter rules the roost. Altoum dodders ineffectively, first pleading with Calaf to leave before he loses his head, and then, when Calaf has won the Riddle Contest, reminding his welching daughter that her vow was, after all, sacred. In the end, love wins out and Altoum lives to see Turandot and Calaf betrothed, while his subjects wish him a reign of ten thousand years.

10. Prince Shuisky is a Boyar in *Boris Godunov* who has his eye on the Czar's throne. He plays on Boris's superstitions and feelings of guilt, first by recounting to him the rumors about Dmitri's supposed return from the dead, and later by bringing the old monk Pimen into the Kremlin to tell Boris of the miracles the dead Dmitri had wrought. This narrative triggers Boris's fatal heart attack.

11. Prince Orlofsky is the wealthy, bored nobleman (usually sung by a woman) who throws the gala masked ball in *Die Fledermaus*. At this party, Dr. Falke is able to play out the farce he has created around his philandering friend Eisenstein. The Prince is smitten by the charms of Eisenstein's maid, Adele, and ultimately agrees to underwrite her career as an actress.

12. Duchess Federica is the young woman in Verdi's *Luisa Miller* who loves Count Rodolfo. Rodolfo, however, loves Luisa, and

Federica refuses to release Rodolfo from the marriage of state which will bind him to her. At the final curtain, Rodolfo has slain Luisa, the villainous Wurm, and himself. Federica, presumably, ends up alone.

13. Prince Gremin, in Tchaikovsky's *Eugene Onegin*, is the mature nobleman who marries the shy Tatyana. She doesn't love Gremin the way she loved Onegin, who had once rejected her, but when the chastened Eugene begs her to leave her husband, Tatyana has sufficient character not to abandon the loving, if fatherly, Gremin.

14. The Count of Saxony, otherwise known as Maurizio, is the rather caddish beloved of the heroine in Cilea's *Adriana Lecouvreur*. Maurizio's duplicitous treatment of Adriana and the Princess di Bouillon results in Adriana's murder.

15. Duchess Elena is the politically suspect heroine of Verdi's *I Vespri Siciliani*. Elena is part of the conspiracy that wants to drive the French forces from Sicily. A complication arises when it turns out that her lover, Arrigo, who shares Elena's political ideas, is actually the son of Montforte, the French governor of Sicily. The well-intentioned Montforte tries to smooth things over, but the radical Procida, who would now be considered a terrorist, leads a massacre of the French as Montforte proclaims Arrigo and Elena man and wife.

76. ELEVEN DONS AND A DONNA

1. Don Pizarro in Beethoven's *Fidelio*.
2. Don Giovanni in Mozart's opera.
3. Don Andres in Offenbach's *La Périchole*.
4. Don Ruy Gomez de Silva in Verdi's *Ernani*.
5. Don Alvaro in Verdi's *La Forza del Destino*.
6. Don Fernando in *Fidelio*.
7. Don Alonso (Count Almaviva) in Rossini's *Il Barbiere di Siviglia*.
8. Don José in *Carmen*.
9. Don Alfonso in Mozart's *Così Fan Tutte*.

10. Don Curzio in Mozart's *Le Nozze di Figaro*.
11. Don Rodrigue in Massenet's *Le Cid*.
12. Donna Elvira in *Don Giovanni*.

77. THREE GUYS NAMED DON CARLO

1. Don Carlo, in Verdi's *Don Carlo*, based on Schiller's tragedy about the Spanish court, is a tenor.
2. Don Carlo in *Forza* is an unmitigated louse.
3. Don Carlo in *Forza*.
4. Don Carlo in *Don Carlo*.
5. Don Carlo in *Ernani*.
6. Don Carlo in *Forza*.
7. Don Carlo in *Don Carlo*.
8. Don Carlo in *Ernani*.
9. Don Carlo in *Don Carlo*.
10. Don Carlo in *Forza*.
11. Don Carlo in *Forza*.
12. Don Carlo in *Don Carlo*. There are several versions of this scene. In the one most often performed, Don Carlo is spirited away from the forces of the Inquisition by a friar who *might* be the ghost of Charles V. Another edition follows the ending of the Schiller play, with Don Carlo simply being handed over to the Inquisition.
13. Don Carlo in *Ernani*.
14. Don Carlo in *Don Carlo*.
15. Don Carlo in *Don Carlo*.
16. Don Carlo in *Ernani*.
17. Don Carlo in *Ernani* turns up in Verdi's *Don Carlo*, in which he is referred to as Charles V. He is either a ghost or the still living king, who has falsified his own death and gone to live out his days as a monk. He is the grandfather of the opera's eponymous Don Carlo and the father of the opera's darkest character, King Philip II.

78. THEIR MASTERS' VOICES

1. Violetta's faithful maid in *La Traviata* is Annina (soprano).
2. Falstaff is served by those two oafs Bardolfo (tenor) and Pistola (bass) in *Falstaff*.
3. In the first scene of *La Forza del Destino*, Leonora is served by Curra (mezzo-soprano).
4. Selim owns the villainous Osmin (bass) in Mozart's *The Abduction from the Seraglio*.
5. Bartolo's servant in the Rossini *Barbiere* is the sneezing Berta (soprano in the original score; if the Rosina is a soprano, however, Berta sings the mezzo line in the opera's first-act finale).
6. Medea's confidante is Neris (mezzo-soprano) in Cherubini's opera.
7. In *La Fille du Régiment*, Hortentius (bass) looks after the Marquise's varied needs.
8. Timur, the old king and Calaf's father in Puccini's *Turandot*, is aided by the slave Liù (soprano).
9. Rigoletto employed Giovanna (mezzo-soprano) as housekeeper and duenna to his daughter, Gilda.
10. Sarastro in *Die Zauberflöte* owns the evil slave Monostatos (tenor).
11. In *Fidelio*, Rocco is aided by both his turnkey, Jaquino (tenor), who loves Rocco's daughter, Marzelline, and the supposed youth "Fidelio," who is actually Leonore (soprano) disguised as a boy in order to attempt to free her husband, Florestan. Florestan is unjustly imprisoned in the jail that Rocco tends.
12. Donizetti's Mary, Queen of Scots, is aided by her lady-in-waiting Anna Kennedy (mezzo-soprano).
13. Alice Ford, in *Falstaff*, has four young servants, Ned, Will, Isaac, and John (all mute), who together find it heavy going to toss a laundry basket (into which Falstaff has been crammed) into the Thames.
14. In *Eugene Onegin*, Madame Larina, the heroine's mother, is the owner of many serfs, among them the elderly nurse Filippyevna (mezzo-soprano).

15. In Puccini's *Tosca*, Scarpia has two leering henchmen, Spoletta (tenor) and Sciarrone (baritone), to do his dirty work for him.
16. Elisabetta, in Verdi's *Don Carlo*, has the young page Tebaldo (mezzo-soprano) and the mute Countess of Aremberg to attend her. Elisabetta's cruel husband, King Philip II of Spain, dismisses the countess, who allowed Elisabetta to have a private meeting with her stepson, Don Carlo.
17. Desdemona, in the *Otello* of both Verdi and Rossini, has Emilia (mezzo-soprano) as her maid-of-all-work.
18. Juliette, in Gounod's *Roméo et Juliette*, is attended by her nurse, Gertrude (mezzo-soprano).
19. Belinda (mezzo-soprano).
20. Susanna (soprano).

79. SERVANTS, SLAVES, AND COMPANIONS

1. Annina is Violetta's maid in Verdi's *La Traviata*. She doesn't have too much to do beyond faithfully serving Violetta until the heroine's death. Her one action that has bearing on the plot is to deliver Violetta's reply to Flora's invitation.
2. Mariandl is not really a servant at all, but merely the disguise put on by Octavian in Richard Strauss's *Der Rosenkavalier*, first to avoid embarrassing the Marschallin when her cousin, Baron Ochs, comes to call. Later—as part of the plot to embarrass Ochs—Octavian as "Mariandl" pretends to want a rendezvous with Ochs in a rustic inn.
3. Robin is the page in Verdi's *Falstaff* who delivers Sir John's love notes to Mistress Alice and Mistress Meg, when Falstaff's own servants, Bardolf and Pistola, refuse to do so.
4. Aida, in Verdi's opera, offends her mistress, the Princess Amneris, by falling in love with Radames, whom Amneris loves. Since Radames loves Aida, Amneris's jealousy leads to Radames' and Aida's deaths, and to her own bitter unhappiness.
5. Brangäne is Isolde's servant in Wagner's *Tristan und Isolde*. Although she means well, her substitution of a love potion for the death draft Isolde has commanded her to prepare for Tris-

tan and herself leads to the ultimate destruction of the lovers.

6. Adele is Rosalinde's chambermaid in Johann Strauss's *Die Fledermaus*. More interested in good times than in washing the windows, Adele sneaks off to the same ball that her mistress and master attend and, wearing one of Rosalinde's gowns, captures the fancy of Eisenstein, Warden Frank, and Prince Orlofsky.

7. Suzuki is Cio-Cio-San's faithful companion in Puccini's *Madama Butterfly*. Cynical and wiser than her mistress, Suzuki foresees disaster but is powerless to prevent it from occurring.

8. Bersi is Maddalena's servant in Giordano's *Andrea Chénier*. Although the upheaval of the French Revolution leads Bersi into a life of prostitution, she is loyal to her noble mistress and uses her earnings to support Maddalena. She also sets up the fatal assignation for Chénier and Maddalena.

9. Carlo Gérard is a colleague of Bersi's in the Coigny household in *Andrea Chénier*. First, he leads the house servants in a job action that disrupts a soiree, resulting in his discharge. Later, Gérard becomes a leader of the Revolution, abusing his power to try to press his attentions on Maddalena, whom he has always loved. Too late, he repents and attempts, unsuccessfully, to free Chénier, whom Gérard's false testimony has sent to the guillotine.

10. Curra in *La Forza del Destino* is Leonora's maid, and her only function is to help the hesitating girl to pack for her planned elopement with Alvaro. In Verdi's *Ernani*, Curra is Elvira's maid.

11. Despina serves the sisters Fiordiligi and Dorabella in Mozart's *Così Fan Tutte*. The scheming Don Alfonso enlists Despina's aid in introducing the girls' disguised sweethearts into the household. To add to the confusing fun, Despina later impersonates both a doctor and a notary.

12. Frantz is Councillor Crespel's deaf servant in the Antonia Act of Offenbach's *Les Contes d'Hoffmann*. (The running order of the second and third main segments of the opera is often switched these days; traditionally, "Antonia" is performed after "Giulietta" but today, as Bellini once remarked, "Anything

goes!") Frantz does not understand Crespel's order not to let anyone into the house, and promptly admits Hoffmann, who is in love with Crespel's daughter, Antonia.

13. David is Hans Sachs's apprentice in Wagner's *Die Meistersinger von Nürnberg*. Besides providing a love interest for Eva's companion Magdalene, thereby becoming the fifth voice in the great quintet, David, with his jealous attack on Beckmesser, whom he wrongly believes is serenading Magdalene, precipitates the brawl that concludes the second act of this great comedy.

14. Monostatos is Sarastro's slave in Mozart's *Die Zauberflöte*. His lust for Pamina earns him a thrashing, and his assistance to the evil (but funky) Queen of the Night in her attempt to kidnap her own daughter (Pamina) leads to his destruction, along with the Queen and her three ladies-in-waiting.

15. Antonio is the gardener employed by Count Almaviva in Mozart's *Le Nozze di Figaro*. His drunken interruption all but foils the plans of Figaro, Susanna, and the Countess Almaviva.

16. Addie and Cal are the servants of Regina and Horace Giddons in Marc Blitzstein's *Regina*, the operatic version of Lillian Hellman's *The Little Foxes*. Good, gentle people, this pair despises the scheming Regina and are exceptionally devoted to the ailing Horace and to Zan, the Giddons's adolescent daughter.

17. Leopold, in Richard Strauss's *Der Rosenkavalier* (a mute character, by the way), is the loutish manservant whom Baron Ochs keeps close at hand. One is given to understand that he is Ochs's love child.

18. In Barber's *Antony and Cleopatra*, Charmian is one of Cleopatra's most devoted handmaidens, helping her mistress commit suicide before grasping an asp herself.

19. Dimitri, in Giordano's *Fedora*, is the stableboy of Fedora's murdered fiancé Vladimiro. After considerable prodding by his elders, Dimitri manages to put a name to the face he recognized at the murder scene—Loris Ipanoff. Dimitri is a "trouser" role, and was once recorded by Kiri te Kanawa.

20. Billy is Minnie's rather sleazy jackrabbit of all trades in *La Fanciulla del West*. Billy does one good deed. Urged on by

Nick, he runs off to get Minnie so that she can save Dick Johnson from the lynch-mob that is already chanting the words "Doodah, doodah day!" in a most alarming and menacing manner.

80. DOCTOR, DOCTOR!

1. Dr. Grenvil, in *La Traviata*, is unable to cure Violetta Valery of consumption. He does, however, have an admirable bedside manner.
2. Dr. Miracle, one of the four demonic villains in Offenbach's *Les Contes d'Hoffmann*, uses all sorts of supernatural tricks to make certain that his patient, Antonia, dies of a strange ailment that is exacerbated by the girl's singing.
3. In Barber's *Vanessa*, the Doctor is a loyal friend of Vanessa and her family, but doesn't immediately understand the cause of the depression suffered by the title character's niece, Erika. He does, however, successfully treat Erika after her self-induced abortion.
4. In Berg's *Wozzeck*, the Doctor performs fiendish and gross medical experiments on the unresisting soldier Wozzeck, who survives them but goes on to become mad and murder his common-law wife, Marie.
5. The Surgeon in *La Forza del Destino* is able to save Don Alvaro from death from a bullet wound. This good news fills the vengeful Don Carlo with joy. Carlo, you see, wants the pleasure of killing Alvaro himself, in order to avenge the (accidental) shooting of his father.
6. Dr. Malatesta in Donizetti's *Don Pasquale* appears to practice psychology. Curing Pasquale of his absurd idea of marrying the young Norina (a.k.a. "Sofronia") is almost worse than the disease, but all turns out well in this jolly *opera buffa*.
7. In Poulenc's *Dialogues des Carmélites*, Dr. Javelinot not only fails to save the life of the old Prioress but he bungles the dosage of her medicine, and the terrified old lady perishes in agony.

8. In Verdi's *Macbeth*, a hapless Physician attends Lady Macbeth after she goes mad. All he does is mutter helplessly during the Lady's Sleepwalking Scene, and he is unable to prevent her death one scene later.

9. Dr. Boroff, in Giordano's *Fedora*, is a friend of tenor Loris Ipanoff. He discovers that Fedora is responsible for the deaths of Loris's mother and brother. When he arrives at the villa shared by Fedora and Loris, Fedora has not only confessed to Loris, but has taken poison. The crushed Loris implores Dr. Boroff to save his mistress's life. Boroff seems unable to reverse the poison's effect, but one is not convinced that the doctor is trying very hard.

10. In *Porgy and Bess*, as Bess lies delirious and fever-wracked, the saintly Serena, who practices faith-healing, calls upon "Dr. Jesus" to save Bess. Moments later, as the clock strikes three, Bess regains her health. By the end of the opera, Serena quite possibly regrets having helped her.

81. HOLY MEN AND WOMEN

1. Zaccaria (bass) is the high priest of the Hebrews held captive by Nabucco and Abigaille in Verdi's *Nabucco*. (Zaccaria himself is not a captive.) The priest takes Fenena—Nabucco's daughter—hostage, hoping to have the Hebrews freed, but Fenena falls in love with the Hebrew Ismaele and embraces Judaism. Nabucco frees the Hebrews and converts, too.

2. Varlaam (bass) is one of a pair of mendicant monks who arrive with the runaway Grigori at an inn at the Lithuanian border in Mussorgsky's *Boris Godunov*. Varlaam is the more jocular of the two and sings the familiar drinking song in that scene. When soldiers arrive searching for Grigori, Grigori reads the warrant (the soldiers are illiterate) and changes the description to fit Varlaam. Varlaam, realizing that there is trouble in store for him, painfully attempts to read the document himself ("When it comes to hanging, I can read!") and sees that the wanted man is the runaway. Grigori escapes, and Varlaam and

his partner Missail turn up again during the opera's Kromy Forest Scene.

3. In Saint-Saëns's *Samson et Dalila*, the High Priest of Dagon (baritone) orders the very willing Dalila to seduce Samson and learn the secret of his strength. She does so, and, in the final scene, the priest leads the worship that culminates in the miraculous destruction of the pagan temple.

4. In Verdi's *Aida*, Ramfis (bass) is the High Priest of Phthà. His influence is great indeed: He consecrates Radames as commander of the Egyptian army; warns the king of Egypt to hold Aida and Amonasro as hostages when, per Radames's request, the other Ethiopian captives are freed; sentences Radames to death following Radames's inadvertent treason; and defies Amneris's frantic plea that Radames be spared.

5. In Poulenc's *Dialogues des Carmélites*, De Croissy (mezzo-soprano) is the prioress who accepts Blanche as a novice in the Carmelite order. Her terrifying death scene is a dramatic high point of the opera, as this disciplined, strong woman curses God on her deathbed, lacking the strength to meet her end with the dignity that has otherwise characterized her life.

6. Cardinal Brogni (bass) is the villain in Halévy's *La Juive*. This elderly anti-Semite persecutes Eléazar and his presumed daughter to death, only to learn that Rachel is actually his own, illegitimate daughter, whom Eléazar had adopted.

7. In *Nabucco* the High Priest of Baal (bass) conspires with Abigaille to wrest power from Abigaille's adoptive father (Nabucco), who has been rendered insane by a thunderbolt as punishment for announcing that he is God. Nabucco, however, is returned to sanity when he decides to convert to the Hebrew faith, and although the libretto doesn't specifically describe the High Priest's eventual fate, one assumes that he will not have an easy time after the final curtain descends.

8. The Bonze (bass) is Butterfly's fanatical Buddhist uncle in Puccini's *Madama Butterfly*. He breaks up her wedding reception, cursing her for leaving her ancestral faith to become a Christian.

9. In Massenet's *Thaïs*, Athanaël (baritone) is the repressed, mas-

ochistic monk who attempts to salvage the soul of the courtesan Thaïs. In fact, Athanaël merely lusts after Thaïs. She, however, sincerely converts to Christianity. Thaïs dies of exhaustion while traveling to a cloister with Athanaël. He lives on with his guilt.

10. In *Boris Godunov*, Rangoni (baritone) is a Jesuit who urges the Polish Princess Marina to seduce the Pretender Dmitri, in order to pave the way for the ascension of Roman Catholicism in Russia.

11. In Gounod's *Roméo et Juliette*, as in Shakespeare, Frère Laurent (bass) is Roméo's friend and performs his marriage to Juliette. He later gives Juliette the potion that induces her presumed death. As in Shakespeare, Roméo learns only that Juliette is dead, and, thanks to the friar's well-intentioned meddling, both young lovers commit suicide for real.

12. In Meyerbeer's *Le Prophète*, John of Leyden (tenor) is a Dutch innkeeper whom treacherous Anabaptist intriguers pass off as a holy prophet and then crown king. John becomes their corrupt tool, but months later, after his beloved Berthe kills herself as a result of his cruelty, John succumbs to his own tortured conscience and incinerates himself, his mother, and his enemies in his castle.

13. Titurel (bass), in Wagner's *Parsifal*, is the old, ailing head of the Knights of the Holy Grail, and the father of the suffering Amfortas. Titurel is heard only in the musical drama's first act, and offstage at that.

14. Olin Blitch (bass) is an itinerant preacher in Floyd's *Susannah*. Blitch seduces the title character and is shot for this outrage by Susannah's quick-tempered brother, Sam.

15. The Abbé (tenor), in Cilea's *Adriana Lecouvreur*, has no priestly function whatsoever, beyond serving as a nattering sycophant of the Prince and Princess di Bouillon.

16. Mme. Lidoine (soprano) in Poulenc's *Dialogues des Carmélites*, is the new prioress who becomes head of the order after the death of Mme. de Croissy. She leads the sisters throughout their ordeal at the hands of the Revolutionary Tribunal, and is the first to walk bravely to her death at the end of the opera.

17. Baldassare (bass) in Donizetti's *La Favorita* is the head of the order of monks from which the opera's hero, Fernando, withdraws when he falls in love with Leonora. Baldassare publicly berates Leonora for her illicit relationship with the King of Spain, and eventually welcomes Fernando back to the monastery.

18. The Grand Inquisitor (bass) in Verdi's *Don Carlo*, is a ninety-year-old blind monk who attains great power in Spain during the reign of Philip II. He forces Philip to have Rodrigo murdered because of his "liberal" beliefs, and is prepared to preside over the arrest of Don Carlo and Queen Elisabetta at the end of the opera.

19. At last, a benign religious figure and in a comedy, yet! Rabbi David (baritone) is Fritz's friend in *L'Amico Fritz* by Mascagni. David is a bit of a matchmaker and tactfully brings together the diffident bachelor Fritz and the adoring, if shy, Suzel.

20. Padre Guardiano (bass) in Verdi's *La Forza del Destino*, is the head of the monastery where first Leonora, and later Don Alvaro, are granted refuge. He agrees to let Leonora live as a hermit away from the other monks, in an otherwise unused cave. At the end of the opera, he tries to comfort the dying Leonora and the grieving Don Alvaro.

82. HI, MOM! HI DAD!

1. Oroveso is the errant priestess Norma's father in Bellini's *Norma*. Although he condemns her to death for her liaison with the Roman Pollione, Norma prevails upon her father to spare her two children.

2. Peter and Gertrude are the parents of Hänsel and Gretel, in Humperdinck's *Hänsel und Gretel*. The stern Gertrude sends them off into the woods to pick strawberries after Hänsel spills a pitcher of milk. Peter, the kindly broommaker, warns Gertrude that the woods are haunted by a witch. The parents set out to hunt for their children, and find them, none the worse for wear, at the opera's conclusion.

3. Archibaldo is the old, blind king who strangles his daughter-in-law in Montemezzi's *L'Amore dei Tre Re*. Archibaldo kills Fiora because he suspects (correctly) that she is betraying his son, Manfredo. To trap Fiora's lover, Archibaldo paints Fiora's dead lips with poison. Sure enough, Avito sneaks into the chapel to kiss Fiora once more, and dies. Unfortunately for Archibaldo, Manfredo also kisses Fiora, leaving the old man childless.

4. La Cieca is the old, blind mother of La Gioconda, in Ponchielli's opera. Cieca falls into the clutches of the evil spy, Barnaba, who lusts for La Gioconda. Although she in no way returns Barnaba's love for her, she agrees to "surrender herself," as they used to say in program synopses of the opera, in return for Cieca's freedom. As the villain approaches her, Gioconda stabs herself. As she dies, Barnaba shouts that he has drowned Cieca anyway!

5. Mamma Lucia is Turiddu's mother in Mascagni's *Cavalleria Rusticana*. Her chief dramatic function is to listen unhappily as Santuzza tells her that Turiddu has betrayed her and gone back to Lola. Lucia runs the village tavern and serves Turiddu the wine with which he toasts Lola. The tipsy Turiddu then loses the inevitable knife fight with Lola's husband. Mamma Lucia is left by fate (and the librettist) to weep over Turiddu's death and to "be a mother to Santuzza."

6. In Mozart's *Le Nozze di Figaro*, Marcellina spends the first two acts trying to trap Figaro into marrying her, and not Susanna. In Act III, however, it is revealed that Marcellina is Figaro's long-lost mother. From that point on, she becomes a staunch ally of Figaro and Susanna in their battle to keep Count Almaviva from exercising his *droit du seigneur*.

7. Antonio, also from *Le Nozze di Figaro*, is the count's gardener and father of Barbarina, the pretty lass who captures Cherubino's heart after his flirtations with Susanna and the Countess. Antonio's big moment comes in the finale to the second act, when he complains that somebody (actually Cherubino) has jumped into the garden, ruining some plants.

8. Rocco is Marzelline's father in Beethoven's *Fidelio*. As he is

the jailer in the prison where Leonore's husband is being held, it is to Rocco's house that Leonora comes disguised as the youth Fidelio. Rocco's daughter promptly falls in love with Fidelio, and Rocco encourages Leonore to pay court to Marzelline. He also allows Fidelio to help him dig the grave intended for Florestan, thus enabling Leonore to rescue Florestan.

9. Strominger is Wally's strange old father in Catalani's *La Wally*. When Wally refuses to marry Gellner as her father wishes, Strominger disowns her, forcing her to live in the Alps, and cueing the soprano for Wally's famous aria, "Ebben? ne andrò lontano."

10. Erda, the earth goddess, appears in two of the *Ring* operas, *Das Rheingold* and *Siegfried*. She bears Wotan's nine Valkyrie daughters and the three Norns who weave the Rope of Fate in *Götterdämmerung*, thereby providing the cycle with its heroine, Brünnhilde, and the narrators who begin *Götterdämmerung* with a summary of the *Ring*'s first three music dramas.

11. In Charpentier's *Louise*, only Louise and her lover, the artist Julien, are given names. La Mère and Le Père, thus, are Louise's folks. The mother is quite a nasty lady who disapproves of Louise's affair with Julien. Louise's father loves her, and is gentler than his wife. (So is Attila the Hun!) However, her father's stifling possessiveness finally drives Louise away from home, back into Montmartre, one assumes, forever.

12. Simon Boccanegra, in Verdi's opera of that name, has a daughter named Maria who is reared by others under the name Amelia Grimaldi. Simon, the Doge of Genoa, is asked by his henchman Paolo for permission to marry Amelia. When Boccanegra discovers that the girl is his daughter, he refuses to allow the marriage, and, in retaliation, the treacherous Paolo poisons him.

13. The Marquise is Marie's mother in Donizetti's comedy *La Fille du Régiment*. Pretending at first that she is Marie's aunt, the Marquise takes the bumptious girl away from the soldiers who have raised her, and tries to make Marie into a debutante. Ultimately, it all ends happily, with the Marquise acknowl-

edging Marie as her own child and allowing "the Daughter of the Regiment" to marry her soldier love, Tonio.

14. Mamm'Agata is the conniving, loud mother of a young prima donna in another Donizetti *opera buffa, Le Convenienze ed Inconvenienze Teatrali.* Mamm'Agata creates havoc at an operatic rehearsal, insulting the other singers and showing the wretched conductor how opera should be sung. Since this work is a satirical farce, it is perhaps not surprising that Mamm'Agata is sung by a baritone.

15. Azucena, in Verdi's *Il Trovatore,* is believed by all to be Manrico's mother. Actually, as she triumphantly announces to the shocked Count di Luna, she is only Manrico's foster mother. Her real son died because the absentminded Gypsy tossed him into the fire where her own mother had been burned as a witch. Azucena then kidnapped the count's brother to avenge her mother's death at the hands of the count's father. She raised the boy as her own and achieves a peculiar revenge indeed when Manrico is beheaded on Di Luna's orders. (Now, why does everyone say that the plot of *Il Trovatore* is hard to follow?)

16. Stankar, in Verdi's rarely performed *Stiffelio,* is the father of the minister Stiffelio's errant wife, Lina. Stankar is quite contemptuous of his weak-willed daughter, and fiercely protective of his son-in-law's honor. While Stiffelio is willing to forgive Lina for her indiscretion and intends to let Raffaele, her lover, off without punishment, Stankar runs the stud through with his sword.

17. Alberich, in Wagner's *Der Ring des Nibelungen,* renounces love early on, but manages to sire the arch-villain Hagen, who, among other bad deeds, murders Siegfried, in *Götterdämmerung.* Alberich counsels his offspring to take possession of the ring, but like everyone else, Hagen is done in by his father's curse. He is dragged to his death by the Rhinemaidens at the very end of *Götterdämmerung.*

18. In Wagner's *Die Meistersinger von Nürnberg,* Pogner is the goldsmith member of the Mastersingers' Guild, who offers the hand of his daughter, Eva, to the winner of the Song

Contest—provided, of course, that Eva approves. Since the winner is Walther, her beloved, Eva could hardly be more pleased.

19. In Verdi's *Macbeth*, Banco (Banquo in Shakespeare) is a Scottish general, once a friend of Macbeth, and the father of Fleance. Macbeth orders Banco and his son killed, in order to protect his own bloody grip on Scotland's throne. A chorus of murderers dispatches poor Banco, but Fleance escapes. Banco, or at least his ghost, promptly shows up at the Macbeths' dinner party and (as Thurber would have said) scares the haggis out of the host!

20. Madame Larina, in Tchaikovsky's *Eugene Onegin*, is the mother of two daughters, the lively Olga and the quiet Tatyana. Olga is affianced to the young poet Lenski, while Tatyana falls in love with Lenski's visiting friend, Eugene Onegin. Larina's most notable action is to give Tatyana a birthday party that ends in shattered friendships and the promise of bloodshed.

21. Cio-Cio-San in *Madama Butterfly* reveals herself in Act II to be the mother of Pinkerton's son, a boy whom she has yclept "Dolore" (Trouble) but whom she promises to rename "Gioia" (Joy) when his seafaring papa comes back to Nagasaki. But when Pinkerton arrives, he is with his American wife, Kate. The Pinkertons ask to take the child back to America to raise and Cio-Cio-San consents, moments before she blindfolds the boy and commits suicide with him in the room.

22. In Verdi's *Falstaff*, Ford is the father of Nannetta Ford. Ford, for some bizarre reason, wishes Nannetta to marry the idiotic Dr. Caius, but when all the dust settles, is tricked into letting Nannetta wed the young man of her choice.

23. In Mozart's *Die Zauberflöte*, the Queen of the Night is the mother of the lovely Pamina. The Masonic leader Sarastro has kidnapped Pamina from the Queen, whom he considers to be a wicked woman. The Queen sends Tamino and Papageno to rescue Pamina, but they ally themselves with Sarastro and the Queen is destroyed.

24. Siegmund, in *Die Walküre*, is the father of Siegfried, whom

we don't meet until *Siegfried*. Enough has been said about Siegmund, Sieglinde, and their baby boy not to warrant any further discussion!

25. Nabucodonosor, known by one and all as Nabucco in Verdi's opera, is the natural father of Fenena, and the adoptive father of the low-born Abigaille. Following Fenena's lead, Nabucco frees his Hebrew captives and embraces Judaism. The unpleasant Abigaille dies ignominiously.

83. FOUR GALS NAMED LEONORA

1. Leonora in *La Favorita*.
2. Leonore in *Fidelio*.
3. Leonora in *Il Trovatore*.
4. Leonora in *Il Trovatore*.
5. Leonore in *Fidelio*. Beethoven's first three versions of the opera were entitled *Leonore*.
6. Leonora in *La Forza del Destino*. "Non imprecare, umiliati."
7. Only Leonore in *Fidelio*.
8. Leonora in *Il Trovatore*. "Di quella pira."
9. Leonora in *La Favorita*.
10. Leonora in *La Favorita*. The aria was "O mio Fernando."
11. Leonore in *Fidelio*.
12. Ponselle sang the Leonoras in *Il Trovatore* and *Forza*.
13. Leonora in *La Favorita*.
14. Leonora in *La Favorita* is deemed unworthy of the "pure" Fernando because she has been the "favorite" of King Alfonso of Spain.
15. The Leonoras of *Fidelio* and *Forza* are not loved by the baritone characters in their respective operas.
16. Leonore in *Fidelio*. The opera is also called *Leonore*.
17. Leonora in *Forza*.
18. *La Favorita*.
19. Leonora in *Il Trovatore*. She agrees to make love to Di Luna if he frees Manrico. When Di Luna discovers that Leonora is dying, he has Manrico executed.

20. The Leonoras in *Il Trovatore* and *La Favorita*.
21. None. They are *all* Spanish.
22. Leonora in *Il Trovatore*.

84. WHAT'S MY LINE?

1. Adriana Lecouvreur, the title character in Cilea's opera, is a leading member of the Comédie-Française.
2. Nedda, in Leoncavallo's *Pagliacci*, is a member of a troupe of players led by her husband.
3. La Gioconda, the title character of Ponchielli's *La Gioconda*, is a street singer. So, by the way, is La Périchôle, in Offenbach's operetta.
4. Peter, the father of Hänsel and Gretel in Humperdinck's opera, is a broom maker.
5. Papageno, in Mozart's *Die Zauberflöte*, is a birdcatcher.
6. In Leoncavallo's *Pagliacci*, Canio is head of the company and its principal clown. Beppe and Tonio are the other two *pagliacci*. (Verdi's Rigoletto is a court jester and is an acceptable answer, too.)
7. Dr. Malatesta, in Donizetti's *Don Pasquale*, helps Norina and Ernesto get married by first presenting Norina to Ernesto's rich uncle, Don Pasquale, as "Sofronia," a prospective bride who almost drives the old man out of his mind. Although Malatesta is a medical doctor, his specialty seems to be *raising* the blood pressure of his patients.
8. Eléazar, in Halévy's *La Juive*, and David, in Mascagni's *L'Amico Fritz*, are rabbis. (During the last years of Mussolini's reign in Italy, when Hitler pressured the Italians to persecute their Jewish citizens, Rabbi David's profession was changed to physician when this opera was presented in Italy.)
9. Marcello in Puccini's *La Bohème*, Mario Cavaradossi in Puccini's *Tosca*, and Flammen in Mascagni's *Lodoletta* are painters. Marcello is a bohemian unknown who must scrounge for commissions. Mario is a wealthy young man who paints mostly for pleasure. Still, someone must have commissioned him to

paint in the church of Sant' Andrea della Valle. Flammen is the Dutch-born artist living in Paris whose chance meeting with Lodoletta in a small town in Holland leads to tragedy.

10. Figaro, in Mozart's *Le Nozze di Figaro*, is the valet of the irascible Count Almaviva. In the 1991 Corigliano-Hoffman opera *The Ghosts of Versailles*, Figaro and Almaviva are still locked in that relationship.

11. The unforgettably named Marianne Leitmetzerin is Sophie's duenna in Richard Strauss's *Der Rosenkavalier*.

12. Minnie, in Puccini's *La Fanciulla del West*, not only owns the Polka Saloon, but serves drinks, sells cigars, and acts as general "den mother" to the miners who patronize her establishment.

13. Five soldiers might include Wozzeck and Andres in Berg's opera, the strange Old Soldier in Catalani's *La Wally*, Sergeant Belcore in Donizetti's *L'Elisir d'Amore*, and Don José in *Carmen*. If you count officers, there are Verdi's Radames from *Aida*, Cassio and Otello in the two *Otello*s by Verdi and Rossini, and both Don Alvaro and Don Carlo in Verdi's *La Forza del Destino*, who earn officer's commissions under assumed names. You might name Ferrando and Guglielmo in Mozart's *Così Fan Tutte*; Almaviva gives Cherubino an officer's commission in *Nozze*; and, returning to Wozzeck, there are the Captain and Drum Major. Valentin in Gounod's *Faust* is a veteran of military action, too. Watch this space for further listings!

14. Count Carnero in Strauss's *Der Zigeunerbaron* and Belcore in *L'Elisir* are recruiters. Each convinces the tenor lead in his opera, Barinkay and Nemorino, respectively, to join up.

15. Ellen Orford, in Britten's *Peter Grimes*, is a schoolmistress.

16. Carmen, in Bizet's opera, works in a cigarette factory when the opera begins.

17. Jake and Robbins, in Gershwin's *Porgy and Bess*, are stevedores, as are Tinca, Talpa, and Luigi in Puccini's *Il Tabarro*.

18. Barnaba, in Ponchielli's *La Gioconda*, is a spy for the Inquisition. For a man in such a position, he makes a surprising number of blunders.

19. Szupán in *Der Zigeunerbaron* raises pigs.
20. Michonnet in *Adriana Lecouvreur* is a stage manager.

85. DISGUISES

1. Ernani in Verdi's opera.
2. Count Almaviva in Rossini's *Il Barbiere di Siviglia*.
3. Cherubino in *Le Nozze di Figaro*.
4. Martha in Flotow's opera.
5. Donna Anna, Donna Elvira, and Don Ottavio in Mozart's *Don Giovanni*.
6. Eisenstein in Johann Strauss's *Die Fledermaus*.
7. Ferrando and Guglielmo in Mozart's *Così Fan Tutte*.
8. Mefistofele follows Faust in Boito's opera.
9. Magda in Puccini's *La Rondine*.
10. Alberich in Wagner's *Das Rheingold*.
11. Gilda in Verdi's *Rigoletto*.
12. Don Andrès in Offenbach's *La Périchole*.

86. ALIASES

1. Lindoro, in Rossini's *Il Barbiere di Siviglia*, is actually Count Almaviva, who has decided to woo Rosina wearing the guise of a poor student.
2. Don Carlo di Vargas, in Verdi's *La Forza del Destino*, claims to be a student called Pereda as he searches for his sister, Leonora, whom he has sworn to kill.
3. In Verdi's *Simon Boccanegra*, Simon's enemy Jacopo Fiesco uses the name Andrea in order to escape detection in Genoa, from which he has been banished.
4. Amelia Grimaldi, also in *Simon Boccanegra*, is actually Maria Boccanegra, the child that Simon Boccanegra had with Maria Fiesco. Jacopo Fiesco, a member of the Grimaldi family, adopts Maria without being aware of the child's true identity, and passes her off as a Grimaldi (the actual daughter of that

family had died as a small child) in order to protect the family fortune.

5. In Ponchielli's *La Gioconda*, Enzo Grimaldo is an Italian prince banished from Venice by Alvise Badoero, who pretends to be a Dalmatian sailor named Enzo Giordan in order to find his beloved Laura Adorno, whom Alvise has married.

6. In Wagner's *Siegfried*, Wotan, the leader of the Norse gods, wanders through the forests disguised in human form, hoping to learn the whereabouts of his mortal grandson, Siegfried.

7. In *La Forza del Destino*, Don Alvaro flees from the vengeful Carlo and takes holy vows as Padre Raffaele. He finds refuge in the same cloister in which his beloved Leonora has hidden from the outside world.

8. Enrico is the name taken by Faust in Boito's *Mefistofele* after the Devil has transformed him into a handsome youth.

9. In Johann Strauss's *Die Fledermaus*, Eisenstein, due to begin a brief jail term, goes to Orlofsky's party instead, and, at his friend Dr. Falke's suggestion, uses the name Marquis Renard in lieu of his own.

10. In Wagner's *Tristan und Isolde*, the heroine, in Isolde's Narrative, relates how Tristan, calling himself Tantris, wooed her for King Marke.

11. In Richard Strauss's *Der Rosenkavalier*, Octavian, the Marschallin's youthful lover, disguises himself as a housemaid called Mariandl, first to save the Marschallin from embarrassment, but later to foil Baron Ochs's designs on Sophie von Faninal.

12. In another Richard Strauss opera, *Arabella*, the heroine's impoverished family can't afford to bring up two girls in society and thus forces Arabella's younger sister, Zdenka, to masquerade as the boy Zdenko.

13. In Verdi's *Falstaff*, Ford disguises himself as Fontana, mythical suitor to Ford's own wife, Alice, as part of an elaborate plot to punish the fat knight.

14. In Giordano's *Andrea Chénier*, Maddalena bribes a Parisian jailer to allow her to assume the identity of a condemned woman, Idia Legray, so she can die with Chénier.

15. In *Die Fledermaus*, Rosalinde's maid, Adele, attends Orlofsky's party where, in a gown "borrowed" without her mistress's consent, Adele passes herself off as an actress, Mlle. Olga.

16. In Verdi's *Rigoletto*, the Duke of Mantua woos Rigoletto's daughter, Gilda, posing as the poor student Gualtier Maldé.

17. In Donizetti's *Don Pasquale*, Sofronia is the name taken by Norina when she pretends to be the shrewish sister of Dr. Malatesta, in the absurd sham marriage to Don Pasquale.

18. In Puccini's *Gianni Schicchi*, the title character impersonates the recently deceased Buoso Donati in order to change the dead man's will, leaving all the riches to himself.

87. REALLY WEIRD NAMES

1. Handel's *Teseo*
2. Britten's *Gloriana*
3. Janáček's *Katya Kabanova*
4. Janáček's *From the House of the Dead*
5. Mozart's *La Finta Giardiniera*
6. Halévy's *La Juive*
7. Verdi's *Aroldo*
8. Floyd's *Susannah*
9. Bellini's *La Straniera*
10. Alfano's *Risurezzione*
11. Britten's *Billy Budd*
12. Puccini's *La Fanciulla del West*
13. Verdi's *Luisa Miller*
14. Berg's *Lulu*
15. Smetana's *The Bartered Bride* (in the widely performed German-language version of this work, Vasek was rechristened Wencel)
16. Mozart's *L'Impresario*
17. Catalani's *La Wally*
18. Puccini's *Madama Butterfly*
19. Mascagni's *Iris*
20. Giordano's *Fedora*

88. TATTLETALES

1. Tonio, in Leoncavallo's *Pagliacci*, vengefully informs Canio that Nedda, Canio's spouse, is busily betraying her marriage vows in the arms of Silvio. Tonio conveniently forgets to say

that he himself had just tried to force himself upon Nedda, who had responded by striking him with a whip.

2. Tosca, in the second act of Puccini's *Tosca*, can no longer bear the sounds that Mario is making while being tortured. She therefore blurts out to Scarpia that the escaped prisoner Angelotti is hiding in the well in the garden of Mario's villa.

3. Fedora, in Giordano's *Fedora*, having gotten Loris to admit that he has killed her fiancé Vladimiro, reveals this to Grech, an agent of the czar's secret police, before she learns the reason that Loris had done the deed—Vladimiro was a bit of czarist sleaze who had seduced Loris's wife and betrayed Fedora.

4. In Strauss's *Der Rosenkavalier*, Valzacchi and his companion, Annina, are precursors of today's tabloid journalists. They search for gossip and make up the facts if they can't find them. Baron Ochs hires them to find out the background of the supposed "maid" Mariandl. Later, the pair let Ochs know that his fiancée, Sophie, is making eyes at Octavian (which is actually true). Finally, Octavian pays the enterprising couple to betray Ochs.

5. The Princess Amneris, in *Aida*, discovers Aida and Amonasro pleading with Radames not to feel too bad about betraying his country to its enemy. With one word, *traditor*, the Princess attracts the attention of high priest Ramfis and starts the deadly chain of events that leads to the opera's tragic ending.

6. Desideria, in Menotti's *The Saint of Bleecker Street*, suspects that her lover, Michele, harbors incestuous feelings toward his fragile sister, Annina. When Desideria informs the entire neighborhood of her suspicions, Michele stabs her to death.

7. Iago, in *Otello*, tells the Moor that his wife, Desdemona, has become the mistress of Otello's captain, Cassio. This, of course, is completely untrue, but whom is Otello to trust?

8. In *Falstaff*, Bardolph and Pistol betray their corpulent master by informing Master Ford of Falstaff's intention to seduce Mistress Ford, and the fun begins.

9. In Puccini's *Manon Lescaut*, Geronte catches Manon, wearing the luxurious clothes that he has given her, in the arms of her younger lover, Des Grieux. Furthermore, Manon mocks him

cruelly when he reproaches her for her conduct. In vengeance, Geronte denounces Manon to the police as a prostitute. No one thinks of charging Geronte with corrupting the morals of a minor!

10. In Floyd's *Susannah*, the strange youth known as Little Bat makes up the story that he has been seduced by Susannah, whom the local Elders already consider to be of suspect morals. This lie, told by Little Bat to ingratiate himself with the local powers and escape punishment from his father, results in the tragedy that follows.

11. Mrs. Sedley is the evil-minded harridan in Britten's *Peter Grimes* who always thinks the worst of Grimes. She blunders upon the secret of Peter's seeming guilt in the death of his apprentice, John. Mrs. Sedley alerts the villagers to her pernicious theories concerning Grimes.

12. In *Le Nozze di Figaro*, Barbarina angers her father, the gardener Antonio, and embarrasses Count Almaviva when she tells everyone assembled for the count's wedding that the count has flirted with her on earlier occasions.

89. WHO WEARS THE PANTS?

1. Cherubino, in Mozart's *Le Nozze di Figaro*.
2. Smetona in Donizetti's *Anna Bolena*.
3. Fyodor, in Mussorgsky's *Boris Godunov*.
4. Oscar, in Verdi's *Un Ballo in Maschera*.
5. The Composer, in Richard Strauss's *Ariadne auf Naxos*.
6. Stéphano, in Gounod's *Roméo et Juliette*.
7. Octavian, in Strauss's *Rosenkavalier*.
8. Dimitri, in Giordano's *Fedora*.
9. Siebel, in Gounod's *Faust*.
10. Romeo, in Bellini's *I Capuleti ed i Montecchi*.
11. Nicklausse, in Offenbach's *Le Contes d'Hoffmann*. (He and Giulietta sing the Barcarolle.)
12. Prince Orlofsky, in Johann Strauss's *Die Fledermaus*.
13. Walter in Catalani's *La Wally*.

14. Janos in Janáček's *Jenufa*.
15. Idamante in Mozart's *Idomeneo*.

90. IN-LAW TROUBLE

1. In Verdi's *Stiffelio*, the moralistic Stankar values his son-in-law's honor more highly than he values his daughter's happiness. Therefore, Stankar slays Raffaele, who has seduced Lina, Stiffelio's wife.
2. In Puccini's *La Rondine*, the unseen mother of Ruggero fouls the Swallow's lovenest when she pens an ode to her prospective daughter-in-law's virginity. The plot is derivative of *La Traviata*, but the ending is much more civilized.
3. In Richard Strauss's *Die Frau ohne Schatten*, the god Keikobad, who does not actually appear in the opera, causes his son-in-law, the Emperor, to be turned to stone until his wife, Keikobad's quirky daughter, becomes fertile.
4. In Verdi's *Simon Boccanegra*, Simon's daughter, Amelia a.k.a. Maria, wishes to wed Gabriele Adorno, who eventually switches sides to support Amelia's dad.
5. In Puccini's *Turandot*, the aged Emperor Altoum tries but fails to dissuade Calaf from attempting to answer Turandot's trio of enigmas. The price of a wrong answer is death.
6. In Janáček's *Jenufa*, Kostelnicka's savage way with words chases from Steva's mind all thoughts of marrying the old woman's foster daughter, Jenufa, whom he has left with a baby. Kostelnicka avenges the family's honor by first convincing Steva's half-brother, Laca, to marry Jenufa, and then by drowning the infant, whose existence has been kept secret from the local folk, in a nearby stream.
7. In Janáček's *Katya Kabanova*, the vicious Kabanicha heaps all sorts of insults and outrages upon her unhappy daughter-in-law, Katya.
8. In Verdi's *Falstaff*, Ford wants his daughter, Nannetta, to marry the idiotic but wealthy Dr. Cajus. Nannetta, with the support of her mother, Alice Ford, wishes to marry the hand-

some youth Fenton. As an epilogue to the humiliation of the
Fat Knight in Windsor Forest, the marriage of Fenton and
Nannetta is accomplished.

9. In Montemezzi's *L'Amore dei Tre Re*, the blind king Archibaldo kills his daughter-in-law Fiora after managing to catch
her embracing her lover, Avito. But the trap the bitter old
man sets to punish Avito ensnares his own son as well.

10. In Richard Strauss's *Der Rosenkavalier*, Faninal would gladly
overlook the fact that his prospective son-in-law, Baron Ochs
von Lerchenau, is a vulgar, boorish swine, because of the Baron's wealth. But after catching Ochs at play with the maid
Mariandl (actually Octavian in drag), Faninal quickly agrees
to Sophie's engagement to the noble Octavian.

11. In Donizetti's *La Fille du Régiment*, the Marquise of Berkenfeld rejects the idea of Marie, her supposed niece (really her
daughter), marrying Tonio, the humble soldier whom she
loves. The haughty Marquise wants Marie to wed the well-
born but twerpy Duke of Krakentorp. Just in the nick of time,
Maman Dearest relents and all ends happily.

12. In Verdi's *La Forza del Destino*, the Marquis of Calatrava brutally prevents the elopement of his daughter, Leonora, with
her lover, Don Alvaro. The old man makes a point of dispar-
aging Alvaro's racially mixed parentage—his mother was a
Latin American Indian.

91. SINGLE PARENTS

1. Rocco, in Beethoven's *Fidelio*, is the father of Marzelline. This
youngster has a crush on another woman, Leonore, believing
that Leonore is a boy, Fidelio. After everyone's identity is
sorted out, Marzelline pairs off with Rocco's assistant, Jaquino,
who has loved her all along.

2. Boris, in Mussorgsky's opera, has two children. Daughter
Xenia is weepy, having lost her fiancé prematurely. Son Fyodor
is clever and active, and Boris dies naming the boy as the next
Czar. History teaches us that Fyodor was killed soon afterward.

3. Madame Larissa in Tchaikovsky's *Eugene Onegin* has two daughters, Olga and Tatyana. The vivacious Olga comes to grief when her flirtation with Onegin leads to his killing her fiancé, Lenski, in a duel. The troubled Tatyana, however, gets over her own infatuation with Onegin and makes an advantageous marriage with one Prince Gremin.

4. In *Tannhäuser*, Hermann's daughter Elisabeth loves the free-living minstrel of the opera's title. After he disgraces himself by singing "dirty" tunes at a song contest, she pines away while Tannhäuser trudges to Rome to ask for the Pope's forgiveness. Elisabeth dies just moments before Tannhäuser returns from his pilgrimage.

5. Teresa is Amina's foster mother in *La Sonnambula*. Even though Amina has a problem with sleepwalking, her reputation is restored and she weds Elvino, a sturdy, if none too bright, peasant lad.

6. Sir Giorgio in *I Puritani* is the rather distant father of Elvira. Politics and man-trouble threaten to unhinge Elvira, but when Arturo returns to her, she appears poised upon the brink of living happily ever after.

7. The Contessa di Coigny in *Andrea Chénier* is the mother of the emotional, lovelorn Maddalena. Maddalena loses her head over Chénier, in more ways than one!

8. Nabucco, in Verdi's opera, has a natural daughter, Fenena, and an older, adopted girl, Abigaille. Abigaille tries unsuccessfully to seize power from Nabucco when the latter is temporarily rendered insane by a thunderbolt from God, and (we're not making this up, you know!) eventually poisons herself. The sweet Fenena, an early monotheist, marries Ismaele, a nice Jewish boy, and is alive and smiling at the opera's end.

9. Il Re d'Egitto in *Aida* is the father of Amneris, apparently an only child. Amneris's beloved Radames dies and is entombed with his beloved Aida.

10. Strominger, in Catalani's *La Wally*, is the father of the opera's uptight title character. Although he throws her out of his house, Strominger eventually leaves her his fortune. But Wally can't buy love, and when love finally comes to her, it is im-

mediately swept away with her beloved Hagenbach in an avalanche. Wally kills herself, dying rich but unhappy.

11. Emperor Altoum, in Puccini's *Turandot*, is the father of Turandot herself. Although rather bloodthirsty in her dating years, Turandot eventually marries happily.

12. Greedy Daland in *Der Fliegende Holländer* would gladly marry off his daughter, Senta, to the strange sea captain he has just met, since the newcomer is laden with riches. The good news is that Senta has loved the legendary Dutchman all her life; but the bad news is that she is constrained to prove her love for him by jumping into the sea. She has vowed to be faithful unto death. By killing herself, Senta proves her love for the Dutchman and both go straight to heaven.

13. Marie in Berg's *Wozzeck* is a slatternly creature who has borne the soldier Wozzeck a child. Wozzeck kills Marie and drowns himself. The child, who has inherited his mother's good looks and his father's intelligence, runs blithely off to view his mother's corpse, leaving us to worry about his future.

14. Alberich, in the *Ring* Cycle, is the father of a character who is easily as hateful as he himself is—Hagen. After six hours of nefarious deeds, the Rhinemaidens drag Hagen to his doom. Good riddance!

15. In Cilea's *L'Arlesiana*, Rosa Mamai is the bitter mother of the lovelorn Federico.

16. In *La Traviata*, Giorgio Germont is the overbearing father of Alfredo. He breaks up Alfredo's affair with the fallen but noble Violetta, and lives to regret it.

17. Mamma Lucia in *Cavalleria Rusticana* is the overindulgent mother of the skirt-chasing Turiddu, who seems to have needed a good spanking more than he needed all that wine!

18. Banco, in Verdi's *Macbeth*, is the Italianized equivalent of Banquo. His son is Fleance, a mute character in the opera. Macbeth has ordered Banco and Fleance struck down because the Witches have forecast that Banco's descendants will rule over Scotland. Banco is slain, but Fleance escapes.

19. Mime in the *Ring* is not actually a father, but he has brought Siegfried up, however miserably, from birth, often whiningly

reminding Siegfried that he has been both father and mother to him. In the manner of a prehistoric Menendez brother, Siegfried dispatches Mime, fearing (correctly) that Mime will kill him at the first opportunity.

92. HOME WRECKERS

1. Luigi, the stevedore in Puccini's *Il Tabarro*, is the lover of Giorgetta, the wife of Michele, Luigi's boss. Misinterpreting Michele's lighting of his pipe as the signal from Giorgetta that all is ready for the lovers, Luigi is confronted by the jealous Michele, who strangles Luigi and then forces his erring wife to kiss the dead man's lips.
2. Werther, the title character of Massenet's opera, loves Charlotte, who loves him back but wishes to be loyal to her husband, Albert. Albert suspects the truth, and when asked by Werther to lend him his dueling pistols, does so gladly. Werther shoots himself, but Charlotte finds the dying man and assures him of her love as he expires.
3. Adalgisa, in Bellini's *Norma*, is a virtuous young priestess. Although she suffers from guilt pangs, Adalgisa allows Pollione to seduce her. Once she realizes that Pollione is the father of Norma's two sons, Adalgisa breaks off her relationship with him. Overcome by her love for Pollione, Norma confesses her own affair with the Roman rascal, and she and Pollione die at the stake, at the hands of the Druids.
4. Enzo, in Ponchielli's *La Gioconda*, loves Laura Adorno, married to the beastly Alvise Badoero. Aided by the distraught Gioconda, who loves Enzo but has sworn to help Laura, the lovers escape the wrath of Alvise and sail off into the sunset, leaving poor Gioconda to kill herself.
5. Riccardo (a.k.a. Gustavus III) is the tenor hero of Verdi's *Un Ballo in Maschera*. Riccardo loves Amelia, the wife of his loyal secretary, Renato (a.k.a. Count Anckarström). When Renato discovers the affair, which, incidentally, has been confined to the platonic level, he joins the conspiracy to assassinate

Riccardo. Renato shoots Riccardo, who pardons him before expiring.

6. Roberto Devereux, the title character in Donizetti's opera, is loved by Queen Elizabeth I. Inconveniently, he loves Sara, the married Duchess of Nottingham. The queen orders Roberto's execution for treason, and the jealous Duke of Nottingham places his wife under arrest so that she is unable to give the queen Roberto's ring, which under a promise from Elizabeth would have made her pardon Roberto. Thus Roberto is executed, Sara is humiliated, and the Virgin Queen is quite annoyed at the Duke of Nottingham as the final curtain falls.

7. Alfred is the strolling, strutting Italian tenor in Johann Strauss's *Die Fledermaus*. Alfred's frenzied flirtation with Rosalinde, wife of Eisenstein, costs him a night in jail, but all is put right at the end of the operetta, and the confusion is attributed to a general overdose of champagne.

8. Percy, in Donizetti's *Anna Bolena*, has the misfortune to be thought Anna's lover, much to the displeasure of King Henry VIII. Actually, Percy and Anna haven't really been lovers, but Henry has them executed anyway.

9. The countess, in Berg's *Lulu*, is the lesbian lover of the heroine. She helps Lulu escape from prison, where Lulu has been confined after murdering her husband, Dr. Schön. The two women eventually flee to London, where the ever-resourceful Lulu becomes a streetwalker. Her final client is Jack the Ripper, who stabs both Lulu and the countess to death.

10. The Drum Major in Berg's *Wozzeck* seduces Marie, the common-law wife of the title character. Wozzeck suspects Marie's infidelity and stabs her to death before he drowns himself.

11. Paolo da Verruchio, in Zandonai's *Francesca da Rimini*, is the young, handsome, charming brother of Francesca's deformed, mean-tempered, and generally loathsome husband, Gianciotto. Francesca is tricked into marrying the latter, thinking that she is getting Paolo (no wonder they call this opera the Italian *Tristan und Isolde*), but eventually forgives Paolo for his part in the treachery. Gianciotto discovers the situation, and

promptly sends Paolo and Francesca to the place where Dante found them.

12. Erda, the subterranean-dwelling earth goddess, introduces herself to Wotan shortly before *Das Rheingold* ends, and promptly lets him father the nine all-singing, all-riding Valkyries. Fricka, Wotan's prissy wife (as you will recall, Fricka is the Goddess of Marriage), fumes and fusses, but can't do much to alter the situation.

93. VILLAINS

1. Iago, in Verdi's *Otello* (also Rossini's) destroys Otello by falsely convincing him that Desdemona, the Moor's wife, has been unfaithful to him. Otello slays her, and then himself, after Iago's treachery has been revealed.
2. Tonio in Leoncavallo's *Pagliacci*.
3. Count di Luna in Verdi's *Il Trovatore* is this novice-snatching cad.
4. Lady Macbeth, in Verdi's *Macbeth*, uses the cabaletta "Or tutti sorgete" to call for diabolical strength of heart.
5. Abigaille in Verdi's *Nabucco* is the culprit here. Her treachery fails and she kills herself as all the others convert to Judaism.
6. This is Hagen in *Götterdämmerung*, who bumps off Siegfried, and his own half-brother, Gunther, while causing boundless trouble for his half-sister, Gutrune, and Brünnhilde, too. He ends as fishbait, thanks to the Rhinemaidens.
7. Ortrud in Wagner's *Lohengrin* not only turns Elsa's brother, the Duke of Brabant, into a swan, but disrupts the wedding of Lohengrin and Elsa, sowing seeds of doubt into Elsa's rather feeble mind, and destroying the couple's chances for marital bliss.
8. This is the Witch in Humperdinck's *Hänsel und Gretel*. So she changes some brats into gingerbread! Kids are running wild in the forest! Have another helping of dessert!
9. Claggart, in Britten's *Billy Budd*, destroys the title character for the pleasure of doing such a thing. He loses his own life

when Billy, whom Claggart has falsely accused of planning a mutiny onboard their ship, the *Indomitable*, loses his temper and strikes Claggart, who falls, hits his head, and goes off to face his Maker.

10. Barnaba, in Ponchielli's *La Gioconda*.

11. In Beethoven's *Fidelio*, the nasty Don Pizarro's plot to execute Florestan is terminated when the jailer's "boy" assistant, Fidelio, reveals herself as Florestan's wife, Leonore, and, waves a pistol at Pizarro, who desists from tormenting Florestan. Pizarro is soon placed under arrest by the kindly Don Fernando, a king's minister who passes through the vicinity at an opportune moment.

12. Here, we are describing Mime in *Der Ring*. Siegfried, in the second act of that music drama, learns that Mime, his adoptive parent, is about to slay him in order to get that darned golden ring. Siegfried cheerfully runs Mime through with his sword, Nothung.

13. Here we speak of the slimy slave Monostatos, in Mozart's *Die Zauberflöte*. His unwanted attentions to Pamina net him a whipping, and his alliance with the evil Queen of the Night doom him to sink into the earth alongside the Queen and her three Ladies.

14. The Nurse in Strauss's *Die Frau ohne Schatten* is devoted to her mistress, the barren, shadowless demigoddess, the Empress. The Nurse would beguile the unhappy Dyer's Wife of her shadow and thus, her fertility, and magically transfer these to the Empress. The Empress, however, sees the light of righteousness and will have none of this plan. The Spirit Messenger of Keikobad condemns the wretched Nurse to life among the humans she so despises, and she makes her exit with a blood-freezing shriek.

15. Verdi's Macbeth. His final aria is incredibly touching, and one senses throughout the opera the tragedy of a decent man undone by greed.

16. Beckmesser, in Wagner's *Die Meistersinger von Nürnberg*, is a comic figure but a villain nonetheless. He makes Walther miserable, annoys Sachs, and generally irritates the good folk

of Nuremberg, who eventually rally against him at the Song Contest.

94. THREE GALS NAMED ELVIRA

1. Elvira in *Don Giovanni.*
2. Elvira in *Ernani.*
3. Elvira in *I Puritani.*
4. Maria Callas. (Complete *I Puritani*, arias from *Ernani* and *Don Giovanni.*)
5. Leontyne Price. (Complete *Ernani* and *Don Giovanni.*)
6. Elvira in *I Puritani.*
7. Elvira in *Don Giovanni* and Elvira in *Ernani* are left alone. Don Giovanni, Donna Elvira's prey, has been dragged off to Hades by the statue of the Commendatore. Elvira in *Ernani* loses her man when Ernani is forced by Silva to kill himself, moments after he has wed her.
8. Elvira in *Ernani*—that Silva is a bad one!
9. Donna Elvira in *Don Giovanni* is mocked by Don G.'s sharp-tongued servant Leporello in the Catalog Aria, in which Leporello provides the statistics concerning his master's seductions of women all across Europe.
10. Elvira in *I Puritani.*
11. Elvira in *Ernani.*
12. Martina Arroyo.
13. Elvira in *I Puritani.*
14. Elvira in *I Puritani.*
15. Elvira in *Ernani.*

95. GOOD DREAMS . . . BAD DREAMS

1. Pollione, in Bellini's *Norma*, dreams that Norma has pursued him and Adalgisa to Rome to punish Pollione for turning his attentions from Norma to Adalgisa. Norma is, of course, infuriated when she actually learns of Pollione's duplicity, but

after hours of worrying about the situation, she spares Adalgisa's life, admits that she has broken her own vows of chastity, and, with the newly contrite Pollione, goes to her death.

2. In Richard Strauss's *Die Frau ohne Schatten*, the dreaming Empress sees her husband turned to stone. By learning compassion for others, the Empress, with her newly defined humanity, serves to allow the Emperor to turn back to flesh and blood.

3. Klytämnestra, in Richard Strauss's *Elektra*, is haunted by nightmares in which she is murdered by her son Orest as punishment for her own murder of Orest's father, Agamemnon. Her dream comes true.

4. Elsa, in Wagner's *Lohengrin*, sees the arrival of the Swan Knight in a dream. Lohengrin does indeed sail to Brabant and fights for Elsa in a trial by combat. Although he wins, the evil Ortrud eventually undermines Elsa's faith in Lohengrin, leading to his departure from Brabant and Elsa's own death.

5. In Wagner's *Die Walküre*, Sieglinde dreams of her twin brother (and lover) Siegmund's death at the hands of Hunding, her husband. In spite of Brünnhilde's valiant efforts on Siegmund's behalf, the dream comes true.

6. Lady Macbeth, in Verdi's opera, sleepwalks as she relives in her dreams the murders of Duncan, Lady Macduff, and Macduff's children.

7. In Verdi's *Otello*, as in Shakespeare's tragedy, one of the fictions that Iago manufactures in his effort to destroy Otello and Desdemona's happiness is a dream that Iago claims Cassio had, during which he murmured words of love to Desdemona. Otello, of course, swallows Iago's bait, and tragedy results.

8. In Mussorgsky's *Boris Godunov*, Czar Boris suffers a fatal heart attack when the old monk Pimen recounts the story of a blind man who regained his sight after dreaming of the murdered Czarevitch Dmitri.

9. In Bellini's *La Sonnambula*, the sleepwalking Amina dreams that her jealous suitor, Elvino, is restored to her. Elvino, overcome by shame as he watches the innocent Amina walk in her sleep, sinks to his knees in front of her. Thus, Amina awakens to find that her dream has come true.

10. In Gilbert and Sullivan's *Iolanthe*, the Lord Chancellor's bad dream, described in the song "When You're Lying Awake," is a very funny and very realistic description of a foolish but unnerving dream.

11. In Rossini's Cinderella opera, *La Cenerentola*, Don Magnifico (the male equivalent of the wicked stepmother) is mystified by his dream of being turned into a donkey. His subsequent foolish behavior shows that the dream, at least metaphorically, has come true.

12. In Verdi's *I Lombardi*, Giselda, who has experienced more trauma in four acts than even La Gioconda could envision, has her faith restored by a dream/vision of her recently slain lover, Oronte, singing to her from a better world. Shortly thereafter, the Crusaders actually reach Jerusalem, and everyone still breathing is the better for the experience!

13. In the second act of Massenet's *Manon*, the Chevalier des Grieux recounts to Manon his dream of happiness with her. Next thing you know, the poor Chevalier is carried off by thugs hired to free him from Manon's clutches. Manon briefly finds happiness with her next lover, De Brétigny.

14. In Johann Strauss's *Der Ziguenerbaron*, the Gypsy Czipra tells her daughter Saffi and her lover Barinkay that she has had a dream in which Barinkay's late father told her where to find a buried treasure. This one, of course, has a happy ending.

96. LOCO EN EL COCO

1. Elvira, in Bellini's *I Puritani*, sinks into delirium when Arturo, her intended, deserts her at the altar in order to save Enrichetta, widow of Charles I of England, from execution at the hands of Cromwell. As soon as Arturo returns, Elvira recovers her faculties.

2. Ophélie is, of course, Hamlet's cast-off sweetheart in Ambroise Thomas's *Hamlet*. As in Shakespeare, the cumulative effect of Hamlet's strange behavior, which includes the murder of Ophélie's father, Polonius, is too much for the poor girl.

3. *Lucia di Lammermoor* has perhaps the most famous mad scene in all opera. Donizetti's heroine goes mad when, after being tricked into marrying a political ally of her brother's, her true love Edgardo—whom she had believed to be false—arrives to break up the wedding party. Lucia stabs her bridegroom to death.

4. Nabucco, in Verdi's opera, is struck by lightning sent by Jehovah when the Babylonian king announces to the assembled soloists and chorus that he is no longer merely the king, but God himself. There is no aria here for Nabucco, just the lead in the ensemble that ends the act. Nabucco regains his intellect after praying to God for forgiveness.

5. Marguérite, in Gounod's *Faust*, loses her mind after Faust abandons her when she is pregnant with his child. To make matters worse, Faust, aided by Méphistophélès, kills Marguérite's brother Valentin in a duel, and the dying man curses his sister. Marguérite kills her baby and is condemned to death, although her prayers for deliverance from Méphistophélès and Faust lead to her salvation.

6. Peter Grimes, in Britten's opera, is on the edge of emotional collapse throughout the opera. Grimes finally snaps completely when his new apprentice accidentally falls to his death. Grimes knows that he will be blamed.

7. Azucena, in Verdi's *Il Trovatore*, is demented throughout, but especially in the second act, when she is riveted by the memory of her mother being burned at the stake. In her terror, she had thrown her own baby into the flames and has never been the same again.

8. Imogene, in Bellini's *Il Pirata*, goes berserk when her husband executes her pirate lover. Her *scena di pazzia* ends the opera somewhat abruptly. Bellini wasn't interested in the final scene of the libretto, in which various plot angles are straightened out.

9. Boris Godunov, in Mussorgsky's masterpiece, suffers from the guilt he feels for the murder of the Czarevitch Dmitri. The Clock Scene in Act II finds Boris gibbering on the floor, terrified by visions of the slaughtered child's ghost.

10. Juana La Loca, in Gian Carlo Menotti's opera, is the much put-upon daughter of Ferdinand and Isabella of Spain. Betrayed by husband, father, and son, Juana spends her last forty years walled up in a dark corner of the palace. Small wonder she goes crazy, in a mad scene that lasts for almost the entire third act of the opera.

11. Anna Bolena goes mad after she is imprisoned and condemned to death on false charges of adultery, in Donizetti's opera. The second wife of Henry VIII fades in and out of reality as her date with the axe draws near. Her final scene—especially when performed by Callas—is a knockout!

12. Ah-Joe, the leading female character in Leoni's *L'Oracolo*, goes mad after the villainous Cim-Fen slays her fiancé, Uin-San-Lui. The dead youth's father, Uin-Sci, solves the crime and brutally slays the malicious Cim-Fen.

97. SUICIDIO

1. In Catalani's *La Wally*, Wally's unexpected reconciliation with Hagenbach, whom she herself had wanted to kill earlier on, is ruined when the poor tenor is killed in an avalanche. Wally jumps into an icy chasm without so much as a backward glance.

2. In Wagner's *Der Fliegende Holländer*, the title character, condemned to sail the seas eternally unless he finds a wife who will be true unto death, believes that Senta has betrayed him. She proves that she has not by her leap into the sea, an act of love that results in the Dutchman's own death and the pair's mystical reunion in the Great Beyond.

3. Leonora, in Verdi's *Il Trovatore*, drinks poison from her ring in order to die faithful to Manrico. The spiteful Count di Luna, discovering that he has been duped, orders Manrico to the block—only to be told by Azucena that Manrico had been Di Luna's own, long-lost brother.

4. Rodolfo, in Verdi's *Luisa Miller*, is this tragically gullible fel-

low. As he falls dying, he manages to stab Wurm, the spoil-sport who contrived all of Luisa's and Rodolfo's suffering.

5. Peter Grimes, in Britten's opera, takes Captain Balstrode's stern but well-intentioned advice and sinks his boat away from shore, with himself as its only passenger.

6. Aida, in Verdi's opera, plants herself inside Radames's soon-to-be-sealed crypt, so that she may die with the man she loves.

7. This is the penultimate scene of Berg's *Wozzeck*. When Woz-zeck walks into the river, he leaves the body of Marie to be discovered by a band of children, including their own son.

8. In the original version of Verdi's *La Forza del Destino*, per-formed in St. Petersburg, Don Alvaro jumps to his death after Don Carlo kills his sister, Alvaro's beloved Leonora. No one in this version gets to sing that beautiful trio, "Non imprecare, umiliati," which Verdi later crafted to end the opera.

9. Liù, in Puccini's *Turandot*, dies for love, and Puccini expired shortly after composing her death scene.

10. Papageno, in Mozart's *Die Zauberflöte*, decides not to hang himself when the Three Genii remind him that his magic glockenspiel can help him find Papagena.

11. In Massenet's *Werther*, the title character slays himself in that melancholy manner. Werther suffers a lingering death, but is comforted at the end by his darling, distraught Charlotte.

12. Gilda in Verdi's *Rigoletto* allows Sparafucile to slay her instead of the callous Duke of Mantua. The jester discovers his mor-tally wounded child in the sack provided for disposal of the duke's body.

13. This, of course, is the death of Otello in Verdi's opera, one of the most poignant and powerful scenes in the entire lyric theater.

14. Eros, in Barber's *Antony and Cleopatra*, kills himself rather than obey the hesitating Antony's command to kill him.

15. The words etched into the knife given to Cio-Cio-San's father by the Mikado call for an honorable ending to a life stained with dishonor. Cio-Cio-San, therefore, is certain that what she does with that knife is proper.

98. MURDERS MOST FOUL

1. In Cilea's *Adriana Lecouvreur*, the vile Princess di Bouillon dips a bouquet of violets into a poison and sends them to Adriana, implying that the posies have come from Maurizio, to whom Adriana had originally given them. Adriana sniffs the bouquet and dies in Maurizio's arms shortly thereafter.

2. In Puccini's second opera, the all-but-forgotten *Edgar*, the vicious Tigrana stabs the wholesome Fidelia, her virtuous rival for Edgar's affections, to death.

3. In Giordano's *Fedora*, Loris Ipanoff shoots the evil Vladimiro. Fedora is engaged to the murder victim, knowing nothing of her fiancé's darker side. Thus, until we learn Loris's side of the story in Act II, the killing of Vladimiro appears to be a cold-blooded murder.

4. Aegisth, in Richard Strauss's *Elektra*, finds his stepdaughter (the title character) welcoming him home with uncharacteristic joy. The king enters his palace and is surprised by Orest (Elektra's brother and son of the murdered Agamemnon) waiting for him with an axe.

5. Samson, of biblical fame, is the tenor protagonist of Saint-Saëns's *Samson et Dalila*. Dalila ties up Samson and shears off his hair, which, as most of you will recall, is the source of Samson's tremendous strength. Blinded, Samson is led into the temple of Dagon, where the Philistines make sport of him. Samson prays to God for a return of his prowess, then proceeds to push down the columns that support the structure, thus killing his enemies and himself at the same time.

6. Renato (a.k.a. Anckarström) in Verdi's *Un Ballo in Maschera*, believes that his wife, Amelia, and his best friend, Count Riccardo (a.k.a. Gustavus III) are lovers. He therefore assassinates the count at a masked ball. The dying Riccardo pardons him.

7. Lucrezia Borgia, heroine of Donizetti's opera, poisons the wine offered the guests at a dinner party she gives in Ferrara, hoping to destroy Orsini, who had previously insulted her. Her own recently discovered illegitimate son, Gennaro, is Orsini's best

friend and shares the wine with him. Poor Lucrezia has little choice but to sing her *cabaletta* and cater the funeral.

8. Giants Fasolt and Fafner have built Valhalla for the gods in Wagner's *Das Rheingold.* Although at first Wotan had offered them his sister-in-law Freia, the Goddess of Youth, as payment, he later attempts to buy them off with the gold he has just stolen from the dwarf Alberich (who had himself pinched it from the Rhinemaidens). They quarrel over ownership of the ring, and Fafner hits Fasolt over the head.

9. Baron Scarpia, in Puccini's *Tosca,* has dined well and expects to enjoy Tosca as dessert. Tosca has promised herself to the baron in return for the life of her lover, Mario Cavaradossi. Instead, she stabs Scarpia with his own bread knife.

10. Lucia di Lammermoor, the heroine of Donizetti's best-known tragic opera, has been forced into marriage to Arturo Bucklaw. She'd much rather wed her brother's archenemy, Edgardo. So, as the newlyweds slip away to the bridal chamber, Lucia stabs her husband to death during the intermission before the Mad Scene.

11. In Gounod's *Faust,* Faust, aided by Méphistophélès, kills Valentin in a duel. Valentin is the soldier whose sister, Marguérite, Faust has impregnated and abandoned.

12. Shostakovich's Katerina Ismailova, the Lady Macbeth of Mtsensk, could teach Lucrezia Borgia a thing or two about making borscht!

13. Hermann is the unhappy gambler in Tchaikovsky's *Pique Dame* who frightens the Old Countess to death when he barges into her bedchamber demanding her secret for winning at cards. The old lady returns from the other side to help Hermann—or does she?

14. In Debussy's *Pelléas et Mélisande,* Golaud's worst suspicions about his half-brother Pelléas's intentions toward the bizarre Mélisande (Golaud's new spouse) are confirmed. Golaud rather impulsively dispatches Pelléas.

15. In Berg's *Lulu,* the amoral protagonist grabs the gun with which her unhappy husband, Dr. Schön, has menaced her. Lulu wishes to run off with the Countess Geschwitz and won't

let Schön's protests dissuade her. She empties the revolver into her husband.

99. WIDOWS AND WIDOWERS

1. Gutrune, in *Götterdämmerung*, is widowed when Hagen, her half-brother, slays Siegfried. Since Gutrune does little but whine whenever she is onstage, she doesn't elicit much sympathy.
2. In *Ernani*, Elvira is widowed moments after saying "I do," when her hateful Uncle Silva forces Ernani to honor his pledge to kill himself when Silva sounds the hunting horn Ernani has given him.
3. Klytämnestra, in Richard Strauss's *Elektra*, makes herself a widow when she murders her husband Agamemnon.
4. Lucia, in Donizetti's *Lucia di Lammermoor*, is another member of the "Do-It-Yourself Widows Club" when she slays Arturo on their wedding night.
5. Regina, in Blitzstein's opera, allows her husband, Horace, to die of a heart attack. With Horace dead, Regina can regain control of the family fortune.
6. Enrichetta, in *I Puritani*, is the widow of King Charles I, who was toppled from Britain's throne.
7. Serena is widowed early on in *Porgy and Bess* when her husband, Robbins, is slain by Crown in a fight.
8. Canio, in *Pagliacci*, stabs his unfaithful wife, Nedda, during a performance of a comedy in which they tour the map of little Italy. Even though he did it himself, Canio sobs over Nedda's body as the curtain falls.
9. Frank, in Weill's *Street Scene*, also causes his own widowhood when he shoots his unfaithful, but enormously sympathetic wife, Anna, and Anna's lover, Steve.
10. Macduff, in Verdi's *Macbeth*, loses his wife in a scene played offstage (unlike in Shakespeare's tragedy) to murderers enlisted by Macbeth for the purpose.
11. Loris, in *Fedora*, loses his wife, the unseen but witchy Wanda,

when she dies of an illness shortly after Loris has shot her lover, Fedora's infamous fiancé, Vladimiro.

12. The Thane, known to his golfing buddies as Macbeth, loses his Lady when she dies, apparently of a very guilty conscience, shortly after her Sleepwalking Scene.

13. Hanna, the Merry Widow, loses her husband, conveniently, as it turns out, on her wedding night, leaving her very rich and very faithful to Prince Danilo, with whom she is reunited at the end of Lehár's best-known operetta.

100. PRISONERS OF FATE

1. Piquillo (Paquillo in the Metropolitan Opera version) in Offenbach's operetta *La Périchole*, is sent to the Dungeon for Recalcitrant Husbands when he refuses to acquiesce to his wife's being the mistress of the Viceroy of Peru. The wife in question, Périchole, has, of course, no intention of being unfaithful, but angrily insists on Piquillo's arrest when he insults her during her presentation at court. Since *La Périchole* is a comedy, Périchole—after briefly being locked up herself—escapes with Piquillo, eventually winning the Viceroy's forgiveness, and a title in the bargain.

2. Margherita, in Boito's *Mefistofele*, like her counterpart Marguérite in Gounod's *Faust*, is sent to prison under sentence of death for having killed the baby she has borne Faust. Faust and Mefistofele endeavor to manage her escape, but Margherita prays to God for strength and for pardon, and dies in a state of grace.

3. In Puccini's opera, Manon Lescaut and her impoverished lover, Des Grieux, are surprised while making love by Manon's wealthy old protector, Geronte di Ravoir. When the old man storms off in a fury, Manon wastes precious time gathering up her jewelry. Geronte returns with the police, to whom he has denounced the girl as a prostitute. The felony is compounded when Manon is caught hiding the jewels. Manon is

deported to Louisiana where, tended by the faithful Des Grieux, she dies of starvation.

4. In Verdi's *Rigoletto*, Monterone is dragged off to the dungeon because he has dared to publicly berate the Duke of Mantua for seducing Monterone's daughter. Although we never learn Monterone's exact fate, the curse he hurls at Rigoletto is fulfilled by Gilda's murder at the hands of the assassin Sparafucile.

5. Elena, the firebrand heroine of Verdi's *I Vespri Siciliani*, is sent to "death row" after the discovery of her part in the plot against Monforte, the French governor of Sicily. Monforte's son Arrigo is Elena's lover, and she is eventually pardoned and allowed to marry Arrigo. Unfortunately, the Sicilian rebel Procida ruins the wedding party by rushing in with a horde of angry Sicilians, who murder all the French soldiers, including Monforte, the groom's father!

6. In Verdi's *Don Carlo*, the title character is sent to prison after he draws his sword against his father, King Philip II of Spain, in an attempt to win leniency for Protestant Flanders. A change of heart on Philip's part (after a depressing conversation with the Grand Inquisitor) sets Carlo free, but the king attempts to rearrest his son the following evening, believing that Carlo and Philip's young wife, Elisabetta, are lovers. The end of *Don Carlo* is quite confusing, as the Prince is saved from Philip's soldiers by the intervention of a rather scary friar who appears to be the ghost of Charles V, Carlo's doting old grandfather. Charles V leads the lad into the cloister of St. Just, from which he evidently never emerges.

7. In Puccini's *Tosca*, all we know about Angelotti is that he has been sent to prison by the Royalists because he was a Republican consul. The Sardou play on which the opera is based explains that Angelotti is the former lover of the notorious Lady Hamilton. Lady Hamilton, a friend of the Roman Queen, Caroline, fears that Angelotti might embarrass her by revealing her naughty past. She has the works of Voltaire planted in Angelotti's home and thereby seals the poor fellow's doom. In both play and opera, Angelotti escapes from jail (the

Castel Sant'Angelo) and is hidden by the painter Cavaradossi (Tosca's lover) in the well in the garden of Cavaradossi's villa. Cavaradossi refuses, even under torture, to reveal his friend's hiding place, but Tosca, who can't stand hearing her lover's cries of pain, gives Baron Scarpia the information. Angelotti kills himself with poison as the policemen reach him.

8. Massenet's *Manon* differs from Puccini's opera *Manon Lescaut* by having the heroine arrested after a card game at the Parisian Hôtel de Transylvanie. Guillot, the old man whose attentions Manon has been spurning continuously for four long acts, accuses Manon's lover, Des Grieux, of cheating at cards and tells the arresting officers that Manon is Des Grieux's accomplice. The young man's powerful father prevents Des Grieux's arrest, but Manon is dragged off. In the Massenet opera, Manon's release from custody is arranged before deportation to America, but the poor girl has suffered so greatly in prison that she dies in Des Grieux's arms moments after being freed.

9. Eisenstein, in Johann Strauss's *Die Fledermaus*, has been sentenced to five days in jail for assaulting a tax collector. His incompetent lawyer, Dr. Blinde, has so badly bungled the appeal that three additional days are added to his sentence. Eisenstein arrives in prison hours after his sentence has begun, having first gone off to Prince Orlofsky's ball. All the complications are set right at the end of the opera, and Eisenstein serves his sentence a happy man, knowing that his wife, Rosalinde, wasn't really unfaithful to him after all . . . probably.

10. The Old Prisoner in Offenbach's *La Périchole* helps Périchole and Piquillo escape from the viceroy's dungeon. As the plot is resolved, the viceroy recognizes the old man as a dear friend, and asks why he has been shut away in the first place. The Old Prisoner replies that he was guilty of no crime, so therefore there can be no pardon. The old man is led away brandishing his penknife with which—he assures the sympathetic onlookers—he can burrow his way out to freedom in a mere twelve years.

11. Don José, in Bizet's *Carmen*, is jailed because he allows Carmen, who has been arrested for injuring a coworker in a brawl

in the cigarette factory where she works, to escape while he is transporting her to prison. Carmen, of course, has quickly ensnared José with her fabled wiles.

12. Maria Stuarda, in Donizetti's opera, has been imprisoned by Queen Elizabeth I of England for being politically dangerous to her. Maria seals her doom during a meeting with Queen Bess by losing her temper and speaking rudely to her sovereign. First she loses her temper, then she loses her head . . .

13. The Carmelite nuns, in Poulenc's *Dialogues des Carmélites*, run afoul of the forces of the French Revolution because they refuse to give up practicing their religion, which the Tribunal has outlawed.

14. Billy, in Britten's opera, is hanged after he kills the evil Claggart, who has falsely accused Budd of inciting the other sailors to mutiny. Billy, who stammers, is so angered by Claggart's perfidy that he is unable to reply verbally. He strikes Claggart, who falls, hits his head, and dies.

15. Peter, in Gershwin's *Porgy and Bess*, is unjustly arrested by Charleston policemen as a material witness to the murder of Robbins, even though the Catfish Row residents, including Porgy, tell them that Crown killed Robbins.

101. CAPITAL PUNISHMENT

1. The Prince of Persia, in Puccini's *Turandot*, is beheaded because he has failed to answer the princess's three riddles.

2. Mario Cavaradossi, in Puccini's *Tosca*, is shot by Baron Scarpia's soldiers, although Tosca herself believes it to be a mock execution. The shooting was ordered because Mario had aided the escaped political prisoner Angelotti, and, moreover, had insulted Scarpia after having been tortured.

3. Paolo Albiani dies in Verdi's *Simon Boccanegra* for having abducted Doge Simon's daughter. Before his arrest, however, Paolo has poisoned Simon's carafe of drinking water.

4. Maria Stuarda, in Donizetti's opera, dies mourned by all her

retainers. The Queen of Scots had committed treason, in the eyes of Queen Elizabeth I, by calling her a "vil bastarda."

5. Manrico, in Verdi's *Il Trovatore*, is dragged away to the axe-man calling out "Madre, o madre, addio" to Azucena, who he doesn't realize is *not* his mother.

6. Maddalena, in Giordano's *Andrea Chénier*, has bribed a jailer to let her die in place of a condemned woman, Idia Legray, in order to perish with her beloved poet Chénier, who has been sentenced to death for treasonous activities by the minions of the Reign of Terror.

7. The entire convent of Carmelite nuns in Poulenc's *Dialogues des Carmélites* (except for the incognita Mother Marie of the Incarnation) go bravely to their deaths, having defied the French revolutionary government by keeping their religious vows.

8. Don José, in Bizet's *Carmen*, is undoubtedly executed for murdering his Gypsy sweetheart. His last words in the opera are, "You may arrest me. I killed her. Oh, my beloved Carmen." Mérimée's novel is narrated by José, who awaits execution.

9. The Duchess Elena, in Verdi's *I Vespri Siciliani*, craves vengeance for her brother's execution at the hands of the French, who rule Sicily at the time. Her lover, Arrigo, turns out to be the son of Monforte, the French Governor of Sicily. The statesmanlike Monforte is willing to forgive Elena's treasonable acts and let her marry Arrigo. However, Elena's hard-hearted revolutionary colleague insists on assassinating Monforte and all the French just as vespers sound on the day of Elena's marriage to Arrigo.

10. Jokanaan, or John the Baptist, in Richard Strauss's *Salome*, is beheaded at the request of Salome, after Herod has promised his stepdaughter anything she wants, if she would dance for him. After Salome receives Jokanaan's severed head and makes love to it for twenty or so minutes, the shocked Herod orders his soldiers to kill her.

11. Billy Budd is hanged for his accidental killing of the evil Master of Arms Claggart, because not even the excellent Captain Vere can put aside the military code's prescribed punishment for an impressed seaman who kills an officer.

12. Poor Anna Bolena, in Donizetti's opera, loses her head because Henry VIII has lost his heart to Giovanna Seymour!

13. Rabbi Eléazar is executed, at the end of Halévy's *La Juive*, along with his supposed daughter Rachel, because it wasn't easy being Jewish in fifteenth-century Poland, especially if a rather narrow-minded cardinal is one's worst enemy. Eléazar follows Rachel into a cauldron of boiling oil, but not before informing the Cardinal that Rachel is actually the churchman's own, long-lost illegitimate child.

14. John Proctor, in David Ward's *The Crucible*, allows himself to be hanged rather than confess to a baseless charge of witchcraft.

15. Marie-Antoinette, in John Corigliano's *The Ghosts of Versailles*, is the object of a doomed attempt by the playwright Beaumarchais to save her from the guillotine. The plan fails, but playwright and queen are, in this work, united for eternity.

102. FINAL REQUESTS

1. As she lies dying, Violetta, in Verdi's *La Traviata*, hands her beloved Alfredo a locket containing her portrait. She tells Alfredo to give the locket to the innocent young girl he will someday marry, and to tell her that an angel in heaven is praying for her happiness. We never learn whether or not Alfredo marries, but at least Violetta gets her greatest wish— Alfredo returns to her before she dies.

2. Johnson, in Puccini's *La Fanciulla del West*, is about to be lynched by the posse led by Sheriff Jack Rance. He accepts his fate (although he will, of course, be rescued by Minnie) but asks the men to allow Minnie to believe that he is alive and free in another part of the country.

3. Mario, in *Tosca*, asks the jailer to allow him to write a farewell to Tosca. The jailer consents, and we get to hear the aria "E lucevan le stelle."

4. Paolo, in Verdi's *Simon Boccanegra*, has been condemned to death for treason. As he is led off, Paolo tells the haughty Fiesco that he, Paolo, has abducted Fiesco's ward, Amelia. He

begs Fiesco to kill him and thus spare him the indignity of public execution, but Fiesco angrily refuses, leaving Paolo to his fate.

5. Werther, in Massenet's opera, begs his beloved, married Charlotte to bury him beneath the shade of his favorite tree. Not being familiar with the zoning ordinances of eighteenth-century Frankfurt, we are unable to tell you if this melancholy request was granted or not.

6. Amelia, in Verdi's *Un Ballo in Maschera*, takes seriously her husband Renato's vow to kill her after her romantic involvement with Riccardo is revealed. She asks Renato to let her see her son once more before she dies. Renato not only grants this wish, but decides to spare her life and kill Riccardo instead.

7. Boccanegra, in Verdi's *Simon Boccanegra*, having been poisoned by the condemned Paolo, names his new son-in-law, Gabriele Adorno, to be the new doge, after Simon's death. He asks Fiesco, his former enemy, to see that his wish is carried out. Fiesco proclaims Adorno Doge as the curtain falls.

8. Anna Bolena, in Donizetti's opera, awaiting the executioner, hears the offstage celebrations of the wedding of Henry VIII to Jane (Giovanna) Seymour. She claims to forgive her ex-husband and his new bride, and calls down heaven's blessing upon them. Her fiery melody, however, suggests that Bolena is not entirely sincere in her attitude. In reality, the marriage of Henry and Jane was ill-fated. She died in childbirth.

9. Don Alvaro, in Verdi's *La Forza del Destino*, believes himself to be dying from a wound suffered in battle. He asks his new friend, who is actually his sworn enemy Don Carlo, to burn all his personal papers upon his death. Alvaro doesn't die, and Carlo, of course, riffles through these items and discovers Alvaro's true identity, thereby motivating the final hour of the plot.

10. Desideria, in Menotti's *The Saint of Bleecker Street*, has been stabbed by her lover, Michele, during a furious argument in which Desideria insinuates that Michele has incestuous desires for his sister Annina, a frail and devout girl whom the neighbors consider a saint. Desideria falls dying and, in her terror,

asks Annina to pray for her soul. In an electrifying tableau, Annina does so.

11. Mimì, in Puccini's *La Bohème*, is dying in the bohemians' cold garret. She wishes for a muff to warm her hands. Musetta sells her earrings and returns with the muff for Mimì, moments before the heroine slips away.

12. Turiddu, in Mascagni's *Cavalleria Rusticana*, begs his mother, Mamma Lucia, to be a mother to Santuzza if Turiddu should not return. The drunken Turiddu is immediately slaughtered by Alfio in a duel. We never learn what happens to the surviving women, but, since Mamma Lucia doesn't seem to care much for Santuzza to begin with, one rather doubts that they will become close, Turiddu's wish notwithstanding.

13. Desdemona, in Verdi's *Otello*, begs Otello not to kill her until she has had time to say a prayer. The Moor strangles her at once. Moments later, the dying heroine begs Emilia, who has reentered the room, to commend her to her Lord, implying that she has committed suicide. Otello immediately contradicts her, and the final, horrible moments begin.

14. Pagano, in Verdi's *I Lombardi alla Prima Crocciata*, is the parricide turned holy man whom his brother Arvino and the Crusaders encounter in the Holy Land. Fatally wounded in battle, Pagano reconciles with Arvino and begs to be carried to the banks of the Jordan to see Jerusalem. The Crusaders carry him off as the final curtain descends.

15. In Poulenc's *Dialogues des Carmélites*, the Old Prioress, Mme. de Croissy, endures a painful final illness and a fearful death agony. She is ashamed of her weakness and, in her final moment begs the young postulant Blanche to forgive her fear of death. De Croissy expires before Blanche, who fears death herself, can comfort her.

103. OPENING LINES

1. In Puccini's *La Bohème*, Marcello addresses Rodolfo with these words, jokingly blaming the sea in his painting for the cold that pervades their attic flat.

2. In Verdi's *Rigoletto*, the Duke of Mantua opens the opera by discussing his latest sweetheart (actually, Gilda) with the courtier Borsa.

3. As the curtain rises on Verdi's *Otello*, the Cypriots react to the storm that threatens Otello's ship with these first words.

4. In Puccini's *Turandot*, the Mandarin begins the opera by announcing Turandot's decree to the assembled crowd.

5. In Verdi's *Il Trovatore*, the old soldier Ferrando bestirs his resting guardsmen with this admonition, then proceeds to launch into the exposition.

6. In Richard Strauss's *Salome*, the first character to be heard is the captain of the guard, Narraboth, commenting on the beautiful Salome to his colleagues.

7. In Verdi's *La Forza del Destino*, the Marquis of Calatrava begins the turbulent opera on a quiet, tender note, as he bids his daughter Leonora good night.

8. In Mozart's *Le Nozze di Figaro*, the opera begins with Figaro measuring his new room with a yardstick.

9. In Mozart's *Die Zauberflöte*, the first bit of action is Tamino's rushing on stage, screaming for help, as he is being pursued by a vicious-looking serpent.

10. In Gounod's *Faust*, the title character commences the opera with this despairing summation of his life's achievements thus far.

11. At the beginning of Gershwin's *Porgy and Bess*, Clara sings this lullaby to her baby.

12. This line opens Menotti's *The Telephone* as Ben enters and gives Lucy a piece of abstract sculpture.

13. The "spirit" of wine, actually an offstage male chorus, opens Offenbach's melodically alcoholic *Les Contes d'Hoffmann* with this surreal statement.

14. In Massenet's *Werther*, the genial bailiff, father of Charlotte, tries to bring his younger children under control as he attempts to rehearse them in a Christmas carol on a summer afternoon.

15. Samuel Barber's *Antony and Cleopatra* opens with these words of exposition from the chorus of Egyptians.

16. In Puccini's *Tosca*, Angelotti's frantic entrance line gets the opera off to an appropriately nervous start.

17. In Verdi's *Aida*, High Priest Ramfis plunges right into the discussion of the work's political conflict with the strapping young captain, Radames.

18. These bemused words are sung by Fritz Kobus to his friend, Rabbi David, in Mascagni's *L'Amico Fritz*.

19. In Leoncavallo's *La Bohème*, which opens with the Café Momus scene, these words from tavern-keeper Gaudenzio are addressed to Alcindoro.

20. In Alban Berg's *Lulu*, the Ringmaster addresses the audience with these words. Lulu is soon revealed to us as one of the "soulless beasts."

104. FAMOUS FIRST WORDS

1. In Verdi's *La Forza del Destino*, Don Carlo ponders his friend Alvaro's serious war wounds before singing the aria "Urna fatale del mio destino."

2. In Verdi's *Aida*, the heroine wonders about her ill-starred love for Radames as she begins the aria "O patria mia."

3. In Mozart's *Le Nozze di Figaro*, the countess anxiously waits for Susanna in order to set in motion the intrigue planned to stop the count's philandering, and then she thinks about Almaviva's betrayal of their love in the aria "Dove sono."

4. In Puccini's *La Fanciulla del West*, Johnson, about to be lynched by the miners, thanks Sonora for allowing him a few last words, which he addresses to the absent Minnie in the aria "Ch'ella mi creda."

5. Upon her entrance in Act I of Bizet's opera, Carmen greets her admirers with these words before beginning the "Habanera."

6. Lucia, in Donizetti's *Lucia di Lammermoor*, waits for her lover, Edgardo, and describes their passion in the aria "Regnava nel silenzio."

7. Leonora di Vargas, in Verdi's *La Forza del Destino*, sings these words at the beginning of the Convent Scene before singing the aria "Madre, Madre, pietosa Vergine."

8. In Mascagni's *Cavalleria Rusticana*, Mamma Lucia asks this of Santuzza, who responds with the aria "Voi lo sapete, o mamma," letting Lucia and the audience know why she is so unhappy.

9. With these words, Canio in Leoncavallo's *Pagliacci* begins the most famous of all tenor scenes, leading into "Vesti la giubba."

10. In Cilea's *Adriana Lecouvreur*, the actress-heroine dismisses the praise of her backstage visitors, then sings the aria "Io son l'umile ancella."

11. In Puccini's *Madama Butterfly*, Cio-Cio-San tries to calm the agitated Suzuki, as she describes her anticipated joy at Pinkerton's putative return in "Un bel dì vedremo."

12. Donna Elvira, in Mozart's *Don Giovanni*, contemplates Don G.'s bad behavior as she launches into "Mi tradì, quell'alma ingrata."

13. These are the words uttered by Norma in Act I of Bellini's opera as she enters and calms the rebellious Druids with her limpid "Casta Diva."

14. Cilea's *Adriana Lecouvreur*, as Adriana receives the poisoned violets sent to her by her rival, the Princess di Bouillon, she leads into the aria "Poveri fiori."

15. In Verdi's *Il Trovatore*, Leonora dismisses Ruiz, who has brought her to the castle where Manrico is imprisoned. The aria that follows is "D'amor sull'ali rosee."

16. In Verdi's *La Traviata*, Violetta rereads Germont's letter in Act III describing the events that have transpired since Flora's ill-fated party. The aria that follows is "Addio, del passato."

17. In Verdi's *Don Carlo*, Eboli sings these despairing words after the Queen banishes her, leading into the aria "O don fatale."

18. In Massenet's *Manon*, the heroine sings these words after agreeing to become the mistress of De Brétigny, and acquiescing to the abduction of the young man she really loves, Des Grieux. The aria is "Adieu, notre petite fable."

19. In Act IV of Meyerbeer's *Le Prophète*, Fidès begins her

magnificent scene leading to the aria "Adieu, mon pauvre en-fant," in which she bemoans her son Jean's (John of Leyden) transformation from a decent man to a corrupt, pseudo-religious figure.

20. This is the introduction to Dido's aria "When I am laid in earth" from Purcell's *Dido and Aeneas*.

105. DRAMATIC ENTRANCES

1. In Puccini's *Turandot*, the title character, the Princess Tu-randot, plunges directly into her first aria—addressed to her father, the unknown prince, and the assembled throng—in which she explains that her hatred of men stems from the rape of one of her ancestors many years earlier.

2. In Act I of Wagner's *Die Walküre*, Siegmund, exhausted from battle, staggers into Hunding's home (in the hollow of a tree) begging for water and a place to rest, not knowing that he is about to discover his long-lost twin sister, Sieglinde.

3. This succinct, ironic greeting is addressed to Faust by Méph-istophélès, in Gounod's opera. Faust has, you will recall, just summoned Satan to him.

4. In Verdi's *Aida*, Radames is first heard questioning the high priest Ramfis about preparations for the coming war with Ethi-opia, and he is especially interested in the selection of the commander of the Egyptian troops.

5. In Verdi's *La Traviata*, Violetta graciously welcomes her friend Flora Bervoix and other tardy guests with these hospitable words.

6. In Ponchielli's *La Gioconda*, the title character establishes her close relationship with her mother, La Cieca, with her very first words, as she leads the old blind woman into the Piazza San Marco.

7. The lovesick Leonora, in Verdi's *Il Trovatore*, complains thus to her confidante, Ines, as she makes her first appearance in the opera, waiting for Manrico's serenade.

8. Brünnhilde's blustering, if somewhat nonsensical, war cry is

addressed to her father, Wotan, as the Valkyrie rushes onstage in Wagner's *Die Walküre*.

9. In Verdi's *Don Carlo*, the fearsome Grand Inquisitor, brought into Philip II's study, makes plain his desire to confront the king with his very first line.

10. Verdi's lovelorn Aida pleads concern with politics when on her entrance, Amneris begins to question her, suspecting (correctly, as it turns out) that Aida, like Amneris herself, is in love with Radames.

11. In Richard Strauss's *Der Rosenkavalier*, the awakening Octavian caresses the Marschallin, with whom he has spent the night, crooning those tender words to her.

12. Cleopatra, in Barber's *Antony and Cleopatra*, makes a rather petulant entrance with those words, addressed to no one.

13. Marguérite, in Gounod's *Faust*, utters what must be the most modest phrase ever to issue from the lips of a diva, to Faust, when he accosts her during the Kermesse scene.

14. This is Dalila's opening pitch to Samson in Saint-Saëns's *Samson et Dalila*.

15. This odd line is uttered by Anatol to Vanessa, in Barber's *Vanessa*, after she, believing she is speaking to Anatol's now-dead father, asks if he still loves her.

16. Micaela, in Bizet's *Carmen*, offers this reply to the dragoon Moralès, when he asks her for whom she is looking, at the beginning of the first act.

17. This reply by poet Andrea Chénier, in Giordano's opera, is in response to the Contessa di Coigny's attempt to have him recite to her guests.

18. These words are sung by Consul Sharpless, in Puccini's *Madama Butterfly*, while still offstage, as he struggles to reach Pinkerton's new home in time for the wedding ceremony.

19. In Leoncavallo's *Pagliacci*, clown Canio speaks ironically to the crowd that has assembled to welcome him and his company of actors to their village. They have been cheering so vociferously that Canio can't begin his "spiel" about the forthcoming performance.

20. This comment is made by Florestan, in Beethoven's *Fidelio*, as he contemplates yet another day in the dungeon.

106. LOVE DUETS

1. Radames and Aida in Verdi's *Aida*.
2. Faust and Marguérite in Gounod's *Faust*.
3. With these words the great duet for Manon Lescaut and Des Grieux begins in Puccini's *Manon Lescaut*.
4. Lucia and Edgardo in Donizetti's *Lucia di Lammermoor*.
5. Riccardo (Gustavo) and Amelia in Verdi's *Un Ballo in Maschera*.
6. Otello and Desdemona in Verdi's *Otello*.
7. This is the lovely duet sung by Octavian and Sophie in the closing moments of Richard Strauss's *Der Rosenkavalier*.
8. Cio-Cio-San and Pinkerton in Puccini's *Madama Butterfly*.
9. Alfredo and Violetta in Verdi's *La Traviata*.
10. Nedda and Silvio in Leoncavallo's *Pagliacci*.
11. These sarcastic words open the duet for Adalgisa and Pollione, who soon soothes her fears, in Bellini's *Norma*.
12. These are the opening words of the final duet for Turandot and Calaf in Puccini's *Turandot*. (Puccini died before completing this scene, and the duet and finale were finished by Franco Alfano, working from Puccini's sketches.)
13. These are the opening words of the ecstatic duet for Mimì and Rodolfo in Puccini's *La Bohème*.
14. Werther and Charlotte in Act I of Massenet's *Werther*.
15. With these words, Brünnhilde awakens and begins the long duet for her and Siegfried in the final scene of Wagner's *Siegfried*.
16. This is the ecstatic duet for Leonore and Florestan in Beethoven's *Fidelio*.
17. This is the little duet from Mozart's *Le Nozze di Figaro* in which Figaro cools the anger of his bride Susanna, who believes she has caught Figaro flirting.

18. This duet has uncomfortable consequences for Alfred and Rosalinde in Johann Strauss's *Die Fledermaus.*

19. This is the final duet for Maddalena and Chénier in Giordano's *Andrea Chénier.*

20. This is the second of three duets for Don Carlo and Elisabetta in Verdi's *Don Carlo.*

21. With these words begins the Act I duet for Tosca and Mario in Puccini's *Tosca.*

22. Francesca and Paolo in Zandonai's *Francesca da Rimini.*

23. Gilda and the Duke of Mantua in Verdi's *Rigoletto.*

24. This is the Act III duet for Mario and Tosca in *Tosca.*

25. Laura and Enzo in Ponchielli's *La Gioconda.*

26. This is the St. Sulpice scene from Massenet's *Manon,* in which the heroine once again ensnares Des Grieux.

27. This is the brief but passionate duet for Eva and Walther von Stolzing in Act II of Wagner's *Die Meistersinger von Nürnberg.*

107. CABALETTE

1. In Act II of Verdi's *La Traviata,* Alfredo's rhapsodic aria is followed by his crestfallen *cabaletta,* "O, mio rimorso" (Oh, my remorse!), when he learns that Violetta has been selling her property in order to support him.

2. In Act II of Verdi's *Luisa Miller,* Rodolfo's contemplative aria, in which he muses on the happiness that he and Luisa once enjoyed, is followed by the overwrought *cabaletta* "L'ara, o l'avella apprestami" (Make ready the altar or my grave!), in which Rodolfo vows to punish Luisa for her apparent faithlessness.

3. In Act I of Verdi's *Il Trovatore,* Leonora follows her descriptions of Manrico's nocturnal serenades by vehemently casting aside her attendant's skepticism about the sincerity of Manrico's love in the *cabaletta* "Di tale amor" (Of such a love as this).

4. Norma's prayer in Act I of Bellini's opera is closely followed by her *cabaletta* "Ah! bello a me ritorna" (Ah, return to me

the beautiful days of love), in which she prays for the restoration of Pollione's love.

5. In Act I of Verdi's *Macbeth*, Lady Macbeth, upon learning that King Duncan will be spending the night under her roof, ceases her musings on the nature of power and, in the *cabaletta* "Or tutti sorgete, ministri infernale" (O come to me, ye demons of hell!), calls upon evil spirits to give her the strength to induce Macbeth to murder the king.

6. In Bellini's *La Sonnambula*, Amina's dreamy expression of her love for Elvino, who has wrongly accused her of infidelity, is followed by the joyous "Ah! non giunge, uman pensiero" (Ah, human thought cannot comprehend) when Elvino awakens her, begging her forgiveness.

7. In Act I of *La Traviata*, Violetta's introspective aria, in which she wonders if she could seriously love Alfredo, is followed by the determinedly hedonistic "Sempre libera" (Ever free) in which the courtesan vows to continue living solely for pleasure.

8. In Act III of Verdi's *Il Trovatore*, Manrico's tender avowal of his love for Leonora is followed by an anguished vow to save his mother, Azucena, from the family tradition of being burned at the stake. The *cabaletta* is "Di quella pira" (From this pyre). For decades, this piece was known in English as "Tremble, you tyrant!"

9. In Act II of Bellini's *I Puritani*, Elvira's delirious lament over Arturo's continued absence is sweetened by her similarly deluded fantasy in which she imagines that her tenor has returned to her. That *cabaletta* is "Vien, diletto, è in ciel la luna" (Come, my darling. The moon is in the sky).

10. In Act I of Donizetti's *Lucia di Lammermoor*, Lucia describes a lovelorn maiden who drowned herself in the vicinity, telling her confidant, Alise, that the suicide's ghosts haunts the very spot where they are standing, in the *cavatina* "Regnava nel silenzio." Then, Lucia's mood brightens, and, in the *cabaletta* "Quando, rapita in estasi" (When I am transported by ecstasy), she describes the joys of her clandestine love for Edgardo, even though he is her family's sworn enemy.

11. In Act I of Verdi's *Ernani*, Elvira's dreamy *cavatina* in which

she longs for Ernani to carry her away from Silva's castle is followed by her more agitated *cabaletta* "Tutto sprezzo che d'Ernani non favella a questo cor" (Speak no ill of Ernani to me), in which the girl's desires for Ernani grow more intense.

12. In Donizetti's *Roberto Devereux*, the heartbroken Elizabeth, learning that Devereux might have been saved from execution had circumstances been different, now sings "Quel sangue versato" (that spilled blood) in which she laments Roberto's spilled blood and bemoans her shattered existence.

13. In Donizetti's *La Favorita*, Leonora longs for her beloved Fernando. In the *cabaletta* that follows, "Scritto è in cielo il mio dolore" (My pain is written in heaven), she foresees her early death, fearing that she will be condemned for her sins.

14. In Act II of Verdi's *Nabucco*, Abigaille learns of her ignoble birth after she finishes her aria, during which she had been musing upon her younger days, when she was a more *simpatica* person, in love with the Hebrew officer Ismaele. Pausing only to draw breath, the slave raised as a princess vows in the *cabaletta* "Salgo già" (I am already leaping toward greatness) that she will triumph over anyone who tries to stand in her way.

15. In Act II of Verdi's *Rigoletto*, the Duke of Mantua learns that the young woman he thought he had lost is actually awaiting his pleasure, however unwillingly, in his own chamber. Off he goes to score yet again, but not before bringing down the house with his *cabaletta*, "Possente amor" (Powerful love).

108. "I AM WHAT I AM"

1. Iago to Cassio in Verdi's *Otello*.
2. Adriana Lecouvreur to the Prince di Bouillon, the Abbé, and Michonnet, in Cilea's opera.
3. Rodolfo to Mimì in Puccini's *La Bohème*.
4. Mefistofele to Faust in Boito's *Mefistofele*.
5. Anna Maurrant in Weill's *Street Scene*.
6. Cio-Cio-San to Sharpless in Puccini's *Madama Butterfly*.
7. Annina in Menotti's *The Saint of Bleecker Street*, addressing her brother.

8. Norina in soliloquy in Donizetti's *Don Pasquale*.
9. Figaro in soliloquy in Rossini's *Il Barbiere di Siviglia*.
10. Desdemona to Otello in Verdi's *Otello*.
11. La Gioconda to Laura in Ponchielli's opera.
12. Mimì to Rodolfo in Puccini's *La Bohème*.
13. Scarpia in soliloquy in *Tosca*.
14. Nabucco to the Babylonians and Hebrews in Verdi's opera.
15. Pinkerton to Sharpless in *Madama Butterfly*.
16. Minnie to Dick Johnson in Puccini's *La Fanciulla del West*.
17. Bardolph and Pistol to Falstaff in Verdi's opera.
18. Manon in soliloquy in Massenet's opera.
19. Musetta to Marcello and all his friends in Puccini's *La Bohème*.
20. Santuzza to Mamma Lucia in Mascagni's *Cavalleria Rusticana*.
21. Don Carlo to Elisabetta in Verdi's opera.
22. Manon Lescaut to Des Grieux in Puccini's opera.

109. FAMOUS LAST WORDS

1. In Ponchielli's *La Gioconda*, the evil spy Barnaba voices his rage that the heroine, who has just stabbed herself rather than keep her promise to go to bed with him, has expired before he can inform her that he had, the day before, drowned her mother.
2. In Giordano's *Andrea Chénier*, the poet Chénier and his beloved Maddalena di Coigny exclaim this peculiar sentiment as they climb into the tumbrel that will deliver them to the guillotine.
3. In Verdi's *Rigoletto*, the title character cries out in horror as his daughter Gilda dies, killed by the assassin whom Rigoletto had engaged to murder the Duke of Mantua, thus fulfilling the curse that Monterone has placed on the jester.
4. In Massenet's *Werther*, Charlotte exclaims that all has ended as Werther dies in her arms of a self-inflicted wound. Offstage, the village children are heard celebrating Christmas in this effectively Gothic ending.
5. In Verdi's *Don Carlo*, at the moment Philip II orders his sol-

diers to arrest Carlo and Elisabetta, he hears the voice of his
father—supposedly dead for five years—from within the cloister. Philip says these words and Elisabetta cries out, in shock,
to heaven.

6. The assembled at King Gustavus III's (a.k.a. Riccardo) masked
ball in Verdi's *Un Ballo in Maschera*, exclaim in horror as the
king dies after being shot by his so-called best friend, Count
Anckarström (a.k.a. Renato).

7. This simple statement, uttered by the grieving Fernando,
closes Donizetti's *La Favorita*, as the repentant Leonora dies
in Fernando's arms. The phrase is memorable because, while
singing it, the tenor must hit a ringing high C-sharp.

8. With these taunting words, Carmen, in Bizet's opera, seals her
fate. Having the ring thrown in his face snaps Don José's self-
control, and he stabs the Gypsy to death.

9. Violetta, in Verdi's *La Traviata*, feels better just at the moment
that consumption claims her life. Convinced that she is recovering, she tries to embrace Alfredo, falling dead in the
process.

10. Margherita, in Boito's *Mefistofele*, addressing Faust by the alias
he had given her, refuses to let him comfort her as she lies
dying in prison. Her final words crush Faust, whom the Devil
roughly drags away.

11. Verdi's Simon Boccanegra dies stammering the name of both
his daughter and her mother. He has been poisoned by his
treacherous henchman, Paolo Albiani, the abductor of Amelia
Grimaldi, who is actually his long-lost daughter Maria.

12. With these frantic words to Azucena, whom he believes is his
mother, Manrico, the hero of Verdi's *Il Trovatore*, is dragged
to the headsman by Count di Luna's guards, leaving Azucena
to inform the count—and the audience—that Manrico was
not really her son at all, but Di Luna's missing brother Garzia.

13. At the conclusion of Wagner's *Die Walküre*, Wotan invokes
the demigod of fire, leaving his daughter Brünnhilde to sleep
surrounded by magic flames until a hero brave enough to pass
through fire arrives on the scene.

14. With these two loaded words, the Marschallin, in Richard

Strauss's *Der Rosenkavalier*, agrees with Faninals' trite comment on the ways of young folks and, in the process, reveals her heartbreak at losing Octavian to Faninal's daughter, Sophie.

15. Canio, in Leoncavallo's *Pagliacci*, after stabbing both his wife, Nedda, and her lover, Silvio, to death, rings down the curtain on both the play in which he had been appearing and the opera itself.

16. In Barber's *Vanessa*, Erika utters this line as she covers all the mirrors and locks all the gates in the home that Vanessa has given her, just as Vanessa herself had once done. Erika begins to wait for her lover to return to her. Since Erika's lover is Anatol, who has just married Vanessa, this seems unlikely to happen.

17. With these words, which have no equivalent in Shakespeare's tragedy, the title characters in Gounod's *Roméo et Juliette* die together.

18. Having just witnessed her sister Elektra dance herself to death while rejoicing in the deaths of Klytämnestra and Aegisth, Chrysothemis, in Richard Strauss' *Elektra*, frantically calls for help from her brother Orest, who has just sent the wayward couple to their graves.

19. Having wished their emperor a reign of ten thousand years, the people of Peking, as portrayed in Puccini's *Turandot*, end that opera still hailing old Altoum.

20. With these poignant words, Otello, in Verdi's opera, expires after learning that his wife Desdemona, whom he has just strangled, was innocent of infidelity.

21. Bess, in Gershwin's *Porgy and Bess*, hisses this epithet at Sportin' Life, who has gotten her high on cocaine and plans to take her with him to New York. Bess is too weak-willed to get away from Sportin' Life, but she knows that what she is doing is wrong.

22. In Puccini's *Gianni Schicchi*, the wily protagonist asks the audience to forgive his pranks by applauding. Yes, when the opera is given at matinees, the lines are altered.

IV

And Then What Happens?
Opera Plots and Plotting

110. EXTRA! EXTRA! READ ALL ABOUT IT!

1. Ponchielli's *La Gioconda*
2. Wagner's *Lohengrin*
3. Puccini's *Tosca*
4. Verdi's *Luisa Miller*
5. Richard Strauss's *Salome*
6. Any of these: Boito's *Mefistofele*; Gounod's *Faust*; Verdi's *Il Trovatore*
7. Verdi's *Simon Boccanegra*
8. Verdi's *Falstaff* or Nicolai's *Die Lustigen Weiber von Windsor*
9. Wagner's *Die Walküre*
10. Saint-Saëns's *Samson et Dalila*
11. Giordano's *Andrea Chénier*
12. Verdi's *I Vespri Siciliani*
13. Verdi's or Rossini's *Otello*
14. Puccini's *Turandot*
15. Wagner's *Tannhäuser*
16. Britten's *Peter Grimes*
17. Verdi's *La Forza del Destino*
18. Verdi's *Rigoletto*
19. Verdi's *Un Ballo in Maschera*
20. Leoncavallo's *Pagliacci*
21. Verdi's *Aida*
22. Mascagni's *Cavalleria Rusticana*
23. Wagner's *Götterdämmerung*
24. Wagner's *Tristan und Isolde*
25. Wagner's *Die Meistersinger von Nürnberg*
26. Mussorgsky's *Boris Godunov*
27. Catalani's *La Wally*
28. Mozart's *Don Giovanni*
29. Richard Strauss's *Elektra*
30. Donizetti's *Anna Bolena*
31. Puccini's *Manon Lescaut*
32. Donizetti's *Maria Stuarda*
33. Britten's *The Turn of the Screw*
34. Gounod's *Faust* or Boito's *Mefistofele*
35. Puccini's *La Fanciulla del West*
36 Giordano's *Fedora*

111. THE RAIN IN SPAIN

1. In Donizetti's *Lucia di Lammermoor*, Edgardo and Enrico meet in Wolf's Crag Tower, amid crackling thunder and lightning, to challenge one another to a duel.

2. In Massenet's *Thaïs*, the playgirl turned penitent crosses the desert accompanied by the sex-starved Monk Athanaël, and the privations of the journey are too much for Thaïs to bear.

3. In Wagner's *Die Walküre*, Siegmund blunders into a fateful treehouse, seeking refuge from a storm. There he discovers his twin sister, Sieglinde, unhappily married to the brutish Hunding. The twins run off together, and Siegmund fathers Sieglinde's child (who, many years later, grows up to be Siegfried). Unfortunately for Siegmund, Hunding kills him the next day.

4. In Puccini's *La Bohème*, Rodolfo and Marcello have run out of firewood in Act I, so Rodolfo throws a play he has written into the stove, providing a few minutes' warmth.

5. In Mascagni's *Lodoletta*, the title character shivers in front of her beloved Flammen's house, surviving only long enough to perform the opera's best-known aria, "Flammen, perdonami!"

6. In Kurt Weill's *Street Scene*, the overheated neighbors make so many remarks about Anna Maurrant's indiscretion that her ill-tempered husband discovers the truth and murders his wife and her boyfriend, Steve Sankey.

7. In Donizetti's *La Favorita*, the unhappy Leonora, once mistress of a king, staggers through the snow to the monastery where her beloved Fernando has, once again(!), taken holy vows. Fernando finds her dying in a snowdrift, forgives her, and the pair renew their vows of love. Leonora expires before Fernando is forced to contemplate leaping over the wall.

8. In Verdi's *Otello*, the first act opens with a terrible storm, and the opening moments of the opera deal with the frantic attempts to dock safely the battleship that has brought Otello home from the war.

9. In Rossini's *Il Barbiere di Siviglia*, the storm interlude in Act

III gives the singers a few moments of rest while the orchestra conjures a brief summer rainstorm.

10. In Puccini's *La Fanciulla del West*, the irate Minnie tosses Dick Johnson out into the snow after she learns that he is really the bandit Ramerrez, in spite of Dick's protests of moral, if not technical, innocence. Sheriff Rance is lurking near Minnie's cabin, and he shoots Dick. The erstwhile bandit staggers back inside Minnie's place, bleeding, and the soprano finally decides that she loves the tenor in spite of his past. This one has a happy ending.

11. This uniquely realized tempest takes place in the third act of Verdi's *Rigoletto*.

12. This vicious storm provides the background for the second scene of Act I of Britten's *Peter Grimes*.

13. The hurricane that strikes the people of Catfish Row in Gershwin's *Porgy and Bess* is responsible for the deaths of Jake, the crew of his fishing boat, and Jake's wife, Clara.

14. In Wagner's *Der Fliegende Holländer*, a bad storm runs Daland's ship off its course, leading him to cast anchor in a strange town. This brings Daland to his fateful encounter with Philip Vanderdecken.

15. Here we are describing the soul-selling, knee-slapping Wolf's Glen scene from Weber's *Der Freischütz* in which Max, the unlucky huntsman, attempts to barter his soul for the magic bullets offered by Caspar.

112. LITTLE THINGS MEAN A LOT

1. In Rossini's *Il Barbiere di Siviglia*, when Dr. Bartolo finds only four sheets of writing paper, instead of the five he had left there, and notices that some ink has been spilled, he suspects (correctly) that Rosina has been up to some mischief in his absence.

2. In Massenet's *Manon*, the heroine, preparing to leave her impoverished lover Des Grieux for the wealthy De Brétigny, is overcome with remorse and sadness as she bids farewell to the

little table at which she and Des Grieux had shared many meals, and she sings the aria "Adieu, notre petite table."

3. In Act I of *Street Scene* by Kurt Weill, Anna Maurrant gives her little boy, Willie, a dime to buy a Coke on this scorchingly hot night, establishing herself as a sweet and generous person.

4. In Britten's *Peter Grimes,* Ellen's discovery of the sweater she had knitted for Grimes's little apprentice convinces her that the child has come to harm.

5. In Puccini's *Tosca,* the heroine sees a dinner knife innocently adorning Scarpia's supper table, and she suddenly discovers a way out of her unpleasant bargain with him.

6. In Puccini's *Madama Butterfly,* Cio-Cio-San distracts her son by giving the boy a flag to play with while she prepares to commit suicide.

7. In Puccini's *La Bohème,* the flighty Musetta demonstrates the compassion she seldom reveals to Marcello by telling him to pawn her earrings in order to buy some medicine and a muff for the dying Mimì.

8. In Mozart's *Le Nozze di Figaro,* the gardener Antonio punctures the fib that Susanna and the countess have concocted for the count's benefit, when Antonio rushes into the countess's apartment to complain about a plant damaged by a man who jumped out of the countess's window.

9. In Rossini's *L'Italiana in Algeri,* the heroine, Isabella, interrupts the bullies threatening to execute Taddeo when she invites them to join her for coffee.

10. In Verdi's *Otello,* Iago uses the handkerchief his wife had innocently taken from Desdemona to convince Otello that Desdemona has been unfaithful to him. The credulous Otello immediately decides to kill his guiltless wife.

11. In Puccini's *Il Tabarro,* the unfortunate Luigi mistakes his boss Michele's lighting of his pipe for the signal he had arranged with his lover Giorgetta, the boss's wife. He boards the couple's barge—and is promptly caught and killed by Michele.

12. In Ponchielli's *La Gioconda,* La Cieca, Gioconda's blind mother, gives her rosary to Laura, who has saved her life. When La G. discovers that the man she loves, Enzo, has a

lover, she plans to kill the other woman. When she discovers that her rival is Laura (she sees the rosary in Laura's hand), she devotes herself to making possible Laura and Enzo's escape from Venice.

13. In Leoncallo's *Pagliacci*, Nedda, acting the role of Colombina in the play-within-the-opera, fusses over the chicken on which she and Arlecchino will dine, not realizing that she herself will soon be carved up.

14. In Puccini's *Gianni Schicchi*, all of the deceased Buoso Donati's relations ransack his home to find his will. When they do discover the document, they realize that they'll need the help of Gianni Schicchi, a wily lawyer, to change it to their advantage.

15. In Bizet's *Carmen*, the heroine's final act of defiance is to throw the ring Don José had once given her right in his face. Doing what any healthy, normal, obsessed Mama's Boy would do, José stabs her to death.

16. In Donizetti's *L'Elisir d'Amore*, Dr. Dulcamara sells Nemorino a bottle of bordeaux, telling the dopey but simpatico youth that it is Queen Isolde's elixir of love. Nemorino drinks himself to near oblivion, hoping that Adina will admit that she loves him. As a matter of fact, she does.

113. HOT TIMES

1. John of Leyden, in Meyerbeer's *Le Prophète*, devises this drastic method of atoning for his own wicked acts, while taking his even more wicked Anabaptist enemies along with him.

2. Enzo, in Ponchielli's *La Gioconda*, eludes Alvise Badoero, his beloved Laura's husband, by jumping into the Adriatic Sea, after having diverted his enemy's attention.

3. In Act I of Verdi's *Otello*, the Cypriots dance joyously around a fire moments before Iago begins working out his evil designs by getting Cassio drunk.

4. In Bellini's *Norma*, the title character, a Druid Priestess, and

her Roman lover, Pollione, are burned to death for having had a forbidden affair.

5. In Verdi's *Don Carlo*, an auto-da-fé, in which a number of Flemish Protestants are burned at the stake for heresy, serves as the entertainment at the coronation of King Philip II of Spain. Although it must bring them scant comfort, these wretched victims of intolerance are welcomed into heaven by a Celestial Voice who sings one of Verdi's most exquisite melodies.

6. In Mozart's *Don Giovanni*, the unrepentant Don is sent off to Hell while devilish flames reduce his palace to a shell. The Statue of the Commendatore, appearing at Don G.'s party at his bidding, commands the Don to renounce his licentious ways. When Don Giovanni refuses, all hell breaks loose.

7. In Humperdinck's *Hänsel und Gretel*, witch Rosina Daintymouth expects to make a dainty meal of her two young prisoners. Gretel, at Hänsel's urging, pushes the witch into the oven, thus releasing all the children who have been bound by her spell and providing everyone with a tasty gingerbread cookie.

8. Azucena, in Verdi's *Il Trovatore*, throws the wrong baby (her son) into the fire that had devoured her own mother. She thought it was the baby of the old Count Di Luna.

9. In Wagner's *Götterdämmerung*, the fire from Siegfried's funeral pyre rises, destroys what's left of Valhalla (not to mention the Gibichungs' palace), and wipes out almost all of the *Ring*'s population. The exceptions, it appears, are the three Rhinemaidens, who, having finally gotten their accursed lump of gold back, frolic on through the ages.

10. In Verdi's *Giovanna d'Arco*, Joan of Arc is *not* burned by the English, receiving instead a seemingly mortal wound on the battlefield from which she miraculously recovers just in time to take part in the opera's finale. Then, Giovanna dies for good!

11. In Verdi's *Macbeth*, Lady M. glides through the castle, reliving her various misdeeds, lighting her slumbering way with a candle.

12. In Hector Berlioz's *Les Troyens*, violence and chaos reign as the Greeks sack Troy while the Trojan women choose "death with honor."

13. In Richard Strauss's *Die Frau ohne Schatten*, the frustrated Dyer's Wife starts to fry some fish for Barak's dinner. Crackling through the flames come the voices of the woman's unborn children, begging their mother not to sell her shadow—and her fertility—to the Empress and her Nurse, who wish to buy these from her.

14. Mimì, in Puccini's *La Bohème*, meets Rodolfo when her candle is extinguished and she asks him to relight it.

15. In Wagner's *Ring*, the Magic Fire is lit around Brünnhilde at the end of *Walküre*. Siegfried penetrates the flames twice, in Act III of *Siegfried* and Act I of *Götterdämmerung*, when he is disguised as Gunther. Waltraute, Brünnhilde's sister, also shows her mettle by passing through the Magic Fire, in Act I of *Götterdämmerung*, when she visits Brünnhilde and begs her to surrender the ring.

114. HOLIDAYS

1. Christmas Eve figures in the *La Bohème*s of Puccini and Leoncavallo, Massenet's *Werther*, and Menotti's *Amahl and the Night Visitors*. In Puccini's *La Bohème*, Mimì and Rodolfo meet on Christmas Eve and then go to the Café Momus with Rodolfo's bohemian friends to celebrate the holiday and their love. In Leoncavallo's *Bohème*, Mimì and Rodolfo meet for the first time at the Café Momus on Christmas Eve. Sadly, Mimì dies in Rodolfo's bleak attic on Christmas Eve a year later. As Mimì dies, she hears church bells ringing in the holiday. Her last words are "E Natale, è Natale!" (It's Christmas!). *Werther*, which begins with the Bailiff's children rehearsing a Christmas song in July, ends with Werther's suicide on Christmas Eve. The reprise of the joyous song offstage serves as a contrast to Werther's suffering and Charlotte's grief. *Amahl and the Night Visitors* is set on the original Christmas Eve, and the miracle of the crippled boy regaining his health when he offers his

crutch as a gift to the Christ Child gives the opera its happy ending.

2. Mascagni's lurid *Cavalleria Rusticana* is set on Easter Sunday. The opera features an Easter procession, and the violent love triangle leads to Turiddu's murder by Alfio moments after the Easter Mass is celebrated in the village church.

3. Midsummer Night, called *Johannesnacht* in Wagner's *Die Meistersinger von Nürnberg*, is the setting for the opera's second act. In this scene, we witness Walther and Eva's declaration of love, Beckmesser's attempt to serenade Eva, and the walloping administered to Beckmesser by David. In Britten's *A Midsummer Night's Dream*, Shakespeare's comedy of gentle deception and supernatural fun is faithfully retold.

4. Walpurgisnacht, the witches' Sabbath, is the setting for the fifth-act ballet in Gounod's *Faust*, during which Méphistophélès attempts to distract Faust's longings for Marguérite by conjuring up such beautiful women as Helen of Troy. The trick, of course, does not work.

5. The birthday of the mythical Don Andres, Viceroy of Peru, provides the occasion for the merrymaking that opens Offenbach's *La Périchole*.

6. Passover figures in the plot of Halévy's *La Juive*, which boasts a scene during which Eléazar presides over a Passover seder.

7. Good Friday is the setting for the third act of Wagner's *Parsifal*. It is also the setting for the first scene of Menotti's *The Saint of Bleecker Street*, in which Annina's neighbors come to witness her vision of the Crucifixion and the stigmata that appear on her hands.

8. Carnival, or the pre-Lenten celebrations, is mentioned in Ponchielli's *La Gioconda*, Verdi's *La Traviata*, and Johann Strauss's *Eine Nacht in Venedig*. In *La Gioconda*, the festivities surrounding the regatta enable the spy Barnaba to begin his evil intrigues. In *La Traviata*, the dying Violetta listens to the offstage revelry early in the third act and instructs her maid Annina to distribute half their remaining few coins to the poor. Carnival forms the basis for all the merry complications of *Eine Nacht in Venedig* (*A Night in Venice*).

9. In *The Saint of Bleecker Street*, Annina, the feeble, saintly her-

oine, who exhibits the stigmata each year on Good Friday, is forcibly dragged by the Sons of San Gennaro to head the Little Italy parade on the Feast Day.

10. In Leoncavallo's *Pagliacci*, the townspeople celebrate this day by attending the play presented by Canio and his troupe.

115. WINE, PERSONS, AND SONG

1. In Gershwin's *Porgy and Bess*, the vicious Crown stumbles drunkenly into Catfish Row in Act I, scene 1, and soon begins to brawl with the other men, killing Robbins, Serena's husband.

2. In Act I of Bizet's *Carmen*, the heroine bargains with Don José to entertain him at the inn of Lillas Pastia if only he will let her escape from his custody. She promises to dance the *seguedilla* for him and drink *manzanilla* in his company. José cannot resist and ends up with a term in the guardhouse, but he ultimately does meet Carmen at Pastia's. The rest is history.

3. Hoffmann, Offenbach's poet-protagonist in *Les Contes d'Hoffmann*, gets carried away by the fellowship at Luther's tavern and relates the story of his tragic love for the doll Olympia, the courtesan Giulietta, and the doomed girl Antonia. He gets so drunk in the process that he sleeps through the arrival of his current amour, the singer Stella, who cheerfully accepts the attentions of Hoffmann's archenemy, Councillor Lindorf.

4. Lucrezia Borgia, in Donizetti's opera, invites the youths who have insulted her to a dinner party, where she plans to kill them with poisoned wine. Lucrezia is unpleasantly surprised when her own illegitimate son drinks, too, and dies with his pals.

5. In Act II of Puccini's *Tosca*, Baron Scarpia invites the heroine to enjoy his Spanish wine as she ponders his offer to free her lover if she spends the night with him. If the wine gives Tosca courage, it is the courage needed to stab Scarpia with the knife she spots near the wineglass.

6. In Act I of Wagner's *Götterdämmerung*, Siegfried is given a

special brew by the villainous Hagen, which is designed to make the simple hero forget his vows of love for Brünnhilde. Hagen plans to offer his half-sister Gutrune to Siegfried, and then schemes to have Siegfried snatch the ring of the Nibelung from Brünnhilde, who regards it as her wedding ring.

7. Falstaff, in Verdi's opera, orders sherry after the merry wives have had him dumped into the Thames as punishment for the ribald propositions he has made to Alice and Meg. The drink soothes him, but he is soon led by his lechery into the Windsor Forest, where the wives and their friends torment him further.

8. Alfred, in Johann Strauss's *Die Fledermaus*, urges Rosalinde to drink with him now that her husband, Eisenstein, has gone off to jail. In fact, Eisenstein has made a detour first. Before much champagne can be imbibed, Prison Warden Frank arrives to escort Eisenstein to jail. To protect Rosalinde's reputation, gallant Alfred agrees to impersonate her husband.

9. In Samuel Barber's *Vanessa*, Erika, Vanessa's niece, dines with Anatol, the son of the lover Vanessa had expected to join her. Anatol takes after his dad, and after a few too many, Erika spends the night with Anatol, whom she has just met. By the end of the next act, Anatol is engaged to Vanessa, and Erika is pregnant!

10. In *La Traviata*, Violetta listens to Alfredo's toast and soon finds herself considering his declaration of love. She runs off with him, but, as is well known, problems crop up.

11. In Offenbach's *La Périchole*, the title character is plied with food and an exquisite vintage by Don Andres, and therefore agrees to a sham marriage that will allow Don Andres, the Viceroy of Peru, to keep Périchole as his mistress. Whom does she marry? Her lover, Piquillo, who is too drunk to recognize her.

12. The amiable simpleton herein described is Nemorino in Donizetti's *L'Elisir d'Amore*. He drinks wine thinking it is a love potion.

13. Sam Polk in Floyd's *Susannah* dispatches the all-too-human Reverend Olin Blitch after Susannah informs Sam that Blitch has seduced her.

14. In Berg's *Lulu*, there is a macabre yet wildly funny moment in Act II when Lulu, having just emptied a pistol into her husband, Dr. Schön, comforts her dying mate with a glass of the bubbly.

15. In Gounod's *Faust*, Méphistophélès switches vintages on the townsfolk, who promptly chase him off, however briefly, by making the sign of the Cross with their swords.

116. SING IT WITH FLOWERS

1. In Gounod's *Faust*, young Siebel runs afoul of Méphistophélès, who places the lad among the horticulturally deprived. Siebel bathes his hands in holy water, and Satan's whammy is reversed!

2. Lakmé, in Delibes's opera, poisons herself via a venomous snack. She is upset because her English lover, Gerald, has decided to leave her and return with his regiment to Britain.

3. Toward the end of the second act of *Madama Butterfly*, Cio-Cio-San and her servant Suzuki strew cherry blossoms about their hilltop home. Pinkerton's ship has entered the harbor, and Butterfly wants his homecoming to be beautiful in every respect. Unlike her mistress, Suzuki has misgivings concerning the next day's events, and she is right, as Pinkerton has returned to Nagasaki with his new wife, Kate, wishing to take the son that Butterfly has borne him. Butterfly commits hara-kiri.

4. In the first act of *La Traviata*, Violetta offers Alfredo her camellia, inviting him to return it to her when it has faded. In other words, she arranges an assignation with Alfredo for the very next day.

5. In Mascagni's *L'Amico Fritz*, the shy Suzel presents a bouquet to Fritz, whom she loves. Fritz, who fancies himself above affairs of the heart, has barely noticed Suzel growing up on his estate. Men!!!

6. This garden is found in Act II of Wagner's *Parsifal*. The evil Klingsor has created this decadent garden in order to ensnare

the guileless and pure Parsifal. The humanoid singing blossoms are the Flower Maidens, and the cronelike Kundry has been transformed by Klingsor into a temptress. After a turgid half hour, Parsifal, virtue intact, destroys the garden and Klingsor, too, with a wave of Amfortas's spear, which he has caught in midair after Klingsor has chucked it at him!

7. In *L'Elisir d'Amore*, Sergeant Belcore grandiosely presents his garland of posies to Giannetta, but immediately repossesses the flowers and gives them to Adina.

8. In Cilea's *Adriana Lecouvreur*, Adriana gives a bunch of violets to Maurizio as a love token. In the next act, Maurizio gives the violets to the Princess di Bouillon, whom he has come to see about affairs of state. The Princess's interest, however, lies in other kinds of affairs. In Act IV, the Princess, having dipped the withered flowers into a poison, sends them back to Adriana, who inhales the fumes while singing "Poveri fiori," and dies in the arms of the erring Maurizio.

9. In *Der Rosenkavalier*, Octavian is sent to deliver a silver rose to Sophie on the occasion of her betrothal to Baron Ochs.

10. The prima donna is Floria Tosca in Puccini's *Tosca*. The scene takes place in the fictional Attavanti chapel in the very real Church of Sant' Andrea della Valle. The Attavanti chapel is modeled on the actual chapel of the Barberini family in that great church.

11. This is the flower, usually a rose, that Carmen, in Bizet's opera, gives to Don José as she finishes singing the "Habanera" in Act I.

12. Mimì in *La Bohème*, specifically Puccini's version, laments at the end of her first-act aria that the flowers she creates lack fragrance. Not to worry, Rodolfo falls in love with her, all the same.

117. CRIMES MAJOR AND MINOR

1. In Mussorgsky's *Boris Godunov*, the first crime is the murder of the Czarevitch Dmitri, arranged by Boris. The second

crime, at least by the laws of the day, is the escape by Grigori from his monastery. The final crime is the robbing of the Fool, by the band of children who steal his money as he bewails the fate of Russia.

2. One crime in Verdi's *Don Carlo* is the assassination of Rodrigo, arranged by King Philip II and the Grand Inquisitor, and carried out by soldiers of the Inquisition. The next crime is treason, when Don Carlo draws his sword against his father, King Philip. The third crime, this one of a more domestic nature, is Eboli's theft of Elisabetta's jewel box, which contains Carlo's portrait. This is calculated to make the jealous old monarch suspicious of his unhappy young wife. Lastly, there is the crime of adultery, committed by Philip and Eboli.

3. Blackmail occurs in Meyerbeer's *Le Prophète* when the sinister Anabaptists twice threaten to kill Fidès, John of Leyden's mother, if John doesn't agree to go along with their various plans and schemes. We might also mention the mass murder that John commits when he blows up his own castle, taking his enemies, as well as his mother, with him!

4. In Puccini's *Madama Butterfly*, Pinkerton commits bigamy by marrying Kate while still married to Butterfly.

5. In Ponchielli's *La Gioconda*, Alvise Badoero is guilty of the attempted murder of his wife, Laura. Barnaba is the opera's chief malefactor: he is guilty of bearing false witness when he accuses La Cieca of being a witch; of extortion when he threatens to kill Cieca if Gioconda won't go to bed with him (he also kidnaps poor Cieca!); and finally, he's guilty of Cieca's murder.

6. In Puccini's *Manon Lescaut*, the heroine is accused of prostitution and attempted theft when the police apprehend her when she is about to leave Geronte's house with all his jewelry. Geronte himself is also conceivably guilty of corrupting the morals of a minor.

7. In Wagner's *Das Rheingold*, Alberich steals the gold from the Rhinemaidens; Wotan and Loge steal from Alberich the ring he has forged from the gold (as well as the rest of the gold

and the magic Tarnhelm); and Fafner kills his brother Fasolt when the two giants quarrel over possession of the ring.

8. In Verdi's *Simon Boccanegra*, Paolo Albiani abducts Boccanegra's newly discovered daughter, Amelia, and, an act later, murders Simon by poisoning his pitcher of water.

9. In Berg's opera *Lulu*, the protagonist shoots her husband, Dr. Schön, and later, with the aid of the countess, escapes from prison. Later still, Lulu violates London's public morality by walking its streets. The opera's final crimes, however, are committed by none other than Jack the Ripper, whom Lulu brings to her rooms. Jack kills Lulu and the countess.

10. In Britten's *Billy Budd*, Squeak steals Billy's tobacco; Claggart swears falsely that Billy is plotting a mutiny; and Billy, however accidentally, kills Claggart when he strikes him and Claggart cracks his head as he falls to the floor.

11. In Donizetti's *Lucia di Lammermoor*, Enrico, Lucia's brother, sins by forging the letter that convinces Lucia that Edgardo has deserted her. Although Lucia murders Arturo, her husband of less than an hour, she would, one assumes, have been acquitted by reason of insanity had she lived to stand trial.

12. No one commits a "big" crime during Johann Strauss's *Die Fledermaus*, although Adele "borrows" a dress belonging to her employer, Rosalinde, and in Act II, Rosalinde swipes Eisenstein's watch. However, before the operetta actually begins, Eisenstein has been sentenced to a week in jail for having kicked a tax collector, a fact crucial to the development of the farcical plot.

13. In Wagner's *Lohengrin*, Ortrud, a sorceress, transforms her ward Gottfried, the young Duke of Brabant, into a swan. Later, she and her husband, Telramund, swear that the Duke's sister, Elsa, had murdered him. Then, in the third act, Telramund attempts to kill Lohengrin in the bridal chamber he so briefly shares with Elsa.

14. In *Porgy and Bess*, Crown murders Robbins, Sportin' Life sells cocaine to Crown and Bess, Frazier runs a divorce mill, Maria attempts to cheat the Crab Man, the police falsely arrest Peter

the Honey Man, and Porgy kills Crown. Whew! Who says nothing happens in opera?

15. The only crime in Donizetti's *Don Pasquale* is quite minor: someone impersonates a notary and performs a sham marriage of Don Pasquale and "Sofronia" (Norina in disguise).

16. In *Meistersinger*, David assaults Beckmesser, who, hours later, purloins Walther's lyrics for the Prize Song, only to make an utter fool out of himself in the final scene.

17. Aside from all the battle-related deaths among the Crusaders and Moslems, the chief crime in Verdi's *I Lombardi* is the patricide committed by Pagano (later known as the Hermit) in the first act. The smarmy basso wishes to kill his brother and carry off his sister-in-law. He confuses who sleeps in what room, and slays his father by mistake.

118. EAVESDROPPING

1. Mimì, in Puccini's *La Bohème*, hides behind a tree while her lover Rodolfo first complains to their friend Marcello that Mimì is a flirt, and then breaks down and confides to Marcello that Mimì is terribly ill. Mimì cannot restrain her tears and Rodolfo discovers her. The touching finale to the opera's third act begins here, as Mimì and Rodolfo agree to stay together, at least until spring.

2. In the first act of *Le Nozze di Figaro*, the music teacher Don Basilio makes Count Almaviva mighty angry when the count discovers that Basilio has overheard him trying to turn Susanna's head. This incident clearly establishes Almaviva's roving eye and Susanna's skill at deflecting the count's unwanted attentions.

3. In the third act of *Aida*, Amonasro forces his daughter Aida to wheedle some strategic information from Radames, who is the leader of the Egyptian army. Aida is successful, but Amonasro is so overjoyed that he foolishly reveals both his presence and his rank (King of Ethiopia) to Radames. In the ensuing fracas, they are all overheard by Amneris and Ramfis. This

leads to Radames's arrest for treason, the flight of Aida and Amonasro, and, inexorably, the deaths of all three.

4. In the penultimate act of Verdi's *Otello*, Iago gulls the Moor into listening in on portions of a conversation between Iago and Cassio, which Iago directs in such a way as to convince Otello that his wife is guilty beyond all doubt of adultery with Cassio. After this scene, Iago and Otello decide that Desdemona must die that very night.

5. In *Die Meistersinger von Nürnberg*, David overhears Beckmesser's serenade meant for Eva, but thinks the town clerk is serenading David's beloved Magdalene, who has been briefly impersonating Eva. David attacks Beckmesser, and soon a comic battle involving the whole neighborhood takes place.

6. In Richard Strauss's *Der Rosenkavalier*, the professional intriguers Valzacchi and Annina try to take advantage of the blossoming love between Octavian and Sophie by seizing the pair and alerting Baron Ochs, Sophie's fiancé. Very shortly afterward, the couple decides to switch sides and help Octavian make a fool of Ochs.

7. In Act I of *Fidelio*, Leonore overhears the nasty Pizarro force the unwilling Rocco to agree to participate in the planned elimination of Florestan. She, being Florestan's wife, swears to prevent this crime from happening.

8. In Act IV of Gounod's *Faust*, Méphistophélès hides in the shadows of a church while the anguished Marguérite pours out her heart in prayer. Mephisto cruelly mocks her, and terrifies her by howling that she will be damned for all eternity.

9. In *Pagliacci*, the repulsive clown Tonio, having just been lashed by Nedda when he attempted to rape her, is further angered when he discovers Nedda embracing her local boyfriend, Silvio. Tonio runs off to the inn where Canio has gone for a libation and tells him of his wife's misbehavior. Tragedy ensues.

10. In the first act of Cilea's *Adriana Lecouvreur*, while the Prince di Bouillon and his chum the Abbé di Chazeuil scheme their schemes involving the actress La Duclos, four other members of the Comédie-Française blithely comment on the gossip and

infidelities taking place in their midst. Although the tone here is light, the stage is being set for romantic catastrophe.

119. HIDING PLACES

1. In Mozart's *Le Nozze di Figaro*, Cherubino and Susanna take turns hiding in a closet during Act II. Cherubino hides to escape the wrath of Count Almaviva, and Susanna takes his place in order to help her mistress, the Countess Almaviva, teach the count a lesson. Since this is a comedy, all turns out well.

2. In Act III of Puccini's *La Bohème*, Mimì hides behind a tree to eavesdrop on Rodolfo's conversation with Marcello. She learns that Rodolfo still loves her, but that she is dying of consumption.

3. In Puccini's *Tosca*, Angelotti hides in a well in Mario's garden in order to escape from Scarpia's policemen, who are searching for him after his escape from the Castel Sant'Angelo. Mario is later tortured and Tosca, unable to endure his screams of agony, tells Scarpia where Angelotti has been hidden. Angelotti kills himself to avoid recapture.

4. In Puccini's *La Fanciulla del West*, Minnie hides her wounded boyfriend, Dick Johnson, in her loft when Sheriff Rance, who has shot and wounded Johnson, arrives to search Minnie's little cabin. In a grotesque touch, Johnson's blood drips down from the loft, and Rance forces his quarry to climb down. Minnie cheats in a poker game in which the stakes are Johnson's life and freedom. All ends well.

5. Falstaff, in Verdi's opera—as well as in Nicolai's *Die Lustigen Weiber von Windsor*—is hidden by the merry wives in a laundry basket, ostensibly to save the fat knight from the wrath of Master Ford, but actually as a means of tricking the naughty man, who is tossed into the Thames as punishment for attempting to seduce Alice and Meg.

6. In Mozart's *Don Giovanni*, the Don, meeting Leporello in a graveyard, hides behind a marker and torments his servant,

pretending to be a ghost and not realizing that his own doom is about to be sealed in a supernatural encounter with the Commendatore's statue.

7. In Act I of Puccini's *Tosca*, Angelotti hides in the chapel of his sister, the Marchesa d'Attavanti, first when he hears the Sacristan's approach, and later when Tosca comes to pay her morning call on Mario.

8. In Verdi's *Otello*, the Moor hides behind a partition to eavesdrop while Iago converses with Cassio, falsely supplying evidence to Otello that Cassio is Desdemona's lover. This encounter is the final straw for the Moor, and he decides to murder Desdemona that very night.

9. In the last act of Bizet's *Carmen*, Don José mills around in the crowd outside the arena where Escamillo is fighting bulls, until only Carmen (who has seen him, anyway) is left outside. This is the final session for the two former lovers; José stabs Carmen when she refuses to return to him.

10. In Verdi's *La Forza del Destino*, Leonora takes refuge in a cave at the monastery of Hornachuelos, where she plans to live out her life in seclusion. Her lover, Alvaro, coincidentally takes holy vows at the same monastery, and the truth is discovered in the opera's tragic and bloody final scene.

11. In Zandonai's *Francesca da Rimini*, Francesca's lover, Paolo, tries to escape through a trapdoor when Francesca's husband, Paolo's hunchbacked brother, surprises the guilty pair. Unfortunately, Paolo's cape becomes caught in the door as the irate husband enters, and both lovers are stabbed by the deformed cuckold.

12. In Massenet's *Werther*, Charlotte locks herself into her own boudoir closet to escape from Werther's protestations of love. Werther leaves, crestfallen to the point of suicide. Charlotte runs to Werther's house after her husband has lent Werther a pair of pistols. She arrives, in the opera's last scene, to find Werther dying.

13. In Gershwin's *Porgy and Bess*, the murderous Crown flees Catfish Row and lives on Kittiwah Island for several weeks.

14. In Verdi's *Falstaff*, the young lovers Fenton and Nannetta take

refuge from the lunacy going on in the Fords' living room, hiding and kissing behind a screen while everyone else is engaged in searching for Falstaff, or in concealing him.

15. In Berlioz's *Les Troyens*, taking its cue from Homer, Greek soldiers enter Troy inside a wooden horse, a treacherous "peace offering." Priam's daughter Cassandre has an intuition that disaster threatens, but no one believes her until it is too late.

120. INNS AND OUTS

1. In Richard Strauss's *Der Rosenkavalier*, Baron Ochs, much to his eventual regret, keeps a tryst with "Mariandl," the servant girl who is really Octavian in disguise.

2. In Verdi's *Falstaff*, Falstaff uses the Garter Inn to load himself with food and liquor, and plan his ill-fated attempts at seducing Mistresses Ford and Page.

3. An inn in the town of Hornachuelos in *La Forza del Destino* provides for the siblings Leonora and Carlo di Vargas, as well as a sundry group of colorful figures. Leonora is on her way to the local monastery where she plans to hide from the world, and especially her brother Don Carlo, who has sworn to kill her for having disgraced the family and caused their father's death because of her liaison with Don Alvaro. Although they spend the night in the same inn, Don Carlo doesn't find Leonora for years and years.

4. Sparafucile's hostelry in *Rigoletto*, a sort of Renaissance Hot Sheets Motel, is the place where many unsuspecting men have been lured to their deaths and watery burials.

5. In Puccini's *Manon Lescaut*, an inn at Le Havre provides a rest stop for the coach carrying Manon Lescaut, her brother, and the dirty old basso Geronte. Geronte, as you will recall, is smitten by Manon's beauty and grace, and asks her craven brother to help arrange her journey to Paris with him. Manon, of course, having just met Renato des Grieux, has other ideas.

6. In *La Fanciulla del West*, Minnie's Polka Saloon serves more purposes, it seems, than the Mall of America!

7. In Bellini's *La Sonnambula*, innkeeper Lisa is delighted to find the sleepwalking Amina in the bedroom rented by the Count Rodolfo. Happily believing the worst, Lisa wakes up the whole town, calling upon everyone to witness Amina's seeming betrayal of Elvino, whom Lisa herself loves. Don't worry, this one has a happy ending!

8. We never learn if it has a name, but Mamma Lucia's tavern in *Cavalleria Rusticana* is the place where Alfio and Turiddu make plans for the fight that proves fatal to one of them.

9. We never see the inn where the male members of Canio's troupe adjourn for a drink in *Pagliacci*, but that is where Tonio finds his boss and informs him that his wife, Nedda, has been fooling around with Silvio while Canio has been refreshing himself.

10. In Offenbach's charming *La Périchole*, the Three Cousins run a café named after themselves in a Lima, Peru, that suspiciously resembles Paris in the time of the Second Empire. At this watering hole, Périchole and Piquillo entertain, the Viceroy comes to celebrate his birthday, and *Tout* Lima enjoys itself.

11. At the Tavern of Lillas Pastia in *Carmen* (conveniently situated "*Près des ramparts de Seville*"), Carmen entertains, in the second act of the opera, such admirers as Lieutenant Zuniga, the torero Escamillo, and, of course, Don José.

12. In Richard Strauss's *Arabella*, the fortunes of the Waldner family, Count Walter, Countess Adelaide, daughters Arabella and Zdenka, and their suitors Mandryka and Matteo, are unraveled and decided in the foyer of a Viennese hotel that, like the city in which it is located, has seen better days.

13. In the completed third act of Alban Berg's *Lulu*, there is a long scene in a European casino, in which Lulu and her female protector, Countess Geschwitz, cause yet another scandal and lose yet more money. They flee from the resort, going to London, where the ever-resourceful Lulu puts herself to work as a prostitute and one night makes the slight error of bringing

Jack the Ripper back to her rooms. This scene was first performed in 1979, half a century after the opera had been produced in the truncated form left by Berg at the time of his death.

14. In Lehár's *Giuditta*, Ottavio and Giuditta find themselves facing one another after years of separation. She is a chanteuse and he is still a ne'er-do-well. They go their separate ways.

121. GIFTS

1. The Mikado sends a hara-kiri dagger to Butterfly's father, we learn from Goro in the first act of Puccini's *Madama Butterfly*, with the suggestion that the dishonored man use it. The suggestion was accepted. Cio-Cio-San also finds use for the knife.

2. In the first act of Bellini's *La Sonnambula*, Elvino gives his sweetheart Amina a ring that had belonged to his departed mother.

3. Arlecchino (Beppe) brings a bottle of wine to Colombina (Nedda) in the play-within-a-play segment of Leoncavallo's *Pagliacci*.

4. As the curtain descends on Richard Strauss's *Arabella*, Arabella gives her betrothed Mandryka a glass of water, which signifies her purity.

5. In Massenet's opera *Manon*, De Brétigny dries Manon's tears after her impoverished lover, Des Grieux, has been abducted (for "his own good" by his father) by giving her jewelry.

6. Sachs gives Beckmesser the lyrics to Walther's Prize Song, knowing that the town clerk will disgrace himself when he attempts to perform the song at the Mastersingers' contest in Wagner's *Die Meistersinger von Nürnberg*.

7. In Ponchielli's *La Gioconda*, La Cieca gives Laura her rosary after Laura saves Cieca from a mob bent on killing her.

8. In the beginning of the second act of Puccini's *La Bohème*, Rodolfo buys a pink bonnet for Mimì.

9. In Act III of Wagner's *Die Walküre*, Brünnhilde gives Sieglinde the broken pieces of Siegmund's sword. (Years later, of

course, the Walsungs' son Siegfried forges the sword back into its original state.)

10. Adriana Lecouvreur, in Cilea's opera, gives her lover Maurizio a bouquet of violets. Maurizio, trying to placate the Princess di Bouillon, gives the flowers to her later that same evening. Maurizio comes to regret this!

11. In Cilea's *Adriana Lecouvreur*, the generous Michonnet ransoms Adriana's diamonds, which she has pawned with the Prince di Bouillon in order to raise bail money for Maurizio, and gives them to Adriana moments before another, more sinister "present" arrives for her.

12. Orlofsky, in Johann Strauss's *Die Fledermaus*, gives Adele a purse filled with money to gamble with at his gala party. He is not in the least dismayed when Adele promptly loses everything. In fact, he has the purse refilled!

13. Mario, in the first act of Puccini's *Tosca*, gives his friend Angelotti, who has just escaped from prison, the basket of food and wine that the sacristan has provided for Mario's own dinner.

14. Ernani, in Verdi's opera, gives his hunting horn to the vengeful Silva when Silva agrees to help Ernani rescue Elvira, whom they both love, from the clutches of Don Carlo. Ernani (the fool!) swears to forfeit his life when Silva sounds the horn.

15. At the end of the "Venice" segment of Offenbach's *Les Contes d'Hoffmann*, Dapertutto offers Hoffmann the sword with which he kills Schlémil in a duel.

16. In Verdi's *Falstaff*, the disguised Ford brings Falstaff a cask of ale and a purse filled with gold.

17. In *Die Zauberflöte*, the Three Ladies give a magic glockenspiel to Papageno to take with him on his quest to find Pamina.

18. In Gershwin's *Porgy and Bess*, Porgy, upon his release from jail returns to Catfish Row laden with presents for Bess and his friends, including a new bonnet for Lily.

19. In Beethoven's *Fidelio*, Leonore gives food and water to Florestan when she encounters him in Pizarro's prison, even before she is certain that he is indeed her husband.

20. In Puccini's *La Fanciulla del West*, miner Joe brings Minnie a

bouquet of flowers that, he tells her, resemble blossoms from his faraway homeland.

122. MEMBERS OF THE WEDDING

1. In Mozart's *Le Nozze di Figaro*, Susanna agrees to meet Count Almaviva in the palace garden on the evening of her marriage to Figaro. Of course, Susanna does not intend to keep the tryst. The countess will impersonate Susanna who, dressed as the countess, will test Figaro's loyalty. In the end, the countess catches Almaviva, but all ends with forgiveness and merriment.
2. In Wagner's *Götterdämmerung*, Siegfried, disguised as Gunther, kidnaps Brünnhilde, to whom he has pledged eternal faithfulness. Siegfried, however, has been given a potion that makes him forget all about Brünnhilde. Thus Brünnhilde is given to the *real* Gunther, while Siegfried marries Gunther's rather wimpy sister, Gutrune. All of these events occur in fulfillment of the curse of the ring, but before the drama ends, Brünnhilde realizes that Siegfried, slain by her half-brother-in-law Hagen, was a victim of Hagen's treachery. Her love for Siegfried restored, Brünnhilde rides into his flaming pyre to join him in death.
3. In Mozart's *Don Giovanni*, the wedding of Zerlina and Masetto is interrupted when Don Giovanni arrives on the scene and attempts to seduce the not-totally-unwilling Zerlina. Don Giovanni pursues Zerlina intermittently throughout the opera, but he never succeeds in getting her away from Masetto's watchful eye. Once Don Giovanni has been dragged off to hell, Zerlina and Masetto are free to begin their married life.
4. In Wagner's *Lohengrin*, Elsa derails her wedding night with the Swan Knight when, upset by Ortrud's insinuations, she breaks her vow of ignorance and asks Lohengrin his name and where he comes from. For reasons that defy logic, Lohengrin is compelled to leave Elsa, although before he goes he thwarts Ortrud's evil magic by turning his swan back into Elsa's missing brother, the rightful Duke of Brabant.

5. In Verdi's *I Vespri Siciliani*, the wedding of Arrigo to Elena ends in bloodshed when the Sicilian rebels, led by the fiery Procida, suddenly set upon and kill Arrigo's father, the French governor Monforte, and all the assembled French soldiers. (The French were the occupying power in Sicily at the time.)

6. In Donizetti's *L'Elisir d'Amore*, the flirtatious Adina postpones her wedding ceremony because her lovesick suitor Nemorino isn't around for her to make miserable. Also, deep down, Adina must know that she really loves Nemorino and not the foppish Sergeant Belcore, whom she had impulsively promised to marry.

7. In Gounod's *Roméo et Juliette*, as in Shakespeare's play, the secret marriage of Roméo to Juliette is followed almost immediately by Roméo's slaying of Juliette's kinsman Tybalt and his subsequent banishment from Verona, which leads to the lovers' suicides.

8. In Donizetti's *La Fille du Régiment*, the vivandière Marie is rescued from her forced marriage to the puny Duke of Krakentorp by the arrival of her beloved Tonio and the regiment he now commands. When Maria's past as Daughter of the Regiment is revealed, the duke is dragged away by his haughty mother while Marie's own, newly revealed mother, the Marquise of Berkenfeld, belatedly blesses the union of Marie and Tonio.

9. In Verdi's *Aida*, Amneris emerges from the temple, where she has been praying on the eve of her wedding to Radames, only to find her fiancé romancing Aida and revealing the traveling route of the Egyptian army. She denounces Radames as a traitor, but later relents, although she is unable to save Radames from the death sentence handed down by the priests.

10. In Donizetti's *Don Pasquale*, Pasquale is astounded and dismayed when his supposed bride, Sofronia (who is actually Ernesto's fiancée Norina in disguise) changes from shrinking violet to Venus's-flytrap as soon as their wedding (a sham ceremony arranged by Dr. Malatesta in order to teach Pasquale a lesson) is over. Norina bullies Pasquale to the limits of his sanity, but all is resolved at the final curtain.

11. In Bellini's *I Puritani*, Elvira quickly goes mad when she learns that her bridegroom, Arturo, has run away with Henrietta of England, widow of the axed Charles I. Of course, Arturo's reasons are honorable—he saves Henrietta from certain execution by the Puritan Roundheads—and he and Elvira are reunited after two acts of *bel canto* madness from the bride.

12. In Verdi's *Don Carlo*, the rapturous love between Carlo and Elisabetta di Valois is short-circuited after approximately ten minutes of bliss when the princess learns that, as part of a peace agreement between France and Spain, she must marry Carlo's formidable father, King Philip II. This one ends badly for all concerned.

13. In Donizetti's *Lucia di Lammermoor*, the "hapless Lucy," as folks used to call her, stabs her unwanted bridegroom, Lord Arturo, in their bridal chamber and then goes downstairs to deliver the most celebrated mad scene in the standard repertoire!

14. In Janáček's *Jenufa*, the heroine's wedding to Laca is halted when the body of her illegitimate baby is found frozen in the local brook. Everyone is ready to blame Jenufa, but the girl's foster-mother, Kostelnicka, claims responsibility. Best of all, Laca is still willing to marry the thoroughly nonplussed Jenufa!

15. The so-called lawyer Frazier, in Gershwin's *Porgy and Bess*, charges Porgy $1.50 to divorce Bess from Crown, and then pronounces Porgy and Bess man and wife.

16. In Verdi's *Ernani*, no sooner have Elvira and Ernani said their vows than her uncle Silva, who once planned to wed her himself, arrives on the scene. He has been sounding the hunting horn given to him by Ernani as a pledge of his life. He offers Ernani a choice of dagger or poison. Ernani, over Elvira's strenuous lamentations, stabs himself to death.

123. STOP ALL THAT SINGING AND LET US DANCE!

1. In Cilea's *Adriana Lecouvreur*, the ballet "Judgment of Paris" begins as Adriana and her hostess, the Princess di Bouillon,

are about to scratch each other's eyes out. The princess gets the golden apple but Adriana gets those poisoned violets!

2. In Meyerbeer's *Le Prophète*, the dancing patineurs entertain the Anabaptist rebels.

3. This is, of course, the Triumphal Scene ballet in Verdi's *Aida*.

4. In Verdi's *Don Carlo*, the ballet "The Pearl," commissioned by King Philip as an entertainment for his wife, Elisabetta di Valois, is performed in a scene from Act III that is almost always omitted.

5. In Ponchielli's *La Gioconda*, Alvise's slightly premature announcement that he has killed his faithless wife Laura breaks up his party at the conclusion of the "Dance of the Hours."

6. In Gounod's *Faust*, the Walpurgisnacht ballet finds Méphistophélès trying to distract Faust from his guilt over Marguerite's plight by presenting him with such fabled beauties as Helen of Troy.

7. The final scene of Saint-Saëns's *Samson et Dalila* begins with a wild *bacchanale*, a balletic and sexy version of a pagan rite. Unfortunately, Samson, having been blinded by the Philistines, is unable to enjoy it.

8. The waltz that interrupts Act II of Johann Strauss's *Die Fledermaus* may frustrate Eisenstein, but it seems to delight the audience, nonetheless.

9. In the Paris version of Wagner's *Tannhäuser*, the opera's opening scene scene is the Venusberg ballet, after which Tannhäuser begs leave to depart from Venus's lair.

10. This, of course, is Richard Strauss's "Dance of the Seven Veils" from *Salome*. After dancing for Herod, her stepfather, Salome demands (and eventually gets) Jokanaan's (John the Baptist's) head on a platter.

11. In Act II of Gluck's *Orfeo ed Euridice*, the Blessed Spirits and other less well-adjusted shades do their best to keep Orfeo from entering Hades and returning his late wife Euridice to the world of the living.

12. This brief dance takes place in the first act of Giordano's *Andrea Chénier*, when, foreshadowing the coming French Rev-

olution, servant Carlo Gérard leads a march of the downtrodden into the Di Coigny salon.

13. This is Verdi's *Il Trovatore*. Fragments from the "Anvil Chorus" are heard in this pointless Gypsy ballet, which was clumsily inserted into Act III, scene 1, moments before the scene between Azucena and Di Luna.

14. In the final scene of Wagner's *Die Meistersinger*, the merry young folk perform the "Dance of the Apprentices" just before the march of the Mastersingers.

15. In Verdi's *Otello*, even that august composer had no choice but to provide a ballet for the work's Parisian premiere. So, midway through Act III, as the Cypriot population welcomes the Venetian ambassadors, all of the assembled dignitaries are treated to the "Balibiri," a pseudo-oriental suite of short dance pieces. Legend has it that Verdi deeply resented having to provide these pesky ballets for the Paris versions of his operas. His revenge was to deliberately compose inferior music for them. In our opinion, there is more than a grain of truth here.

124. GETTING THERE IS HALF THE FUN

1. In Barber's *Antony and Cleopatra*, Cleopatra sails down the Nile on a barge. In Puccini's *Il Tabarro*, Michele, Giorgetta, and Luigi live and work on their barge, which sails up and down the Seine.

2. Vanderdecken, Wagner's *Fliegende Holländer*, sails a ship with blood-red sails.

3. Lohengrin, in Wagner's opera, arrives in Brabant on a boat drawn by a swan. Incidentally, when he leaves, the swan has once again assumed its original identity, that of Elsa's brother Gottfried, and the boat is propelled by a dove.

4. In Wagner's *Die Walküre*, Fricka arrives (to nag her husband, Wotan) on a cart drawn by a ram.

5. Rosina Daintymouth in Humperdinck's *Hänsel und Gretel*, rides a broomstick with comic gusto.

6. Porgy, in Gershwin's *Porgy and Bess*, rides on a cart drawn by a goat.

7. In Britten's opera *The Turn of the Screw*, the Governess travels by train to the country estate of her mysterious employer.

8. In the Swedish opera *Aniara* by Karl-Birger Blomdahl, all the action takes place in a spaceship millions of miles from Earth.

9. In Menotti's *Help! Help! The Globolinks!*, tone-deaf creatures from outer space invade a school bus.

10. In another Menotti opera, *The Saint of Bleecker Street*, the fugitive Michele rides the subways and arranges to meet his ailing sister Annina in an IRT station.

11. Peter Grimes, in Britten's opera, has various misadventures on his fishing boat.

12. Lieutenant Pinkerton, in Puccini's *Madama Butterfly*, shuttles between the United States and Japan on board the U.S.S. *Abraham Lincoln*.

13. Tannhäuser walks from Thuringia to Rome and back, doing penance for his wicked lifestyle, in Wagner's opera.

14. In *The Rise and Fall of the City of Mahagonny*, the Widow Begbick and her gang of petty crooks drive through the Southwest.

15. In Barber's *Vanessa*, Anatol travels by horse-drawn sleigh to dine with Vanessa.

16. In Puccini's *Manon Lescaut*, Manon and Des Grieux travel from France to Louisiana by ship.

17. In many productions of Donizetti's *L'Elisir d'Amore*, Dr. Dulcamara has been known to arrive and depart in a hot air balloon.

18. In both the Puccini and Massenet versions of *Manon Lescaut*, Manon and Des Grieux make off at the end of Act I in the coach in which an elderly lecher intended to kidnap Manon. In Massenet's work, the coach is chartered by Guillot. In Puccini's opera, the dirty old basso buffo is Geronte.

19. In Leoncavallo's *Pagliacci*, the troupe of players headed by Canio travel in a donkey cart.

20. In Puccini's *La Fanciulla del West*, Minnie and Dick Johnson

ride off into the sunset at the end of the opera (how else?) mounted on a pair of horses.

125. FARAWAY PLACES

1. Delibes's *Lakmé* takes place in India.
2. Janáček's *Jenufa* and Smetana's *The Bartered Bride* are set in Bohemia.
3. Hell is the setting for Offenbach's *Orphée aux Enfers*, as well as the serious treatments of the Orpheus legend, Gluck's *Orfeo ed Euridice* and Monteverdi's *L'Orfeo*.
4. Venice is the setting for Ponchielli's *La Gioconda*, Act I of Donizetti's *Lucrezia Borgia*, Act II of Offenbach's *Les Contes d'Hoffmann*, Britten's *Death in Venice*, and Johann Strauss's *Eine Nacht in Venedig*. You may think of a few others, yourselves!
5. Offenbach's *La Périchole* is set in Lima, Peru.
6. Palestine (and an opening act in Milan) is the setting for Verdi's *I Lombardi alla Prima Crociata*.
7. Gaul is the setting for Bellini's *Norma*.
8. Gaspare Spontini's *Fernand Cortez*, Roger Sessions's *Montezuma*, and *The Royal Hunt of the Sun*, a contemporary opera by Iain Hamilton, are set in Mexico.
9. An inn on the Lithuanian border serves as the setting for the one more or less comic interlude of *Boris Godunov*.
10. Offenbach's *Les Contes d'Hoffmann*, Gounod's *Faust*, and Massenet's *Werther* take place in Frankfurt.
11. Donizetti's *Lucia di Lammermoor* takes place in Scotland. Bellini's *I Puritani* is set in a Scotland that never really existed.
12. Manhattan is the setting for Weill's *Street Scene* and Menotti's *The Saint of Bleecker Street*, and, in part, for Menotti's *The Last Savage*.
13. Renzo Rossellini's *Uno Sguardo del Ponte*, based on Arthur Miller's play *A View from the Bridge*, takes place in Brooklyn.
14. Moore's *The Ballad of Baby Doe* is set in Colorado.

15. Ward's *The Crucible*, based on Miller's play, deals with the witchcraft trials in colonial Salem, Massachusetts.
16. This is the setting for Menotti's *The Consul*.

126. CRUEL AND UNUSUAL

1. Manfredo, in Montemezzi's *L'Amore dei Tre Re*, dies after kissing the poisoned lips of his dead wife, Fiora. His father, King Archibaldo, has poisoned the lips of his unfaithful daughter-in-law—whom the king had previously strangled—hoping to catch her lover Avito in the act of bidding Fiora farewell. That happens, too, but at the unexpected cost of Manfredo's life.
2. Rachel, in Halévy's *La Juive*, is thrown into a vat of boiling oil with her supposed father, Eléazar. These Jewish martyrs are put to death for defying the edicts of the local cardinal. As Rachel is being deep-fried, Eléazar allows himself the last laugh by shouting to his archenemy, the cardinal, that Rachel is actually the churchman's own illegitimate daughter.
3. Cecilia, an early Christian martyr in Refice's opera of that name, is skewered by a brigade of Roman soldiers after having frustrated her husband for three acts by refusing to consummate their marriage. Although stabbed from every direction, Cecilia lives long enough to warble out her final visions of salvation. Some prefer Bernini's Cecilia to Refice's. Presumably, Claudia Muzio favored the opera over the statue.
4. The Queen of the Night (along with Monostatos and the three ladies-in-waiting) is swallowed up into the earth shortly before Mozart's *Die Zauberflöte* reaches its conclusion. The naughty quintet had been planning the destruction of Sarastro's righteous community and seem to get exactly what they deserve.
5. La Cieca is La Gioconda's luckless mother in Ponchielli's opera. She is held hostage by Barnaba, who promises her release if Gioconda will make love to him. Gioconda kills herself instead, but Barnaba gloatingly shouts to the suicide that he had already drowned La Cieca in the canal.
6. Giuseppe Hagenbach, the tenor lead in Catalani's *La Wally*,

survives being tossed over a cliff by Gelner, who does so to avenge the insult Wally had suffered from Giuseppe. The remorseful Wally subsidizes Hagenbach's convalescence, only to lose him in an avalanche, after which, incidentally, Wally jumps off a cliff.

7. Lisa, in Tchaikovsky's *Pique Dame*, chooses a rather picturesque method of doing herself in, namely, jumping into the Neva, when she realizes that her lover, Hermann, has lost his mind in his obsession with winning at cards.

8. Antonia, the saddest of Hoffmann's three loves in Offenbach's *Les Contes d'Hoffmann*, suffers from a strange disease that makes her singing potentially lethal to her. (Conversely, quite a few sopranos suffer from a more common malady that makes their singing potentially fatal to audiences!) The diabolical Dr. Miracle conjures up the voice of Antonia's deceased mother, who had died of the same disease. The mother's voice urges Antonia to sing, and the girl does so until she collapses and dies in her father's arms after completing a gorgeous if strenuous trio with Dr. Miracle and her mother's phantom voice.

9. In Giordano's *Fedora*, the title character is responsible for the arrest and eventual death of the brother of her sometime enemy, otherwise lover, Loris. Loris has killed Fedora's evil fiancé Vladimiro, son of the head of the Czar's secret police. Fedora writes to Moscow implicating Loris (who is in Paris with her) and his brother, Valeriano. Valeriano is drowned when a flood engulfs his dungeon cell, and the boy's poor, old mother expires upon receiving the grim news. These events lead to Fedora's eventual confession and suicide, which is accomplished with a dose of poison concealed in her jeweled crucifix.

10. Lakmé, in Delibes's opera, realizing that her love affair with the Englishman Gérald is doomed, poisons herself by a most exotic means—sniffing the perfume of a poisonous flowering plant.

11. Glauce is Giasone's young second wife in Cherubini's *Medea*. Medea's hatred for Glauce, who has supplanted her in Giasone's heart, is so strong that she sends the girl a wedding dress treated with a poisonous chemical that causes the dress

to catch fire, thus immolating the bride. Then Medea proceeds to prepare a special dinner for Giasone, but that's another story!

12. John and Fidès are consumed in the fire set by the guilt-ridden "prophet" in *Le Prophète*.

13. In Richard Strauss's *Salome*, Jokanaan is beheaded on orders from Salome, who wishes to engage in some very kinky play with the Baptist's severed head.

14. Lulu and the countess, the only one who truly loves her, are brutally hacked to death by Jack the Ripper, whom Lulu, in a moment of imprudence, has mistaken for an ordinary client looking for love, and brings back to her flat.

15. Hunding, the unpleasant husband of Sieglinde, is killed by an irritated Wotan, with a wave of his hand, at the end of the second act of *Die Walküre*. Wotan had been forced by Fricka to let Hunding kill Siegmund in the duel they have fought after Siegmund and Sieglinde have run off together. Wotan, apparently, had made no guarantees to Fricka concerning Hunding's future.

16. Miles is the little boy in Britten's *The Turn of the Screw*. He dies at the end of the psychic tug-of-war his governess has with the evil ghost of his former tutor, Peter Quint. It is a moot point whether the boy is killed by the vengeful Quint, or is merely frightened to death by the governess's mounting hysteria.

17. Rebecca Nurse, in Ward's *The Crucible*, is a nice old woman who is hanged as a witch by those neighborly folks in Salem, Mass.!

V

A Potpourri

127. OPENING NIGHTS

1. Marguerite was sung by Christine Nilsson (no relation to Birgit).
2. Italian.
3. Puccini's *Tosca*, with Dorothy Kirsten in the title role.
4. Enrico Caruso as the Duke of Mantua in Verdi's *Rigoletto*, 1903; Cesare Siepi as King Philip II in *Don Carlo* in 1950; Maria Callas as Bellini's Norma, 1956; George London as Amonasro in Verdi's *Aida*, 1951; Lucine Amara as the Celestial Voice in *Don Carlo*, 1950; Giulietta Simionato as Azucena in Verdi's *Il Trovatore*, in 1959; Ruggero Raimondi as Silva in Verdi's *Ernani*, 1970; Jessye Norman, as Cassandre/Didon in Berlioz's *Les Troyens*, 1983.
5. *Antony and Cleopatra*; music by Samuel Barber; libretto adapted from Shakespeare by Franco Zeffirelli, who also designed and staged the production. Alvin Ailey choreographed the opera, his first assignment at the Met. Justino Díaz and Leontyne Price sang the title roles. Jess Thomas sang Caesar Octavius, Rosalind Elias was Charmian, Ezio Flagello was Enobarbus, and Andrea Velis sang Mardian the Eunuch. Thomas Schippers was the conductor. The date was September 16, 1966.
6. Puccini's *Madama Butterfly* starring Maria Callas.
7. Renata Tebaldi and Maria Callas conducted, at least through their partisans, *the* operatic feud of the 1950s and 1960s. Callas attended the opening-night performance of Cilea's *Adriana Lecouvreur* on September 16, 1968. Tebaldi sang the title role, flanked by Franco Corelli as Maurizio, Irene Dalis as the Prin-

cess, and Anselmo Colzani as Michonnet, with Fausto Cleva conducting. After the final act, Rudolf Bing brought Callas backstage to see Tebaldi. In a scene captured by photographers, the two women fell into each other's arms, weeping with emotion.

8. December 7—Pearl Harbor Day.

9. One year, Caruso allowed Geraldine Farrar to make her debut on opening night. Farrar sang the soprano lead in Gounod's *Roméo et Juliette.*

10. There was a special concert on December 7, 1946, conducted by Arturo Toscanini. The program included the Verdi *Te Deum*, the prologue to Boito's *Mefistofele*, the prayer from Rossini's *Mosè* and the third act of Puccini's *Manon Lescaut.* Three of the singers that night were Mafalda Favero, Tancredi Pasero, and Renata Tebaldi, making her La Scala debut on that occasion.

11. In 1980, there was a musicians' strike of several months' duration at the Met. The opening was postponed three months to mid-December, when Music Director James Levine decreed to the public that the Met would commence its season with the Mahler piece, which Levine himself conducted.

12. Leontyne Price opened the Metropolitan Opera's 1961–62 season singing Minnie in Puccini's *La Fanciulla del West.* Sudden illness forced Miss Price to withdraw from the next performance after the first act. (She was replaced by Dorothy Kirsten.) Leontyne Price never sang Minnie again, although she recorded "Laggiù nel Soledad."

13. *Das Rheingold.*

14. At the world premiere of Puccini's *Turandot*, at La Scala in 1926, conductor Arturo Toscanini ended the performance at the end of Liù's death scene to honor the dead composer, who left the opera unfinished, except for sketches, at that point. Ever since the premiere, the final duet, completed by Franco Alfano under Toscanini's withering supervision, has been performed.

128. OPERA HOUSES AROUND THE WORLD

1. Mozart's *Don Giovanni* had its world premiere at the Prague Opera.
2. Mary Garden managed the Chicago Opera (not related to the Chicago Lyric Opera) for one tempestuous season in the 1920s, during which period the company lost the then-astonishing sum of nearly $1 million.
3. As the Paris Opéra-Comique, the Salle Favart was the scene, on March 3, 1875, of the first performance of Bizet's *Carmen*.
4. *Oberto*, Verdi's first opera, was also his first to be given at La Scala, Milan.
5. *La Bohème* was first produced at the Teatro Regio in Turin. The rebuilt theater opened in 1971 with a not-terribly-successful production of Verdi's *I Vespri Siciliani* staged by Maria Callas and Giuseppe di Stefano.
6. The Metropolitan Opera opened, on October 22, 1883, with a performance of Gounod's *Faust* in Italian. The seven seasons that followed featured operas sung only in German, regardless of their countries of origin.
7. *La Forza del Destino*.
8. The Chicago Lyric Opera was organized in 1954 by Carol Fox, its director, conductor Nicola Rescigno, and Lawrence Kelly.
9. Tebaldi made her American debut in the autumn of 1950 in the title role of *Aida*. The debut took place at the San Francisco Opera, and her Radames that night was Mario del Monaco.
10. Sutherland made her Royal Opera House debut as the First Lady in *Die Zauberflöte*. Her modest success soon led to her appearance as the servant Clotilde in *Norma*, but she could hardly have been noticed in Bellini's opera since the Norma on that occasion was Maria Callas.
11. The Monte Carlo Opera House was home to the first performance of Puccini's *La Rondine* in 1917.
12. Both La Scala and the Vienna State Opera were practically

leveled by Allied bombing. La Scala was the first to reopen, with a gala concert led by Arturo Toscanini in 1946. Vienna had to wait nine more years, until 1955, for the Staatsoper to reopen with a performance of Beethoven's *Fidelio*.

13. The Stockholm Opera has created a production of Verdi's *Un Ballo in Maschera* with a Swedish setting that is sung in Swedish to a libretto that depicts more accurately the events surrounding the assassination of King Gustavus III than the original Italian libretto and the Scribe play on which it is based.

14. Parma is feared by singers around the world for the hostility heaped on offending artists by the local patrons, especially the fanatics who sit in the theater's highest gallery.

15. Gatti-Casazza managed La Scala before he headed the Metropolitan Opera.

16. The Baths of Caracalla in Rome is celebrated for the spectacular stagings of *Aida* that lured thousands of tourists each summer.

17. Puccini's *Madama Butterfly* and *Turandot* were given their premieres at La Scala. The *Butterfly* premiere, in 1904, was conducted by Toscanini with Rosina Storchio as the heroine. The performance was a fiasco, with rude behavior from the audience (an intrigue led by Puccini's enemies was rumored to have been responsible). Puccini immediately withdrew the opera and revised it. *Turandot* was produced at La Scala in 1926, two years after the death of the composer. *Turandot* was led by Toscanini, who terminated the performance with the last music Puccini completed, Liù's death scene in Act III. The Turandot was Rosa Raisa, and the opera was triumphantly received.

18. *La Traviata*'s unsuccessful first night took place at the Teatro La Fenice in Venice.

19. Liebermann turned the Hamburg Opera into a major operatic center before leaving that post for the Paris Opéra.

20. The Edinburgh Festival, in Scotland, had invited the La Scala company to perform Bellini's *La Sonnambula* in a production starring Maria Callas. Callas refused to take part in an extra

performance that was added in response to the great demand for tickets. Her understudy, Renata Scotto, then in her early twenties and virtually unknown in or out of Italy, sang the role of Amina to great acclaim.

21. The Glimmerglass Opera in Cooperstown, New York, is not far from the Baseball Hall of Fame.

22. The Sadler's Wells Theatre was the birthplace of the companies that became known as the English National Opera and the Royal Ballet.

23. The twice burned-out opera house is situated in Frankfurt, Germany.

24. The beautiful Teatro del Liceo in Barcelona fell victim to a devastating fire.

25. This is the Sydney Opera, one of Dame Joan Sutherland's favorite ports of call.

26. The beautiful Teatro La Fenice burned down, for the second time in its long history. Both *Rigoletto* and *La Traviata* were given their first performances at La Fenice. In recent years, nonoperatic artists frequently appeared there, and Woody Allen was scheduled to reopen La Fenice, performing with his Dixieland quartet. Plans are being made to allow the Fenice to once again rise from its ashes.

129. FROM PAGE TO STAGE

1. *Ivanhoe*, by Sir Walter Scott, was the inspiration for Sir Arthur Sullivan's lone serious opera, also named *Ivanhoe*.

2. Henry James's novel *The Wings of the Dove* was adapted for the lyric stage by Douglas Moore and was done at the New York City Opera in 1961.

3. Dickens's novel was renamed *Miss Havisham's Fire* when American composer Dominick Argento created an opera based upon it, produced at the New York City Opera in 1979.

4. Cervantes's *Don Quixote* was adapted as an opera by Jules Massenet, who, of course, gave the title character a French name, *Don Quichotte*. Mention might also be made of Albert

Marré and Mitch Leigh's 1965 musical play *Man of La Man-cha*, which straddles the thin line between "musical" and "grand opera."

5. Doestoevsky's *The Gambler* was used as a subject by Prokofiev, whose opera bears the same title as the novel.

6. The title is a dead giveaway. Walter Scott's somewhat lurid romance was turned by Donizetti into his most popular opera, *Lucia di Lammermoor.*

7. Tolstoi's novel was made into an opera by Prokofiev, and, in addition to being "standard repertoire" in Russia, has been televised in the United States, been a "hit" at the English National Opera, and was done in Italian at La Scala in a production that starred Franco Corelli.

8. The Abbé Prévost's novel about an eighteenth-century nymphet inspired Massenet's *Manon*, Puccini's *Manon Lescaut*, and, before either of those two works, a now-forgotten *Manon Lescaut* by Daniel Auber.

9. The James Cain novel, source of the unforgettable Lana Turner film, was recently made into an opera by American composer Dominick Argento.

10. James's gothic novel inspired one of Benjamin Britten's most popular operas, which retained James's title.

11. Massenet simplified the title of the Goethe novel to *Werther.*

130. PLAY VERSUS OPERA

1. e. Berlioz's *Béatrice et Benedict* is based on Shakespeare's play *Much Ado About Nothing.*

2. h. Johann Strauss's *Die Fledermaus* is based on the comedy by Meilhac and Halévy.

3. i. Verdi's *Luisa Miller* is based on Schiller's tragedy.

4. g. Verdi's *Rigoletto* is based on this play by Victor Hugo.

5. a. Mascagni's *Lodoletta* is adapted from Ouida's novel.

6. j. The *La Bohèmes* of both Puccini and Leoncavallo are based on this autobiographical novel by Henri Murger.

7. f. Verdi's *La Traviata* is based on the novel and play by Alexandre Dumas, *fils*.

8. c. Britten's *Peter Grimes* is based on the poem by George Crabbe.

9. k. Donizetti based *L'Elisir d'Amore* on this comedy adapted by Eugène Scribe from a work by Silvio Malapetta.

10. l. and p. Ponchielli based *La Gioconda* on Victor Hugo's play, which also was the basis for Mercadante's rarely revived *Il Giuramento*.

11. b. Thomas's *Mignon* is based on Goethe's play.

12. m. Berg's *Lulu* is based on Wedekind's play.

13. d. The "Antonia" act of Offenbach's *Les Contes d'Hoffmann* is based on this tale by E. T. A. Hoffmann.

14. n. Janáček's *Jenufa* is based on this Czech play, by Gabriella Preissová.

15. q. Verdi's *La Forza del Destino* is taken from this play by the Duke of Rivas.

131. LIBRETTISTS

1. Antonio Ghislanzoni
2. Giuseppe Giacosa and Luigi Illica
3. Ruggiero Leoncavallo
4. Tobia Gorrio (pseudonym for Arrigo Boito)
5. Temistocle Solera
6. Luigi Illica
7. Eugène Scribe and Charles Duveyrier
8. Lorenzo da Ponte
9. Richard Wagner
10. Henri Meilhac and Ludovic Halévy
11. Giuseppe Adami and Renato Simoni
12. Francesco Maria Piave
13. Montagu Slater
14. Tito Ricordi and Gabriele D'Annunzio
15. Arrigo Boito
16. Hugo von Hofmannsthal
17. Arrigo Boito
18. Hedwig Lachmann
19. Salvatore Cammarano
20. Pyotor and Modest Tchaikovsky
21. Friedrich Kind
22. Georges Bernanos
23. Giuseppe Giacosa and Luigi Illica
24. Jules Barbier and Michel Carré
25. Modest Mussorgsky

132. RECORD COLLECTORS I

1. The nine Metropolitan Operas productions issued by Columbia Records were *La Bohème*, Giuseppe Antonicelli conducting with Bidù Sayão, Richard Tucker, and Mimi Benzell; *Hänsel und Gretel* (in English), Max Rudolf conducting with Risë Stevens, Nadine Conner, and Thelma Votipka; *Faust*, Fausto Cleva conducting with Eleanor Steber, Eugene Conley, and Cesare Siepi; *Madama Butterfly*, Max Rudolf conducting, with Eleanor Steber, Richard Tucker, and Giuseppe Valdengo; *Cavalleria Rusticana*, Fausto Cleva conducting with Richard Tucker and Margaret Harshaw; *Pagliacci*, Fausto Cleva conducting with Richard Tucker and Lucine Amara; *Die Fledermaus* (in English), Eugene Ormandy conducting with Ljuba Weltisch, Lily Pons, John Brownlee, and Richard Tucker; *Così Fan Tutte* (in English), Fritz Stiedry conducting with Eleanor Steber, Richard Tucker, and Roberta Peters; *The Rake's Progress* (in English), Igor Stravinsky conducting with Hilde Gueden, Eugene Conley, Blanche Thebom, Mack Harrell, and Martha Lipton.

2. Victor de Sabata.

3. Wotan is sung by George London in *Das Rheingold*, and by Hans Hotter in *Die Walküre* and *Siegfried*. (In *Siegfried*, of course, Wotan is known as The Wanderer.)

4. Price's first *Il Trovatore*, for RCA, was conducted by Arturo Basile. Her colleagues included Richard Tucker (Manrico), Rosalind Elias (Azucena), and Leonard Warren (di Luna). Price's second *Il Trovatore*, also for RCA, was conducted by Zubin Mehta, and the cast included Plácido Domingo (Manrico), Fiorenza Cossotto (Azucena), and Sherrill Milnes (di Luna). Price's third recording of this role, for EMI, was conducted by Herbert von Karajan, and the other artists included Franco Bonisolli (Manrico), Elena Obraztsova (Azucena), and Piero Cappuccilli (di Luna).

5. Among the operas recorded by the New York City Opera are *Giulio Cesare*; *Lizzie Borden*; *The Crucible*; *Carry Nation*; *The Ballad of Baby Doe*; *Silverlake*; and *Candide*.

6. In this *Pagliacci*, Luciano Pavarotti is heard as Canio, and his father, Fernando Pavarotti, is heard as a villager.

7. EMI.

8. Toscanini's 1954 broadcast of Verdi's *Un Ballo in Maschera* was supposed to have had Jussi Bjoerling singing Riccardo. Owing to Bjoerling's absence from rehearsals, the tenor was replaced by a Toscanini favorite, Jan Peerce. Peerce was miffed because he wasn't the maestro's original choice for the performance and nearly refused to sing, throwing the entire project—Toscanini's final operatic performance—into doubt until he was persuaded to perform.

9. Olivero recorded *Turandot* in 1937 for Parlaphone Records (currently released as a Cetra CD) and *Fedora* in 1969 for Decca/London. In *Turandot*, the soprano sang Liù, while Gina Cigna and Francesco Merli are heard as Turandot and Calaf, respectively. In *Fedora*, Olivero sings the title role, while Mario del Monaco sings Loris and Tito Gobbi sings de Siriex.

10. *Aida.* She was American-born.

11. a. Giacomo Aragall
    b. Plácido Domingo
    c. Alfredo Kraus
    d. Plácido Domingo

12. Carreras's first opera recording was Rossini's *La Pietra del Paragone.*

13. Grace Bumbry sings Leonora, Nicolai Gedda sings Alvaro, and Hermann Prey sings Don Carlo on this recording of highlights from Verdi's *La Forza del Destino*, which is known in German as *Die Macht des Schicksals.*

14. In each copy of this album was a piece of the old Met's gold curtain, which was unceremoniously chopped up when the company moved to Lincoln Center in 1966.

15. Caterina Mancini sang Abigaille opposite the Nabucco of Paolo Silveri in Cetra's recording of *Nabucco.*

16. The opera with Bjoerling that was canceled was Verdi's *Un Ballo in Maschera* for Decca/London. Rumor has it that the Decca vaults contain the first two scenes of this ill-fated re-

cording. The opera was finished with Carlo Bergonzi replacing Bjoerling as Riccardo.

17. Six operas recorded commercially by Milanov include *Cavalleria Rusticana* (Santuzza), *Tosca* (title role), *Il Trovatore* (Leonora), *Aida* (title role), *La Gioconda* (title role), and *La Forza del Destino* (Leonora).

18. Callas was forced to cancel her plans to record *La Traviata* for EMI in 1956 because she had made a recording of this work for Cetra. Her contract for the latter performance had a five-year exclusivity clause that had not yet expired, and from which Cetra would not release her. Antonietta Stella replaced Callas on the EMI set. After Callas's death in 1977, EMI published two of her live *La Traviata* performances, one from Lisbon dating from 1958, and the other the electrifying La Scala performance from 1956. Callas is flanked by Alfredo Kraus and Mario Sereni in the Lisbon performance, conducted by Franco Ghione. Her colleagues on the La Scala recording are Giuseppe di Stefano and Ettore Bastianini, with Carlo Maria Giulini conducting.

19. Maria Callas.

20. Tebaldi and Corelli made *no* complete operatic performances together. They did record a disc of duets from *Aida, Manon Lescaut, Adriana Lecouvreur,* and *Francesca da Rimini* for Decca/London. CDs exist of their live performances in *Andrea Chénier, La Gioconda, La Bohème,* and *Tosca.*

21. Boris Christoff, in each of his two EMI recordings of Mussorgsky's *Boris Godunov,* undertook not only the title role but those of the monks Pimen and Varlaam.

22. Tebaldi, Nilsson, and Bjoerling appear in the RCA *Turandot* and in the gala sequence of the Decca/London *Die Fledermaus* conducted by Herbert von Karajan.

23. Flagstad, worried about her high C, allowed soprano Elisabeth Schwarzkopf to sing those notes, which were spliced into Flagstad's part. Flagstad insisted on utter secrecy, but a recording engineer spread the story hours after the session ended. The mortified Flagstad never forgave EMI and switched her allegiance to Decca for the remainder of her recording career.

24. Santuzza was sung by Lina Bruna Rasa, Turiddu by Beniamino Gigli, and Mamma Lucia by Giulietta Simionato.

25. The opera was *Rigoletto*, and the recording took place in 1950. The leading artists were Erna Berger (Gilda), Jan Peerce (Duke of Mantua), Leonard Warren (Rigoletto), and Nan Merriman (Maddalena). Renato Cellini conducted.

26. The opera was Massenet's *Manon*. The Manon was Janine Micheau.

27. Martina Arroyo.

28. Deutsche Grammophon made the first absolutely complete recording of *Don Carlo*, sung in French. Plácido Domingo sings Carlo, Katia Ricciarelli sings Elisabetta, Ruggero Raimondi sings Philip II, Lucia Valentini-Terrani is Eboli, Leo Nucci sings Rodrigo, and Nicolai Ghiaurov is the Grand Inquisitor. Claudio Abbado conducts the orchestra and chorus of La Scala.

29. Christa Ludwig. Incidentally, she sang the Rossini aria in German.

30. Domingo has recorded the title role in *Il Barbiere di Siviglia*. This is interesting because Figaro is a baritone role. Mr. Domingo, it might be remembered, is one of the "Three Tenors."

133. RUDOLF BING

1. He had been the director of the Glyndebourne Festival in England.

2. Bing replaced former tenor star Edward Johnson, who had run the Met between 1935 and 1950.

3. In the opening-night *Don Carlo*, soprano Delia Rigal (Elisabetta), mezzo Fedora Barbieri (Eboli), bass Cesare Siepi (Philip), and soprano Lucine Amara (Celestial Voice) made their Met debuts. Rigal lasted a decade at the Met (and turned up to replace Amara in the *La Forza del Destino* trio at the closing gala at the old Met); Barbieri visited the company sporadically throughout the next quarter century; Siepi remained

primo basso until 1973; and Amara went on to sing many leading roles over the next forty-one years.

4. Zinka Milanov had been let go for no apparent reason by the Johnson administration. Bing reengaged her, and Milanov went on to sing with the Met until 1966, triumphing in such roles as Aida, both Verdi Leonoras, Santuzza, Tosca, Desdemona, Norma, Elvira (in *Ernani*), and Maddalena.

5. The *Fledermaus* adapters were Garson Kanin (dialogue) and Howard Dietz (lyrics).

6. Igor Stravinsky's *The Rake's Progress*.

7. Bing fired Callas because she refused to sign her Met contract for the 1958–59 season without an alteration of roles. She didn't want to sing both Violetta and Lady Macbeth within a few days of each other. Bing ordered Callas to cable acceptance by a certain hour. When Callas failed to do so, Bing fired her in a move many consider to be his single worst mistake as manager of the Met. In the memoirs of Callas's husband, Battista Meneghini, dictated shortly before his death, the author admitted that he and Callas had deliberately goaded Bing into firing her after having concluded that Callas would have been better off singing in Europe instead of in New York.

8. Karl Liebl, Albert Da Costa, and Ramón Vinay were Nilsson's three Tristans in one night, in December 1959.

9. Lauritz Melchior, whom many rate as the finest Wagnerian tenor of the century.

10. Bing invited Walter Slezak, son of heldentenor Leo Slezak, to appear in the role of Szupan in Johann Strauss's *The Gypsy Baron*. Walter Slezak made his entrance carrying a diapered piglet. He is remembered for his Hollywood villains (*Lifeboat*), Broadway comic turns (*Fanny, My Three Angels*), and many eloquent radio appearances as a Texaco Opera Quiz contestant.

11. Lunt staged *Così Fan Tutte* (in English) in 1952 and *La Traviata* in 1966.

12. Death threats and other mischievous notes directed against soprano Leonie Rysanek were received by the Met hours before a broadcast performance of *Otello* in 1964. Bing felt that cer-

tain members of the Standing Room Regulars were responsible, and he banished all the standees that afternoon. Diva Maria Jeritza is said to have interceded on behalf of the chastened standees, and Sir Rudolf relented in time for the evening performance. Rysanek returned unscathed to perform through 1996. Rysanek was, in fact, a great favorite of Met audiences and received scores of intensely affectionate ovations.

13. Leopold Stokowski earned Bing's wrath during the closing gala at the old Met when, in an unscheduled speech, he pleaded with the audience to save the old Met from being torn down to make room for an office building. Bing had agreed to the old theater's destruction in order to finance the company through lease of the land on which the old Met stood.

14. Because of cold war politics, Boris Christoff was prevented from singing on Bing's first opening night. Although the Bulgarian bass eventually sang in the United States, he never came to terms with the Met. Soprano Sena Jurinac, a darling of the Viennese public, was often invited but never sang at the Met. Beverly Sills, who eventually became a friend of Bing's, was never offered a contract that suited her. Sills's Met debut was made in 1975, during the Schuyler G. Chapin regime.

15. The title role in Gluck's *Alceste*.

16. Ljuba Welitsch. She jumped on tables and onto singers's backs and, it has been alleged, wore no undergarments that evening!

17. Birgit Nilsson, whose tax troubles led to her self-exile from the United States from 1975 to 1979, once claimed Bing as a dependent because he "needed" her.

18. Roberta Peters, who had never sung a professional opera performance (although she was scheduled to debut later that season), made her Met debut as Zerlina, replacing the ailing Nadine Conner, on three hours' notice.

19. The final opera sung at Bing's Met was *Don Carlo* in the same Margaret Webster production that had begun Bing's tenure in 1950. Two artists who sang in the premiere sang in this broadcast matinee: Lucine Amara (Celestial Voice) and Cesare Siepi (Philip). Also heard that day were Franco Corelli (Carlo), Montserrat Caballé (Elisabetta), Grace Bumbry (Eboli), and

Frederica Von Stade (Tebaldo.) The performance survives as a CD on the Foyer label. That evening, Sir Rudolf Bing was honored by a gala concert featuring most members of the company.

20. After leaving the Met, Sir Rudolf Bing taught a course in opera at Brooklyn College, and became a member of the board of directors of Columbia Artists. He wrote two volumes of memoirs: *5000 Nights at the Opera* and *A Knight at the Opera*. Although in failing health, Sir Rudolf is, at this writing, ninety-three years of age. I take this opportunity to express my respect and affection for this great man, and offer my profound gratitude for his many kindnesses to me through the years.

134. FAMOUS OPERATIC CONDUCTORS

1. Cleofonte Campanini
2. Arturo Toscanini
3. Franco Faccio
4. Tullio Serafin
5. Thomas Schippers
6. Hans von Bülow
7. Sarah Caldwell
8. Nicola Rescigno
9. Pietro Mascagni
10. Herbert von Karajan
11. Gustav Mahler
12. Sir Georg Solti
13. Mstislav Rostropovich (married to Galina Vishnevskaya)
14. Guido Cantelli
15. Bruno Walter
16. Karl Böhm
17. Richard Bonynge (married to Joan Sutherland)
18. Wilfred Pelletier
19. Pierre Boulez
20. James Levine
21. Victor de Sabata
22. Clemens Krauss
23. Sir Thomas Beecham
24. Wilhelm Furtwängler
25. Julius Rudel
26. Rafael Kubelik
27. Carlos Kleiber
28. Leonard Bernstein (Cherubini's *Medea* in 1955, with Maria Callas)
29. Calvin Simmons
30. Kurt Herbert Adler
31. Claudio Abbado
32. John Crosby
33. Kent Nagano
34. Riccardo Muti
35. James Conlon

135. THE NEW YORK CITY OPERA

1. The first N.Y.C.O. performance was *Tosca*, in 1945. It took place at the City Center.
2. Leinsdorf replaced Laszlo Halasz. Leinsdorf was succeeded by Julius Rudel.
3. Williams was the first African-American soprano engaged to sing leading roles by a major New York opera company. She is especially well remembered for her Cio-Cio-San.
4. Enzo Mascherini.
5. Washington, D.C., and Los Angeles.
6. Patricia Brooks.
7. The role was Cleopatra in the 1966 N.Y.C.O. production of Handel's *Giulio Cesare*. Phyllis Curtin had been the first choice for the role.
8. José Carreras, twenty-five years of age and quite unknown, made his N.Y.C.O. debut as Pinkerton in *Madama Butterfly* in the spring of 1972.
9. Nilsson joined the City Opera for one performance in the title role of *Tosca* in Los Angeles in 1974. She replaced Beverly Sills, who had canceled her L.A. engagement with the company because she had to undergo cancer surgery, from which she fully recovered. Nilsson was partnered on that occasion by José Carreras.
10. Sills sang the following Donizetti roles: Marie in *The Daughter of the Regiment*, Elisabeth in *Roberto Devereux*, and the title roles in *Maria Stuarda*, *Anna Bolena*, *Lucrezia Borgia*, and *Lucia di Lammermoor*.
11. Tito Capobianco.
12. *Susannah*.
13. Abigaille in *Nabucco* and the title role in Cherubini's *Medea*.
14. The opera was Janáček's *The Makropoulos Case*. The enterprising director was Frank Corsaro.
15. a. *Regina*.
16. Louis Quilico.
17. Milnes returned to the N.Y.C.O. to sing the title role in Am-

broise Thomas's *Hamlet*. In 1996 he came back to sing the title role in Verdi's *Falstaff*.

18. *Tito Capobianco*.
19. *Julius Rudel*.
20. *Johanna Meier*.
21. *Jerry Hadley*.
22. *Cavalleria Rusticana* and *Pagliacci*.
23. Tosca in Puccini's opera.
24. In this silly treatment of *Carmen*, the Gypsy girl was embroiled in the Spanish Civil War on the side of the anti-Fascists. Don José was engaged in fighting for Franco. Olé!
25. Christopher Keene; Hindemith's *Mathis der Maler*.
26. Paul Kellogg.

136. SATURDAY AFTERNOONS AT THE MET

1. Kirsten Flagstad made her debut singing Sieglinde in *Die Walküre* in 1935. In 1940, Astrid Varnay debuted singing that role and being heard coast-to-coast, too.
2. The only Met broadcast with Callas was a December 1956 performance of *Lucia di Lammermoor*, with Callas in the title role.
3. Tenor Giovanni Martinelli collapsed from food poisoning as he attempted to sing "Celeste Aida" one afternoon in the 1940s. The performance resumed after a break. Standby Frederick Jagel, listening to the broadcast from a nearby hotel, rushed to the opera house and took over the role.
4. Baritone Cornell MacNeil rushed from Italy to the Met overnight to make his debut, replacing Robert Merrill in the broadcast performance of *Rigoletto* that took place early in 1959.
5. Sutherland's broadcast debut occurred less than a month after her Met debut. In both performances, she sang the title role in *Lucia di Lammermoor*. Richard Tucker was her tenor partner.

6. *Hänsel und Gretel* was the recipient of the first complete broadcast from the Met, on Christmas Day, 1931.

7. Texaco.

8. Geraldine Farrar joined Cross at the microphone back in the good old days.

9. The first complete opera broadcast from Lincoln Center was Barber's *Antony and Cleopatra*, at its world premiere on opening night of the new Met, September 16, 1966.

10. Peerce's twenty-fifth anniversary was in 1966, and he was honored during the broadcast of *Don Giovanni* in which he sang Don Ottavio. Milanov was feted during a 1963 broadcast of *Andrea Chénier* in which she sang Maddalena. Tucker celebrated his twenty-fifth anniversary at the Met in 1970 in a broadcast of *La Bohème*, in which he sang Rodolfo.

11. Pamela Coburn was replaced by Anne Evans.

12. A performance of Verdi's *Macbeth* was terminated after the *third* act because a member of the audience jumped to his death from an upper balcony during the intermission.

13. Schwarzkopf sang Donna Elvira in *Don Giovanni* in the opera's first performance that season, a broadcast in January 1966. (This was, coincidentally, Jan Peerce's twenty-fifth-anniversary performance, noted in #10.) The soprano was suffering an indisposition, and this highly disciplined artist uncharacteristically canceled the remainder of her engagement, and never sang at the Met again.

14. Cross was replaced, after his death in January 1975, by Peter Allen.

15. March 14, 1964, marked Renata Tebaldi's rapturously received return to the Met, in a broadcast performance of Puccini's *La Bohème*, in which she sang Mimi. Sándor Kónya sang Rodolfo.

16.

a. 1977	f. 1966
b. 1994	g. 1960
c. 1957	h. 1966
d. 1977	i. 1968
e. 1974	j. 1959

17. The all-Wagner concert featured Birgit Nilsson and Jon Vickers. James Levine conducted.

18. On February 2, 1963, the scheduled performance of *Der Fliegende Holländer* had to be canceled when tenor Karl Liebl, the Erik, found himself voiceless (don't forget, Liebl was the tenor whose indisposition caused the Night of the Three Tristans in 1959). This time, there was no one at all to sing Erik, so the bill was changed to *Ariadne auf Naxos*, getting its first-ever broadcast (it had received its Met premiere less than two months earlier). The artist least inconvenienced by the crisis was Leonie Rysanek, who was scheduled to sing both Senta in *Holländer* and the title role in *Ariadne*.

19. Menotti's opera *The Last Savage* was broadcast from the Met in 1964. Leading artists included Roberta Peters, George London, Nicolai Gedda, Morley Meredith, and, in one of her first leading roles in a Met broadcast, Teresa Stratas.

20. Farrell was heard as Alceste in Gluck's opera in 1961, Leonora in *La Forza del Destino* (1961), *La Gioconda* in 1962, and Santuzza in *Cavalleria Rusticana* in 1964. The *Cavalleria Rusticana* and *Gioconda* performances can be found on CD.

137. OPERA ON THE SILVER SCREEN

1. *Carmen* (with Geraldine Farrar); *La Bohème* (with Lillian Gish as Mimì); and *Der Rosenkavalier* (with Maria Jeritza as the Marschallin).

2. Aida: Renata Tebaldi; Radames: Giuseppe Campora; Amneris: Ebe Stignani; Amonasro: Gino Bechi; conductor: Giuseppe Morelli.

3. In the film *Salome*, the Princess of Judea was a good girl and a convert to the preaching of John the Baptist! She performed the dance of the seven veils in order to win John's release from Herod!

4. Sylvia Sidney played Butterfly; Cary Grant was Pinkerton.

5. Eileen Farrell was the "voice" of Miss Lawrence.

6. Dorothy Kirsten and Lucine Amara.

7. Franco Corelli was heard in a 1958 film of *Tosca*, in which the title role was sung by Maria Caniglia but acted by Franca Duval. Corelli appeared on the screen.

8. Callas made a film of *Medea*, directed by Pier Paolo Pasolini, in 1970.

9. Stevens's best-known film is *Going My Way*, in which she costarred with Bing Crosby and sang the "Habanera." She also starred with Nelson Eddy in a film of *The Chocolate Soldier* and was seen in *Carnegie Hall*.

10. In the Salzburg Festival *Der Rosenkavalier* film, the conductor was Herbert von Karajan. Elisabeth Schwarzkopf, Sena Jurinac, and Otto Edelmann were seen, respectively, as the Marschallin, Octavian, and Baron Ochs.

11. The soprano starlet Wilhelminia Wiggins Fernandez was featured in the film *Diva*. In the movie, Fernandez sings "Ebben, ne andrò lontana" from Catalani's *La Wally*. Her 1982 City Opera debut was as Musetta in Puccini's *La Bohème*.

12. Grace Moore filmed Charpentier's *Louise* in Paris, with Georges Thill as Julien. The film, a heavily cut but charming production, can be found on video.

13. Franco Zeffirelli.

14. Novotna filmed *The Bartered Bride*, playing the title role.

15. Miss Horne dubbed the songs for Dorothy Dandridge in Otto Preminger's film of *Carmen Jones*.

16. The film was *Moonstruck*. The recording was the Decca/London version with Tebaldi and Bergonzi.

17. The film was *La Traviata* in the 1982 Zeffirelli film. Plácido Domingo sang Alfredo and Cornell MacNeil sang Germont. James Levine conducted.

18. Joseph Losey directed. Zerlina was sung by Teresa Berganza.

19. The film was *Carmen*. Lorin Maazel conducted.

20. The film was *Meeting Venus*. Kiri Te Kanawa dubbed the music for Glenn Close.

138. OPERA ON TV

1. The National Broadcasting Company created the NBC Opera Company.
2. The opera was Gounod's *Faust*, which they broadcast from Japan (Tokyo) and the United States (Chicago).
3. On *The Ed Sullivan Show*, Callas made her U.S. television debut singing a very truncated version of the second half of Act II of *Tosca*. George London sang Scarpia, while Dimitri Mitropoulos conducted.
4. The debut took place at the Paris Opéra. La Callas began with a concert that included "Casta Diva" from *Norma*, "Una voce poco fa" from *Il Barbiere di Siviglia*, and "D'amor sull'ali rosee" followed by the "Miserere" from *Il Trovatore*. After an intermission, the second act of *Tosca* was presented, fully staged, with Albert Lance as Mario and Tito Gobbi as Scarpia. Georges Sebastian conducted.
5. Renata Scotto had to contend with unruly detractors while singing the title role in Verdi's *Luisa Miller* "live" from the Met.
6. Judith Blegen and Kathleen Battle; Katia Ricciarelli and Aprile Millo.
7. a. Simionato was heard as Santuzza in *Cavalleria Rusticana* and Amneris in *Aida*.
   b. Del Monaco was seen in the title roles of *Otello* and *Andrea Chénier*, and as Radames in *Aida* and Canio in *Pagliacci*.
   c. Gobbi sang Iago in *Otello*.
   d. Tebaldi was seen in the title role in *Tosca* and as Maddalena in *Andrea Chénier*.
   e. Tucci was heard in the title role in *Aida*, Nedda in *Pagliacci*, and Desdemona in *Otello*.
   f. Protti appeared as Amonasro in *Aida*, Gérard in *Andrea Chénier*, and Tonio in *Pagliacci*.
8. *Manon, Il Barbiere di Siviglia*, and *Il Turco in Italia*.
9. Ludmila Filatova.
10. The program was *The Voice of Firestone*. Each broadcast

opened with the guest singer performing "If I Could Tell You" and closed with his/her rendition of "In My Garden." These songs were composed by Idabelle Firestone, a musically inclined member of the family of the tire magnate whose company sponsored the broadcasts.

11. The opera was Puccini's *La Bohème*, reset in the Paris of the 1950s (the Latin Quarter was a "vision" in neon!). The star tenor was David Hobson.

12. James McCracken walked out on the Met after plans to telecast him in the title roles of *Otello* and *Tannhäuser* were scuttled.

13. The prima donna was Leontyne Price. Her farewell performance was as Aida.

139. RECORD COLLECTORS II

1. Maria Huder.

2. Among Cossotto's supporting roles recorded early in her career were Suzuki in *Madama Butterfly* for London/Decca, Bersi in *Andrea Chénier* for EMI, Teresa in *La Sonnambula* for EMI, and the Madrigal Singer in *Manon Lescaut* for EMI.

3. Serafin agreed to conduct *La Traviata* at La Scala for an EMI recording. Callas was the announced Violetta, but owing to a five-year wait-clause in her recording contract with Cetra (with whom she had done a *La Traviata* less than five years earlier), she was unable to record the work with Serafin, Giuseppe di Stefano, and Tito Gobbi. The angry, disappointed Callas was replaced on the EMI set by Antonietta Stella, and she regarded Serafin's continued participation in the project as a personal affront. Although the diva and the aged maestro eventually resumed their friendship, Callas refused to work with Serafin for more than a year after the *Traviata* affair.

4. Gobbi recorded *Il Tabarro* with soprano Margaret Mas and tenor Giacinto Prandelli. The conductor of this still-available EMI performance was Vincenzo Bellezza.

5. Carreras's first *Tosca*, released in 1977, boasts Montserrat Ca-

ballé in the title role and Ingvar Wixell as Scarpia. Sir Colin Davis conducts this Philips recording. Carreras's second *Tosca*, released in 1980, features Katia Ricciarelli as Tosca and Ruggero Raimondi as Scarpia. Herbert von Karajan conducts this Deutsche Grammophon set. His third recording, for Sony, offers Eva Marton in the title role, and Juan Pons sings Scarpia. The conductor is Michael Tilson Thomas.

6. The three operas the Met recorded for RCA are: Samuel Barber's *Vanessa*, with the "original cast": Eleanor Steber, Rosalind Elias, Giorgio Tozzi, Nicolai Gedda, and Regina Resnik, conducted by Dimitri Mitropoulos; Rossini's *Il Barbiere di Siviglia* with Roberta Peters, Robert Merrill, Cesare Valletti, Giorgio Tozzi, and Fernando Corena, conducted by Erich Leinsdorf; and Verdi's *Macbeth*, with Leonard Warren, Leonie Rysanek, Carlo Bergonzi, and Jerome Hines, conducted by Erich Leinsdorf.

7. Stella recorded Verdi's *Un Ballo in Maschera*, *Il Trovatore*, and *Don Carlo* for Deutsche Grammophon. She was the first soprano to record the Fontainebleau Scene of the latter opera. The tenors were Gianni Poggi, Carlo Bergonzi, and Flaviano Labó, respectively.

8. Corena's non-buffo roles included Schaunard in *La Bohème*, Geronte in *Manon Lescaut*, and the King of Egypt in *Aida*.

9. The 1970 Bolshoi *Eugene Onegin* released in the West by EMI posed difficulties to the Soviet authorities after its soprano and conductor, Galina Vishnevskaya and Mstislav Rostropovich, defected to the West and were stripped of their Soviet citizenship. Although the couple still lives in America, the post-Soviet Russian government restored their Russian citizenship, and the pair have returned to their homeland for visits.

10. Callas's only non-Italian opera set is the 1964 EMI *Carmen*, sung in French, with Nicolai Gedda and Robert Massard, conducted by Georges Prêtre. Recordings of live performances of Callas singing in such non-Italian operas as *Parsifal* and *Alceste* (both sung in Italian) also exist.

11. Spanish tenor José Soler sang Chénier opposite Tebaldi on her first *Andrea Chénier* set, released by Cetra.

12. Warren and Vinay recorded the Recognition Scene from *Simon Boccanegra*, an opera they sang at the Met in 1949.

13. Nelli, of course, was a favorite of Arturo Toscanini's. She broadcast and recorded the *Requiem, Otello, Falstaff, Aida*, and *Un Ballo in Maschera* with him.

14. On the Decca/London *Ring*, Hans Hotter is Nilsson's Wotan, and Wolfgang Windgassen is her Siegfried. On the Philips *Ring*, the soprano is flanked by Theo Adam as Wotan and, once again, Windgassen as Siegfried.

15. Metella in *La Vie Parisienne* (EMI), and the title roles in *La Périchole* (Erato) and *La Grande-Duchesse de Gérolstein* (CBS).

16. Alberto Erede conducted all six.

17. Simionato's early Countess di Coigny was sung in the company of Beniamino Gigli (Chénier), Maria Caniglia (Maddalena), and Gino Bechi (Gérard). Oliviero de Fabritiis conducted.

18. Pavarotti's debut recording was Bellini's *Beatrice di Tenda* in which he received third billing after Joan Sutherland and Josephine Veasey.

19. Eugenio Fernandi sang Calaf to Callas's Turandot.

20. Price replaced the ailing Leonie Rysanek in the *Aida* set, now available on the Decca/London label.

21. Karen Huffstadt. She replaced Teresa Stratas. The recording is sung in French.

22. *Eugene Onegin*, on the EMI label.

23. The opera was *Pagliacci*. McCracken refused to record the opera's final lines until the argument was settled. He dubbed those lines into the otherwise completed recording more than a year after the rest of the set was finished.

24. Nicholas Harnoncourt.

25. They were recording *Aida* in 1960, a joint project for RCA and Decca/London.

26. The love duet from the first act of *Tosca*.

27. The EMI *Turandot* made at La Scala boasts Callas in the title role and Schwarzkopf as Liù.

28. Christa Ludwig (Carmen), Rudolf Schock (Don José), and Hermann Prey (Escamillo). Horst Stein conducts.

29. a. Luciano Pavarotti
     b. Plácido Domingo
     c. José Carreras
     d. Nicolai Gedda
     e. Anton Dermota
30. The role was Amneris in *Aida* under Jonel Perlea's baton for
    RCA, and under Herbert von Karajan's direction for EMI.

140. OLD VIENNA

1. Paris.
2. Saffi, although reared by Gypsies, is really an Austro-Hungarian
   princess.
3. Emmerich Kálmán.
4. China.
5. Camille de Rossillon.
6. Baron Mirko Zeta.
7. *Die Fledermaus.*
8. The Vienna Volksoper is the chief theater for operetta in the
   world today; and also presents "grand" opera in German.
9. Hanna's celebrated number is the "Vilia-Lied."
10. a. Orlofsky is the bored Russian prince who hosts the ball in
        Act II of Johann Strauss's *Die Fledermaus.*
     b. Mi is the prince's lovesick younger sister in Lehár's *The
        Land of Smiles.*
     c. Giuditta is the siren heroine in Lehár's *Giuditta.*
     d. Barinkay is the tenor hero of Johann Strauss's *Der
        Zigeunerbaron.*
     e. These three girls are dancers of whom Danilo is enamored
        in Lehár's *The Merry Widow.*
     f. Frosch is the comic jailer in *Die Fledermaus,* a speaking
        part.
     g. Wittenburg is Maritza's love interest in Emmerich Kál-
        mán's *Countess Maritza.*
     h. Sonja is the love interest in Lehár's *The Czarevitch.*
     i. Gabrielle is the leading lady in Strauss's *Wiener Blut.*

j. Bella Giretti is the opera singer whom Paganini admires in Lehár's *Paganini*.

11. Danilo is an habitué of Maxim's.

12. *Wiener Blut* is a pastiche of Strauss's music.

13. Robert Stolz.

14. The six "Champagne Operettas" were: *Die Fledermaus, The Merry Widow, The Gypsy Baron, A Night in Venice, Wiener Blut*, and *The Land of Smiles*. All were vehicles for Elisabeth Schwarzkopf and Nicolai Gedda.

15. c. Saffi.

16. Lisa decides to return home after her husband, Prince Sou Chong, informs her that, although he loves only her (in "Dein ist mein ganzes Herz"), he is forced by Chinese law to marry three other wives.

17. Chevalier played Danilo in the 1930s version of *The Merry Widow* made by MGM.

18. *Die Fledermaus.*

19. Dame Joan Sutherland.

20. Three Broadway shows that are often performed at the Volksoper are *My Fair Lady, Kiss Me Kate*, and *Show Boat.*

21. *The Land of Smiles* was composed for Richard Tauber.

22. Tebaldi sang "Vilia"; Nilsson sang "I Could Have Danced All Night"; Bjoerling sang "Dein ist mein ganzes Herz"; Price sang "Summertime"; Welitsch offered "Vienna, My City of Dreams"; and Simionato and Bastianini teamed up for a hilarious rendition of "Anything You Can Do" from *Annie, Get Your Gun.*

23. Ljuba Welitsch.

24. Niccolo Paganini.

25. Kálmán was born in Hungary. He was forced to flee to the United States by the Nazis.

26. Maria Jeritza at a special "Gala."

141. THEY HAD SOME SONGS TO SING, O

1. The work that required a curtain-raiser was Offenbach's *La Périchole*, and the G & S work that filled the bill was *Trial by Jury*.

2. D'Oyly Carte was the theatrical producer who brought G & S together and organized the D'Oyly Carte Opera Company in London that performed their operas continuously until 1982, when financial pressure forced it out of business, although it was revitalized several years later.

3. a. *H.M.S. Pinafore.* Dick is the comic villain. He informs Captain Corcoran of the impending elopement of Ralph and Josephine.

   b. *Ruddigore.* Rose is the young girl who loves the shy Robin.

   c. *The Yeomen of the Guard.* Fairfax is the dashing young prisoner in the Tower of London whose escape is arranged by means of a "sham" marriage to Elsie, with bittersweet results.

   d. *The Gondoliers.* Luiz is the humble youth who turns out to be the heir to a much disputed throne.

   e. *The Sorcerer.* Wells is the title character.

   f. *The Yeomen of the Guard.* Jack Point is the single tragic figure in G & S lore. He is the itinerant jester who loses his partner and lady-love to Colonel Fairfax.

   g. *H.M.S. Pinafore.* Hebe is the meddlesome but good-hearted relative of Sir Joseph Porter, K.C.B., who, when the plot is sorted out, marries that august gentleman.

   h. *Trial by Jury.* Angelina is the plaintiff, who sues the defendant for breach of promise.

   i. *Iolanthe.* Strephon is the half-mortal, half-fairy (a source of amusement in the United States) son of the fey Iolanthe and the pompous Lord Chancellor.

   j. *Princess Ida.* Hilarion is Ida's long-suffering fiancé.

   k. *Ruddigore.* Mad Margaret is one of the mildly balmy characters who appear in this slightly supernatural libretto.

   l. *The Mikado.* Peep-bo is the least important of the "three little maids from school."

   m. *Iolanthe.* When we first meet him, the Lord Chancellor is smitten with Phyllis. Later on, it turns out that his first love was the long-vanished Iolanthe, Phyllis's new mother-in-law.

   n. *H.M.S. Pinafore.* Josephine is Captain Corcoran's

daughter, loved by Sir Joseph but in love with 'umble Ralph Rackstraw.

o. *The Pirates of Penzance.* Ruth is the "piratical maid of all work" and nanny to Frederick, the reluctant pirate.

4. Mrs. Cripps.

5. Captain Shaw was the chief of London's fire department at the time *Iolanthe* was written. He was a handsome, popular figure. The reference to him is made in the Queen of the Fairies' song, "Oh foolish fay," in which she warns her fairies—who may not marry mortals under pain of death— that Captain Shaw will not put out the fires in their hearts should they fall in love.

6. Richard D'Oyly Carte built the Savoy Theatre.

7. Gilbert loved to satirize *Il Trovatore,* in which Gypsy Azucena mixes up two children, as do Buttercup in *H.M.S. Pinafore* and Inez in *The Gondoliers.*

8. Sullivan's other works include the opera *Ivanhoe,* the hymn "Onward, Christian Soldiers," and the song "The Lost Chord."

9. Victoria was insulted by Gilbert's sly use, in *The Pirates of Penzance,* of the command "Surrender in Queen Victoria's name," to which the pirates reply, "With all *our* faults we love our Queen." Edward VII knighted Gilbert.

10. *The Pirates of Penzance* had its official premiere in the United States, but the night before that performance took place, a touring company of *H.M.S. Pinafore* hastily ran through *Pirates* in England to protect its British copyright.

11. *The Yeomen of the Guard* opens not with a chorus but with Phoebe's doleful spinning song, "When maiden loves."

12. *Princess Ida.*

13. The last two G & S operas are *Utopia Limited* and *The Grand Duke.*

14. John Reed.

15. a. The chorus of Yum-Yum's friends in *The Mikado.*
   b. Josephine in *H.M.S. Pinafore.*
   c. Sir Joseph, Captain Corcoran, and Josephine in *H.M.S. Pinafore.*

    d. The Lord Chancellor in *Iolanthe*.

    e. Grosvenor in *Patience*.

    f. Ruth in *The Pirates of Penzance*.

    g. The Defendant in *Trial by Jury*.

    h. The Grand Inquisitor in *The Gondoliers*.

    i. Robin and Rose in *Ruddigore*.

    j. Patience in *Patience*.

16. Martyn Green played in the Hollywood attempt at *The Mikado*.

17. Archibald Grosvenor in *Patience* seems to have been modeled on Wilde.

18. a. *The Lass That Loved a Sailor*

    b. *The Slave of Duty*

    c. *The Peer and the Peri*

    d. *The Town of Titipu*

19. *The Mikado*.

20. Iolanthe. Iolanthe, a fairy, has married a mortal man. Ordinarily, the punishment for this injudicious act is death, but the Queen of the Fairies commuted poor Iolanthe's sentence to a lifetime of penal servitude. For reasons best explained by the libretto itself, Iolanthe chooses a pond, in that odd position.

21. According to playbills from D'Oyly Carte performances of *The Mikado*, *toko* was nineteenth-century London schoolboy slang for punishment. Deprivation of something sweet, for instance a yam, would, therefore, be a punishment for minor misbehavior. It is an odd reference, since, as all those who have read *Tom Brown's School Days* know, disciplining British schoolboys rarely involved depriving them of yams!

22. In the ensemble "Farewell, my love," sung as Ralph is being led to the brig, the others comment that "He'll hear no word from the maiden he loves so well/ No telephone communicates with his cell."

142. SHAKESPEARE SUNG

1. The play is *Romeo and Juliet.* The opera is Gounod's *Roméo et Juliette.*
2. Elements of *Henry IV, Part 1* were combined with the plot and characters of *The Merry Wives of Windsor* by Verdi and his librettist Boito, and the result was *Falstaff.*
3. *Macbeth* by Shakespeare became *Macbeth* (a.k.a. *Macbetto*) by Verdi.
4. The play? *Much Ado About Nothing.* The opera? Hector Berlioz's *Béatrice et Bénédict.*
5. *The Merry Wives of Windsor* inspired Verdi's *Falstaff* in part (see Question #2) and was also the model for Nicolai's *Die Lustigen Weibern von Windsor,* now rarely performed but, in its day, a major work.
6. *A Midsummer Night's Dream.* Benjamin Britten composed an opera based on it, by the same name.
7. Ambroise Thomas's *Hamlet* leaves the Sweet Prince alive, if somewhat bewildered, at the end of the performance.
8. William Walton composed an opera taken from *Troilus and Cressida,* keeping the original title.
9. *Othello.* Both became *Otello* in the operas by Rossini and Verdi.
10. The play was *King Lear.* Verdi's opera would probably have been called *Re Lear.* Reimann's work is called *Lear.*
11. Play and opera are known as *Antony and Cleopatra.* Catherine Malfitano sang the role of Cleopatra at the Chicago Lyric Opera.
12. Richard Wagner's second opera, *Das Liebesverbot,* was based on *Measure for Measure.*

143. OPERAS SET IN PARIS

1. *La Bohème* (either Puccini's or Leoncavallo's).
2. Corigliano and Hoffman's *The Ghosts of Versailles.*

3. Massenet's *Manon.*
4. Puccini's *Il Tabarro.*
5. Poulenc's *La Voix Humaine*, with text adapted from Cocteau's play.
6. Cilea's *Adriana Lecouvreur.*
7. Verdi's *La Traviata.*
8. Mascagni's *Lodoletta.*
9. Puccini's *La Rondine.*
10. Giordano's *Andrea Chénier.*
11. The opera is Gustave Charpentier's *Louise.* The aria is "Depuis le jour."
12. Gustave Charpentier's *Julien* is the sequel to his rather more successful *Louise.*

144. OPERA FOR THE BIRDS

1. In *Siegfried*, once Siegfried has tasted the blood of the dragon (né Fafner) that he has slain, he can understand the words of the Forest Bird, who warns the youth that Mime intends to murder him, and tells him about the sleeping Brünnhilde.
2. In *Der Freischütz*, it is huntsman Max's run of bad luck as a hunter of game birds that leads him to strike his silly deal with the Devil for magic bullets.
3. Lohengrin, in Wagner's opera, is often called the Swan Knight, as his transportation consists of a boat drawn by a swan. At the end of the opera, when the swan is miraculously transformed back into Gottfried, Elsa's younger brother and the rightful Duke of Brabant, Lohengrin's boat is powered by a rather surprisingly strong dove.
4. Parsifal, in Wagner's opera, is first noticed by the Grail Knights when he shoots one of their lovely swans. Hours later, the opera ends when Parsifal, grown wise and compassionate, returns Amfortas's spear to the Knights, and a dove miraculously appears to signify God's love and forgiveness.
5. In *Götterdämmerung*, two ravens fly ominously across the sky

in the instant before the treacherous Hagen slays Siegfried with his spear.

6. In *Pagliacci*, Nedda wistfully watches a flock of birds in the sky as she sings her aria "Stridono lassù" and, trapped in her unhappy marriage to Canio, envies them for their freedom. Later in the opera, during the doomed "Commedia," Nedda, as Colombina, fusses over another kind of bird, a roast chicken that she has prepared for Arlecchino.

7. In *Les Contes d'Hoffmann*, the suffering Antonia is first heard singing a song about a turtledove that has flown away.

8. In *Gianni Schicchi*, the clever lawyer Schicchi sends his daughter off to feed the birds as he plots his impersonation of the recently deceased Buosi Donati with the greedy relatives of the dead man.

9. Magda, the heroine, is nicknamed by her poet friend Prunier "La Rondine" (the swallow) because, although she tries to leave her luxurious nest for a stab at "true love" with the young Ruggero, Prunier is certain that she'll someday return to her demimondaine lifestyle.

10. In *Frau*, the Emperor's mascot falcon is injured by her master after she attacks the Empress, who has transformed herself into a gazelle. The falcon remains staunch and true to the Emperor all the same. The Emperor searches for the bird shortly before he is temporarily turned to stone by his father-in-law, the god Keikobad.

11. In the "Habanera," Carmen eloquently compares love to a wild bird that has never been subjected to human law.

12. In *Die Zauberflöte*, the charming Papageno is a bird-catcher, and is invariably costumed with feathers as he searches for his soul and nest mate, Papagena.

13. In *Porgy and Bess*, a buzzard flying low over Catfish Row is a harbinger of the trouble that will soon overtake the leading characters. The frightened Porgy sings the haunting "Buzzard Song" here.

14. In *Madama Butterfly*, the heroine embarrasses the American Consul Sharpless when he comes to inform her that Pinkerton has remarried while in America. Butterfly naively asks him if

robins nest more or less frequently in America than in Japan. Pinkerton, it develops, has promised his Japanese bride that he will return to her when the robins nest. Sharpless has no satisfactory answer for her, but Butterfly learns a new word: *ornithologia.*

15. In *Salome*, the craven Herod, desperate to avoid killing Jokanaan (John the Baptist) after his stepdaughter Salome demands his head as reward for having danced for Herod, offers Salome his collection of peacocks. Salome, as we all know, demurs.

145. WOMEN'S WORLD

1. Countess Clara Maffei.
2. Thea Musgrave.
3. Geraldine Souvaine.
4. Judith Somogi.
5. Cosima Wagner. She was the illegitimate daughter of Franz Liszt and the wife of Richard Wagner.
6. The Opera Company of Boston.
7. Carol Fox, head of the Chicago Lyric from 1954 through 1981, was the force behind Callas's American debut in 1955.
8. Eve Queler, founder of the Opera Orchestra of New York.
9. Margherita Wallman.
10. Mrs. August Belmont, known on the stage as Eleanor Robson.
11. Winifred Wagner was the wife of Wagner's son Siegfried. She was stripped of control over the Bayreuth Festival because of her ardent support of Hitler. Frau Wagner was born in Great Britain.
12. Claudia Cassidy of the Chicago *Tribune*.
13. Pauline de Ahna, wife of Richard Strauss. The opera is *Intermezzo*.
14. Giuseppina Strepponi.
15. Doria Manfredi.
16. Margaret Webster.
17. Alberta Maisiello.

146. OPERAS SET IN ITALY

1. Wagner's *Rienzi*.
2. Puccini's *Gianni Schicchi*—the city is Florence.
3. Britten's *Death in Venice*.
4. Puccini's *Tosca*. The first Tosca was Haridea Dardée.
5. *Così Fan Tutte*.
6. Johann Strauss's *Eine Nacht in Venedig*.
7. Zandonai's *Francesca da Rimini*. Note: Rachmaninoff composed an opera on the same subject.
8. *Simon Boccanegra*.
9. The subject was Nero, the operas each called *Nerone*, composed by Boito and Mascagni.
10. Mantua became the subject of Verdi's *Rigoletto*, for reasons discussed in the *Rigoletto* quiz. The opera was supposed to have been set in France, before the censors intervened.
11. Ponchielli's *La Gioconda*.
12. Gounod's *Roméo et Juliette*.
13. Leoncavallo's *Pagliacci*.
14. The "Siciliana" comes from Mascagni's *Cavalleria Rusticana*.
15. Donizetti's *Lucrezia Borgia*.
16. Refice's *Cecilia*, composed for the incomparable Claudia Muzio.

147. OFF THE BEATEN PATH

1. The best-known opera to have come out of Poland is Stanislaw Moniuszko's *Halka*.
2. Matti Salminen.
3. Milanov was born Zinka Kunc (pronounced *Kuntz*).
4. Soprano Gabriella Tucci, tenor Nicolai Gedda, and bass Jerome Hines sang the final trio from Gounod's *Faust*.
5. *One Night of Love* was a vehicle for Grace Moore.
6. Renata Scotto's feud with Pavarotti exploded into the public eye during an April 1980 documentary film that combined

behind-the-scenes moments with excerpts from a San Francisco Opera revival of *La Gioconda*, which was shown on PBS television throughout the United States.

7. Soprano Helen Traubel was the star of Rodgers and Hammerstein's unsuccessful musical, *Pipe Dream*, which opened on Broadway in October 1955.

8. Ponchielli's *La Gioconda*, the second opera to be performed at the first Metropolitan Opera House, was a seven-year-old newcomer to America when the Met opened in 1883. By September 1966, however, *La Gioconda*, which was heard at the Met's second night at Lincoln Center, was familiar enough to be considered the first "bread and butter" opera to be presented by the Met in its new theater.

9. Miss Martin performed an excruciatingly funny version of "Un bel dì." The performance survives on the DRG label and is highly recommended.

10. Pinza's TV show about a music-loving widower with a houseful of children was called *Bonino*.

11. Callas's nemesis was Richard "Eddie" Bagarozy, who claimed to have been engaged by Callas in 1947 to act as her manager.

12. Nellie Melba, Marjorie Lawrence, and Joan Sutherland.

13. Massenet's *Werther*, which failed to interest Paris impresarios, had its first performance in Vienna in a German translation.

14. Elisabeth Schwarzkopf, beginning her career as a chorister in Berlin, is heard on that famous recording conducted by Sir Thomas Beecham.

15. Arrigo Boito, composer of *Mefistofele* and *Nerone*, provided for Verdi the libretti of the revised *Simon Boccanegra*, and the composer's two final masterpieces, *Otello* and *Falstaff*. Under the alias Tobia Gorrio, Boito created the luridly endearing text for Ponchielli's *La Gioconda*. Gian Carlo Menotti, composer of *Amahl and the Night Visitors* and *The Consul*, provided his long-time friend Samuel Barber with the libretto for *Vanessa*.

16. The following gentlemen (plus Puccini) all had a hand in the *Manon Lescaut* libretto: Luigi Illica, Giuseppe Giacosa, Giulio Ricordi, Ruggiero Leoncavallo, Domenico Oliva, and Marco Praga.

17. Rosa Ponselle.
18. Poulenc's *Dialogues des Carmélites* was adapted from a film of that name.
19. Francesco Cilea, of *Adriana Lecouvreur* fame, wheedled Olivero into agreeing to sing Cilea's best-known work after a decade's absence from performing. Unfortunately, the composer died shortly before Olivero reactivated her career.
20. Umberto Giordano, composer of *Andrea Chénier* and *Fedora*.
21. Fittingly, the opera performed at the Vienna State Opera hours before its near-destruction was Wagner's *Götterdämmerung*.
22. Robinson was the author of *Caruso: His Life in Pictures* and *Celebration*, a pictorial history of the Metropolitan Opera.
23. Flotow's *Martha* is best remembered for the tenor aria immortalized by Caruso in its Italian version, "M'apparì." The soprano aria, based on the folk ballad "The Last Rose of Summer," was for many years a favorite encore item on soprano recital programs.
24. The Jockey Club ruled the opera, as well as the race track, in Paris. It was this club that stipulated that all operas performed at the Paris Opéra have a ballet.
25. Ticker, Perlmutter, and Angelovich are better known under their stage names: Richard Tucker, Jan Peerce, and Gianna d'Angelo.
26. Kirsten was the protégée of another blond American beauty —Grace Moore.
27. Siepi appeared in *Bravo, Giovanni* in 1962 and *Carmelina* in 1979. In both ill-fated musicals, Siepi played restaurant owners.
28. Nellie Melba and Luisa Tetrazzini had culinary treats named for them. For Melba, there was the peach, raspberry, and ice cream dessert, Peaches Melba. For the portly Tetrazzini, a casserole of pollo and pasta, Chicken Tetrazzini, was created.
29. Ezio Pinza was arrested and imprisoned for several weeks after another Met bass told the police that Pinza was a fascist spy. Pinza was completely exonerated.
30. Bass-baritone George London was the first American to sing

at the Bolshoi. His debut role was the title character in Mussorgsky's *Boris Godunov*.

31. Nicolai Rimsky-Korsakov and Dimitri Shostakovich each orchestrated *Boris Godunov*. Both editions are occasionally used to this day, although Mussorgsky's own orchestration has now been adopted by many opera companies.

32. Baritone John Shirley-Quirk, of the Royal Opera, Covent Garden, was the ubiquitous character who pursued the opera's protagonist through plague-ridden Venice in seven guises.

33. Sybil Seligman.

34. In the Philips *La Traviata* that boasts Kiri Te Kanawa in the title role, tenor Alfredo Kraus, who sings the callow Alfredo Germont, could easily be the father of baritone Dmitri Hvorostovsky, who portrays Papa Germont.

35. Nellie Melba had her own railroad car in those glorious, pre-airplane days.

148. DON'T BELIEVE EVERYTHING YOU READ I

1. False. *Carmen* was Bizet's last opera. The composer died three months after the first performance.

2. True.

3. True.

4. True.

5. False. Azucena informs the count that her supposed son Manrico was the count's long-lost brother.

6. False. Callas's first American success was because of the recordings of *I Puritani*, *Lucia di Lammermoor*, and *Tosca* that she had made in Europe. Callas starred in a nonoperatic film version of *Medea* in 1970.

7. True. (The "Honor Monologue" was taken from *Henry IV, Part 1*.)

8. False. Butterfly's father has been dead for years before the action of Puccini's opera begins. It is her uncle who is a Buddhist priest, and who curses her.

9. False. It was Montserrat Caballé who was very impressed by

Carreras when he sang the role of Flavio to her *Norma* in Bellini's opera at the Teatro Liceo in Barcelona in 1970.

10. False. Leoni, composer of *L'Oracolo,* never turned his affections toward Manon. Daniel Auber was the other composer of a *Manon Lescaut* opera.

11. True.

12. False. Pinza and Merman never worked together. Pinza's Broadway costar in *South Pacific* was Mary Martin.

13. True.

14. False. It was Arturo Toscanini.

15. True.

16. False. Siegfried marries Gutrune while in an altered state of consciousness. Sieglinde, who dies in between *Die Walküre* and *Siegfried,* is the hero's mother.

17. False. Gigli died at home, in bed, on November 30, 1957. Leonard Warren died onstage during a Met *La Forza del Destino* on March 4, 1960.

18. False. In the Rossini opera, there is no wicked stepmother at all, only a foolish, but not terribly wicked, stepfather, Don Magnifico. Giselda is the heroine of Verdi's *I Lombardi.*

19. True.

20. True.

21. False. The Molière play in question is *Le Bourgeois Gentilhomme.*

22. True.

23. False. Although Sills did succeed Rudel at the New York City Opera, she has been married to Peter Greenough since 1956.

24. False. Toscanini conducted.

25. False. Schmidt actually was less than five feet tall.

26. True.

27. False. Violetta gives Alfredo a locket with a portrait of herself inside, and tells him to give it to his future bride.

28. True.

29. False. Callas never sang Adina, but did sing and record Fiorilla in Rossini's *Il Turco in Italia,* as well as Rosina in the same composer's *Il Barbiere di Siviglia.*

30. True.

149. OPERATIC SCAVENGER HUNT

1. Mimì in *La Bohème* (Puccini and Leoncavallo) and Violetta in *La Traviata*.
2. The *Il Trovatore* Leonora and La Gioconda kill themselves rather than surrender to those creepy baritones, Count di Luna and Barnaba, respectively. Tosca has a much better idea—she simply murders the baritone, Scarpia!
3. Mignon, in Ambroise Thomas's opera of that name, is a "good," wholesome Gypsy.
4. Italian tenor wife-killers include *Pagliacci*'s Canio, who does in the adulterous Nedda; Otello in both Verdi's and Rossini's operas; and in *Luisa Miller*, Rodolfo kills his betrothed, Luisa, under the mistaken impression that she has been unfaithful.
5. Amina in *La Sonnambula* and Elvira in *I Puritani* each have mad scenes (Amina's is a dreamy sleepwalking sequence) but recover their mental capacities when their men return to them.
6. Three operatic fathers who are directly responsible for the deaths of their children would include the Cardinal in Halévy's *La Juive*, who orders Rachel's execution not knowing that she is actually his own, illegitimate daughter; Rigoletto, who sets in motion the plot to assassinate the Duke of Mantua, which his daughter aborts by taking the Duke's place; and Archibaldo in *L'Amore dei Tre Re*, who sets a trap for his daughter-in-law's lover, and catches his own son, Manfredo, as well.
7. Many villains don't get away. Don Pizarro in *Fidelio* is denounced by Rocco, Florestan, and Leonore and is subsequently arrested by Don Fernando; Monostatos and the Queen of the Night in *Die Zauberflöte* are crushed by the powers of good embodied by Sarastro; the Nurse in *Die Frau ohne Schatten* is condemned by the very god she serves, Keikobad; Telramund in *Lohengrin*, influenced by his evil wife, Ortrud, is slain by Lohengrin when he attempts to attack the Swan Knight; Macbeth, another character influenced by a nasty spouse who pushes him to regicide and other murders, is killed by Macduff; in *Don Giovanni*, that original "anti-hero" is dis-

patched to hell by the Commendatore's animated statue; and Normanno, who has encouraged Ashton in his plots to thwart the love of Lucia di Lammermoor and Edgardo, is publicly denounced by Raimondo after Lucia has gone mad and killed her husband. Iago's guilt is established at the end of *Otello*, and he runs out of the Moor's bedchamber, chased by members of the chorus. One assumes that he will be caught. There are undoubtedly other possibilities, too.

8. Three operas that include scenes at masked balls are Verdi's *I Vespri Siciliani*, Ponchielli's *La Gioconda*, and Rossini's *Il Turco in Italia*.

9. Two German operas based on Shakespearean dramas are Wagner's *Das Liebesverbot*, based on *Measure for Measure*, and Nicolai's *Die Lustigen Weiber von Windsor*, based on *The Merry Wives of Windsor*. Reimann's *Lear* is also based on Shakespeare—*King Lear*.

10. Thomas Pasatieri's *The Seagull*.

11. Turiddu, in Mascagni's *Cavalleria Rusticana*, loses his life in a fight with Alfio shortly after leading the Easter celebrants in "Viva il vino spumeggiante." John of Leyden leads his guests in a drinking song in the final scene of Meyerbeer's *Le Prophète*, shortly before his castle is blown up on his own orders.

12. Operatic characters who are beheaded include Manrico in Verdi's *Il Trovatore*; Donizetti's Roberto Devereux, Maria Stuarda, and Anna Bolena; Andrea Chénier and Maddalena di Coigny in Giordano's opera; Paolo Albiani in Verdi's *Simon Boccanegra*; and almost the entire convent of Carmelite nuns in Poulenc's *Dialogues des Carmélites*.

13. Susanna (married to Figaro) in Mozart's *Le Nozze di Figaro*, and Tatyana (married to Prince Gremin) in Tchaikovsky's *Eugene Onegin* are happily wed.

14. Three operatic fratricides include Di Luna in *Il Trovatore*, Gianciotto in Zandonai's (and, for that matter, Rachmaninoff's) *Francesca da Rimini*, and Count Walter in Verdi's *Luisa Miller*.

15. Three evil high priests include the High Priest of Baal in Verdi's *Nabucco*, Ramfis (not so much evil as reactionary and

rigid, perhaps) in *Aida*, and the High Priest of Dagon in Saint-Saëns's *Samson et Dalila*.

16. Five baritone "good guys" might include Rabbi David in Mascagni's *L'Amico Fritz*; Dr. Malatesta in Donizetti's *Don Pasquale*; Gianni Schicchi in Puccini's comedy; Michonnet in Cilea's *Adriana Lecouvreur*; Marcello in Puccini's *La Bohème*; and, of course, Rossini's Figaro in *Il Barbiere di Siviglia*.

17. Five evil sopranos might include the scheming Abigaille in Verdi's *Nabucco*; the Queen of the Night in Mozart's *Die Zauberflöte*; Verdi's Lady Macbeth; and Ortrud in Wagner's *Lohengrin* (the latter two roles have been shared by sopranos and mezzos). Medea in Cherubini's opera is a wronged wife, but her extreme vengefulness—not to mention the fact that in order to help Jason acquire the golden fleece, she murdered her father and brother—place her in the "naughty" category.

18. Two operatic wives who whack their husbands are Susanna in Mozart's *Le Nozze di Figaro*, who strikes Figaro whenever she thinks he is paying court to such ladies as Marcellina or the Countess Almaviva; and Norina, who, while play-acting the role of "Sofronia" in Donizetti's *Don Pasquale*, smacks her "husband," Pasquale, when he scolds her for her bitchy behavior.

19. Dr. Miracle in Offenbach's *Les Contes d'Hoffmann* kills Antonia with his bizarre spells. The doctor in *Wozzeck* is a quack, too.

20. Operas set in what is now the United States might include Verdi's *Un Ballo in Maschera* (sometimes set in Boston); *The Crucible*, by David Ward (Salem, Massachusetts); Menotti's *Saint of Bleecker Street* (set in New York City); Marc Blitzstein's *Regina* (Alabama); Franco Leoni's *L'Oracolo* (San Francisco's Chinatown); Puccini's *La Fanciulla del West* (California); Weill's *The Rise and Fall of the City of Mahagonny* (the mythical Southwest); Floyd's *Susannah* (Tennessee); Levy's *Mourning Becomes Electra* (New England); Puccini's *Manon Lescaut* (Act IV takes place in Louisiana); and Moore's *The Ballad of Baby Doe* (Colorado and Washington, D.C.).

21. Mascagni's lesser-known operas include *Nerone*, *Il Piccolo Ma-*

rat, Le Maschere, Guglielmo Ratcliff, Lodoletta, Isabeau, Zanetto, and *Iris.*

22. Verdi's *I Vespri Siciliani* (based on *Les Vêpres Siciliennes*); Donizetti's *L'Elisir d'Amore* (based on *Le Philtre*); and Verdi's *Un Ballo in Maschera* (based on *Le Bal Masqué*).
23. Piave wrote the libretti for *La Traviata, Rigoletto,* and *Macbeth.*
24. Lotte Lehmann, Friedrich Schorr, and Elisabeth Schumann.
25. The title character in Janáček's *The Cunning Little Vixen.*
26. Tchaikovsky's *The Queen of Spades* (the Old Countess).
27. *Le Nozze di Figaro* (Cherubino) and *Der Rosenkavalier* (Octavian).

150. DIRECTORS

1. Franco Zeffirelli.
2. Frank Corsaro.
3. Peter Sellars.
4. Harry Kupfer.
5. Wieland and Wolfgang Wagner.
6. Werner Herzog.
7. Colin Graham.
8. Elijah Moshinsky.
9. John Dexter.
10. Peter Hall.
11. Gian Carlo del Monaco.
12. Gian Carlo Menotti.
13. Harold Prince.
14. Herbert von Karajan.
15. Cyril Ritchard.
16. Goeran Gentele. He was replaced for *Carmen* by Bodo Igesz.
17. Otto Schenck.
18. Jean-Pierre Ponnelle.
19. Jonathan Miller.
20. Alfred Lunt.

151. DON'T BELIEVE EVERYTHING YOU READ II

1. False. Verdi's first opera was *Oberto.*
2. False. Rosa Raisa was the first Turandot. Rosina Storchio was the first Butterfly.
3. True. Beethoven composed three overtures for *Leonore,* and then he wrote a fourth for the final revision of the work, which was renamed *Fidelio.*

4. False. Tebaldi never sang *Adriana Lecouvreur* under Toscanini's baton. In 1946, however, she did sing for the great maestro at the gala concert that celebrated the opening of the rebuilt La Scala, which had been heavily damaged during World War II.

5. True.

6. True.

7. True.

8. True.

9. True.

10. False. Marian Anderson was the first black artist to sing at the Metropolitan, on January 7, 1955, in the role of Ulrica in *Un Ballo in Maschera*. Price made her Met debut six years later, as Leonora in *Il Trovatore*.

11. False. Catalani never had anything to do with *La Bohème*. Puccini stole *La Bohème* from Ruggiero Leoncavallo whose own *La Bohème* was first produced two years after Puccini's masterpiece. Although Leoncavallo's opera is quite pleasant, it does not survive comparison with Puccini's indisputable masterpiece.

12. True.

13. False. Da Ponte was a little ahead of Verdi's time. He was the librettist for three of Mozart's greatest operas, *Don Giovanni*, *Le Nozze di Figaro*, and *Così Fan Tutte*. Da Ponte eventually emigrated to New York, where he taught at King's College (now Columbia University). He is buried on Staten Island.

14. True.

15. False. Meneghini was Callas's husband. The head of La Scala then was Antonio Ghiringhelli.

16. False. Puccini's favorite Tosca was Maria Jeritza.

17. False. Phyllis Curtin was the original Susannah, but Treigle was the first Blitch.

18. False. Milanov and Peerce had no feud. Milanov was not fond of her frequent costar Kurt Baum, while Peerce didn't speak to his tenor colleague Richard Tucker, who was Peerce's brother-in-law!

19. True. In fact, Simionato recorded the role of Mamma Lucia with Mascagni himself conducting.

20. False. Donizetti reworked *La Fille du Régiment* to an Italian text, supplying sung recitatives to replace the spoken dialogue of the French version, and adding an aria for Tonio. The Italian version was titled, simply, *La Figlia del Reggimento*.

21. False. Verdi composed *I Masnadieri* for Lind.

22. False. Caruso did indeed sing Johnson at *La Fanciulla del West's* premiere in December 1910. However, this performance took place *not* at Covent Garden, but at the Metropolitan in New York.

23. False, *Stiffelio* became *Aroldo*. *I Lombardi*, with a heavily revised French libretto, was rechristened *Jérusalem*.

24. True.

25. True.

26. False. The "Hymn to the Moon" is sung in Dvořák's *Rusalka*, early in that opera's first act. *Iris* opens with a chorus entitled "Hymn to the Sun."

27. False. Callas's last role, sung in Paris in 1965, was Norma. The final performance of the run was terminated after the third act, as Callas was simply out of voice.

28. True.

29. False. The opera was *Simon Boccanegra*.

30. True.

152. DON'T SING WITH YOUR MOUTH FULL

1. In *La Traviata*, Act II, scene 2, the invitation to dine temporarily cools down the quarrel brewing between Alfredo, whom Violetta has just abandoned (for the noblest reasons, as you will recall) and the Baron Douphol, her former "protector," to whom she has returned.

2. In Act II, scene 5 of *Don Giovanni*, the ghostly statue of the Commendatore, having kept his promise to appear at Don G.'s dinner party, informs his startled host that those who have eaten heavenly victuals have no need for the earthly variety.

3. In Rossini's *L'Italiana in Algeri*, the silly Mustafa stuffs himself while Isabella makes plans to flee with Lindoro, thinking this

is part of an initiation rite into the nonsensical and nonexistent fraternal order "Papataci."

4. In *Hänsel und Gretel,* those naughty children eat up all the berries they have gone into the woods to collect for their family's dinner. After spending the night in the forest, the kids discover that lovely gingerbread cottage belonging to a certain Miss Daintymouth . . .

5. The opera is Barber's *Vanessa.* The title character's niece Erika is observed ordering this four-star meal as the opera begins. Erika ends up dining on the shellfish and poultry with the opportunistic Anatol. To paraphrase Fanny Brice in *Funny Girl,* guess who's gonna be dessert!

6. In Act II of Puccini's *La Bohème,* Mimì dines with Rodolfo and friends at the Café Momus, and orders a dish of ice cream.

7. In the first act of *Les Contes d'Hoffmann,* Hoffmann slips away from Spalanzani's dinner party in order to make time with his host's "daughter," Olympia. Olympia could not care less about food, for she is a mechanical doll.

8. In the "commedia" in *Pagliacci,* Colombina (Nedda) fusses over a chicken dinner for her beau Arlecchino (Beppe) only to be interrupted onstage and in "real life" by Pagliaccio (Canio).

9. In Britten's *Billy Budd,* the seaman Dansker defies the rules and brings the condemned Billy a little something to eat moments before his execution.

10. In *La Forza del Destino's* fourth act, Fra Melitone chafes at his duty of feeding the homeless folks who have gathered at the monastery, and, in a rage, dumps the kettle of soup on the ground, to the disapproval of the Padre Guardiano.

11. In *Amahl and the Night Visitors,* Amahl's poverty-stricken Mother has nothing to serve the three visiting Wise Men who have encamped *chez elle* on their way to Bethlehem. She is helped out by her neighbors, who drop by with hors d'oeuvres.

12. In the first act of Massenet's *Werther,* Charlotte offers dinner to her younger brothers and sisters and then offers her arm to the already lovesick poet Werther.

13. In Puccini's *Suor Angelica,* Sister Genovieffa, who has a weak-

ness for sweets, passes the goodies around to the other nuns.

14. In Act I of *Tosca*, the Sacristan has prepared a lunch basket for the painter Mario Cavaradossi, who donates the food to his friend, Cesare Angelotti, who has escaped from prison and sought refuge in the church where Mario is working. Baron Scarpia discovers the now-empty basket and guesses that Mario has helped Angelotti in his escape.

15. In *Tosca*'s second act, Scarpia makes small talk with the heroine, noting that the torture of Mario has wrecked his concentration on his supper. Between chasing Tosca around and being stabbed to death by that resourceful lady, the poor Baron never gets to find out what's for dessert!

16. At the conclusion of *Falstaff*, Master Ford invites all assembled to dine with Falstaff. But first, they take a moment to sing that incomparable fugue, "Tutto nel mondo è burla!"

17. This comic larceny is performed by Maria in *Porgy and Bess*, during that charming scene in Act II when the local vendors advertise their wares.

18. In *Die Fledermaus*, the tenor Alfred, whose eye is on Rosalinde von Eisenstein, sits down to dinner with that lady in her Viennese home, when the prison warden Frank comes to arrest Eisenstein, and escort him to jail. As the real Eisenstein has already left the premises, Alfred, whom Frank mistakes for his quarry, has little choice but to save Rosalinde's reputation and go off to jail.

153. OUT IN THE COLD

1. All four ladies are leading mezzo-soprano roles in operas by Verdi—*Don Carlo, Nabucco, Aida,* and *Luisa Miller*. Federica, however, is the misfit. The other three ladies are princesses; Federica is only a duchess.

2. One way of looking at this group would be to find that none of these operas, with the exception of *Turandot*, has a role for a leading tenor. However, it might also be noticed that *Das Rheingold* is the only German-language opera of the four.

3. Of the four Bellini operas given, *Norma* is exceptional because it does not have a "mad scene" for its heroine. Technically, the sleepwalking Amina in *La Sonnambula* is not insane. However, her aria "Ah non credea mirarti" is sung during an altered state of consciousness, and therefore, qualifies as a mad scene.

4. Of the four gentlemen in question, Des Grieux is the only tenor character not taken from a play by Victor Hugo.

5. On the one hand, Dalila is the only one of these four mezzo characters who is *not* a Gypsy. However, Preziosilla, a denizen of Verdi's *La Forza del Destino*, is the only Italian-speaking character among her three French colleagues.

6. All four of these characters are murdered. But *Tosca's* Scarpia, Adriana, and Gennaro in Donizetti's *Lucrezia Borgia* are killed by women. Only Luisa is dispatched by a man.

7. Leonora di Vargas, the Spanish heroine of Verdi's *La Forza del Destino*, is the only non-French character listed, even though all are from Italian operas.

8. The Met is the only one of these four great opera houses that is not subsidized by the government of its nation.

9. All four operas are masterpieces by Verdi. Three of them were composed to Italian texts, as one would expect, but *Don Carlo*, commissioned by the Paris Opéra, was first composed and produced in French (as *Don Carlos*). And, of these four works, *Falstaff* is the lone comedy.

10. Of those four noted sopranos, Garden, Moore, and Kirsten share a common artistic heritage, as Garden coached Moore, who coached Kirsten, leaving the talented Munsel out of the foursome. You might also note that Mary Garden is the only Scotswoman among the three American ladies listed here.

11. *Linda, Parisina,* and *Emilia* are relatively obscure operas by Donizetti. *Elisabetta*, however, is a little-known work by Rossini (who reused its overture in *Il Barbiere di Siviglia*).

12. One might note that all of these characters are servants, except Mariandl in *Der Rosenkavalier*, who is a sham servant, really Octavian in disguise. Or it could be said that Mariandl is the only one of the four who does *not* appear in a Mozart opera.

13. *Mitridate* is the only one among these Mozart operas whose libretto was not written by Lorenzo da Ponte.

14. Although each of these artists is (or was) of Greek heritage, Callas alone was born in the United States, although conceived in the "old country."

15. One the one hand, Alfredo Kraus is not one of the so-called "Three Tenors" of Rome and Hollywood fame. On the other hand, Pavarotti is the only one of these four gentlemen born not in Spain, but in Italy.

16. *Vanessa* is the only one of these four excellent American operas to have been produced—indeed, premiered—at the Metropolitan Opera.

17. *Götterdämmerung* is the only one of these four Wagnerian favorites that has no "title character." Also, in *Der Fliegende Holländer*, the tenor character, Erik, is less than a truly leading role.

18. Although Emmy Destinn, Dorothy Kirsten, Barbara Daniels, and Renata Tebaldi all were celebrated as Minnie in *La Fanciulla del West*, Destinn, the first Minnie, did not, of course, sing the role at the new Met, nor is there an available "live" recording of her performance in the role.

19. Although all four divas are American citizens, Ms. Cruz-Romo was born in Mexico.

20. Of this quartet of European-born conductors, Karajan was the only "Aryan" and therefore did not have to flee from the Nazis.

154. RECORD COLLECTORS III

1. *Fidelio* was the first digital-process opera. The 1979 London release is conducted by Sir Georg Solti and features Hildegard Behrens, Peter Hofmann, and Hans Sotin.

2. Cossotto sings Cherubino in the EMI *Le Nozze di Figaro* led by Carlo Maria Giulini, with such artists as Elisabeth Schwarzkopf, Anna Moffo, Rolando Panerai, and Eberhard Wächter.

3. Beverly Sills, Joan Sutherland, Patrice Munsel, Lisa della Casa, and Dorothy Kirsten.

4. Mario Filippeschi.

5. Elisabeth Schwarzkopf.

6. Maria Vitale.

7. Anita Cerquetti completed a magnificent *La Gioconda* for Decca/London (available on CD), led by Gianandrea Gavazzeni and flanked by Mario del Monaco, Cesare Siepi, Ettore Bastianini, and Giulietta Simionato.

8. Renata Tebaldi and Mirella Freni have recorded the three heroines of *Il Trittico*: Giorgetta, Suor Angelica, and Lauretta.

9. Ligabue recorded Alice Ford in *Falstaff* in two complete performances, and one disc of highlights. She sang the role complete for Leonard Bernstein (CBS) and Sir Georg Solti (RCA), now available on Decca/London. The recorded highlights of *Falstaff* was for Decca/London, conducted by Sir Edward Downes.

10. Vickers sang his first recorded Florestan opposite Christa Ludwig's Leonore on the EMI set led by Otto Klemperer. Several years later, Vickers recorded the opera, again for EMI, opposite Helga Dernesch, under Herbert von Karajan's direction.

11. Martina Arroyo replaced the chronically ailing Montserrat Caballé.

12. Anna Moffo sang Musetta for EMI and Mimi for RCA. Lucine Amara, the Musetta on the beloved Beecham recording of *Bohème* currently released by EMI, sings Mimì in an abridged version of *La Bohème* issued by the Metropolitan Opera Record Club in 1957. Renata Scotto, twice a recorded Mimì, may be seen as Musetta in the Bel Canto videotape of her 1982 performance at the Metropolitan Opera.

13. The title role in Strauss's *Arabella*, with Josef Metternick as Mandryka.

14. Moffo sang Musetta in *La Bohème*, Nanetta in *Falstaff*, and Susanna in *Le Nozze di Figaro*. Her tenors were Giuseppe di Stefano in *Bohème* and Luigi Alva in *Falstaff*. There is no leading tenor role in *Nozze*; Moffo was partnered by Rolando Panerai.

15. The Callas recording of Puccini's *Manon Lescaut* was delayed for several years until Callas could be persuaded to approve the set for release. Giuseppe di Stefano was her Des Grieux; Tullio Serafin conducted.
16. John Culshaw.
17. Ljuba Welitsch sings Marianne, Sophie's duenna, on the Von Karajan EMI *Der Rosenkavalier*.
18. *Oberto* and *Alzira* were released in the mid-1980s.
19. Puccini's *La Bohème*.
20. Marilyn Horne sings Mignon on the CBS recording of Thomas's opera.
21. Leo Nucci.
22. *Anna Bolena; Roberto Devereux; Rigoletto; I Vespri Siciliani; Norma; Medea; Caterina Cornaro; Aida; Il Trovatore; Elisabetta, Regina d'Inghilterra.*
23. Teldec.
24. Waltraud Meier is the world's first recorded mezzo Isolde. In a recording released by Teldec in 1995, she is partnered by Siegfried Jerusalem as Tristan, with Daniel Barenboim conducting.
25. Swedish.

155. RECORD COLLECTORS IV

1. Rosina in *Il Barbiere di Siviglia* and the title role in *La Cenerentola.*
2. Alagna and Fabriccini share the leads in Sony's *La Traviata.* Riccardo Muti conducts the performance given at La Scala, Milan.
3. Verdi's *Ernani.*
4. Mirella Freni is the soprano, Plácido Domingo the tenor, and bass Samuel Ramey sings the baritone role of Scarpia. Giuseppe Sinopoli conducts and DG released the set.
5. Malfitano's video *Salome* features Simon Estes as Jokanaan and Leonie Rysanek as Herodias. Daniel Barenboim conducts. On Malfitano's audio *Salome*, issued by London, Bryn Terfel is

heard as Jokanaan and Hannah Schwarz sings Herodias. Christoph von Dohnányi conducts.

6. *Parsifal,* on DG.

7. These would include Mussorgsky's *Khovanschina,* Tchaikovsky's *Pique Dame,* Borodin's *Prince Igor,* and Prokofiev's *The Fiery Angel.*

8. Lauritz Melchior is the Tristan, Kirsten Flagstad is the Isolde, and the two conductors are Sir Thomas Beecham and Fritz Reiner.

9. The opera is *La Traviata,* and the singers are Angela Gheorghiu as Violetta, Frank Lopardo as Alfredo, and Leo Nucci as Germont. The label is Decca/London.

10. *Faust* (EMI), *Rigoletto* (Teldec), and *La Bohème* (Erato).

11. The opera is *Armida,* recorded at the Teatro La Fenice in Venice.

12. Gino Penno.

13. b. Callas never, as far as can be ascertained, sang Micaela's aria from *Carmen.*

14. The opera is *Billy Budd,* and the baritone is Theodor Uppman.

15. The opera is Massenet's *Hérodiade.* The EMI performance, conducted by Michel Plasson, stars Cheryl Studer, Nadine Denize, Ben Heppner, and Thomas Hampson. On Sony, one can enjoy Renée Fleming, Dolora Zajick, Plácido Domingo, and Juan Pons, in a performance conducted by Valery Gergiev.

16. Antonella Banaudi.

17. Nimbus. Ten male singers found on the Prima Voce series would include Enrico Caruso, John McCormack, Giovanni Martinelli, Tito Schipa, Fyodor Chaliapin, Beniamino Gigli, Richard Tauber, Mattia Battistini, Jussi Bjoerling, and Ezio Pinza. Ten female stars would include Geraldine Farrar, Kirsten Flagstad, Adelina Patti, Rosa Ponselle, Conchita Supervia. Amelita Galli-Curci, Claudia Muzio, Frieda Hempel, Nellie Melba, and Lotte Schoën. Nimbus has devoted discs to three opera houses: La Scala, Bolshoi, and Il Liceo (Barcelona).

18. *Visions of Love.*

19. Plácido Domingo and Ruth Ann Swenson.

20. Maria Callas.

21. Naxos.
22. Richard Bonynge is the conductor. Bonynge's wife, the unforgettable Dame Joan Sutherland also sang that repertoire with distinction and may be a little envious.
23. Thomas Hampson is the Onegin, and Dame Kiri Te Kanawa is the Tatyana.
24. Elena Suliotis (a.k.a. Souliotis) is heard as the Zia Principessa in the London-Decca recording of Puccini's *Suor Angelica*. The title role is sung by Mirella Freni.
25. Marilyn Horne is surrounded in this RCA album by Jerry Hadley, Samuel Ramey, Spiro Malas, and Thomas Hampson.
26. In the EMI *Die Fledermaus*, Domingo not only conducts but sings the role of Alfred.
27. Jane Eaglen.
28. *La Belle et la Bête*, released by Teldec.
29. The series is "Entartete Musik," or "Forbidden Music," named to reflect the infamous Nazi ban on these works. Among the operas already released in this series are Krenek's *Jonny Spielt Auf*, Ullman's *Der Kaiser von Atlantis*, Korngold's *Das Wunder der Heliane*, and Korngold's *Die Gezeichneten*.

156. ULTIMATE, ULTIMATE WAGNER

1. There are thirty-four separate vocal parts in the *Ring*, and one choral group.
2. *Ring* characters in order of appearance:

Das Rheingold	Donner	Hunding
Woglinde	Loge	Brünnhilde
Wellgunde	Froh	Gerhilde
Flosshilde	Mime	Helmwige
Alberich	Erda	Schwertleite
Fricka		Ortlinde
Wotan	*Die Walküre*	Waltraute
Freia	(New characters)	Siegrune
Fasolt	Siegmund	Rossweise
Fafner	Sieglinde	Grimgerde

Siegfried	*Götterdämmerung*	Gunther
(New characters)	(New characters)	Hagen
Siegfried	First Norn	Gutrune
Wanderer (actually	Second Norn	The Vassals
Wotan in	Third Norn	
disguise)		
Forest Bird		

157. PHOTO QUIZ

1. On the left is Giuseppe di Stefano; on the right, the author, Kenn Harris. Di Stefano was signing recordings at New York's J and R Music World.

2. Leontyne Price and Franco Corelli are shown taking curtain calls after an *Aida* at the Metropolitan Opera.

3. Maria Spacagna. Her Met debut was in Verdi's *Luisa Miller*.

4. José Carreras is shown as Rodolfo in Puccini's *La Bohème* at the Metropolitan Opera, a few years before his near-fatal bout with leukemia. The production was designed by Franco Zeffirelli.

5. Birgit Nilsson is seen as Elektra in Strauss's opera of that name.

6. Plácido Domingo is shown as Stiffelio, in Verdi's opera of that name.

7. Frederica Von Stade as Mélisande in Debussy's *Pelléas et Mélisande*.

8. Leonard Warren.

9. Soprano Lotte Lehmann is holding a portrait of Arturo Toscanini.

10. Eileen Farrell.

11. Soprano Astrid Varnay is shown with director Wieland Wagner. They worked together at the Bayreuth Festival during the 1950s.

12. Rosalind Elias, like Mansfield something of a publicity hound, is costumed as the Marquise de Berkenfeld in Donizetti's *La Fille du Régiment*.

13. Kathleen Battle is shown as Zdenka in Strauss's *Arabella*.

14. Mirella Freni is seen as Adriana Lecouvreur in Cilea's opera of that name.

15. Shirley Verrett is seen as Dalila in Saint-Saëns's *Samson et Dalila*.

16. Giulietta Simionato. She appears here as Amneris in *Aida*.

17. Vladislav Piavko and Irina Archipova, of Moscow's Bolshoi, are shown as Don José and Carmen in Bizet's opera. These two artists are married to one another.

18. Maria Callas is shown as Tosca in Puccini's opera of that name.

19. Eva Marton is dressed to sing the title role in Puccini's *Manon Lescaut*.

20. Giulietta Simionato.

21. Mario del Monaco is pictured as Otello in Verdi's opera.

22. Fiorenza Cossotto is seen as Santuzza in *Cavalleria Rusticana*.

23. From left: José Carreras, Herbert von Karajan, and Mirella Freni. The three recorded together frequently in the 1980s.

24. Marilyn Horne, seen here in *The Ghosts of Versailles*.

25. Pavarotti sang Oronte in Verdi's *I Lombardi*, which premiered in 1993.

26. Teresa Stratas is seen here as Marenka in *The Bartered Bride*.

27. From left: diva suprema Renata Tebaldi (Met 1955–73), Schuyler G. Chapin, former General Manager of the Met, and New York City Mayor Rudy Giuliani. Mayor Giuliani had proclaimed December 11, 1995, "Renata Tebaldi Day" and presided at a City Hall ceremony in Tebaldi's honor. Giuliani occasionally hosts gala performances at the Met and has played comic "guest" roles there in *Die Fledermaus*.

28. Samuel Ramey as Pagano in *I Lombardi*.

29. Alfredo Kraus and Mirella Freni are seen as Faust and Marguérite in Gounod's *Faust*.

30. Christa Ludwig.

31. Lauritz Melchior. The Heldentenor was celebrated for such roles as Siegmund, Siegfried, Tristan, Lohengrin, and Parsifal.

32. Dame Joan Sutherland.

33. Eleanor Steber. Barber composed "Knoxville, Summer of 1916" for her. She also created the title role in his opera *Vanessa*.

34. From left: Carlo Bergonzi and Alfredo Kraus.
35. Piero Cappuccilli, costumed as Giorgio Germont in *La Traviata*.
36. Victoria de los Angeles is shown in a rare appearance as Agathe in Weber's *Der Freischütz*.
37. Jon Vickers as Samson in Saint-Saëns's opera.
38. Leonie Rysanek as the Old Countess in Tchaikovsky's *Pique Dame*.
39. Victoria de los Angeles as Mimì in Puccini's *La Bohème*.
40. Anna Russell.
41. Lucine Amara.
42. Renata Tebaldi visits Franco Corelli backstage in Parma. Corelli sang Pollione in *Norma* that night.
43. Mr. New.
44. Kenn Harris!

FOR THE BEST IN PAPERBACKS, LOOK FOR THE

In every corner of the world, on every subject under the sun, Penguin represents quality and variety—the very best in publishing today.

For complete information about books available from Penguin—including Puffins, Penguin Classics, and Arkana—and how to order them, write to us at the appropriate address below. Please note that for copyright reasons the selection of books varies from country to country.

In the United Kingdom: Please write to *Dept. JC, Penguin Books Ltd, FREEPOST, West Drayton, Middlesex UB7 0BR.*

If you have any difficulty in obtaining a title, please send your order with the correct money, plus ten percent for postage and packaging, to *P.O. Box No. 11, West Drayton, Middlesex UB7 0BR*

In the United States: Please write to *Consumer Sales, Penguin USA, P.O. Box 999, Dept. 17109, Bergenfield, New Jersey 07621-0120.* Visa and MasterCard holders call 1-800-253-6476 to order all Penguin titles

In Canada: Please write to *Penguin Books Canada Ltd, 10 Alcorn Avenue, Suite 300, Toronto, Ontario M4V 3B2*

In Australia: Please write to *Penguin Books Australia Ltd, P.O. Box 257, Ringwood, Victoria 3134*

In New Zealand: Please write to *Penguin Books (NZ) Ltd, Private Bag 102902, North Shore Mail Centre, Auckland 10*

In India: Please write to *Penguin Books India Pvt Ltd, 706 Eros Apartments, 56 Nehru Place, New Delhi 110 019*

In the Netherlands: Please write to *Penguin Books Netherlands bv, Postbus 3507, NL-1001 AH Amsterdam*

In Germany: Please write to *Penguin Books Deutschland GmbH, Metzlerstrasse 26, 60594 Frankfurt am Main*

In Spain: Please write to *Penguin Books S. A., Bravo Murillo 19, 1° B, 28015 Madrid*

In Italy: Please write to *Penguin Italia s.r.l., Via Felice Casati 20, I-20124 Milano*

In France: Please write to *Penguin France S. A., 17 rue Lejeune, F–31000 Toulouse*

In Japan: Please write to *Penguin Books Japan, Ishikiribashi Building, 2–5–4, Suido, Bunkyo-ku, Tokyo 112*

In Greece: Please write to *Penguin Hellas Ltd, Dimocritou 3, GR–106 71 Athens*

In South Africa: Please write to *Longman Penguin Southern Africa (Pty) Ltd, Private Bag X08, Bertsham 2013*